Charles John Ann Hereford

The history of France

from the first establishment of that monarchy, brought down to, and including a complete narrative of the late revolution

Charles John Ann Hereford

The history of France
from the first establishment of that monarchy, brought down to, and including a complete narrative of the late revolution

ISBN/EAN: 9783742800930

Manufactured in Europe, USA, Canada, Australia, Japa

Cover: Foto ©ninafisch / pixelio.de

Manufactured and distributed by brebook publishing software (www.brebook.com)

Charles John Ann Hereford

The history of France

CONTENTS.

	Page
PREFACE BY THE EDITOR	VII
I. JOHN WYCLIFFE. 1324—1384.	
St. John's Gospel	1
II. GEOFFREY CHAUCER. 1328—1400.	
Canterbury Tales. (The Story of patient Grisilde)	59
III. STEPHEN HAWES. 15. Cent.	
The Pastime of Plesure. (Chap. I. II.)	95
IV. SIR THOMAS MORE. 1480—1535.	
The Descripcion of Richard III.	109
V. EDMUND SPENSER. 1553—1599.	
The Faerie Queene. (Book I. Canto I. Book II. Canto IX. X.)	127
VI. BEN JONSON. 1554—1637.	
The Alchemist	177
VII. JOHN LOCKE. 1632—1704.	
Some thoughts concerning Education	277
VIII. THOMAS GRAY. 1716—1771.	
Poems. (Odes. Miscellaneous)	389

PREFACE BY THE EDITOR.

It is with feelings of high satisfaction and most sincere gratitude, that I beg leave to offer to the Public the five hundredth volume of my Collection of British Authors.[*]

Never could I have flattered myself, that I should be able to achieve such a result, when more than eighteen years ago, I published the first volume [**] of the Series, incited to the undertaking by the high opinion and enthusiastic fondness, which I have ever entertained for English literature: a literature springing from the self same root as the literature of Germany, and cultivated in the beginning by the same Saxon race, which is still flourishing on this and on the other side of the Atlantic. As a German-Saxon it gave me particular pleasure to

[*] A glance at my list of authors will shew that America has contributed no small part to my Collection. Nevertheless I did not deem it necessary to alter the title under which my undertaking was started as I thought that the term "*British* Authors" might not improperly be applied to writers employing the language common to the two nations on either side of the Atlantic.

[**] "Pelham, by Sir Edward Bulwer Lytton," published Sept. 1st 1841.

promote the literary interest of my Anglo-Saxon cousins, by rendering English literature as universally known as possible beyond the limits of the British Empire. This extension, which I conceived to be dependent in some degree on the realisation of my scheme, I am really proud to say has been accomplished.

And why should I not be proud, when looking upon the splendid series formed by these five hundred volumes, containing the works of the classical aristocracy of English literature, especially of modern times? Few names can be mentioned of those, who have essentially contributed to the literary glory of Great-Britain, that have not found their representatives in this "Collection," which is, I believe, unrivalled in extent as well as in the influence it has exercised upon the public not only in Germany, or even in Europe, but throughout the whole civilised world by diffusing the standard works of British literature in cheap, correct and elegant editions.

Neither must I omit to mention that this Collection was the first undertaking in which the principle of international copyright was respected and carried on to a practical result. The *Treaties* now concluded between many of the civilised nations for the protection of literary property have created a new era in that part of legislation. May they prove to be the forerunners of *Laws* of general authority.

I was fortunate enough to win for my undertaking the approbation of a great majority of the most eminent

PREFACE BY THE EDITOR.   IX

among living British authors, who encouraged me in
the most friendly manner, by words* as well as by
deeds, privileging me, to publish their productions in
my "Collection." To all of them this volume may
convey my best thanks for their kindness. Its com-
panion volumes may at the same time prove a monument of my gratitude to the public, adorned by such a
glorious galaxy of literary names.**

* One of them, celebrated alike as novelist and statesman
said: "It is with extreme satisfaction, that I have assented to
the wish of Mr. Bernhard Tauchnitz of Leipzig, to prepare an
edition of ..... for continental circulation and especially for
the German public. The sympathy of a great nation is the
most precious reward of authors, and an appreciation, that is
offered us by a foreign people has something of the character
and value which we attribute to the fiat of posterity."

** I append a list, in alphabetical order, of writers,
whose works have appeared in the Collection: *Miss Aguilar,
W. H. Ainsworth, Currer Bell, Ellis & Acton Bell, Lady
Blessington, Rev. W. Brock, Sir Edward Bulwer Lytton, John
Bunyan, Robert Burns, Miss Burney, Lord Byron, Thomas
Carlyle, W. Collins, Fennimore Cooper, Miss Cummins, Ch.
Dickens, B. Disraeli, E. B. Eastwick, George Eliot, Fielding,
Lady G. Fullerton, de Foe, Mrs. Gaskell, Oliver Goldsmith,
Mrs. Gore, N. Hawthorne, Th. Hughes, Washington Irving,
G. P. R. James, Douglas Jerrold, S. Johnson, Miss Kavanagh,
R. B. Kimball, Kinglake, Ch. Kingsley, Ch. Lever, G. H. Lewes,
H. W. Longfellow, Lord Macaulay, Lord Mahon, Mansfield,
Captain Marryat, Mrs. Marsh, Milton, Thomas Moore, Miss
Mulock, Hon. Mrs. Norton, Ossian, Mrs. Paul, Mrs. Pike, Pope,
Ch. Reade, Walter Scott, Miss Sewell, Shakespeare, Smollett,
Sterne, Mrs. Stowe, Swift, Baroness Tautphoeus, Alfred Tennyson,
W. M. Thackeray, Thomson, Anthony Trollope, Warburton,
S. Warren, Miss Warner, Miss Yonge.*

PREFACE BY THE EDITOR.

In the present volume it has been my intention to trace out the development of the English language during the last five centuries — from *John Wycliffe*, the venerable founder of the modern English in the middle of the Fourteenth Century, to *Thomas Gray*, the mild star on the sky of English poetry in the middle of the Eighteenth Century — in characteristic specimens. It constitutes a supplementary part to those ancient authors, whose works have already appeared in this "Collection," namely, Shakespeare, Swift, Thomson &c.

And so I will proceed with this undertaking, with the same zeal and spirit that have hitherto marked its progress.

LEIPZIG, February 1. 1860.

BERNHARD TAUCHNITZ.

L

JOHN WYCLIFFE.

1324—1384.

.... "This Version (of the New Testament by *Wycliffe*) is interesting from the circumstances under which it was made, and its connexion with one of the greatest names of our country, so curious a monument of the language of that period, of so much philological importance, illustrating, as it does, the formation of our own mother tongue and exhibiting it in its transition-state, and also so valuable, as showing incidentally, and therefore the more surely, how certain questions of theology, were regarded by him whom we term our earliest reformer, and what was, in his day, and by him, considered the most authentic as a standard and, as it were, an original text."

Preface of "The New Testament in English translated by J. W. etc. Printed for Will. Pickering."
London 1848.

þe euuangelie of Joon

In þe bigynnynge was þe worde (þat is goddis sone)/ and þe worde was at god · & god was þe worde/ þis was in þe bigynnynge at god/ alle þingis ben made by hym: and wiþouten hym is made nou3t/ þat þing þat is made: in hym was liif/ and þe liif was þe li3te of men/ and þe li3te schyneþ in dirkenessis & dirkenessis comprehenden (or taken) not it/ a man was sente fro god: to whom þe name was ioon/ þis man came into witnessynge· þat he schulde bere witnessynge of þe li3t· þat alle men schulde bileue by hym/ he was not þe li3t: but þat he schulde bere witnessynge of þe li3t· it was verrey li3te þe whiche li3teneþ eche man comynge into þis worlde/ he was in þe worlde· & þe worlde was made by hym: and þe worlde knewe hym not/ he came into his owne þingis: and hes receyueden hym not/ forsoþe hou manye euer receyueden hym: he 3aue to hem power for to be made þe sones of god: to hem þat bileueden in his name

Ioon

name/ þe whiche not of bloodis· neþer of wille of fleyſche·
neþer of wille of man: but ben borne of god/ and þe worde
(þat is goddis ſone): is made fleyſche (or man)· ⁊ haþ dwellide in us/ and we hane ſeen þe glorie of hym: þe glorie as
of þe one bigoten of þe fadir/ þe ſone ful of grace ⁊ treuþe//
¶ Ion beriþ witneſſynge of hym: and crieþ ſeyinge/ þis it
was of whom I ſeyde/ he þat is to come aftir me· is made
bifore me· for he was þe former þan I/ and of þe plenty
of hym: we alle hane taken ⁊ grace for grace/ for þe lawe
is youen by moyſes: forſoþe grace ⁊ treuþe is made by ihū
criſt/ no man euer ſiȝe god· no but þe one bigoten ſone þat
is in þe boſum of þe fadir: he haþ tolde oute/ and þis is þe
witneſſynge of Ioon· whanne Iewis ſenten fro iriſm priſtis ⁊
dekenes to hym: þat þei ſchulden are hym/ who art þou/ and
he knowelechide ⁊ denyede not/ and he knowelechide: for I
am not criſt/ and þei axiden hym/ what þerfore art þou
helie? and he ſeyde I am not/ art þou a prophete? and he
anſweride/ nay/ þerfore þei ſeyden to hym/ who art þou:
þat we yyue anſwere to þes þat ſenten us/ what ſeiſt þou
of þi ſelf? he ſeiþ/ I (am) a voyce of (a man) cryinge in
deſerte: dreſſe ȝee þe weye of þe lorde· as yſaie þe prophete
ſeyde/ and þei þat weren ſente: weren of þe phariſees/ and
þei axiden hym ⁊ ſeyden to hym/ what þerfore baptiſiſt þou·
yif þou art not criſt· neþer helie· neþer a prophete? Ioon
anſweride to hem ſeyinge/ I baptiſe in water· ſoþely þe
mydil (man) of you ſtood whom ȝee knewen not/ he it is þat
aftir me is to come· þat is made bifore me· of whom I am
not worþi þat I vnbynde þe þwonge of his ſchoo/ þes þingis
ben done in bethanye ouer iordan: where Ioon was baptiſynge/
anoþer day Ioon ſiȝe ihū comynge to hym: and he ſeiþ/ lo
þe

Joon

þe lombe of god: lo þat doiþ awey þe synnes of þe worlde/
þis is he of whom I seyde/ aftir me comeþ a man þat is
made bifore me· for he was þe former þan I/ I knewe
hym not/ but þat he be schewide in isrl þerfore I came
baptisynge in water: and Joon bare witnessynge: seyinge/ for
I sixe þe spirit comynge as a culuer from heuene· & dwellynge
vpon hym· & I knewe hym not/ but he þat sente me for to
baptise in water: seyde to me/ vpon whom þou schalt se þe
spirit comynge doune· & dwellynge vpon hym· þis is it þat
baptisiþ in þe holy goost/ and I sixe & bare witnessynge· for
þis is þe sone of god// ¶ Anoþer day Joon stode & two of
his disciplis/ and he biholdynge ihū walkynge: seiþ/ to þe
lombe of god/ and two disciplis herden hym spekynge: and
folowiden ihū/ soþely ihc conuertide (or turnyde axen)· & seinge
hem suynge hym: seiþ to hem/ what seeken xee? þe whiche
seyden to hym/ raby þat is interpretide mayster· where dwelleſt
þou? he seith to hem/ come xee & se xee/ þei camen & sixen
where he dwellide: and dwelten at hym in þat day/ soþely
þe houre was at þe tenþe/ forsoþe andrew broþer of Symount
petre was one of þe two þat herden of Joon: and hadden
suede hym/ þis fonde firste his broþer symount: and he seiþ/
we haue founden messias· þat is interpretiue crist/ and he ledde
hym to Jhū/ soþely biholdynge hym: seyde/ þou art symount
þe sone of Johanna· þou schalt be clepide cephas· þat is interpretide petre/ fforsoþe on þe morotwe he wolde gon oute into
galilee: and he fonde philip/ and Jhc seiþ to hym sue þou me/
philip was of bethsayda þe cytee of andrewe & petre/ Philip
fonde nathanael: and he seiþ to hym/ we haue founden Jhū
þe sone of Joseph of nazareth· whom moyses wrote in þe lawe
& prophetis/ and nathanael seyde to hym/ of nazareth may sum
þing

Joon

kyng of good be/ Philip seiþ to hym/ come & se/ and Ihc̄ siȝe nathanael comynge to hym: and seiþ to hym/ lo verreyley a man of isrl· in whom is no gile/ nathanael seiþ to hym/ wher of hast þou knowen me/ Ihc̄ answeride & seiþ to hym/ bifore þat philip clepide þee· whanne þou were vndre þe fyge tree: I siȝe þee/ nathanael answeride to hym: & seiþ raby· þou art þe sone of god: þou art kyng of isrl/ Ihc̄ answeride & seyde to hym/ for I seyde to þee· I siȝe þee vndre þe fyge tree: þou bileuest/ þou schalt se more þan þes þingis/ and he seyde to hem/ treuely I seye to you· ȝee schulen se heuene openyde· & þe aungels of god steyȝynge vp & comynge doune vpon mannes sone//

Cm 2m And þe þridde day weddyngis ben made in þe chane of cuntre of galilee: and þe modir of ihū was þere/ soþely Ihc̄ is clepide & his disciplis to þe weddyngis/ and wiþn sayynge: þe modir of ihū seyde to hym/ þei haue not wiȝn/ and Ihc̄ seiþ to hire/ what to me & to þee wommanÞ myn houre came not ȝit/ þe modir of hym seiþ to þe mynystres/ what euer þing I schal seye to you: do ȝee/ forsoþe þere weren putte sixe stonen pottis aftir þe clensing of iewis: takyng eche two or þre mesures/ Ihc̄ seiþ to hem/ fille ȝee þe pottis wiþ water/ and þei filliden hem vnto þe hiȝest parte/ & ihc̄ seyde to hem/ drawȝee nowȝ & beriþ to architriclyn (þat is prynce of þe hous of þre stagis)/ and þei tooken/ and as architriclyn tastide þe water made wiȝn· & he wiste not wher of it was· soþely þe mynystres wisten þat drowen þe water: architriclyn clepiþ þe spouse & seiþ to hym/ eche man puttiþ firste good wiȝn· and whanne men schulen be fulfilde: þan þat þat is worse/ soþely þou hast kepte good wyn vnto nowe/ Ihc̄ dide þis bigynnynge
of

Joon

of signes in þe chaunc of galilee· & schewide his glorie: & his disciplis bileueden into hym/ aftir þes þingis he came doune to capharnaum· & his modir & his breþeren & his disciplis: & þei dwelten þere not manye dayes/ and þe pasке of iewis was nyȝ: and ihc̄ wente vp to irl̄m/ & he fonde in þe temple men sellynge scheep & oxen & culueris & money chaungers sittynge/ and whanne he hadde made of smale coordis as a scourge: he caste oute alle of þe temple· & scheep & oxen/ and he schedde oute money of chaungers: and turnede vpso-doune þe boordis/ and he seyde to hem þat solden culuers/ takiþ awey hens þes þingis· & nyl ȝee make þe hous of my fadir: an hous of marchaundise/ forsoþe his disciplis hadden mynde: for it is writen/ þe ȝeele (or feruoure of loue) of þin hous haþ eten me/ þerfore þe iewes answeriden & seyden to hym/ what signe (or token) schewist þou to vs· for þou doist þis þingis? Ihc̄ answeride & seyde to hem/ vndo ȝee þis temple· & in þre dayes I schal reyse it aȝen/ þerfore þe iewis seyden/ in fourty & sixe ȝeer þis temple is bildide: and þou in þre dayes schalt aȝen   / forsoþe he seyde of þe temple of his body· (þat wiþ outen comparisoune was more)/ þerfore whanne he had risen fro deade (men): his disciplis hadden mynde· for he seyde þis þing/ and þei bileueden to þe scripture: and to þe worde þat ihc̄ seyde// ¶ forsoþe whanne ihc̄ was at irl̄m in pasкe in þe feest day· many bileueden in his name· seinge þe signes of hym þat he dide/ soþely ihc̄ hym self· bileefede not hym self to hem· for þat he knewe alle men· & for it was not neede to hym: þat any man schulde bere witnessynge of man/ soþely he wiste what was in man//

Joon

C· 3· Forsoþe þer was a man of þe pharisees nychodeme by name: a prynce of Iewis/ he came to Jhū in þe nyȝt: and seyde to hym/ raby we witen· for of god þou hast comen mayster/ Soþely no man may do þes signes þat þou doist: but ȝif god were wiþ hym/ Jhc̄ answeride & seyde to hym/ treuly treuly I seye to þee· but ȝif a man schal be borne aȝen: he may not se þe kyngdom of god/ nychodeme seyde to hym/ how may a man be borne whanne he olde is/ wher he may entre aȝen into his modir wombe· & be borne aȝen/ Jhc̄ answeride/ treuly treuly I seye to þee· but ȝif a man schal be borne aȝen of water· & þe holy gost: he may not entre into þe kyngdom of god/ þat þat is borne of fleysche: is fleysche/ and þat þat is borne of þe spirit: is spirit/ wondre þou not for I seyde to þee it bihoueþ ȝou for to be borne aȝen/ þe spirit breþeþ (or quykeneþ) where it wole: and þou herest his voyce: but þou woste not fro whens he comeþ· or whidir it goiþ/ so is eche man þat is borne of þe spirit/ nychodeme answeride: and seyde to hym/ how mowne þes þingis be done/ Jhc̄ answeride & seyde to hym/ art þou a mayster in Isr̄l· & knowest not þes þingis/ treuly treuly I seye to þee· for þat þat we witen we speken· & þat þat we haue seen· we witnessen: & ȝee taken not oure witnessyng/ ȝif I haue seyde to ȝou erþely þingis· & ȝee bileuen not: how ȝif I schal seye to ȝou heuenely þingis schulen ȝee bileue/ & no man styȝeþ vp into heuene: but he þat came doune fro heuene· mannes sone þat is in heuene/ and as moyses reride vp a serpent in desert̄e: so it bihoues mannes sone for to be reyside vp/ þat eche man þat bileueþ into hym perische not: but haue euerlastynge lijf// ¶ fforsoþe god louede so þe worlde· þat he gaue his one bigotten sone· þat eche man þat bileueþ into hym·
perische

Joon

perische not: but haue euerlastynge lijf/ sothely god sente not his sone into þe worlde þat he iuge þe worlde: but þat þe worlde be sauede by hym/ he þat bileueþ into hym: is not demyde (or dampnyde)/ forsoþe he þat bileueþ not· is now demyde: for he bileueþ not in þe name of þe one bigotten sone of god/ soþely þis is þe doom/ for liȝte came into þe worlde: and men loueden more dirkenessis þan liȝte/ forsoþe here werkis weren euyl/ soþely eche man þat doiþ euyl: hatiþ liȝt/ and comeþ not to liȝt: þat his werke be not reproued (or vndirnomen)/ soþely he þat doiþ treuþe· comeþ to liȝt· þat his werkis be schewide: for þei ben in god/ aftir þes þingis Jhc came & his disciplis into þe lande of Jude: and þere he dwellide wiþ hem & baptizide/ soþeli Joon was baptisynge in ennon bisidis salym · for manye watris weren þere: and þei camen· & weren baptiside/ soþely Jon was not ȝit sente into prisoune/ soþely a questioun (or arisinge) is made of Jones disciplis wiþ þe Jewis of þe purificacon (or clensynge)/ and þei camen to Joon: and seyden to hym/ raby (or mayster)· he þat was wiþ þee ouer Jordan to whom þou hast borne witnessynge: lo he baptisiþ· and alle men comen to hym/ Jon answeride & seyde/ a man may not take any þing: but ȝif it be ȝouen to hym/ from heuene/ ȝee ȝoure self beren witnessynge to me þat J seyde J am not Crist: but for J am sente bifore hym/ he þat haþ a spouse (or wijf): is þe spouse (or housbonde)/ Forsoþe a frende of þe spouse þat stondiþ & heriþ hym ioyeþ in ioye· for þe voyce of þe spouse/ þerfore in þis þing: my ioye is fulfilde/ it bihoueþ hym for to waxe: forsoþe me for to be munyschide (or made lasse)/ he þat came from aboue: is vpon alle/ he þat is of þe erþe: spekiþ of þe erþe/ he þat comeþ fro heuene: is aboue alle/ and þis þing þat
he

Ioon

he siȝe & herde· he witnessiþ/ & no man takiþ his witnessynge/ forsoþe he þat haþ taken his witnessynge: haþ markide þat god is soþefast/ forsoþe he whom god sente: spekiþ þe wordis of god/ forsoþe not to mesure· god ȝyueþ þe spirit/ þe fadir loueþ þe sone· & he haþ ȝouen alle þingis in his hande/ he þat bileueþ into þe sone: haþ euerlastynge liif/ forsoþe he þat is vnbileueful to þe sone: schal not se euerlastynge liif· but þe wraþþe of god dwelliþ on hym/

Cm 4m   Therfore as Ihū knewe þat pharisees herden þat Ihū makiþ mo disciplis & baptisiþ þan Ion: þouȝ ihc baptiside not but his disciplis: he lefte Iude & wente aȝen into galilee/ soþely it bihouede hym to passe by samarie/ þerfore Ihc came by a cytee of samarie· þat is seyde sicar· bisidis þe maner (or feelde) þat Iacob ȝaue to Ioseph his sone/ forsoþe þe welle of Iacob was þere/ soþely ihc made wery (or faynte) of þe iourney: satte þus at þe welle/ soþely þe houre was as þe sixte (or vndrun)/ a womman came of samarie for to drawe water/ Ihc seiþ to hire/ ȝyue me for to drynke/ forsoþe his disciplis hadden gon into þe cytee: þat þei schulden bye metis/ þerfore þe ilke womman of samarie· seiþ to hym/ how þou whanne þou art a Iewe arist of me for to drynke: þat am a womman of samarie/ forsoþe Iewis vsen not to comoune wiþ samaritans/ Ihc answeride & seyde to hire/ ȝif þou wistist þe ȝifte of god· & who it is þat seiþ to þee· ȝyue to me for to drynke: parauenture þou schuldist haue axide of hym· & he schulde haue ȝyue to þee quycke water/ þe womman seiþ to hym/ Sire neþer þou hast in what þing þou schalt drawe: & þe pitte is deep/ þerfore wher of hast þou quycke water/ wher þou art more þan oure fadir Iacob
þat

Joon

þat ȝaue to us þe pitte· & he dranke þerof· & his sones & his beestis/ Ihc̄ answeride & seyde to hir/ eche man þat drynkiþ of þis water: schal þirste eftesones/ forsoþe he þat schal drynke of þe water þat I schal ȝyue to hym: schal not þriste into wiþ outen ende/ but þe water þat I schal ȝyue to hym: schal be made to hym a welle of spryngyng up water: into euerlastyng liff/ þe womman seiþ to hym/ sire ȝyue to me þis water þat I þriste not· neþer come hidir for to drawe/ Ihc̄ seiþ to hire/ go clepe þin housbonde & come hidir/ þe womman answeride & seyde/ I haue not an housbonde/ Ihc̄ seiþ to hire/ þou seydist wel· for I haue not an housbonde/ for þou hast hadde fyue housbondis/ and he whom þou hast: is not þin housbonde/ þis þing þou seydist soþely/ þe womman seiþ to hym/ lorde I se: for þou art a prophete/ oure faderis worschipeden in þis hil· & ȝee seyn for at irl̄m is place· where it bihoueþ for to worschip/ Ihc̄ seiþ to hire/ womman bileue þou to me for þe houre schal come· whanne neþer in þis hil· neþer in irl̄m: ȝee schulen preye (or worschip) þe fadir/ ȝee worschipen þat ȝee witen not: we worchipen þat we witen· for helþe is of Iewis/ but þe houre comeþ & now it is· whan trewe worschipers schulen worschip þe fadir in spirit & treuþe/ for whi & þe fadir seekiþ suche: þat schulen worschip hym/ god is a spirit· & it bihoueþ hem þat worschipen hym/ for to worschip in spirit & treuþe/ þe womman seiþ to hym/ I woot for messyas is comen: þat is seyde crist/ þerfore whanne he schal come: he schal telle to us alle þingis/ Ihc̄ seiþ to hire/ I am: þat speke wiþ þee/ and anone his disciplis camen & wondriden for he spac wiþ þe womman/ neþeles no man seyde what sekist þou· or what spekist þou wiþ hire/ þerfore þe womman lefte hire water potte· & wente

into

Joon

into þe cytee & seiþ to þe men/ come ȝee & se ȝee a man þat seyde to me alle þingis· what euer þingis I haue done/ wher he is crist? and þei wenten oute of þe cytee: and þei camen to hym/ In þe menewhile his disciplis preyeden hym seyinge/ raby (or mayster) ete/ soþely he seyde to hem/ I haue mete for to ete þat ȝee witen not/ perfore disciplis seyden to geðir/ wher any man brouȝte to hym for to ete? þE seiþ to hem/ my mete is þat I do þe wille of hym þat sente me: and þat I parfourme þe werke of hym/ wher ȝee seyn not· for ȝit foure moneþes· ben & ripe corne comeþ? lo I seye to ȝou· liste vp ȝoure yȝen· & se ȝee þe regiouns (or cuntrees) for nowe þei ben whiȝt to ripe corne/ and he þat reepiþ takiþ hire (or meede): and he þat geðiriþ fruyte into euerlastynge liff/ þat & he þat sowiþ haue ioye to geðir & he þat reepiþ/ In þis þing soþely is þe worde trewe· for anoþer is þat sowiþ: & anoþer þat reepiþ/ I sente ȝou for to reepe þat þat ȝee traueyliden not/ oþer men traueyliden: and ȝee entriden into here traueylis/ forsoþe of þat cytee manye samaritans bileueden into hym: for þe worde of þe womman berynge witnessynge· for he seyde to me alle þingis what euer þingis I dide/ perfore whanne samaritans camen to hym: þei preyeden hym þat he schulde dwelle þere/ and he dwellide þere two dayes/ and many mo bileueden for his worde· & seyden to þe womman/ for now not for þi speche we bileuen/ forsoþe we haue herde & we witen: for þis is verreyly þe saueour of þe worlde// ¶ fforsoþe aftir two dayes he wente þens· & wente into galilee/ Soþely he bare witnessynge· for a prophete in his owne cuntre· haþ not honoure (or worschip)/ perfore whanne he came into galilee: men of galilee receyueden hym· whanne þei hadden seen alle þingis þat he hadde done in irlm

Joon

In þe feeſt day (or halyday)/ and ſoþely þei hadden comen to þe feeſt day/ þerfore he came eftſone into þe chane of galilee· wher he made þe water wyn/ and ſum litil king was: whos ſone was ſijk at capharnaum/ whanne he þis had herde· þat Jhū ſchulde come fro Jude into galilee: he wente to hym & preyede hym· þat he ſchulde come doune & heele his ſone/ forſoþe he bigan for to dye/ þerfore Jhē ſeyde to hym/ no but ȝee ſchulen ſe tokenes & grete wondris: ȝee bileuen not/ þe litil kyng ſeiþ to hym/ lorde come doune bifore my ſone dye/ Jhē ſeiþ to hym/ go þi ſone lyueþ/ þe man bileuede to þe worde þat Jhū ſeyde to hym: and he wente/ ſoþely now hym comynge doune: þe ſeruauntis camen aȝenes hym· & tolden hym ſeyinge for his ſone lyuede/ þerfore he axide of hem þe houre in whiche he hadde hym better/ & þei ſeyden to hym/ for ȝiſtirday in þe ſeueneþ houre· þe feuer lefte hym/ þerfore þe fadir knewe þat þe ilke houre it was in whiche Jhē ſeyde to hym þi ſone lyueþ/ and he bileuede & al his hous/ Jhū dide efte þis ſecounde token: whanne he came fro Jude into galilee//

Aftir þis þing was a feeſt day of Iewis/ and Jhē wente into Irlm̄/ forſoþe in Irlm̄ is a ſtondynge water of beeſtis· þat in ebrewe is nampde bethſayda· hauyng fyue litil ȝatis/ in þis lay a greet multitude of langwiſchynge men· blynde & crokide· drie· abydynge þe ſtyrynge of þe water/ forſoþe þe aungel of þe lorde aftir tyme·came doune into þe ſtondynge water: and þe water was mouede/ and he þat firſt came doune in þe ceſterne· aftir þe mouynge of þe water: was made hool· of what ſekeneſſe he was holden// ⁋ fforſoþe ſumman was þere hauyinge & þritty ȝeeris in his ſekeneſſe/
whanne

Cm 5m

Joon

whanne Jhū hadde seen hym liggynge· ⁊ had knowen· for
nowe he hadde myche tyme: he seiþ to hym/ wolte þou be
made hool? þe sijk man answeride to hym/ lorde I haue not
a man þat whanne þe water is turblide· he sende me into
þe cesterne/ forsoþe þe while I come: anoþer goiþ doune
bifore me/ Jhū seiþ to hym/ rise vp take þi bed ⁊ wandre/
and anone þe man is made hool: I took vp his bed ⁊
wandride/ and saboth was in þat day/ þerfore þe Iewis seyden
to hym þat was made hool/ it is saboth it is not leueful to
þee: for to take þi bed/ he answeride to hem/ he þat made
me saaf: seyde to me/ take þi bed ⁊ wandre/ þerfore þei
ariden hym/ who is þat man þat seyde to þee· take þi bed
⁊ wandre/ soþely he þat was made hool: wiste not who it
was/ forsoþe Jhū bowide fro þe cumpanye ordeynyde (or sette)
in þe place/ aftirwarde Jhū fonde hym in þe temple: and
seyde to hym/ lo þou art made hool· now nyl þou synne·
leste any þing bifalle to þee/ þe ilke man wente ⁊ tolde to
þe Iewis· for it was Jhū þat made hym hool/ þerfore þe
Iewis pursueden Jhū: for he dide þis þing in þe saboth/
forsoþe Jhū answeride to hem/ my fadir worchiþ til now: ⁊
I wirche/ þerfore þanne þe Iewis souȝten more to slee hym/
for not onely he brake þe saboth· but ⁊ he seyde his fadir
god· makyng hym euen to god/ and so Jhū answeride ⁊ seyde
to hem/ trewely trewely I seye to ȝou· þe sone maye not of
hym self do any þing: no but þat þing þat he schal se þe
fadir doyinge/ what euer þingis soþely he doiþ: þes þingis
also ⁊ þe sone doiþ/ forsoþe þe fadir loueþ þe sone: ⁊
scheuiþ to hym alle þingis þat he doiþ/ and he schal schewe
to hym more werkis þan þes þat ȝee wondre/ forsoþe as þe
fadir repsiþ deade men ⁊ quykeniþ so ⁊ þe sone quykeniþ
whom

Joon

whom he wole/ soþely neþer þe fadir iugiþ any man: but haþ ȝyue al þe dome to þe sone· þat alle men honoure þe sone· as þei honouren þe fadir/ he þat honoureþ not þe sone: honoureþ not þe fadir þat sente hym/ treuely treuely I seye to ȝou· for he þat heriþ my worde· ⁊ bileueþ to hym þat sente me: haþ euerlastynge liff· ⁊ comeþ not into doom: but passiþ fro deþ into liff/ treuely treuely I seye to ȝou· for þe houre comeþ ⁊ now it is· whanne deade men schulen here þe voyce of goddis sone: ⁊ þei þat heren schulen lyue //
⁋ Soþely as þe fadir haþ liff in hym self: so he ȝaue ⁊ to the sone· for to haue liff in hym self/ and he ȝaue hym power for to make doom: for he is mannes sone/ nyl ȝee wondre þis þing· for þe houre comeþ in whiche alle men þat ben in biriels schulen here þe voyce of goddis sone/ and þei þat haue done good þingis: schulen come forþ into rysinge aȝen of liff/ forsoþe þei þat haue done euyl þingis into risynge aȝen of doom/ I may not of my self do any þing: but as I here I iuge ⁊ my doom is iuste for I seek not my wille: but þe wille of þe fadir þat sente me/ ȝif I bere witnessynge of my self: my witnessynge is not trewe/ anoþer is þat beriþ witnessynge of me: and I woot for his witnessynge is trewe þat he beriþ of me/ ȝee senten to Joon: and he bare witnessynge to þe treuþe/ soþely I take not witnessynge of man: but I seye þes þingis þat ȝee be saaf/ he was a lanterne brennynge· ⁊ schynynge (or ȝyuynge) liȝte/ forsoþe ȝee wolden glade at an houre in his liȝte/ soþely I haue more liȝt þan Joon/ forsoþe þe werkis þat my fadir ȝaue to me þat I parfourme hem: þe ilke werkis þat I do beren witnessynge of me: for þe fadir sente me/ and þe fadir þat sente me: he bare witnessynge of me/ neþer ȝee herden euer his voyce:

neþer

Ioon

neþer siȝen his lickenesse (or fourme)/ and ȝee haue not his worde dwellynge in ȝou: for ȝee bileuen not to hym whom he sente/ seeke ȝee scriptures in whiche ȝee wenen for to haue euerlastynge lijf: & þo it ben þat beren witnessynge of me/ and ȝee wolen not come to me: þat ȝee haue lijf// ¶ I take not clerenesse of men: but I haue knowen ȝou· for ȝee haue not þe loue of god in ȝou/ I came in þe name of my fadir: and ȝee tooken not me/ ȝif anoþer schal come in his owne name: ȝee schulen receyue hym/ how mowne ȝee bileue þat receyuen glorie eche of oþer: & ȝee seeken not þe glorie þat is of god al one} nyl ȝee gesse þat I came to accuse you anentis þe fadir/ it is moyses þat accusiþ ȝou in whom ȝee hopen/ forsoþe ȝif ȝee bileueden to moyses: parauenture ȝee schulden bileue & to me/ sopely he wrote of me/ sopely ȝif ȝee bileuen not to his lettris: how schulen ȝee bileue to my wordis}

Cm 6m Aftir þes þingis Ihū wente ouer þe see of galilee· þat is tiberiadis· & a greet multitude suede hym· for þei siȝen þe tokenes þat he dide on hem þat weren sijk/ þerfore Ihū wente into an hil· & satte þere wiþ his disciplis/ forsoþe pask was ful nyȝ: a feest day of þe lewis/ þerfore whanne Ihū hadde lifte vp þe yȝen & had seen for a greet multitude came to hym: he seiþ to philip/ wherof schulen we bie loues· þat þes men ete} sopely he seyde þis þing temptynge hym/ forsoþe he wiste what was to do/ philip answeride to hym/ þe looues of two hundride pens sufficen not to hem· þat eche man take a litil what/ one of his disciplis andrewe þe broþer of symount petre seiþ to hym/ one childe is here þat haþ fyue barly looues & two fischis· but what ben þes þingis

amonge

Joon

amonge so many men/ þerfore Jhc seiþ/ make ȝee men for to sitte at þe mete/ for þere was myche hay in þe place/ þerfore men saten at þe mete in nowmbre of fyue þousandis/ þerfore Jhc took þe fyue looues/ & whanne he had done þankyngis: he departide to men sittynge at þe mete/ also & of þe fischis: as myche as þei wolden/ forsoþe as þei ben fulfillde: he seyde to his disciplis/ gadir ȝee þe relifes þat ben lefte. þat þei perische not/ þerfore þei geberiden & filliden twelue cofyns of relifes. of þe fyue barly loues & two fischis þat leften to hem þat hadden eten/ þerfore þo men whanne þei hadden seen þe token (or myracle) þat he had done: seyden/ for þis is verreyley a prophete þat is come into þe worlde/ forsoþe whanne Jhu had knowen þat þei weren to come þat þei schulden raupsche hym & make hym kyng: he al one fleyȝe eȝt into an hyl/ sooþely as euen was made: his disciplis wenten doune to þe see/ and whanne þei hadden steyȝede vp into þe boot/ þei camen ouer þe see into capharnaum/ and dirkenessis weren now made: and Jhc had not now comen to hem/ forsoþe a greet wynde blowynge: þe see roos vp/ þerfore whanne þei hadden rowide as fyue & twenty furlongis or þritty: þei siȝen Jhu walkynge on þe see & to be made nerre to þe boot & þei dredden/ sooþely he seyde to hem/ J am: nyl ȝee drede/ þerfore þei wolden take hym into þe boot/ & anone þe boot was at þe lande to whiche þei wenten// ¶ on þe toþer day þe cumpanye þat stoode ouer þe see: siȝe for þer was none oþer boot þere. no but one/ & for Jhc entride not wiþ disciplis into þe boot. but his disciplis weren al one. forsoþe oþer bootis camen fro tiberiadis. bisidis þe place where þei eten brede. doinge þankingis to god/ þerfore whanne þe cumpanye had seen for Jhu was

not

Joon

not þere neþer his disciplis: þei steyȝeden into bootis, & camen into capharnaum. seekyng Jhū/ and whanne þei hadden founden hym ouer þe see: þei seyden to hym/ raby how hast þou comen hidir? Jhc̄ answeride to hem & seyde/ treuely treuely I seye to ȝou. ȝee seeken me not for ȝee siȝen þe tokenes (or myraclis): but for ȝee eten of looues & ben fulfilde/ wirche ȝee not mete þat perischiþ: but þat dwelliþ into euerlastynge liff. þe whiche mete mannes sone ȝyueþ to ȝou/ forsoþe god þe fadir bitokenyde (or markide) hym/ þerfore þei seyden to hym/ what schulen we do. þat we wirche þe werkis of god? Jhc̄ answeride & seyde to hem/ þis is þe werke of god. þat ȝee bileue into hym. whom he sente/ þerfore þei seyden to hym/ þerfore what token dost þou. þat we se. & bileue to þee? what wirchist þou? oure faderis eten manna in deserte: as it is writen/ he ȝaue to hem brede fro heuene for to ete/ þerfore Jhc̄ seiþ to hem/ treuely treuely I seye to ȝou. not moyses ȝaue to ȝou verrey breed fro heuene: but my fadir ȝyueþ to ȝou verrey breed fro heuene/ soþely it is verrey breed þat comeþ doune fro heuene. & ȝyueþ liff to þe worlde/ þerfore þei seyden/ lorde euermore ȝyue to vs þis breed/ soþely Jhc̄ seyde to hem/ I am breed of liff/ he þat comeþ to me: schal not hungre/ & he þat bileueþ in me: schal neuer þirste/ but I seye to ȝou. for & ȝee haue seen me: and ȝee bileueden not/ al þing þat þe fadir ȝyueþ to me: schal come to me/ & I schal not caste oute hym þat comeþ to me/ for I came doune fro heuene. not þat I do my wille: but þe wille of hym þat sente me/ forsoþe þis is wille of hym þat sente me þe fadir: þat alle þing þat þe fadir ȝaue to me. I leese nouȝt of it but aȝen reyse it in þe laste daye/ soþely þis þe wille of my fadir þat sente me. þat eche man þat

seeþ

Joon

seeþ þe sone & bileueþ into hym: haue euerlastynge liff: & I schal aȝen reyse hym: in þe laste day/ þerfore iewis grucchiden of hym: for he had seyde· I am breed þat camen doune from heuene· & þei seyden/ wher þis is not· Jhc̄ þe sone of Joseph:-whos fadir & modir we haue knowen/ þerfore how seiþ he þis· for I came doune from heuene/ þerfore Jhc̄ answeride & seyde to hem/ nyl ȝee grucche togedir/ no man may come to me: no but þe fadir þat sente me schal drawe hym/ and I schal aȝen reyse hym in þe laste daye/ it is writen in prophetis· & alle men schulen be able for to be tauȝte of god/ eche man þat haþ herde of þe fadir & lernyde: comeþ to me/ not for any man siȝe þe fadir· no but þis þat is of god: þis siȝe þe fadir/ soþely soþely I seye to ȝou· he þat bileueþ in me: haþ euerlastynge liff/ I am breed of liff/ ȝoure faderis eten manna in deserte: and ben deade/ þis is breed comyng doune from heuene· þat ȝif any man schal ete þerof: he dieþ not/ I am quycke breed þat came doune fro heuene/ ȝif any man schal ete of þis breed: he schal lyue wiþouten ende/ & þe breed þat I schal ȝyue: is my fleysche· for liff of þe worlde/ þerfore þe iewis chidden togeder seyinge/ how may he þis ȝyue to us his fleysche for to ete/ þerfore Jhc̄ seiþ to hem/ treuely treuely I seye to ȝou· no but ȝee schulen ete þe fleysche of mannes sone· & drynke his blood: ȝee schulen not haue liff in ȝou/ he þat etiþ my fleysche & drynkiþ my blood: haþ euerlastynge lyfe/ & I schal aȝen reyse hym in þe laste day/ forsoþe my fleysche is verreyly mete: & my blood is verreyly drynke/ he þat etiþ my fleysche & drynkiþ my blood: dwelliþ in me & I in hym/ as my fadir lyuynge haþ sente me: & I lyue for þe fadir/ and he þat etiþ me: & he schal lyue for me/ þis is breede þat came doune fro heuene/

Joon

heuene/ not as ȝoure fadris eten manna & ben deade/ he þat etiþ þis breed· schal lyue wiþouten ende/ he seyde þes þingis in þe sinagoge: techynge in capharnaum/ þerfore manye of his disciplis heerynge: seyden/ þis worde is harde & who may here hym/ soþely Jhc witynge at hym self· for his disciplis grucchiden of þis þing: seyde to hem/ þis þing sclaundeirþ ȝou/ þerfore ȝif ȝee schulen se mannes sone steyȝing vp where he was bifore: it is þe spirit þat quykeneþ· þe fleysche profiteþ no þing/ þe wordis þat J haue spoken to ȝou: ben spirit & liff/ but þere ben summe of ȝou þat bileuen not/ soþely Jhc wiste at þe bigynnynge· whiche weren bileuynge: & who was to bitraye hym/ and he seyde/ þerfore J seye to ȝou· þat no man may come to me: no but it were ȝoueu to hym of my fadir/ fro þis tyme manye of his disciplis wenten abak: and nowe wenten not wiþ hym/ þerfore Jhc seyde to þe twelue/ wher & ȝee wolen go aweye? þerfore Symon petre answeride to hym/ lorde to whom schulen we gon? þou haſt wordis of euerlastynge liff/ and we hane bileuede & knowen: for þou art crist þe sone of god/ þerfore Jhc answeride to hem/ wher J chees not ȝou twelue: and one of ȝou is a sende/ forsoþe he seyde of Judas of Symount scarioth/ forsoþe he þis was to bitraye hym: whanne he was one of þe twelue.//

Cm 7¹⁰ Forsoþe aftir þes þingis Jhc walkide into galilee/ for he wolde not walke into Judee: for Jewis souȝten for to slee hym/ soþely þer was in þe nexte a feest day of Jewis senophogia· (þat is a feest of tabernaclis) forsoþe his breþeren seyden to hym/ passe fro hens & go into Jude· þat & þi disciplis se þe werkis þat þou doist/ forsoþe no man doiþ any þing in hide place (or pryueþ): & he sechiþ for to be into open/ ȝif þou doist

Joon

doist þis þingis schewe þi self to þe worlde/ forsoþe neiþer his
breþeren bileueden into hym/ perfore Iħc seiþ to hem/ my
tyme came not ʒit but ʒoure tyme is euermore reedy/ þe worlde
may not haue hatide/ [   ] sopely it haþ me: for I
bere witnessynge þerof· for þe werkis of it ben euyl/ steyʒe
ʒee vp at þis feest day· but I schal not steyʒe vp at þis feest
day· for my tyme is not ʒit fulfilde/ whanne he had seyde þes
þingis he dwellte in galilee/ fforsoþe as his breþeren steyʒeden
vp at þe feest days þanne ⁊ he steyʒede vp· not oppnly but
as in pryueþ/ perfore þe iewis souʒten hym in þe feest day
⁊ seyden/ where is he? and myche grucchynge was of hym:
in þe cumpanye of puple/ forsoþe summe seyden for he is
gode· forsoþe oþer seyden nayes but he deceyueþ þe cumpa-
nyes/ neþeles no man spac oppnly of hym: for drede of
Iewis/ forsoþe nowe þe feest day medelynge (or goinge bi-
twixe): Iħc wente vp into þe temple· ⁊ tauʒte/ and þe iewis
wondriden seyinge/ how can þis (man) lettris· siþen he haþ
not lerned? Iħc answeride hem and seyde my doctryne is
not myn: but his þat sente me/ ʒif any man wole do his
wille: he schal knowe of þe techyng· wher he be of god/ or
I speke of myself/ he þat spekiþ of hymself: seekiþ his owne
glorie/ forsoþe þat seekiþ þe glorie of hym þat sente hym:
þis is soþefast ⁊ vnriʒtwesnesse is not in hym/ wher moyses
ʒaue not a lawe: and no man of ʒou doiþ þe lawe: what
seeken ʒee for to slee me? þe cumpanye answeride ⁊ seyde/
þou hast a deuyl/ who seekiþ for to slee þee? Iħc answeride
⁊ seyde to hem/ I haue done one werke: ⁊ alle ʒee wondren/
perfore moyses ʒaue to ʒou circumcisioñ· not for it is of moyses: but of faderis/ ⁊ in þe saboth ʒee circumciden a man/ ʒif
a man take circumcisioñ in þe saboth· þat þe lawe of moyses
be

Joon

be not broken: haue ȝee indignacōn or wraþþe to me· for I
made al þe man hool in þe saboth/ nyl ȝee deme after þe
face but deme ȝee a riȝtful doom/ þerfore sammen of irl͞m
seyden/ wher þis is not whom þe iewis seeken for to slee/
and lo he spekiþ openly: & þei seyn no þing to hym/ wher
þe prynces knewen verreyly· for þis is crist/ but we witen
þis man of whens he is/ forsoþe whanne crist schal come:
no man woot of whens he is/ þerfore Ih͞c criede in þe temple
techynge & seyinge/ and ȝee witen me of whens I am/ and
I came not of my self: but he is trewe þat sente me: whom
ȝee knowen not/ I woot hym· & ȝif I schal seye for I woot
hym not: I schal be lijk to ȝou a lier/ and I woot hym· for
of hym I am: & he sente me/ þerfore þei souȝten for to
take hym· and no man sente into hym hondis· for his houre
came not ȝit/ soþely many of þe cumpanye bileueden into
hym· & seyden/ whanne c͞rt schal come· wher he schal do mo
tokenes þan þis doiþ/ pharisees herden þe cumpanye of puple
grucchynge of hym þes þingis/ and þe prynces of pharisees
senten mynystris· þat þei schulden take hym/ þerfore Ih͞c
seyde to hem/ ȝit a litil tyme I am wiþ ȝou: & I go þe fadir
þat sente me/ ȝee schulen seeke me & ȝee schulen not fynde·
& where I am· ȝee may not come/ þerfor iewis seyden to
hem self/ whidir is he þis to go: for we schulen not fynde
hym/ wher he is to go into scaterynge (or distruyinge) of heþen
men/ and is to techynge heþen men/ what is þis worde þe
whiche he seyde· ȝee schulen seeke me· & ȝee schulen not
fynde/ & where I am ȝee may not come// fforsoþe in þe laste
day of þe greet feste: Ih͞c stoode & criede seyinge/ ȝif any
man þristiþ: come he to me & drynke he/ he þat bileueþ
into me as þe scripture seiþ: flodis of quycke water schulen
flowe

Joon

flowe of his wombe/ sopely he seyde þis þing of þe holy
gost· whom men bileuynge into hym· weren to take/ forsoþe
þe spirit was not ȝit ȝouen: for ihē was not ȝit glorifiede/
þerfore of þat cumpanye whan þei hadden herde þes wordis
of hym þei seyden/ þis is uerreyly a prophete/ oþer seyden·
þis is crist/ forsoþe summe seyden· wher crist comeþ fro
galilee: wher þe scripture seiþ not þat of þe seed of dauyd·
& of þe castel of bethlem where dauyd was crist comeþ /
and so discencon is made in þe cumpanye for hym/ forsoþe
summe of hem wolden haue taken hym: but no man sente
to handis vpon hym/ þerfore þe mynystris camen to þe
bischopes & to þe pharisees: and þei seyden to hem/ whi
brouȝten ȝee not hym / þe mynystris answeriden/ neuer man
spac so: as þis spekiþ/ þerfore þe pharisees answeriden to
hem/ wher & ȝee ben deceyuede / wher any of þe prynces
bileueden into hym· or of þe pharisees / but þis cumpanye
of puple þat knewe not þe lawe: ben curside/ nychodeme
seiþ to hem· he þat came to hym by nyȝt: þat was one of
hem/ wher oure lawe demeþ a man· no but firste it haue
herde of hym: and knowe what he doiþ/ þei answeriden &
seyden to hym/ wher & þou art a man of galilee / seeke
þou scriptures & se: for a prophete risiþ not of galilee/ and
þei turneden aȝen eche into his owne hous//

Forsoþe ihē wente into þe mounte of olyuete: and erly C^m 8^m
efte he came into þe temple/ & al þe puple came to hym:
& he sittynge tauȝte hem/ forsoþe scribis & pharisees ledden
to a womman taken in anoutrie· & sette hire into þe mydel:
and seyde to hym/ mayster þis womman is nowe taken in
auoutrie/ forsoþe in þe lawe moyses comaundide vs for to

B

Ioon

stoon suche / perfore what seyst þou? sobely þei seyden þis þing temptynge hym: þat þei myȝte accuse hym / forsoþe Ihē bowyng doune hym self: wrote wiþ þe fynger in þe erþe / sobely whanne þei lastiden aringe hym: he replide hym self · & seyde to hem / he whom of you is wiþ outen synne: firste sende a stoon into hire / and eft he bowyng hym self: wrote in þe erþe / sobely þei beryinge þes þingis wenten aweye · one aftir anoþer · þei byggynnynge at þe eldre men / and Ihē dwelte al one: and þe womman stondynge in þe mydil / sobely Ihē reysynge hym self: seyde to hire / womman where ben þei þat accusen? no man dampnyde þee / þe whiche seyde / no man lorde / Ihē seyde to hire / neþer I schal dampne þee / go þou: and nowe aftirwarde nyl þou do synne // ¶ perfore Ihē eft spac to hem seyinge / I am þe liȝte of þe worlde / he þat sueþ me · walkiþ not in dirkenessis: but he schal haue þe liȝte of liff / perfore þe pharisees seyden / þou berest witnessynge of þi self: þi witnessynge is not trewe / Ihē answeride & seyde to hem / and ȝif I bere witnessynge of myself: my witnessynge is trewe / for I wote fro whens I came: & whidir I go / forsoþe ȝee witen not fro whens I came or whidir I go / forsoþe ȝee demen aftir þe fleysche: I deme not any man / and ȝif I deme: my dome is trewe / for I am not al one: but I & þe fadir þat sente me / & in ȝoure lawe it is writen · for þe witnessynge of two men is trewe / I am þat bere witnessynge of myself: and þe fadir þat sente me · beriþ witnessynge of me / perfore þei seyden to hym: where is þi fadir? Ihē answeride neþer ȝee witen (or knowen) me: neþer ȝee witen my fadir / ȝif ȝee wisten me: parauenture & ȝee schulden witte my fadir / Ihē spac þes wordis in þe tresorie: techynge in
þe

Joon

þe temple/ and no man took hym: for his houre came not
ȝit// ☙ þerfore efte Jhc̄ seyde to hem/ lo I go & ȝee schulen
seeke me: and ȝee schulen die in ȝoure synne/ whidir I go:
ȝee mowne not come/ þerfore þe Iewis seyden/ wher he schal
slee hym self/ for he seiþ whidir I go ȝee mowne not come/
& he seyde to hem/ ȝee ben of byneþes I am of aboue/ ȝee
ben of þis worlde: I am not of þis worlde/ þerfore I seyde
to ȝou· for ȝee schulen die in ȝoure synnes/ forsoþe ȝif ȝee
schulen not bileue for I am: ȝee schulen dye in ȝoure synnes/
forsoþe þei seyden to hym/ who art þou/ Jhc̄ seyde to hem/
þe bygynnynge (or þe firste of alle þing)· þe whiche I speke
to ȝou/ I haue many þingis for to speke of to deme of ȝou:
but he þat sente me is soþefaste/ & I speke in þe worlde
þes þingis þat I herde of hym/ and þei knewen not for he
seyde his fadir god/ þerfore Jhc̄ seiþ to hem/ whanne ȝee
haue reysude mannes sone: þanne ȝee schulen knowe for I
am/ and of my self I do no þing: but as my fadir tauȝte
me· I speke þes þingis/ and he þat sente me is wiþ me· &
lefte me not al one: for I do euermore þo þingis þat ben
plesaunt to hym// ☙ hym spekynge þis þingis: manye
bileueden into hym/ þerfore Jhc̄ seyde to hem þe Iewis þat
bileueden into hym/ ȝif ȝee schulen dwelle in my worde:
verreyly ȝee schulen be my disciplis/ and ȝee schulen knowe
þe treuþe: and treuþe schal delyuer ȝou/ þerfore þe Iewis
answeriden to hym/ we ben þe seed of abraham: and to
no man we euer serueden/ how seyst þou· for ȝee schulen
be fre: Jhc̄ answeride to hem treuly treuly I seye to ȝou:
for eche man þat doiþ synne: is seruaunt of synne/ soþely
þe seruaunt dwelliþ not in þe hous into wiþ outen ende/
þerfore ȝif þe sone schal delyuer ȝou: verreyly ȝee schulen be
fre/

Joon

free/ I woote for ȝee ben abrahams sones· but ȝee seeken for to slee me· for my woorde takiþ not in ȝou/ and I speek þo þingis þat I siȝe at my fadir: & ȝee done þo þingis þat ȝee siȝen at youre fadir/ þei answeriden & seyden to hym/ abraham is oure fadir/ Ihē seiþ to hem/ ȝif ȝee ben þe sones of abraham: do ȝee þe werkis of abraham/ soþely nowe ȝee seeken for to slee me· a man þat haue spoken to you þe treuþe þat I herde of god/ abraham dide not þis þing/ ȝee done þe werkis of ȝoure fadir/ and so þei seyden to hym/ we ben not borne of fornicacōn: we haue one fadir god/ þerfore Ihē seyde to hem ȝif god were ȝoure fadir: soþely ȝee schulden loue mee/ forsoþe I procedide (or came forþ) of god: and came/ neþer soþely I came of my self: but he sente me/ whi knowen ȝee not my speche· for ȝee mowne not here my woord/ ȝee ben of þe fadir þe deuyl: and ȝet wolen do þe desires of ȝoure fadir/ he was a man sleer fro þe bigynnynge: and in treuþe he stood not· for treuþe is not in hym/ whanne he spekiþ lesynge: he spekiþ of his owne þingis· for he is a lier· & fadir of it/ soþely ȝif I seye treuþe: ȝee bileuen not to me/ who of ȝou schal reproue me of synne/ ȝif I seye treuþe: whi bileuen ȝee not to me/ he þat is of god heriþ þe wordis of god/ þerfore ȝee heren not: for ȝee ben not of god/ þerfore þe Iewis answeriden & seyden/ wher we seyn not wel· for þou art a samaritan· & hast a deuyl: Ihē answeride & seyde/ I haue not a deuyl· but I honoure my fadir· & ȝee haue vnhonouride me/ forsoþe I seek not my glorie: þer is þat sechiþ & demeþ/ treuely treuly I seye to ȝou· ȝif any man schal kepe my worde: he schal not se deþ into wiþ outen ende/ þerfore þe Iewis seyden/ now we haue knowen· for þou hast a deuyl/ abraham

Joon

ham is deade ⁊ þe prophetis ⁊ þou seist ȝif ony schal kepe
þi worde· he schal not taste deþ into wiþ outen ende/ wher
þou art more þan oure fadir abraham þat is deade· ⁊ þe
prophetis ben deade/ whom makist þou þi silf? Ihc̄ answer-
ide/ ȝif I glorifie my silf: my glorie is nouȝte/ my fadir is
þat glorifieþ me· whom ȝee seyn for he is ȝoure god· ⁊ ȝee
haue not knowen hym/ forsoþe I haue knowen hym/ ⁊ ȝif
I seye for I woot hym not: I schal be a lier lijk to ȝou/
but I woot hym: and I kepe his worde/ abraham ȝoure fadir
gladide (or ful oute ioȝȝede)· þat he schulde se my day· ⁊ he
siȝe ⁊ ioȝȝede/ þerfore þe iewis seyden to hym/ þou haþ not
ȝit fifty ȝeer· ⁊ hast þou seen abraham? þerfore ihc̄ seyde to
hem/ treuely treuely I seye to ȝou· bifore þat abraham was
made: I am/ þerfore þei token stones· þat þei schulden caste
into hym/ soþely Ihc̄ hid him: and wente oute of þe temple //

And Ihc̄ passynge siȝe a man blynde fro þe birþe/ and
his disciplis axiden hym/ raby þat is mayster· who synnede·
þis man or his fadir ⁊ modir· þat he schulde be borne blynde/
Ihc̄ answeride/ neþer þis man synnede· neþer his fadir ⁊
modir: but þat þe werkis of god be schewide in hym/ it
bihoueþ me for to wirche þe werkis of hym þat sente me· þe
while day is/ þe nyȝt schal come: whanne no man may wirche/
how longe I am in þe worlde: I am þe liȝte of þe worlde/
whanne he had seyde þes þingis: he spitte into þe erþe· ⁊
made cleye of þe spotil: and layde (or balmede) þe cley on
his yȝen· ⁊ seyde to hym/ go ⁊ be þou waschen in þe water
of siloy: þat is interpretide sente/ þerfore he wente ⁊ waschide:
and came seȝinge: and so neyȝebors ⁊ þei þat hadden seen
hym bifore· for he was a begger: seyden/ wher þis is not he
þat

Joon

þat satte & beggide/ oþer men seyden: for þis it is/ oþer men seyden nay: but it is a liche of hym/ forsoþe he seyde for I am he/ þerfore þei seyden to hym/ hou ben þin yȝen openyde to þee? he answeride/ þe ilke man þat is seyde Jhc: made cleye & anoyntide myn yȝen: and seyde to me/ go þou to þe water of siloye: and wasche/ & I wente & waschide & siȝe/ and þei seyden to hym/ where is he/ he seiþ I woot not/ þei ledden hym þat was blynde to þe pharisees/ forsoþe it was saboth whanne Jhc made cleye & openyde his yȝen/ efte þe pharisees ariden hym: hou he had seyn? and he seyde to hem/ he puttide to me cleye on þe eȝȝen: and I waschide & I siȝe/ þerfore summe of pharisees seyden/ þis man is not of god: for he kepiþ not þe saboth/ oþer men seyden/ hou may a man synner do þes signes (or myraclis)? and dyuysion was amonge hem/ þerfore þei seyn eftesone to þe blynde man/ what seyst þou of hym þat openyde þin yȝen? soþely he seyde: for he is a prophete/ þerfore iewis bileueden not of him for he was blynde & had seen: til þei clepiden his fadir & modir þat had seen/ and þei ariden hem: seinge/ þis is ȝoure sone· whom ȝee seyn for he is borne blynde: hou þerfore seeþ he nowe? his fadir & modir answereden to hem we witen for þis is oure sone: & he is borne blynde/ soþely hou he seeþ now we witen not: or who openyde his yȝen we witen neuer/ are ȝee hym/ he haþ age: speke he of hym self/ his fadir & modir seyden þes þingis: for þei dredden þe iewes/ forsoþe nowe þe iewes hadden conspirit· þat ȝif any man knowelechide hym crist: he schulde be done oute of þe synagoge/ þerfore his fadir & modir seyden/ for he haþ age: are ȝee hym/ þerfore eftesone þei clepiden þe man þat was blynde: and seyden to hym/

true

Joon

ʒyue þou glorie to god/ we witen for þis man is a synner/ þerfore he seyde/ ʒif he is a synner I woot nere/ one þing I woot· for whanne I was blynde nowe I se/ þerfore þei seyden to hym/ what dide he to þee: howe openyde he þin yʒen ʒ he answeride to hem/ I seyde to ʒou now· & ʒee herden· what wolen ʒee eftesone ʒ wher & ʒee wolen be made his disciplis ʒ þerfore þei cursiden hym & seiden/ be þou his disciple· we ben þe disciplis of moyses/ we witen for god spac to moyses: forsoþe we witen not þis of whens he is/ þe ilke man answeride & seyde to hem/ forsoþe in þis þing is wondreful þat ʒee witen not of whens he is· & he haþ openyde myn yʒen/ sothely we witen: for god hereþ not synners/ but ʒif any man is worschiper of god & doiþ his wille: hym he heriþ/ fro þe worlde it is not herde þat any man openiþ þe yʒen of blynde borne men/ no but þis were of god: he myʒt not do any þing/ þei answereden & seyden to hym/ þou art al borne in synnes· & þou techist vs ʒ and þei casuden hym oute/ Ihc̄ herde for þei hadden caste hym oute/ and whanne he hadde founden hym: he seyde to hym/ bileuest þou into þe sone of god ʒ he answeride & seyde/ lorde who is he: þat I bileue in hym ʒ and Ihc̄ seyde to hym/ and þou hast seen hym: and he it is þat spekiþ wiþ ʒee/ and he seiþ lorde I bileue/ and he fallynge doune: worschipide hym/ þerfore Ihc̄ seyde to hym/ I came into þe worlde· into doom· þat þei þat seen not· se/ and þei þat seen· be made blynde/ and summe of þe pharisees herden þat weren wiþ hym: and þei seyden to hym/ wher & we ben blynde ʒ Ihc̄ seyde to hem/ ʒif ʒee weren blynde: ʒee schulen not haue synne/ but now ʒee seyn for we seen: ʒoure synne dwelliþ //

Treuly

Joon

C⁓ 10⁓ Treuly treuly I seye to you· he þat comeþ not in by þe
dore· into þe foolde of scheep· but steyȝeþ vp by anoþer weye
he is nyȝt þeef ⁊ day þeef/ forsoþe he þat entriþ by þe dore:
is þe scheperde of þe scheep/ to hijs þe porter openyþ: and
þe scheep heren his voyce/ and he clepiþ his owne scheep by
name: and leediþ hem oute/ whanne he haþ sente oute his
owne scheep: he goiþ bifore hem· and þe scheep suen hym·
for þei knowen his voyce/ soþely þei suen not an alien: but
fleen fro hym· for þei hane not knowen þe voyce of aliens/
Jhc seyde to hem this prouerbe/ forsoþe þei knowen not what
he spac to hem/ þerfore Jhc seyde to hem eftesone/ treuely
treuely I seye to you· for I am þe dore of scheep/ alle how
many euer camen: ben nyȝt þeefes ⁊ day þeefes· but þe
scheep herden not hem/ I am þe dore/ ȝif any man schal
entre by me/ he schal be sauede/ and he schal go in ⁊ schal
go oute: ⁊ he schal fynde lesowis/ a nyȝt þeef comeþ not·
but þat he stele ⁊ slee ⁊ leese/ I came þat þei haue liff:
and haue more plenteuously/ I am a gode scheperde/ a good
scheperde ȝyueþ his soule (þat is liff) for his scheep/ forsoþe
a marchaunt (or hiride hyne)· ⁊ þat is not a scheperde: whos
ben not þe scheep his owne: seeþ a wolfe comynge· ⁊ he
leeueþ þe scheep ⁊ fleeþ/ ⁊ þe wolfe rauysschiþ (or scateriþ)
þe scheep/ forsoþe þe marchaunt fleeþ· for he is a marchaunt:
and it parteynyþ not to hym of þe scheep/ I am a gode herde·
⁊ I knowe my scheep: (⁊ my scheep) knowen me/ as þe fadir
haþ knowen me: ⁊ I knowe þe fadir· ⁊ I putte my liff for
my scheep/ ⁊ I haue oþer scheep þat ben not of þis folde:
and bihoueþ me for to leede hem to· ⁊ þei schulen here my
voyce/ and it shal be made one folde ⁊ one scheperde/ þerfore þe fadir loueþ me: for I putte my soule þat eftesone I
take

Joon

take it/ no man takiþ it fro me: but I putte it fro my self/
I haue power for to putte it: and I haue power for to take
it aweȝ/ þis mandement haue I taken of my fadir/ and so
dissencōn was made amonge þe iewis: for þes wordis/ forsoþe many of hem seyden/ he haþ a deuyl & maddiþ (or
wariþ wood)/ what heren ȝee hym/ oþer men seyden/ þes
wordis ben not of a man hauynge a fende/ wher a deuyl
may open þe yȝen of blynde men? forsoþe newe feestis of
halowynge of þe temple ben made in irłm: and it was wyn-
ter/ and Ihc walkide in þe temple: in þe porche of salomon/
þerfore iewis enuyrouneden hym: and seyden to hym/ hou
longe doist þou aweye oure soule? ȝif þou art Crist/ seye to vs
pleynly (or openly)/ Ihc answeride to hem/ I speke to ȝou:
and ȝee bileuen not/ þe werkis þat I do in name of my fadir:
þes beren witnessynge of me/ but & ȝee bileuen not: for ȝee
ben not of my scheep/ my scheep heren my voyce: and I
knowe hem· & þei suen me/ and I ȝyue to hem euerlastynge
lijf: & þei schulen not perische into wiþ outen ende/ and any
man schal not rauysche hem of myne hande/ þat þing þat
my fadir ȝaue to me is more þan alle/ þerfore no man may
rauysche fro my fadris hande/ I & þe fadir ben one þing/
Iewes token vp stones: for to stoon hym to deþ/ Ihc answeride to hem/ I haue schewide to ȝou manye werkis of
my fadir: for whiche werkis of hem stonen ȝee me? þe iewes
answeriden to hym/ we stoonen þee not of good werkes: but
of blasfemye/ & for þou siþen þou art a man: makist þiself
god/ Ihc answeride to hem/ wher it is not writen in ȝoure
lawe· for I seye ȝee ben goddis? ȝif he seyde hem goddis·
to whom þe worde of god is made· & þe scripture whiche þe
fadir halowide & sente into þe worlde may not be vndone· &

Joon

ȝee seyn for I blasfeme· for I seyde I am goddis sone? ȝif I do not þe werkis of my fadir: nyl ȝee bileue to me/ soþely ȝif I do· þouȝ ȝee wolen not bileue to me: bileue ȝee to þe werkis/ þat ȝee knowe & bileue: for þe fadir is in me· & I in þe fadir/ þerfore þei souȝten for take hym: & he wente oute of here handis/ and he wente eftesone ouer Jordan· into þat place where Joon was firste baptysynge: and he dwelte þere/ and manye camen to hym & seyden: for soþely Jon dide no signe (or myracle) forsoþe alle þingis what euer Joon seyde of þis: weren soþe/ and many bileueden into hym //

Cm 11m   Forsoþe þer was sum sijk man lazarus of bethanye of þe castel of mary & marthe his sistris/ forsoþe it was mary þe whiche anoyntide þe lorde wiþ oynement· & wepte his feet wiþ hire heres· whos broþer lazarus was sijk/ þerfore his sistris senten to hym seyinge/ lorde lo he whom þou louest is sijk/ forsoþe Ihc̄ heerynge: seyde to hem/ þes seekenesse is not vnto þe deþ: but for þe glorie of god· þat mannes sone be glorisiede by it/ soþely Ihc̄ louede martha & hire sister marie & lazarus/ þerfore as he̅ herde for he was sijk: þanne soþely in þe same place two dayes/ þer of aftir þes þingis· he seyde to his disciplis/ go we efte into Jude/ þe disciplis seyn to hym/ raby (or mayster) nowe þe Iewis souȝten for to stoon þee· & efte þou gost þidir? Ihc̄ answeride/ wher þer ben not twelue houres of þe day? ȝif any man schal wandre in þe day: he hurtiþ not· for he seeþ þe liȝte of þe worlde/ soþely ȝif he schal wandre in þe nyȝt: he hurtiþ for liȝte is not in hym/ þes þingis he seiþ/ and aftir þes þingis: he seiþ to hem/ lazarus oure frende slepiþ: but I go for to reyse hym fro sleep/ þerfore his disciplis seyden/ lorde ȝif he slepiþ: he
schal

Joon

schal be saaf/ forsoþe Jhc̄ had seyde of his deþ/ but þei
gessiden haþ-he seyde of slepynge of sleep/ þanne þerfore Jhc̄
seyde opynly/ lazarus is deade: and I enioye for you þat ȝee
bileue for I was not þere/ but go we to hym/ þerfore thomas
þat is seyde didymus: seyde to euen disciplis/ and go we:
þat we die wiþ hym/ and so Jhc̄ came · & fonde hym hauynge
nowe foure dayes in þe graue/ sopely bethanye was biside
irim as fiftene furlonges/ forsoþe many of Jewis camen to
mary & marthe · for to coumforte hem of here broþer/ þerfore
as martha herde for Jhū cames sche rennep to hym/ mary
forsoþe sette at home/ þerfore martha seyde to Jhū/ lorde ȝif
þou haddist ben here: my broþer had not ben deade/ but &
nowe I woot · þat whateuer þingis þou schalt are of god: god
schal ȝyue to þee/ Jhc̄ seiþ to hire/ þi broþer schal rise aȝen/
martha seiþ to hym/ I woot for he schal rise aȝen in þe aȝen
rysyng in þe laste day/ Jhc̄ seiþ to hire/ I am aȝen risynge
& liff/ he þat bileueþ into me: ȝhe ȝif he schal be deade:
schal lyue/ and eche þat lyueþ & bileueþ into me: schal not
die into wiþ outen ende/ bileuest þou þis þing? sche seiþ to
hym/ forsoþe (or ȝhe) lorde/ I haue bileuede for þou art crist·
þe sone of quycke· [   ] þat haste comen into þis worlde/
and whanne sche had seyde þis þing · sche wente & clepide
mary hire sister in silence or (stillenesse) seyinge/ þe mayster
comeþ & clepiþ þee/ sche as sche herde roos anone: and came
to hym/ sopely Jhc̄ came not ȝit into þe castel: but he was
ȝit in þat place · where martha had comen aȝenes hym/ þerfore þe Iewis þat weren wiþ hire in þe hous & comfortiden
hire · whanne þei sien mary · for soone sche roos & wente
oute: sueden hire seyinge/ for sche goiþ to þe graue: for to
wepe þere/ forsoþe mary whanne sche hadde seyn where Jhc̄
was:

Joon

was / seinge hym selue to his feet· ⁊ seyde to hym/ lorde ȝif
þou haddist ben / my broþer had not ben deade/ þerfore as
Jhc siȝe hire weppnge ⁊ þe iewis þat weren wiþ hire weppnge /
he made noyse in spirit ⁊ trublide hym self ⁊ seyde/ where
haue ȝee putte hym/ þei seyden to hym/ lorde come and se /
and Jhc wepte/ þerfore þe Jewis seyden lo how he louede
hym/ forsoþe summe of hem seyden/ wher þis man þat
openyde þe yȝen of þe borne blynde· myȝte not make· ⁊ þis
diede not / þerfore efte Jhc makynge noyse of hymself / come
to þe graue / forsoþe þer was a den / and a stoon putte þer
on/ Jhc seiþ take ȝee awey þe stoon/ martha þe sister of hym
þat was deade / seiþ to hym/ lorde he stynkiþ nowe· soþely
he is of foure dayes/ Jhc seiþ to hire/ haue I not seyde to
þee/ for ȝif þou schalt bileue / þou schalt see glorie of god /
þerfore þei token awey þe stoon/ forsoþe þe yȝen reyside
vpwarde / Jhc seyde/ fadir I do þankyngis to þee / for þou
euermore herdist me/ forsoþe I wiste þou euermore herist
me / but for þe puple þat stondiþ aboute I seyde þat þei
bileue· for þou haste sente me/ whanne he had seyde þes
þingis / he criede wiþ greet voyce/ laȝar come þou forþ/ and
anone he þat was deade / came forþ· bounden þe handis ⁊
þe feet wiþ bondis/ and his face was bounden wiþ a sudarie
(or swetynge cloþ/) Jhc seiþ to hem/ vnbynde ȝee hym / and
suffre ȝee go awey/ þerfore many of þe iewis þat camen to
mary ⁊ martha· ⁊ siȝen what þingis he dide / bileueden in
hym/ soþely summe of hem wenten to þe pharisees· ⁊ seyden
to hem what þingis Jhc dide// ¶ þerfore þe bisschopes ⁊ þe
pharisees gederiden a counseyl aȝenes Jhu / ⁊ seyden/ what
done we· for þis man doþ manye signes (or myraclis /) ȝif
we leeuen hym þus / alle men schulen bileue into hym/ and
                                                        romayns

Ioon

romayns schulen come: and schulen take oure place ⁊ folc/ forsoþe one of hem cayphas by name· whanne he was bischop of þat ȝeer seyde to hem/ ȝee witen no þing· for it spediþ to ȝou þat one man die for þe puple: and þat al þe folc perische not/ forsoþe he seyde not þis þing of hym self· but whanne he was bischop of þat ȝeer· he propheciede for Ihc was to dye for þe folc/ and not onely for þe folc: but þat he schulde gedir into one þe sones of god þat weren scateride/ þerfore fro þat day: þei þouȝten for to slee hym// ¶ þerfore Ihc walkide not nowe opynly at þe Iewes: but he wente into a regioñ (or cuntre) bisidis deserte: into a cyte þat is seyde effraym· and þere he dwellide wiþ his disciplis/ forsoþe þe paske of Iewes was nexte: and many of þe cuntre steyȝeden vp to irlm: and þe day bifore pask· for to halowe hem self/ þerfore þei souȝten Ihc: and spaken to gedir· stondynge in þe temple/ what gessen ȝee for he comeþ not to þe feest day/ forsoþe þe bischopis ⁊ pharisees hadden ȝouen a maundement· þat ȝff any man knewe where he is· he schewe· þat þei take hym//

Therfore Ihc bifore sixe dayes of paske came to bethanȝe C⁰ 12ᵘ where laȝarus was deade· whom Ihc reyside/ forsoþe þei maden to hym a soper þere: and martha mynystride to hym/ laȝarus forsoþe was one of þe men sittynge at þe mete wiþ hym/ þerfore mary toke a pounde of oynement precious spikenarde· ⁊ anoyntide þe feet of Ihc wiþ hire heris/ and þe hous is fulfilde of þe sauour of þe oynement/ þerfore Iudas scarioth one of his disciplis þat was to bitraye hym: seyde/ whi is þis oynement not solde for þre hundride pens ⁊ is ȝouen to nedy men/ forsoþe he seyde þis þing· not for it parteynede to hym of nedy men: but for he was a þeef· ⁊

he

Joon

he hauynge purses· bare þo þingis þat weren sente/ þerfore Jhū seyde/ suffre 3ee hire· þat into þe day of my biryinge sche kepe þat/ forsoþe 3ee schulen euermore haue pore men wiþ you: soþely 3ee schulen not euermore haue me/ þerfore myche cumpanye of lewis knewen þat Jhc was þere/ and þei camen not oonly for Jhū: but for to se lazarus whom he reyside fro deade/ ¶ fforsoþe þe princes of pristis þou3ten for to slee lazarus· for manye of þe lewis for hym wenten awey & bileueden into Jhū/ forsoþe þe morow a myche cumpanye þat came to gedir at þe feest day· whanne þei hadden herde whanne Jhū comeþ to Jrlm· tooken braunchis of palmes· & camen forþe a3ens hym & crieden/ osanna blessid is he þat comeþ in þe name of þe lorde kyng of isrl/ and Jhc fonde a litil asse· & satte vpon hym: as it is writen/ þe dou3ter of sion nyl 3ou drede/ lo þi kyng comeþ· sittynge on þe colte of a sche asse/ his disciplis knowen not firste þes þingis: but whanne ihc is glorifiede: þanne þei recordiden (or hadden mynde) for þes þingis weren writen of hym· & þes þingis þei diden to hym/ þe cumpanye bare witnessynge þat was wiþ hym· whanne he clepide lazarus fro þe graue· & reyside hym fro deade/ þerfore and þe cumpanye came metynge to hym: for þei herden hym to haue þis signe/ þerfore þe pharisees seyden to hem self/ 3ee seen for we profiten no þing/ lo al þe worlde wente aftir hym// ¶ fforsoþe þere weren summe heþen men of hem þat hadden sti3ede vp for to worschip in þe feest day/ þerfore þes came to philip· þat was of bethsayda of galilee: and preyede hym seyinge/ sire we wolen se Jhū/ philip comeþ & seiþ to andrewe/ efte andrew & philip seyden to ihū/ soþely ihc answeride to hem seyinge þe houre comeþ þat mannes sone schal be clarifiede/ treuely treuely I seye

Joon

to ȝou· no but þe corne of wheet fallynge into þe erþe schal
be deade: it dwelliþ al one/ soþely ȝif it schal be deade: it
bryngis myche fruyte/ he þat loues his soule (þat is lijf:) schal
leese it/ and he þat hatiþ his soule (þat is lijf) in þis worlde:
kepiþ it into euerlastynge lijf/ ȝif any man serue to me: sue
he me/ and where I am þere ȝ mynystre (or seruaunt) schal
be/ ȝif any man schal mynystre to me: my fadir schal worschip
hym// ¶ Now my soule is turblide/ and what schal I seye ȝ
fadir saue me fro þis houre/ but for þat þing I came into
þis houre/ fadir clarifie þi name/ þerfore a voyce came fro
heuene: seyinge/ and I haue clarificde: and ȝit I schal cla-
rifie/ þerfore þe cumpanye þat stood ȝ herde: seyde þundre
for to be made/ oþer men seyden an aungel spac to hym/
Ihū answeride ȝ seyde/ þis voyce came not for me: but for
ȝou/ ¶ now is doom of þe worlde/ now þe prynce of þis
worlde schal be caste oute/ and ȝif I schal be enhaunside fro
þe erþe: I schal drawe alle þingis to my self/ soþely þis
þing he seyde: signyfyinge by what deþ he was to die/ þe
cumpanye answeride to hym/ we haue herde of þe lawes for
crist dwelliþ into wiþ outen ende/ how seist þou it biþoueþ
mannes sone for to be areride/ who is þis mannes sone ȝ þerfore Ihū seiþ to hem/ ȝit a litil liȝt is in ȝou/ walke ȝee þe
while ȝee haue liȝt: þat dirkeneslis cacche ȝou not/ and he
wandriþ in dirkeneslis: woot nere whidir he goiþ/ þe while
ȝee haue liȝte: bileue ȝee into liȝt· þat ȝee be þe sones of
liȝte/ Ihū spac þes þingis: and wente ȝ hidde hym fro hem/
¶ Soþely whanne he hadde done so manye signes bifore hem:
ȝei bileueden not in hym/ þat þe worde of ysaie þe prophete
schulde be fulfilde· whiche he seyde/ lorde who bileuede to
oure heerynge· ȝ to whom is þe arme of god schewide/ þerfore

Joon

fore þei myʒten not bileue· for eftesone ysaye seyde/ he haþ
blyndide here yʒen· ⁊ he haþ enduride (or made harde) þe
herte of hem· þat þei se not wiþ yʒen ⁊ vndirstande wiþ
herte· ⁊ þat þei be conuertide (or al turnyde)· ⁊ I hele hem/
ysaie seyde þes þingis· whanne he siʒe þe glorie of hym· ⁊
spac of hym/ neþeles ⁊ of þe pryncees manye bileueden into
hym/ but for þe pharisees þei knowelechiden not· þat þei
schulden not be caste oute of þe synagoge/ forsoþe þei loueden
þe glorie of mens more þan þe glorie of god/ forsoþe Iħc
criede ⁊ seyde· he þat bileueþ into me· bileueth not into me·
but into hym þat sente me/ he þat seeþ me· seeþ hym þat
sente me/ I liʒte came into þe worlde· þat eche man þat
bileueþ into me· dwelle not in dirkenesses/ and any man schal
here my wordis ⁊ schal not kepe· I deme hym not/ forsoþe
I came not þat I deme þe worlde· but þat I make þe worlde
saaf/ he þat dispisiþ me ⁊ takiþ not my wordis· haþ hym
þat schal iuge hym/ þe worde þat I haue spoken· þat schal
deme hym in þe laste daye/ for I haue not spoken of my
self· but þe fadir þat sente me· he ʒaue to me a maunde-
ment· what I schal seye ⁊ what I schal speek/ and I woot
for his maundement· is euerlastynge liff/ þerfore þo þingis
þat I speek· as þe fadir seyde to me· so I speek//

Cap 13m   Forsoþe bifore þe feest day of pask· Iħc witynge for his
houre comeþ· þat he passe of þis worlde to þe fadir· whan
he had loued his þat weren in þe worlde· into þe ende he
louede hem/ and þe soper made whanne þe deuyl had sente
nowe into þe herte of Iudas· þat Iudas of symount scarioth
schulde bitraye hym· he witynge for þe fadir ʒaue alle þingis
to hym into his handis· ⁊ þat he wente oute fro god· and goþ

to

Ioon

to god/ risiþ fro þe soper & puttiþ his cloþes/ & whanne he
had taken a lynnen clooþ/ he bifore girde hym/ aftirwarde he
sente water into a basyn/ and bigan for to wasche his disciplis
feet· & to wipe wiþ lynnen cloþe· wiþ whiche he was bifore
girde/ þerfore he came to Symount petre· & petre seiþ to hym/
lorde what þou waschist to me þe feet/ Ihē answeride & seyde
to hym/ what þingis I do þou woost not nowe/ forsoþe þou
schalt wite aftirwarde/ petre seiþ to hym/ þou schalt not wasche
to me þe feet/ into wiþ outen ende/ Ihē answeride to hym/
ȝif I schal not wasche þee/ þou schalt not haue parte wiþ me/
Symount petre seiþ to hym/ lorde not onely my feet/ but &
þe handis & þe heede/ Ihē seyde to hym/ he þat is wasche
haþ no nede/ no but þat he wasche þe feet· but he is clene
al/ and ȝee ben clene/ but not alle/ for he wiste wel· who
schulde bitraye hym/ þerfore he seyde/ ȝee ben not clene alle/
þerfore aftir warde þat he waschide þe feet of hem/ he toke
his cloþes/ and whanne he had reside aȝen/ efte he seyde
to hem/ ȝee witen what I haue done to ȝou/ ȝee clepen me
mayster & lorde/ & ȝee seyn wel/ forsoþe I am/ þerfore ȝif
I lorde & mayster haue waschen ȝoure feet/ & ȝee schulen
wasche anoþer þe toþers feet/ for I haue ȝouen ensaumple
to ȝou· þat as I haue done to ȝou/ so & ȝee do/ ¶ Treuely
treuely I seye to ȝou/ þe seruaunt is not more þan his lorde/
neþer apostle is more/ þan he þat sente hym/ ȝif ȝee witen
þes þingis/ ȝee schulen be blesside· ȝif ȝee schulen do hem/
I seye not of ȝou alle/ I woote þe whiche I haue chosen/ but
þat þe scripture be fulfilde· he þat etiþ my breede/ schal
reyse heel aȝens me/ treuly treuly I seye to ȝou· bifore it be
done· þat whanne it schal be done/ ȝee bileuen for I am/
treuly treuly I seye to ȝou· he þat takiþ whom euer I schal
sende/

Joon

sende: receyueþ me/ for he þat receyueþ me: receyueþ hym
þat sente me/ whanne Ihū had seyde þes þingis: he was
turblide ⁊ seyde/ treuly treuly I seye to you· for one of you
schal bitraye me/ þerfore þe disciplis lokeden to gedir: dout-
ynge of whom he seyde/ þerfore one of his disciplis was rest-
ynge in þe bosum of Ihū: whom Ihū louede/ þerfore symount
petre bileuyde to hym: and seiþ to hym/ who is it of þe whiche
he seiþ/ and so whanne he had restide ayen vpon þe breste
of Ihū: he seiþ to hym/ lorde who is it? Ihē answeride/ he
it is to whom I schal dresse breed indippide/ and whanne he
had dippide in breed: he yaue to Iudas of Symount scarioth/
and aftir þe mussel: þanne sathanas entrede into hym/ and
Ihē seiþ to hym/ what þingis þou doest: do þou sunner/ forsoþe no man of sittynge at þe mete wiste þis þing: to what
þing he seyde to hym/ forsoþe summe gessiden for Iudas had
pursis: þat Ihē had seyde to hym/ bie þou þo þingis þat
ben nedeful to vs: at þe feest day: or þat he schulde yyue
sum þing to nedy men/ þerfore whanne he had taken þe
mussel: he wente oute anone/ forsoþe it was nyyt/ þerfore
whanne he hadde gon oute: Ihē seyde mannes sone is clarifiede ⁊ god is clarifiede in hym: ⁊ god schal clarifie hym in
hym self· ⁊ anone he schal clarifie hym/ litil sones· yit a litil
I am wiþ you/ yee schulen seek me· ⁊ as I seyde to þe
Iewis: whidir I go yee mowne not come/ and to you I seye
now/ I yyue you a newe maundement· þat yee louen to gedir
as I louede you: þat ⁊ yee louen to gedir/ in þis þing alle
men schulen knowe· þat yee ben my disciplis: yif yee schulen
haue loue to gedir/ Symount petre seiþ to hym/ lorde whidir
goste þou? Ihē answeride: whidir I go þou maȝt not sue
me nowe· but þou schalt sue aftirwarde/ petre seiþ to hym/
whi

Joon

whi may I not sue þee nowe? I schal putte my soule þat is my lijf:) for þee/ Ihū answeride/ þou schalt putte þi soule (þat is þi lijf) for me/ treuly treuly I seye to þee· þe cocke schal not crowe til þou schalt denye me þries/ ⁊ he seiþ to his disciplis//

Be not ȝoure herte distourblide: ne drede it/ ȝee bileuen Cm 14m into god: ⁊ bileue ȝee into me/ in þe hous of my fadir: ben many dwellyngis/ ȝif any lesse: I schulde haue seyde to ȝou· for I go for to make redy to ȝou a place/ ⁊ ȝif I schal go aweye, ⁊ schal make redy to ȝou a place: eftesone I come· ⁊ schal take ȝou to my silf/ þat where I am: ⁊ ȝee be/ and whidir I go ȝee witen: ⁊ ȝee wite þe weye/ thomas seiþ to hym/ lorde we witen not whidir þou goest/ and how mowne we wite þe weye/ Ihū seiþ to hym/ I am weye treuþe ⁊ liff/ no man comeþ to þe fadir: no but by me/ ȝif ȝee hadden knowe me: sopely ȝee hadden knowen ⁊ my fadir/ ⁊ aftirwarde ȝee schulen knowe hym: and ȝee haue seen hym/ philip seiþ to hym/ lorde schewe to vs þe fadir: and it sufficeþ to vs/ Ihū seiþ to hym/ so myche tyme I am wiþ ȝou· ⁊ haue ȝee not knowen me? philip he þat seeþ me· seeþ ⁊ þe fadir/ how seyste þou schewe to vs þe fadir/ bileuest þou not· for I in þe fadir ⁊ þe fadir is in me/ I speke not of myself: þe wordis þat I speke to ȝou/ sopely þe fadir dwellynge in me: he doiþ þe werkis/ bileue ȝee not for I in þe fadir ⁊ þe fadir is in me/ ellis bileue ȝee for þe ilke werkis/ treuly treuly I seye to ȝou· he þat bileueþ into me: and he schal do þe werkis þat I do/ ⁊ he schal do more werkis þan þes· for I go to þe fadir/ and what euer þing ȝee schulen axe þe fadir in my name: I schal do þis þing· þat þe fadir be glorifiede

Joon

in þe sone/ ȝif ȝee schulen are ony þing in my name; I schal do þis þing· þat þe fadir be glorifiede in þe sone/ ȝif ȝee schulen are ony þing in my name; I schal do it/ ȝif ȝee louen me; kepe ȝee my comaundementis/ & I schal preye þe fadir; and he schal gife to ȝou anoþer confortoure· þat he dwelle wiþ ȝou into wiþ outen ende· þe spirit of treuþe/ whiche (spirit) þe worlde may not take; for it seeþ not hym neþer woot hym/ forsoþe ȝee schulen knowe hym; for he schal dwelle at ȝou· & he schal be in ȝou/ I schal not leeue ȝou fadirles; I schal come to ȝou/ ȝit a litil & þe worlde seeþ not me now/ forsoþe ȝee schulen se me; for I lyue; and ȝee schulen lyue/ in þat day ȝee schulen knowe· for I am in my fadir; & ȝee in me· & I in ȝow/ he þat haþ my comaundementis & kepiþ hem; he it is þat loueþ me/ forsoþe he þat loueþ me schal be loued of my fadir/ & I schal loue hym; & I schal schewe to hym my self/ Judas seiþ to hym· not he of scarioth/ lorde what is done; for þou art to schewe to us þi self· & not to þe worlde/ Jhc answeride & seyde to hym/ ȝif ony man loueþ me; he schal kepe my worde/ and my fadir schal loue hym· & we schulen come to hym· & we schulen make dwellynge at hym/ he þat loueþ not me; kepiþ not my wordis/ and þe worde whiche ȝee haue herde is not myn; but his þat sente me þe fadris/ þes þingis I haue spoken to ȝou; dwellynge at ȝou/ forsoþe þe holy gost comfortoure whom þe fadir schal sende in my name; he schal teche ȝou al þingis/ and schal schewe to ȝou all þingis; what euer I schal seye to ȝou/ pees I leeue to ȝou; my pees I ȝyue to ȝou/ not as þe worlde ȝyueþ; I ȝyue to ȝou; be not ȝoure herte distourblide; ne drede it/ ȝee haue herde for I seyde to ȝou; I go & come to ȝou; ȝif ȝee loueden me; forsoþe ȝee schulen ioye· for I go to þe fadir·

Joon

fadir· for þe fadir is more þan I/ and nowe I haue seyde to ȝou bifore it be done: þat whanne it schal be done: ȝee bileue/ now I schal not speke many þingis to ȝou/ forsoþe þe prynce of þis worlde comeþ: and he haþ not in me any þing/ but þat þe worlde knowe: for I loue þe fadir/ and as þe fadir ȝaue to me comaundement: so I do/ rise ȝee: go we hens//

I am a verrey vyne: and my fadir is an erþe tiller/ eche C⁰ 15ᵐ syon (or braunche) not berynge fruyte in me: he schal do it aweye/ ⁊ eche þat beriþ fruyte: he schal purge it· þat it more bere fruyte/ nowe ȝee ben clene: for þe worde þat I haue spoken to ȝou/ dwelle ȝee in me: ⁊ I in ȝou/ as a sioune (or braunche) may not make fruyte of it self: no but it schal dwelle in þe vyne tree: so neþer ȝee no but ȝif ȝee schulen dwelle in me/ I am a vyntree: ȝee þe siouns (or braunchis)/ who þat dwelliþ in me ⁊ I in hym: þis beriþ myche fruyte/ for wiþ outen me: ȝee moune no þing do/ ȝif any man schal not dwelle in me: lo he schal be sente oute as a sciounc· ⁊ schal waxe drie/ and þei schulen gedir hym· ⁊ þei schulen sende hym into þe fire· ⁊ he brenneþ/ ȝif ȝee schulen dwelle in me· ⁊ my wordis dwelle in ȝou: what euer þing ȝee schulen wille· ȝee schulen axe· ⁊ it schal be done to ȝou/ in þis þing my fadir is clarified: þat ȝee brynge moste fruyte· ⁊ ȝee be made my disciplis/ as my fadir louede me: ⁊ I louede ȝou/ dwelle ȝee in my loue/ ȝif ȝee schulen kepe my maundementis: ȝee schulen dwelle in my loue· as I haue kepte þe maundementis of my fadir/ and I dwelle in his loue/ þes þingis I spac to ȝou þat my ioye be in ȝou: and ȝoure ioye be fulfilde// ¶ þis is þe comaundement· þat ȝee loue togedir as I
louede

louede ȝou/ no man haþ more loue þan þis: þat any putte
his soule for his frendis/ ȝee ben my frendis· ȝif ȝee schulen
do þes þingis þat I comaunde ȝou/ nowe I schal not seye
ȝou seruauntis: for þe seruaunt woot not what his lorde schal
do/ forsoþe I haue seyde ȝou frendis: for alle þingis what
euer I herde of my fadir: I haue made knowen to ȝou/ ȝee
haue not chosen me/ but I chees ȝou· & putte ȝou þat ȝee
go & brynge fruyte: and ȝoure fruyte dwelle/ þat what euer
þing ȝee schulen aske þe fadir in my name: he ȝyue to ȝou/
þes þingis I comaunde to ȝou þat ȝee loue togedir/ ȝif þe
worlde hate ȝou: wite ȝee for it hadde me in haate firste þan
ȝou/ ȝif ȝee hadden ben of þe worlde: þe worlde schulde loue
þat þing þat was his/ but for ȝee ben not of þe worlde· but
I chees ȝou fro þe worlde: þerfore þe worlde hatiþ ȝou: haue
ȝee mynde of my worde· þe whiche I seyde to ȝou: þe seruaunt
is not more þan his lorde/ ȝif þei haue pursuede me: & þei
schulen pursue ȝou/ ȝif þei haue kepte my worde: and þei
schulen kepe ȝoure/ but þei schulen do to ȝou alle þes þingis
for my name: for þei witen not hym þat sente me/ ȝif I had
not comen & hadde not spoken to hem þei schulden not haue
synne/ forsoþe now þei haue not excusacōn of here synne/ he
þat hatiþ me: hatiþ & my fadir/ ȝif I hadde not done werkis
in hem· þe whiche none oþer man dide: þei schulden not haue
synne/ forsoþe nowe & þei haue seen & hatide me: & my fadir/
but þat þe worde be fulfilde þat is writen in ȝoure lawe: for
þei hadden me in hate wiþ outen cause/ forsoþe whanne þe
comfortoure schal come· þe whiche I schal sende to ȝou fro þe
fadir· a spirit of treuþe· þe whiche procediþ (or comeþ forþe)
of þe fadir: he schal bere witnessynge of me/ and ȝee schulen
bere witnessynge: for ȝee ben wiþ me fro þe bygynnynge.//

Thes

Ioon

Thes þingis I haue spoken to ȝou: þat ȝee be not Cm 16m
sclaunderide/ þei schulen make ȝou wiþ outen synagogis/ but
þe houre comeþ· þat eche man þat sleeþ ȝou: deme hym
for to ȝyue seruyce to god/ and þei schulen do to ȝou þingis:
for þei haue not knowen þe fadir neþer me/ but þes þingis
I spac to ȝou· þat whanne þe houre of hem schal come: ȝee
haue mynde for I seyde to ȝou/ ¶ I seyde not to ȝou þes
þingis fro þe bigynnynge: for I was wiþ ȝou/ & nowe I go
to hym þat sente me: & no man of ȝou axiþ me whidir gost
þou/ but for I haue spoken to ȝou þes þingis· sorowe or
heuynesse haþ fulfilde ȝoure herte/ but I seye to ȝou treuþe:
it spediþ to ȝou þat I go/ soþely ȝif I schal not go aweye:
þe confortoure schal not come to ȝou/ forsoþe ȝif I schal go
aweye: I schal sende hym to ȝou/ and whanne he schal come:
he schal reproue þe worlde of synne & of riȝtwelnesse & of
doom/ forsoþe of synne for ȝee haue not bileuede into me/
soþely of riȝtwesnesse: for I go to þe fadir· & nowe ȝee schulen
not se me/ forsoþe of doom: for þe prynce of þis worlde is
now demyde// ¶ ȝit I haue many þingis for to seye to ȝou:
but ȝee mowne not here now/ soþely whanne þe ilke spirit
of treuþe schal come: he schal teche ȝou al treuþe/ soþely
he schal not speke of hym self: but what euer þingis he schal
here: he schal speke/ & he schal telle ȝou: þes þingis þat ben
to come/ he schal clarifie me: for of myn he schal take· &
schal telle to ȝou/ alle þingis what kyn þingis þe fadir haþ:
ben myne/ þerfore I seyde to ȝou: for of myn he schal take
& telle to ȝou/ ¶ A litil & nowe ȝee schulen not se me: &
eftesone a litil· & ȝee schulen se me· for I go to þe fadir/
þerfore somme of his disciplis seyden to geþir/ what is þis
þing þat he seiþ to vs· a litil & ȝee schulen not se me: for

I

Joon

I go to þe fadir/ þerfore þei seyden what is þis þat he seiþ to us a litil / we witen not what he spekiþ/ forsoþe Ihc̄ knewe for þei wolden axe: and he seyde to hem/ of þis þing ȝee seeken amonge ȝou: for I seyde/ a litil & ȝee schulen not se me: & eftesone a litil & ȝee schulen se me/ treuely treuly I seye to ȝou· for ȝee schulen mourne & wepe: forsoþe þe worlde schal enioye/ for ȝee schulen be sorowful: but ȝoure sorowe (or heuynesse): schal turne into ioye/ soþely a womman whanne sche bereþ childe: haþ sorowe for hire houre comeþ/ forsoþe whanne sche haþ borne a sone: nowe sche þenkiþ not of þe pressure (or peyne) for ioye· for a man is borne into þe worlde/ & þerfore ȝee haue nowe sorowe/ soþely eftesone I schal se ȝou: and ȝoure herte schal enioye/ and no man schal take fro ȝou ȝoure ioye/ & in þat day ȝee schulen not axe me any þing/ treuly treuly I seye to ȝou· ȝif ȝee schulen axe þe fadir any þing in my name: he schal ȝyue it to ȝou/ til nowe ȝee axiden not any þing in my name/ axe ȝee: and ȝee schulen take þat ȝoure ioye be ful/ I haue spoken to ȝou þes þingis in prouerbis (or dirke saumples)/ þe houre comeþ· whanne nowe I schal not speke to ȝou in prouerbis: but oppenly of my fadir I schal telle to ȝou/ in þat day ȝee schul axe in my name/ & nowe I seye to ȝou· for I schal preye þe fadir of ȝou/ forsoþe he þe fadir loueþ ȝou: for ȝee haue louede me· & haue bileuede for I wente oute fro god/ I wente oute fro þe fadirs and I came into þe worlde/ eftesone I leeue þe worlde: & I go to þe fadir/ his disciplis seyden/ lo nowe þou spekest oppenly: and þou seist no prouerbe/ nowe we witen for þou woste alle þingis: & it is no nede to þee· þat any man axe þee/ in þis þing we bileuen: for þou wentist oute fro god/ Ihc̄ answeride to hem/ now ȝee bileuen/ lo þe houre comeþ· & nowe it comeþ:

þat

Ioon

þat ȝee be disparplide (or scateride)· eche into his owne þingis/ and leeue me al one/ and I am not al one: for þe fadir is wiþ me/ þes þingis I haue spoken to ȝou: þat ȝee haue pees in me/ in þe worlde ȝee schulen haue pressynge (or ouerleyinge)/ but triste ȝee I haue ouercomen þe worlde //

Thes þingis Jhc̄ spac· & þe iȝen lifte vp into heuenes he seyde/ fadir þe houre comeþ· clarifie þi sone· þat þi sone clarifie þee/ as þou hast ȝouen to hym power of eche fleysche (or man) þat alle þing þat þou hast ȝouen to hym/ he ȝyue to hem euerlastynge liff/ forsoþe þis is euerlastynge lijf: þat þei knowe þee al one verrey god· & whom þou sentist Jhū crist/ I haue clarifiede þee on erþe: I haue endide þe werke þat þou hast ȝouen to me þat I do/ and nowe fadir clarifie þou me at þi self· wiþ clereneste þat I had at þee: bifore þe worlde was made/ I haue schewide þi name to þe men whom þou hast ȝouen to me of þe worlde/ þei weren þin· & þou hast ȝouen hem to me: & þei haue kepte þi worde/ and nowe þei haue knowen· for alle þingis þat þou hast ȝouen to me: ben of þee/ for þe wordis þat þou hast ȝouen to me: I ȝaue to hem/ & þei haue taken & haue knowen verreyly· for I wente oute fro þee· & þei bileueden· for þou sentist me/ I preye for hem· not for þe worlde: but for hem þat þou hast ȝouen to me/· for þei ben þin· & þi þingis ben myne: and I am clarifiede in hem/ and now I am not in þe worlde & þes ben in þe worlde & I come to þee/ holy fadir kepe hem in þi name· whom þou ȝauest to me· þat þei ben one as & we/ whanne I was wiþ hem: I kepte hem in þi name/ whom þou ȝauest to me I kepte: & no man of hem perischide· no but þe sone of perdicōn (or dampnacōn)· þat þe scripture be fulfilde/ forsoþe

Cᵐ 17ᵐ

Joon

forsoþe nowe I come to þee · & þes þingis I speek in þe worlde: þat þei haue my ioye fulfilde in hem self/ I ȝaue to hem þi worde · & þe worlde had hem in hate · for þei ben not of þe worlde · as I am not of þe worlde/ I preye not þat þou take hem aweye of þe worlde: but þat þou kepe hem fro euyl/ þei ben not of þe worlde: as I am not of þe worlde/ halowe þou hem in treuþe/ þi worde is treuþe/ as þou sentist me into þe worlde: & I sente hem into þe worlde/ & I halowe myself for hem: þat & þei ben halowide in treuþe/ soþely I preye not onely for hem: but & for hem þat ben to bileue into me · bi þe worde of hem/ þat alle ben one · as þou fadir in me · & I in þee · þat & þei in vs ben one · þat þe worlde bileue for þou hast sente me/ and I haue ȝouen to hem þe clerenesse þat þou hast ȝouen to me: þat þei ben one · as we ben one/ I in hem & þou in me: þat þei ben endide into one/ & þat þe worlde knowe þat þou sentist me & hast louede hem: as & þou hast louede me/ fadir I wole þat & þei whom þou ȝauest to me: be wiþ me where I am/ þat þei se my clerenesse whiche þou hast ȝouen to me · for þou louedist me bifore þe makynge of þe worlde/ fadir Iust (or riȝtful) · þe worlde knewe þee not · forsoþe I knewe þee: & þes knowen for þou sentist me/ and I haue made þi name knowen to hem · & schal make knowen: þat þe loue by whiche þou hast louede me: be in hem · & I in hem/|

Cm 18m &Whanne Ihē hadde seyde þes þingis: he wente oute wiþ his disciplis ouer þe strounde of cedron where was a ȝerde · into whiche he entride & his disciplis/ soþely & Iudas þat bitrayede hym · wiste þe place: for ofte ihē came to gedir þidir wiþ his disciplis/ þerfore whanne Iudas hadde taken a cumpanye of knyȝtis & of bischopis & pharisees mynystris: he came þidir wiþ lanternes

Joon

lanternes & brondis & armes/ and so iħc witynge alle þingis þat weren to come vpon hym: wente forþ & seiþ to hem/ whom seeke ȝee? þei answeriden to hym/ Jħu of nazareth/ Jħc seiþ to hem/ I am/ forsoþe & Judas þat bitrayede hym/ stode wiþ hem/ þerfore as he seyde to hem I am: þei wenten abac & felden doune into þe erþe/ eftesone he axide hem/ whom seeke ȝee? forsoþe þei seyden Jħu nazarene/ he answeride to hem/ I seyde to ȝou· for I am/ þerfore ȝif ȝee seeken me: suffre ȝee þes to go aweye/ þat þe worde whiche he seyde be ful-filde: for he loste not any of hem· þe whiche þou hast ȝouen to me/ þerfore symount petre hauynge a swerde drowe it oute & smote þe seruaunt of þe bischop· & kitte of his litil riȝt ere/ forsoþe þe name to þe seruaunt was malcus/ þerfore Jħc seyde to petre/ sende þou þe swerde into þe schepe/ wolte þou not þat I drynke þe like cuppe· þat my fadir ȝaue to me? þerfore þe cumpanye of knyȝtis & þe tribune & þe mynystris of Iewis token Jħu & bounden hym· & ledden hym first to annas/ soþely he was þe fadir of caypphas wife: þat was bischop of þat ȝeer/ soþely it was cayphas þat ȝaue counseyl to þe Iewis· þat it spediþ one man for to die for þe puple/ fforsoþe Symount petre suede Jħu: and anoþer disciple/ fforsoþe þe ilke disciple was knowen to þe bischop: and he entride in wiþ Jħu· into þe halle of þe bischop/ forsoþe petre stoode at þe dore wiþ oute forþ/ þerfore þe toþer disciple þat was knowen to þe bischop wente oute: & seyde to þe womman kepynge þe dore· & ledde in petre/ þerfor þe handemayden keper of þe dore: seyde to petre/ wher & þou art of þe disciplis of þis man? he seyde I am not/ forsoþe þe seruauntis & þe mynystris stoden at þe coolis· for it was colde: & þei warmeden hem/ soþely & petre was wiþ hem stondynge & warmynge hym/ þerfore þe bischopis
axide

Joon

axide Jhū of his diſciplis: and of his techynge/ Jhē anſweride to hym/ I haue ſpoken opynly to þe worlde/ I tauȝte euer‑more in ſynagoge ⁊ in temple· whider alle þe iewis camen to gedir· ⁊ in pryuete I ſpac no þing/ what axiſt þou me: axe hem þat herden· what I haue ſpoken to hem/ lo þei witen· what þingis I haue ſeyde/ whanne he had ſeyde· one of þe myȝyſtris ſtondynge nyȝ: ȝaue a buffet to Jhū· ſeyinge/ an‑ſwereſt þou ſo to þe biſchop? Jhē anſweride to hym/ ȝif I haue ſpoken euyl: bere þou witneſſynge of euyl/ ſoþely ȝif wel: whi ſmyteſt þou me: and annas ſente hym bounden to capphas þe biſchop/ forſoþe Symount petre was ſtondynge ⁊ warmyng hym/ þerfore þei ſeyden to hym/ wher ⁊ þou art his diſciple? he denyede ⁊ ſeyde/ I am not/ one of þe biſchopis ſeruauntis coſyn of hym whos litil ere petre kitte of: ſeyde/ wher I ſiȝe þee not in þe ȝerde wiþ hym? þerfore petre efteſone denyede/ and anone þe cocke crewe/ ⁋ þerfore þei ledden hym into þe mote halle/ ſoþely it was morowtynge/ and þei entride not into þe mote halle· þat þei ſchulden not be defoulide: but þat þei ſchulden ete paſke/ þerfore pilate wente oute wiþ outen forþ to hem: and ſeyde/ what accuſynge bryngen ȝee aȝenes þis man? þei anſwereden to hym ⁊ ſeyden/ ȝif þis man were not a myſdoer: we hadden not bitaken hym to þee/ þerfore pilate ſeiþ to hem/ take ȝee hym: ⁊ deme ȝee hym aftir ȝoure lawe/ þerfore þei ſeyden to hym/ it is not leueful to vs: for to ſlee any man/ þat þe worde of Jhū ſchulde be fulfilde þe whiche he ſeyde/ ſignyfyinge by what deþ he was to die/ þerfore pilat efteſone entride into þe moot hall: and clepide Jhū ⁊ ſeyde to hym/ art þou kyng of Jewis/ Jhū anſweride ⁊ ſeyde to hym/ ſeiſt þou þis þing of þi ſelf: or oþer to þee ſeyden of me? pilate anſweride/ wher I am a iewe? þi folc ⁊ þi biſchopis

bitoken

Ioon

bitoken þee to me/ what hast þou done? Ihc̄ answeride/ my kyngdom is not of þis worlde/ ȝif my kyngdom were of þis worlde: soþely my mynystris schulden stryue· þat I schulde not be bitaken to þe iewis/ nowe forsoþe my kyngdom is not of hens (or of þis place/) and so pilate seyde to hym/ þerfore þou art kyng? Ihc̄ answeride/ þou seist for I am a kyng/ I in þis þing am borne· ⁊ to þis I came into þe worlde: þat I bere witnessynge to treuþe/ eche man þat is of treuþe: heriþ my voyce/ pilate seiþ to hym/ what is treuþe/ and whanne he had seyde þis þing: eftesone he wente oute to þe iewis/ ⁊ seyde to hem/ I fynde no cause aȝenes hym/ forsoþe it is a custom to ȝou· þat I leeue (or delyuer) one to ȝou in paske/ þerfore wole ȝee I schal dismytte to ȝou þe kyng of Iewes? þer-fore þei crieden eftesone alle seyinge/ not þis: but barrabas/ forsoþe barrabas was a þeef //

Therfore pilate took Ihc̄ ⁊ scourgide/ ⁊ knyȝtis foldynge C^m 19to a crowne of þornes: puttiden to his heede/ ⁊ diden aboute hym a cloþe of purpur: and camen to hym ⁊ seyden to hym [   ] buffetis/ eftesone pilate wente oute: and seyde to hem/ lo I leede hym to ȝou wiþ oute forþe· þat ȝee knowe: for I fynde no cause in hym/ þerfore Ihc̄ wente oute berynge a crowne of þornes: and a cloþe of purpur/ ⁊ he seiþ to hem/ lo þe man/ þerfore whanne þe bischopis ⁊ mynystris hadden seen hym þei crieden seyinge crucifie crucifie hym/ pilate seiþ to hem/ take ȝee hym: and crucifie ȝee/ soþely I fynde no cause in hym/ þe iewis answeriden to hym/ we haue a lawe· ⁊ aftir þe lawe he schal die: for he made hym goddis sone/ þerfore whanne pilate had herde þis worde: he dredde more/ ⁊ he wente into þe moot halle: eftesone he seyde

to

Joon

to Jhū/ of whens art þou? and Jhē ȝaue not anſwere to hym/ and pilate ſeiþ to hym/ ſpekiſt þou not to me? woſte þou not for I haue power for to crucifie þee: and I haue power for to deſpuer þee? Jhē anſwteride/ þou ſchuldiſt not haue any power aȝenes me: no but it were ȝouen to þee from aboue/ þerfore he þat bitrayede me to þee: haþ þe more ſynne/ þerof (or fro þens): pilate ſouȝte for to deſpuer hym/ forſoþe þe lewis crieden ſeyinge/ ȝif þou leeueſt hym þus þou art not frende of ceſar/ for eche man þat makiþ hymſelf kyng: aȝen ſeiþ ceſar/ þerfore pilate whan he had herde þes wordis: ledde Jhū forþ· & ſatte for domeſman· in a place þat is licoſtratos· in ebreu forſoþe galgatha· in engliſche place of caluarie/ forſoþe it was þe euentide of paſke· as þe ſirte houre (or half day)/ and he ſeiþ to þe lewis/ lo ȝoure kyng/ forſoþe þei crieden ſeyinge/ do awey do awey: crucifye hym/ pilate ſeiþ to hem/ ſchal I crucifie ȝoure kyng? þe biſchopis anſwteriden/ we haue not a kyng: no but ceſar/ þerfore þanne pilate bitoke hym to hem: þat he ſchulde be crucifiede/ forſoþe þei token Jhū & ledden oute/ & he berynge to hym ſelf a croſſe· wente oute into þat place þat is ſeyde of caluarie· in ebreu galgatha· where þei crucifieden hym/ and oþer two wiþ hym· on þis ſide & on þat ſide: þerfore Jhē þe mydle/ forſoþe & pilate wrote a title: & putte on þe croſſe/ ſoþely it was writen/ Jhū naȝareth kyng of Jewes/ þerfore many of þe Jewis redden þis title: for þe place where Jhū is crucifiede was nyȝ þe cytee/ & it was writen in ebreu greek & latyn/ þerfore þe biſchopis of Jewes ſeyden to pilate/ nyl þou write kyng of Jewes: but for he ſeyde I am kyng of lewes/ pilate anſwteride/ þat þat I haue writen· I haue writen/ þerfore þe knyȝtis whanne þei hadden crucifiede hym: token hys clopes & maden foure

parties·

Joon

parties· to eche knyʒt a parte/ and a coot/ forſoþe þe coote was wiþouten ſeem: and aboue wouen by al/ þerfore þei ſeyden to gedir/ kitte we not it: but laye we lotte whos it is/ þat þe ſcripture be fulfilde: ſeyinge þei partiden my cloþes to hem: ⁊ into my clooþ þei ſenten lotte/ and ſoþely knyʒtis diden þes þingis/ ⁋ fforſoþe biſidis þe croſſe of Jhū ſtoden his modir· ⁊ þe ſiſter of his modir· mary cleophe ⁊ mary maudeleyn/ þerfore whanne Jhū hadde ſeen þe modir· ⁊ þe diſciple ſtondynge whom he louede: he ſeiþ to his modir/ womman lo þi ſone/ aftirwarde he ſeyde to þe diſciple/ lo þi modir/ ⁊ fro þat houre: þe diſciple took hire into his modir// ⁋ Aftirwarde Jhū witynge for now alle þingis ben endide: þat þe ſcripture ſchulde be fulfilde: he ſeiþ/ I þriſte/ ſoþely a veſſel was putte ful of vynegre/ þei forſoþe puttynge aboute wiþ yſope þe ſpounge ful vynegre: offerden to his mouþ/ þerfore whanne Jhū hadde taken þe vynegre: he ſeyde/ it is endide/ and þe heed bowide doune: he bitoke þe ſpirit/ forſoþe for it was paſke euen· þat þe bodies ſchulden not dwelle in þe croſſe in þe ſaboth· for þe ilke day of ſaboth was greet/ þe Iewes preyeden pilate þat þe hippis of hem ſchulden be broken ⁊ taken awey/ þerfore knyʒtis camen· ⁊ ſoþely þei braken þe þies of þe firſte· ⁊ of þe toþer þat was crucifiede wiþ hym/ ſoþely whanne þei hadden comen to Jhū: as þei ſiʒen hym deade· þei braken not his þies: but one of þe knyʒtis openyde his ſide wiþ a ſpere/ ⁊ anone blood ⁊ water wente oute/ and he þat ſiʒe bare witneſſynge: ⁊ his witneſſynge is trewe· for he woot þat he ſeiþ trewe þingis: þat ʒee bileue/ forſoþe þes þingis ben done: þat þe ſcripture ſchulde be fulfilde/ ʒee ſchulen not breke (or make leſſe) a boon of hym/ ⁊ eftſone anoþer ſcripture ſeiþ/ þei ſchulen ſe into whom þei putten hourʒ/ Soþely aftir

þes

Joon

þes þingis Joseph of armathie preyede pilate þat þei schulden take awey þe body of Jhū / forþi ꝫ nychodeme came þat had comen to Jhū firste in þe nyʒt · berynge a medelynge of myrre ꝸ aloes / as an hundride pounde / þerfore þei token þe body of Jhū ꝸ bounde it in lynnen cloþes wiþ swete oynementis (or spices) / as it is custom to Jewes for to birie / soþely in þe place where he was crucifiede / was a ʒerde / ꝸ in þe ʒerde a newe graue / in þe whiche not ʒit any man was putte / þerfore þere for þe paske euen of Iewis · for þat þe graue was nyʒ / þei puttiden Jhū //

Cm 20m   Forsoþe in one (day) of þe saboth (þat is þe woke) / mary maudeleyn came erly to þe graue · whanne ʒit dirkenessis weren / and sche siʒe þe stoon turnyde aʒen fro þe graue / þerfore sche ran ꝸ came to Symount petre ꝸ to anoþer disciple whom Jhc louede / ꝸ seiþ to hem / þei haue taken þe lorde fro þe graue / and we witen not where þei haue putte hym / þerfore petre wente oute ꝸ þe ilke oþer disciple / and þei camen to þe graue / forsoþe þe two runnen togedir · ꝸ þe ilke oþer disciple ranne bifore sunner þan petre / and came firste to þe graue / and whanne he had inbowide hym / he siʒe þe schetis putte · neþeles he entride not in / þerfore Symount peter came suynge hym / and he entride into þe graue / and he siʒe þe schetis putte · ꝸ þe sudarie þat was on his heede · not putte wiþ þe scheetis / but bi it self wlappide into one place / þerfore þanne ꝸ þe ilke disciple þat came firste to þe graue / entride ꝸ siʒe ꝸ bileuede / forsoþe þei wisten not þe scripture / for it bihofte hym for to rise aʒen fro deade / þerfore þe disciplis wenten eftesone to hem self / forsoþe mary stood at þe graue wiþ outen forþe wepynge / þerfore þe while sche wepte / sche
bowide

Joon

bowlde hire & bihelde forþ into þe graue· & sche si3e two
aungels sittynge in white· one at þe heede & one at þe feet
where þe body of Jhū was putte/ þei seyn to hire/ womman
what wepist þou? sche seyde to hem/ for þei haue take awey
my lorde· & I woot not wher þei haue putte hym/ and whanne
sche hadde seyde þes þingis: sche is turnede abac· & si3e Jhū
stondynge & wiste not for it was Jhū/ Jhc seiþ to hire/ womman
what wepist þou: whom seekist þou? sche gessynge for he was
a gardener: seiþ to hym/ sire 3if þon hast taken hym: seye
to me where þou hastse putte hym· & I schal take hym awey/
Jhc seyde to hire/ mary/ sche conuertide (or al turnede): seiþ
to hym/ rabony (þat is seyde mayster) Jhc seiþ to hire/ nyl
þou touche me/ for I haue not 3it assendide to my fadir/ forsoþe go to my breþeren/ and seye to hem/ I stey3e vp to my
fadir & 3oure fadir: to my god & 3oure god/ mary maudeleyn
came tellynge to þe disciplis· for I haue seen þe lorde/ and
þes þingis he seyde to me/ whan euen was in þat day in one
of þe sabotis· & þe 3atis weren schitte where þe disciplis weren
gederide for drede of þe lewis: Jhc came & stood in þe mydle
of þe disciplis & seiþ to hem/ pees to 3ou/ and whanne he had
seyde þis þing: he schewide to hem handis & syde/ þerfore
þe disciplis io3reden: þe lorde seen/ þerfore he seiþ to hem
efte/ pees to 3ou/ as þe fadir haþ sente me: and I sende 3ou/
whan he had seyde þes þingis: he blewe & seyde to hem/ take
3ee þe holy gost/ whos synnes 3ee schulen for3yue: þei ben
for3ouen/ and whos 3ee schulen wiþ holde: þei ben wiþ holden/
forsoþe thomas one of þe twelue þat is clepide didymus: was
not wiþ hem whanne Jhc came/ þerfore disciplis seyden/ we
haue seen þe lorde/ forsoþe he seyde to hem/ no but I schal
se in his handis þe ficchynge of naylis· & schal sende my
fyngeris

Ioon

fyngeris into þe places of þe naylez· ⁊ schal sende myn hande into hys side: I schal not bileue/ and aftir eyʒte dayes· eftesone his disciplis weren wiþinne: and thomas wiþ hem/ Ihc̄ came þe ʒatis schitte: and stode in þe mydle ⁊ seyde/ pees to ȝou/ aftirwarde he seiþ to thomas/ brynge in þi fynger hidir· ⁊ se myn handis ⁊ brynge to þin hande· ⁊ sende (or putte) it into my side· ⁊ nyl þou be vnbileueful· but feiþful/ thomas answeride ⁊ seyde to hym/ my lorde ⁊ my god/ Ihc̄ seiþ to hym/ thomas for þou hast seen me: þou bileuedest/ blesside bei þat seen not: and haue bileuede/ forsoþe ⁊ many oþer signes Ihc̄ dide in þe siʒte of his disciplis· þe whiche ben not writen in þis booc/ forsoþe þes ben writen þat ʒee bileue for Ihc̄ is þe sone of god/ and þat ʒee bileuynge: haue liff in his name//

Cm 21m Aftirwarde Ihc̄ eftesone schewide hym to his disciplis at þe see of tyberiadis: soþely he schewide þus/ þer weren togedir Symount petre ⁊ thomas þat is seyde didymus· ⁊ nathanael þat was of chana galilee· ⁊ þe sones of ȝebedee· ⁊ oþer of his disciplis tuo [   ]
þei seyn to hym/ and we comen wiþ þee/ and þei wenten oute ⁊ steyʒeden into a boot· ⁊ in þat nyʒt þei token no þing/ forsoþe þe morowe made: Ihc̄ stood in þe brynke/ neþeles þe disciplis knewen not: for it is Ihc̄/ þerfore Ihc̄ seiþ to hem: children wher ʒee haue any souþyng þing/ þei answereden nay/ he seyde to hem/ sende ʒee þe nette into þe riʒthalfe of þe rowynge: and ʒee schulen fynde/ þerfore þei senten þe nette ⁊ nowe þei myʒten not drawe it· for multitude of fischis/ þerfore þe ilke disciple þe whiche Ihc̄ louede: seyde to petre/ it is þe lorde/ Symount petre whanne he had herde for it is

þe

Joon

þe lorde: girde hym wiþ a coot/ soþely he was nakide· ⁊ sente hym into þe see/ soþly oþer disciplis camen bi boot/ for þei weren not fer fro þe lande· but as two hundride cubitis: drawynge þe nette of fischis/ þerfore as þei camen doune into þe lande: þei sizen coolis putte· ⁊ a fische putte þeron· ⁊ breed: Ihс̄ seiþ to hem/ brynge zee of þe fischis: þe whiche zee haue taken nowe/ Symount petre stezzede vp· ⁊ drowe þe nette into þe lande ful of greet fischis· an hundride fifty ⁊ þre/ and whanne þei weren so manye: þe nette is not broken/ Ihс̄ seiþ to hem/ come zee: ete zee/ and no man of þe sittynge at mete durste are hym· who art þou· witynge for it is þe lorde/ and Ihс̄ came ⁊ tooke breede ⁊ zaue to hem· ⁊ þe fische also/ nowe þis þridde tyme/ Ihс̄ is schewide to his disciplis: whan he roos azen fro deade // ¶ þerfore whanne þei hadden eten: Ihс̄ seiþ to Symount petre/ Symount of Joon louest þou me· more þan þes⸗ [   ] þe lorde· þou woste for I loue þee/ Ihс̄ seiþ to hym/ fede þou my lambren/ efte he seiþ to hym/ Symount of Jon louest þou me⸗ [   ] þe lorde þou woste for I loue þee/ [   ] he seiþ to hym þe þridde tyme/ Symount of Jon louest þou me⸗ petre is heuy (or soory) for he seiþ þe þridde tyme louest þou me/ and he seiþ to hym/ lorde þou woste alle þingis· þou woste for I loue þee/ Ihс̄ seiþ to hym/ feet my scheep/ treuely treuely I seye to þee· whan þou were zonger þou girdist þee ⁊ wandrist where þou woldist/ soþely whanne þou schalt waxe elder: þou schalt holde forþe þin handis· ⁊ anoþer schal girde þee· ⁊ leede þee whidir þou wolte not/ soþely he seyde þis þing· signyfyinge by what deþ he was to glorifie god/ ¶ And whanne he had seyde þes þingis: he seiþ to hym/ sue þou me/ petre conuertyde (or turnyde) size þe ilke disciple

Joon

disciple sayinge whom ihc̄ louede· ⁊ þe whiche restide in þe
soper on his breste: and seyde to hym/ lorde who is it þat
schal bitraye þee? þerfore whanne petre had seen his: he
seiþ to Jhū/ lorde what forsoþe his? Jhc̄ seiþ to hym/ so I
wole hym dwelle til þat I come· what to þee/ sue þou me/
þerfore his worde wente oute amonge breþeren: for þe ilke
disciple dieþ not/ and Jhc̄ seyde not to hym for he dieþ not:
but so I wole hym dwelle til þat I come/ what to þee/ his
is þe ilke disciple þat beriþ witnessynge of þes þingis: and
wrote þes þingis/ and we witen for his witnessynge is trewe/
forsoþe þer ben ⁊ manye oþer signes (or myraclis) þat Jhc̄
dide: þe whiche ȝif þei ben writen by eche by hym self: I
gesse neþer þe worlde hym self motone taken þe bookis þat
ben to be writen //

II.

GEOFFREY CHAUCER.
1328—1400.

GEOFFREY CHAUCER is properly designated the Father of English Poetry. He acquires his right to that title not only on the ground of being our earliest poet, but because the foundations he laid still support the fabric of our poetical literature and will outlast the vicissitudes of taste and language. His greatest contemporaries and successors have recognized and confirmed his claim to this distinction. Lydgate calls him the "chief poete of Bretayne," and the "lode-sterre" (leading-star) of our language and says, that he was the first to distil and rain the gold dewdrops of speech and eloquence into our tongue; Occleve calls him "the fynder of our fayre langage;" Roger Ascham describes him as the "English Homer" and considers "his sayinges to have as much anthority as eyther Sophocles or Euripides in Greke;" and Spenser speaks of him as "the pure well-head of poetry" and "the well of English undefiled."

Rob. Bell in the "Introduction" to his Edition
of the "Poetical Works of G. Ch."
London 1854.

CANTERBURY TALES.

THE STORY OF PATIENT GRISILDE.

[THAT the original of this story was older than Boccaccio's novel admits of no doubt. Petrarch was acquainted with it many years before it was related by Boccaccio, whom he had himself, probably, supplied with the chief incidents. But, while we have many subsequent forms of it, the novel in the *Decameron* is the earliest now known to exist. The French are entitled to the credit of having first introduced it to the stage, a play on the subject having been produced at Paris in 1393, about nineteen years after Petrarch's death. Dramas were afterwards founded upon it in Italy, Germany, and England. Chaucer's tale is the earliest narrative in our language of the woes and virtues of *Patient Grissell*, since rendered familiar to the English reader by the prominent place it occupies in our ballad literature. Few stories enjoy so wide a popularity. The incredible resignation of the heroine may be said to have passed into a proverb.

Although Chaucer was indebted to Petrarch for his materials, the story acquires originality in his hands from the sweetness and tenderness of expression he has infused into the relation. Charles James Fox, who had never seen Petrarch's version, describes with accuracy the character of this poem when he observes, in one of his letters to Lord Holland, that it closely resembles the manner of Ariosto.]

Ther is at the west ende of Ytaile,
Doun at the root of Vesulus the colde,
A lusty playn, abundaunt of vitaile,
Wher many a tour and toun thou maist byholde,
That foundid were in tyme of fadres olde,
And many anothir delitable sight,
And Saluces this noble contray hight.
    A marquys whilom duellid in that lond,
As were his worthy eldris him bifore,
And obeisaunt ay redy to his hond,
Were alle his liegis, bothe lesse and more.
Thus in delyt he lyveth and hath don yore,
Biloved and drad, thurgh favour of fortune,
Bothe of his lordes and of his comune.
    Therwith he was, as to speke of lynage,
The gentileste born of Lumbardye,
A fair persone, and strong, and yong of age,
And ful of honour and of curtesie;
Discret y-nough his contre for to gye,
Savynge in som thing he was to blame;
And Wautier was this yonge lordes name.
    I blame him thus, that he considered nought
In tyme comyng what mighte bityde,
But on his lust present was al his thought,
As for to hauke and hunte on every syde;
Wel neigh al othir cures let he slyde,
And eek he nolde (that was the worst of al)
Wedde no wyf for no thing that might bifal.
    Only that poynt his poeple bar so sore,
That flokmel on a day to him thay went,
And oon of hem, that wisest was of lore,

(Or ellis that the lord wolde best assent
That he schuld telle him what his poeple ment,
Or ellis couthe he schewe wel such matiere)
He to the marquys sayd as ye schuln hiere.
"O noble marquys, youre humanite
Assureth us and giveth us hardynesse,
As ofte as tyme is of necessite,
That we to yow may telle oure hevynesse;
Acceptith, lord, now of your gentilesse,
That we with pitous hert unto yow playne,
And let your eeris my vois not disdeyne.
"And have I nought to doon in this matere
More than another man hath in this place,
Yit for as moche as ye, my lord so deere,
Han alway schewed me favour and grace,
I dar the better ask of yow a space
Of audience, to schewen oure request,
And ye, my lord, to doon right as yow lest.
"For certes, lord, so wel us likith yow
And al your werk, and ever han doon, that we
Ne couthen not ourselve devysen, how
We mighte lyve more in felicite;
Save oon thing, lord, if that your wille be,
That for to be a weddid man yow list,
Than were your poeple in sovereign hertes rest.
"Bowith your neck undir that blisful yok
Of sovereignete, nought of servise,
Which that men clepe spousail or wedlok;
And thenketh, lord, among your thoughtes wise,
How that our dayes passe in sondry wyse;
For though we slepe, or wake, or rome, or ryde,
Ay fleth the tyme, it wil no man abyde.
"And though your grene youthe floure as yit,
In crepith age alway as stille as stoon,
And deth manasith every age, and smyt
In ech estat, for ther ascapith noon.
And as certeyn, as we knowe everychon

That we schuln deye, as uncerteyn we alle
Ben of that day that deth schal on us falle.
"Acceptith thanne of us the trewe entent,
That never yit refusid youre hest,
And we wil, lord, if that ye wil assent
Chese yow a wyf, in schort tyme atte lest,
Born of the gentilest and the heighest
Of al this lond, so that it oughte seme
Honour to God and yow, as we can deme.
"Deliver us out of al this busy drede
And tak a wyf, for hihe Goddes sake.
For if it so bifel, as God forbede,
That thurgh your deth your lignage schuld aslake,
And that a straunge successour schuld take
Your heritage, O! wo were us on lyve!
Wherfor we pray yow hastily to wyve."
Her meeke prayer and her pitous chere
Made the marquys to han pite.
"Ye wolde," quod he, "myn owne poeple deere,
To that I never erst thought constreigne me.
I me rejoysid of my liberte,
That selden tyme is founde in mariage;
Ther I was fre, I mot ben in servage.
"But natheles I se youre trewe entent,
And trust upon your witt, and have doon ay;
Wherfor of my fre wil I wil assent
To wedde me, as soon as ever I may.
But ther as ye have profred me to day
To chese me a wyf, I wol relese
That choys, and pray yow of that profre cesse.
"For God it woot, that childer ofte been
Unlik her worthy eldris hem bifore;
Bounte cometh al of God, nought of the streen[1]
Of which thay ben engendrid and i-bore.
I trust in Goddes bounte, and therfore

---

[1] Virtue comes from God, and not from the *streen*, or strain (race) from which men are descended.

My mariage, and myn estat and rest,
I him bytake, he may doon as him lest.
"Let me aloon in chesyng of my wif,
That charge upon my bak I wil endure.
But I yow pray, and charge upon your lyf,
That what wyf that I take, ye me assure
To worschip whil that hir lif may endure,
In word and werk, bothe heer and every where,
As sche an emperoures doughter were.
"And forthermor thus schul ye swer, that ye
Ageins my chois schuln never grucche ne stryve.
For sins I schal forgo my liberte
At your request, as ever mot I thrive,
Ther as myn hert is set, ther wil I wyve.
And but ye wil assent in such manere,
I pray yow spek no more of this matiere."
  With hertly wil thay sworen and assentyn
To al this thing, ther sayde no wight nay,
Bysechyng him of grace, er that thay wentyn,
That he wold graunten hem a certeyn day
Of his spousail, as soone as ever he may;
For yit alway the peple som what dredde
Lest that the marquys wolde no wyf wedde.
  He graunted hem a day, such as him lest,
On which he wolde be weddid sicurly;
And sayd he dede al this at her requeste.
And thay with humble hert ful buxomly,
Knelyng upon her knees ful reverently,
Him thanken alle, and thus thay have an ende
Of her entent, and hom agein they wende.
  And herupon he to his officeris
Comaundith for the feste to purveye,
And to his prive knightes and squyeres
Such charge gaf as him list on hem leye;
And thay to his comaundement obeye,
And ech of hem doth his diligence
To doon unto the feste reverence.

PARS SECUNDA.

Nought fer fro thilke palys honurable,
Wher as this marquys schop his mariage,
Ther stood a throp, of sighte delitable,
In which that pore folk of that vilage
Hadden her bestes and her herburgage,
And after her labour took her sustienaunce,
After the erthe ğaf hem abundaunce.
  Among this pore folk there duelt a man,
Which that was holden porest of hem alle;
But heighe God som tyme sende can
His grace unto a litel oxe stalle.
Janicula men of that throp him calle.
A doughter had he, fair y-nough to sight,
And Grisildes this yonge mayden hight.
  But for to speke of hir vertuous beaute,
Than was sche oon the fayrest under sonne;
For porely i-fostered up was sche,
No licorous lust was in hir body ronne;
Wel ofter of the welle than of the tonne
Sche dronk, and for sche wolde vertu plese,
Sche knew wel labour, but noon ydel ease.
  But though this mayden tender were of age,
Yet in the brest of her virginite
Ther was enclosed rype and sad corrage;
And in gret reverence and charite
Hir olde pore fader fostered sche;
A fewe scheep spynnyng on the feld sche kept,
Sche nolde not ben ydel til sche slept.
  And whan sche com hom sche wolde brynge
Wortis and other herbis tymes ofte,
The which sche schred and seth for her lyvyng,[1]
And made hir bed ful hard, and no thing softe.
And ay sche kept hir fadres lif on lofte,[2]

[1] Which she sliced and boiled, or seethed for her food.
[2] She kept her father's life from sinking, that is, supported him.

With every obeissance and diligence,
That child may do to fadres reverence.
　Upon Grisildes, the pore creature,
Ful ofte sithes this marquys set his ye,
As he on huntyng rood peraventure.
And whan it fel he mighte hir espye,
He not with wantoun lokyng of folye
His eyghen cast upon hir, but in sad wyse
Upon hir cheer he wold him oft avise,
　Comendyng in his hert hir wommanhode,
And eek hir vertu, passyng other wight
Of so yong age, as wel in cheer as dede.
For though the poeple have no gret insight
In vertu, he considereth aright
Hir bounté, and desposed that he wolde
Wedde hir oonly, if ever he wedde scholde.
　The day of weddyng cam, but no wight can
Telle what womman it schulde be;
For which mervayle wondrith many a man,
And sayden, whan they were in privite:
"Wol nought our lord yit leve his vanite?
Wol he not wedde? allas, allas the while!
Why wol he thus himself and us bigyle?"
　But natheles this marquys hath doon make
Of gemmes, set in gold and in asure,[1]
Broches and rynges, for Grisildes sake,
And of hir clothing took he the mesure,
By a mayde y-lik to hir of stature,
And eek of other ornamentes alle
That unto such a weddyng schulde falle.
　The tyme of undern of the same day
Approchith, that this weddyng schulde be,
And al the palys put was in array,
Bothe halle and chambur, y-lik here degre,
Houses of office stuffid with plente;

---

[1] Azure, or blue, was the colour of truth.

Ther maystow se of deyntevous vitayle,
That may be founde, as fer as lastith Itaile.
  This real marquys, really arrayd,
Lordes and ladyes in his compaignye,
The which unto the feste were prayed,
And of his retenu the bachelerie.[1]
With many a soun of sondry melodye,
Unto the vilage, of which I tolde,
In this array the right way han they holde.
  Grysild of this (God wot) ful innocent,
That for hir schapen was al this array,
To fecche water at a welle is went,
And cometh hom as soone as sche may,
For wel sche had herd say, that ilke day
The marquys schulde wedde, and, if sche might,
Sche wold have seyen somwhat of that sight.
  Sche sayd: "I wol with other maydenes stonde,
That ben my felawes, in oure dore, and see
The marquysesse, and therfore wol I fonde
To don at hom, as soone as it may be,
The labour which that longeth unto me,
And thanne may I at leysir hir byholde,
As sche the way into the castel holde."
  And as sche wold over the threisshfold goon,
The marquys cam and gan hir for to calle.
And sche set doun her water-pot anoon
Bisides the threisshfold of this oxe stalle,[2]
And doun upon hir knees sche gan falle,
And with sad countenaunce she knelith stille,
Til sche had herd what was the lordes wille.
  This thoughtful marquys spak unto this mayde
Ful soberly, and sayd in this manere:
"Wher is your fader, Grisildes?" he sayde.
And sche with reverence in humble cheere
Answerd, "Lord, he is al redy heere."

[1] The knights or bachelors. [2] In Italy, and other continental countries, the peasantry to this day live in the same houses with their cattle.

And in sche goth withouten lenger let,
And to the marquys sche hir fader fet.
  He by the hond than takith this olde man,
And sayde thus, whan he him had on syde:
"Janicula, I neither may ne can
Lenger the plesauns of myn herte hyde;
If that ye vouchesauf, what so bytyde,
Thy doughter wil I take er that I wende
As for my wyf, unto hir lyves ende.

  "Thow lovest me, I wot it wel certeyn,
And art my faithful leige-man i-bore,
And al that likith me, I dar wel sayn,
It likith the, and specially therfore
Tel me that poynt, as ye have herd bifore,
If that thou wolt unto that purpos drawe,
To take me as for thy sone-in-lawe."

  The sodeyn cass the man astoneyd tho,
That reed he wax, abaischt, and al quakyng
He stood, unnethe sayd he wordes mo,
But oonly this: "Lord," quod he, "my willyng
Is as ye wol, agenst youre likyng
I wol no thing, ye be my lord so deere;
Right as yow list governith this matiere."

  "Yit wol I," quod this markys softely,
"That in thy chambre, I and thou and sche
Have a collacioun, and wostow why?
For I wol aske if it hir wille be
To be my wyf, and reule hir after me;
And al this schal be doon in thy presence,
I wol nought speke out of thyn audience."

  And in the chamber, whil thay were aboute
The tretys, which as ye schul after hiere,
The poeple cam unto the hous withoute,
And wondrid hem, in how honest manere
And tendurly sche kept hir fader deere;
But outerly Grisildes wonder might,
For never erst ne saugh sche such a sight.

No wonder is though that sche were astoned,
To seen so gret a gest come into that place;
Sche never was to suche gestes woned,
For which sche loked with ful pale face.
But schortly this matiere forth to chace,
These arn the wordes that the marquys sayde
To this benigne, verray, faithful mayde.

"Grisyld," he sayde, "ye schul wel understonde,
It liketh to your fader and to me,
That I yow wedde, and eck it may so stonde,
As I suppose ye wil that it so be;
But these demaundes aske I first," quod he,
"That sith it schal be doon in hasty wyse,
Wol ye assent, or elles yow avyse?

"I say this, be ye redy with good hert
To al my lust, and that I frely may
As me best liste do yow laughe or smert,
And never ye to gruch it, night ne day;
And eek whan I say ye, ye say not nay,
Neyther by word, ne frownyng contenaunce?
Swer this, and here swer I oure alliaunce."

Wondryng upon this word, quakyng for drede,
Sche sayde: "Lord, undigne and unworthy
I am to thilk honour that ye me bede;
But as ye wil your self, right so wol I;
And here I swere, that never wityngly
In werk, ne thought, I nyl yow disobeye
For to the deed,[1] though me were loth to deye."

"This is y-nough, Grisilde myn!" quod he.
And forth goth he with a ful sobre chere,
Out at the dore, and after that cam sehe;
And to the pepul he sayd in this manere:
"This is my wyf," quod he, "that stondith heere!
Honoureth hir, and loveth hir, I yow pray,
Who so me loveth; ther is no more to say."

[1] This is still the construction in the vulgar language of East Anglia, where it is common to say "I am frozen to deed," meaning to death.

And for that no thing of hir olde gere
Sche schulde brynge unto his hous, he bad
That wommen schuld despoilen hir right there,
Of which these ladyes were nought ful glad
To handle hir clothes wherein sche was clad;
But natheles this mayde bright of hew
Fro foot to heed they schredde han al newe.

Hir heeres han thay kempt, that lay untressed
Ful rudely, and with hir fyngres smale
A coroun on hir heed thay han i-dressed,
And set hir ful of nowches gret and smale.
Of hir array what schuld I make a tale?
Unnethe the poeple hir knew for hir fairnesse,
Whan sche translated was in such richesse.

This marquis hath hir spoused with a ryng
Brought for the same cause, and than hir sette
Upon an hors snow-whyt, and wel amblyng,
And to his palys, er he lenger lette,
(With joyful poeple, that hir ladde and mette) [1]
Conveyed hire, and thus the day they spende
In revel, til the sonne gan descende.

And schortly forth this tale for to chace,
I say, that to this newe marquisesse
God hath such favour sent hir of his grace,
That it ne semyd not by liklynesse
That sche was born and fed in rudenesse,
As in a cote, or in an oxe stalle,
But norischt in an emperoures halle.

To every wight sche waxen is so deere,
And worschipful, that folk ther sche was born,
And from hir burthe knew hir yer by yere,
Unnethe trowed thay, but dorst han sworn,
That to Janicle, of which I spak biforn,
Sche doughter were, for as by conjecture
Hem thought sche was another creature.

[1] Accompanied and met her.

For though that ever vertuous was sche,
Sche was encresed iu such excellence
Of thewes goode, i-set iu high bounte,
And so discret, and fair of eloquence,
So benigne, and so digne of reverence,
And couthe so the poeples hert embrace,
That ech hir loveth that lokith in hir face.

Nought oonly of Saluce in the toun
Publissched was the bounte of hir name,
But eek byside in many a regioun,
If oon sayd wel, another sayd the same.
So sprad of hire heigh bounte the fame,
That men and wommen, as wel yong as olde,
Gon to Saluce upon hir to byholde.

Thus Walter louly, nay but really,[1]
Weddid with fortunat honestete,
In Goddes pees lyveth ful esily
At home, and outward grace y-nough hath he;
And for he saugh that under low degre
Was ofte vertu y-hid, the poeple him helde
A prudent man, and that is seen ful selde.

Nought oonly this Grisildes thurgh hir witte
Couthe al the feet of wifly homlynesse,
But eek whan that the tyme required it,
The comyn profyt couthe sche redresse;
Ther nas discord, rancour, ne hevynesse
In al that lond, that sche ne couthe appese,
And wisly bryng hem alle in rest and ese.

Though that hir housbond absent were anoon,
If gentilmen, or other of hir contre,
Were wroth, sche wolde bryngo hem at oon,
So wyse and rype wordes hadde sche,
And juggement of so gret equite,
That sche from heven sent was, as men wende,
Poeple to save, and every wrong to amende.

[1] This Walter wedded humbly, or (I should rather say) royally — *scil.*, because of his wife's virtue.

Nought longe tyme after that this Grisilde
Was wedded, sche a doughter hath i-bore;
Al had hir lever hon had a knave[1] childe,
Glad was this marquis and the folk therforo,
For though a mayden child come al byfore,
Sche may unto a knave child atteigne
By liklihed, sith sche nys not barcigne.

INCIPIT TERTIA PARS.

Ther fel, as fullith many times mo,
Whan that this child hath souked but a throwe,
This marquys in his herte longith so
Tempte his wyf, hir sadnesse[2] for to knowe,
That he ne might out of his herte throwe
This mervaylous desir his wyf t'assaye;
Nedeles, God wot, he thought hir to affraye.
 He had assayed hir y-nough bifore,
And fond hir ever good, what needith it
Hire to tempte, and alway more and more?
Though som men prayse it for a subtil wit,
But as for me, I say that evel it sit
T'assay a wyf whan that it is no neede,
And putte hir in anguysch and in dreede.
 For which this marquis wrought in this manere;
He com aloone a-night ther as sche lay
With sterne face, and with ful trouble cheere,
And sayde thus: "Grisild," quod he, "that day
That I yow took out of your pore array,
And putte yow in estat of heigh noblesse,
Ye have not that forgeten, as I gesse.
 "I say, Grisild, this present dignite
In which that I have put yow, as I trowe,
Makith yow not forgetful for to be

---

1 *Knave* means here, a boy (German, *knabe*).
2 To know her sincerity.

That I yow took in pore estat ful lowe,
For eny wele ye moot your selve knowe.[1]
Tak heed of every word that I yow say,
Ther is no wight that herith it but we tway.
"Ye wot your self how that ye comen heere
Into this hous, it is nought long ago;
And though to me that ye be leef and deere,
Unto my gentils ye be no thing so. .
Thay seyn, to hem it is gret schame and wo,
For to ben subject and ben in servage
To the, that born art of a smal village.
"And namely syn thy doughter was i-bore,
These wordes han thay spoken douteles.
But I desire, as I have doon byfore,
To lyve my lif with hem in rest and pees;
I may not in this caas be reccheles;
I moot do with thy doughter for the best,
Not as I wolde, but as my pepul lest.
"And yit, God wot, this is ful loth to me.
But natheles withoute youre wityuge
Wol I not doon; but this wol I," quod he,
"That ye to me assent as in this thing.
Schew now your paciens in your wirching,
That thou me hightest and swor in yon village,
That day that maked was oure mariage."
Whan sche had herd al this sche nought ameevyd
Neyther in word, in cheer, or countenaunce,
(For, as it semed, sche was nought agreeved);
She sayde: "Lord, al lith in your plesaunce!
My child and I, with hertly obeisaunce,
Ben youres al, and ye may save or spille
Your oughne thing; werkith after your wille.
"Ther may no thing, so God my soule save,
Liken to yow, that may displesen me;
Ne I desire no thing for to have,

[1] You were in a full low state for any goods that you possessed your own right.

Ne drede for to lese, save oonly ye.
This wil is in myn hert, and ay schal be,
No length of tyme or deth may this deface,
Ne chaunge my corrage to other place."
　Glad was this marquis for hir answeryng,
But yit he feyned as he were not so.
Al dreery was his cheer and his lokyng,
Whan that he schold out of the chambre go.
Soon after this, a forlong way or tuo,
He prively hath told al his entent
Unto a man, and unto his wyf him sent.
　A maner sergeant was this prive man,
The which that faithful oft he founden hadde
In thinges grete, and eek such folk wel can
Don execucioun in thinges badde;
The lord knew wel that he him loved and dradde.
And whan this sergeant wist his lordes wille,
Into the chamber he stalked him ful stille.
　"Madame," he sayd, "ye most forgive it me,
Though I do thing to which I am constreynit;
Ye ben so wys, that ful wel knowe ye,
That lordes hestes mow not ben i-feynit.
They mowe wel be biwaylit or compleynit;
But men moot nede unto her lust obeye,
And so wol I, there is no more to seye.
　"This child I am comaundid for to take."
And spak no more, but out the child he hent
Dispitously, and gan a chiere make,
As though he wold han slayn it, er he went.
Grisild moot al suffer and al consent;
And as a lamb sche sitteth meeke and stille,
And let this cruel sergeant doon his wille.
　Suspecious was the defame of this man,
Suspect his face, suspect his word also,
Suspect the tyme in which he this bigan.
Allas! hir doughter, that she loved so,
Sche wend he wold han slayen it right tho;

But natheles sche neyther weep ne siked,
Conformyng hir to that the marquis liked.
  But atte last spcke sche bigan,
And mekely sche to the sergeant preyde,
So as he was a worthy gentilman,
That she most kisse hir child, er that it deyde.
And on hir arm this litel child sche leyde,
With ful sad face, and gan the child to blesse,
And lullyd it, and after gan it kesse.
  And thus sche sayd in hir benigne vois:
"Farwel, my child, I schal the never see;
But sith I the have marked withe the croys,
Of thilke fader blessed mot thou be,
That for us deyde upon a cros of tre;
Thy soule, litel child, I him bytake,
For this night schaltow deyen for my sake."
  I trowe that to a norice in this caas
It had ben hard this rewthe for to see;
Wel might a moder than have cryed allas.
But natheles so sad stedefast was sche,
That she endured al adversite,
And to the sergeant mekely sche sayde:
"Have her agayn your litel yonge mayde.
  "Goth now," quod sche, "and doth my lordes heste.
But o thing wil I pray yow of your grace,
That but my lord forbede yow atte leste,
Burieth this litel body in som place,
That bestes ne no briddes it to-race."
But he no word wil to the purpos say,
But took the child and went upon his way.
  This sergeant com unto this lord agayn,
And of Grisildes wordes and hir cheere
He tolde poynt for poynt, in schort and playn,
And him presentith with his doughter deere.
Somwhat this lord hath rewthe in his manere,
But natheles his purpos huld he stille,
As lordes doon, whan thay woln have hor wille;

And bad the sergeaunt that he prively
Scholde this childe softe wynde and wrappe,
With alle circumstaunces tendurly,
And carry it in a cofre, or in his lappe;
Upon peyne his heed of for to swappe
That no man schulde knowe of this entent,
Ne whens he com, ne whider that he went;
But at Boloygne, to his suster deere,
That thilke tyme of Panik[1] was countesse,
He schuld it take, and schewe hir this matiere,
Byseching her to doon hir busynesse
This child to fostre in all gentilesse,
And whos child that it was he bad hir hyde
From every wight, for ought that mighte bytyde.
The sergeant goth, and hath fulfild this thing.
But to this marquys now retourne we;
For now goth he ful fast ymaginyng,
If by his wyves cher he mighte se,
Or by hir word apparceyve, that sche
Were chaunged, but he hir never couthe fynde,
But ever in oon y-like sad and kynde.
As glad, as humble, as busy in service
And eek in love, as sche was wont to be,
Was sche to him, in every maner wyse;
Ne of hir doughter nought o word spak sche;
Non accident for noon adversite
Was seyn in hir, he never hir doughter name
Ne nempnyd sche, in ernest ne in game.

INCIPIT QUARTA PARS.

In this estaat ther passed ben foure yer
Er sche with childe was, but, as God wolde,
A knave child sche bar by this Waltier,

---

[1] The Marquis's sister was married to the Count of Panico.

Ful gracious, and fair for to biholde;
And whan that folk it to his fader tolde,
Nought oonly he, but al his contre merye
Was for this child, and God thay thank and herie.
  Whan it was tuo yer old, and fro the brest
Departed fro his noris, upon a day
This markys caughte yit another lest
To tempt his wif yit after, if he may.
O! needles was sche tempted in assay;
But weddid men ne knowen no mesuro,
Whan that thay fynde a pacient creature.
  "Wyf," quod this marquys, "ye han herd er this
My poeple sckly berith oure mariage,
And namly syn my sone y-boren is,
Now is it wors than ever in al our age;
The murmur sleth myn hert and my corrage,
For to myn ecris cometh the vois so smerto,
That it wel neigh destroyed hath myn herte.
  "Now say thay thus: whan Wauter is agoon,
Than schal the blood of Janicle succede,
And ben our lord, for other have we noon.
Suche wordes saith my poeple, out of drede.
Wel ought I of such murmur taken heede,
For certeynly I drede such sentence,
Though thay not pleynly speke in my audience.
  "I wolde lyve in pees, if that I might;
Wherfor I am disposid outrely,
As I his suster servede by night,
Right so thynk I to serve him prively.
This warn I you, that ye not sodeinly
Out of your self for no thing schuld outraye:
Beth pacient, and therof I yow pray."
  "I have," quod scho, "sayd thus and ever schal,
I wol no thing, ne nil no thing certayn,
But as yow list; nought greveth me at al,
Though that my doughter and my sone be slayn
At your comaundement; this is to sayne,

I have not had no part of children twayne,
But first syknes and after wo and payne.
　"Ye ben oure lord, doth with your owne thing
Right as yow list, axith no red of me;
For as I left at hom al my clothing,
Whan I first com to yow, right so," quod sche,
Left I my wille and my liberte,
And took your clothing; wherfor I yow preye,
Doth youre plesaunce, I wil youre lust obeye.
　"And certes, if I hadde prescience
Your wil to knowe, er ye youre lust me tolde,
I wold it doon withoute negligence.
But now I wot your lust, and what ye wolde,
Al your plesaunce ferm and stable I holde;
For wist I that my deth wold doon yow ease,
Right gladly wold I deye, yow to please.
　"Deth may make no comparisoun
Unto your love." And whan this marquys say
The constance of his wyf, he cast adoun
His eyghen tuo, and wondrith that sche may
In pacience suffre as this array;
And forth he goth with drery countenaunce,
But to his hert it was ful gret plesaunce.
　This ugly sergeaunt in the same wise
That he hir doughter fette, right so he,
Or worse, if men worse can devyse,
Hath hent hir sone, that ful was of beaute.
And ever in oon so pacient was sche,
That sche no cheere made of hevynesse,
But kist hir sone, and after gan him blesse.
　Save this sche prayed him, if that he mighte,
Her litel sone he wold in eorthe grave,
His tendre lymes, delicate to sight,
From foules and from bestes him to save.
But sche noon answer of him mighte have.
He went his way, as him no thing ne rought,
But to Boloyne he tenderly it brought.

This marquis woudreth ever the lenger the more
Upon hir pacience, and if that he
Ne hadde sothly knowen therbifore,
That parfytly hir children loved sche,
He wold have wend that of some subtilte
And of malice, or of cruel corrage,
That sche had suffred this with sad visage.
　But wel he knew, that, next himself, certayn
Sche loved hir children best in every wise.
But now of wommen wold I aske fayn,
If these assayes mighten not suffice?
What couthe a stourdy housebonde more devyse
To prove hir wyfhode and her stedefastnesse,
And he contynuyng ever in stourdynesse?
　But ther ben folk of such condicioun,
That, whan they have a certeyn purpos take,
Thay can nought stynt of her entencioun,
But, right as thay were bounden to a stake,
Thay wil not of her firste purpos slake;
Right so this marquys fullich hath purposed
To tempt his wyf, as he was first disposed.
　He wayteth, if by word or countenaunce
That sche to him was chaunged of corage.
But never couthe he fynde variaunce,
Sche was ay oon in hert and in visage;
And ay the ferther that sche was in age,
The more trewe, if that were possible,
Sche was to him, and more penyble.
　For which it semyd this, that of hem tuo
Ther nas but oo wil; for as Walter lest,
The same plesaunce was hir lust also;
And, God be thanked, al fel for the best.
Sche schewed wel, for no worldly unrest
A wyf, as of hir self, no thing ne scholde
Wylne in effect, but as hir housbond wolde.
　The sclaunder of Walter ofte and wyde spradde,
That of a cruel hert he wikkedly,

For he a pore womman weddid hadde,
Hath morthrid bothe his children prively;
Such murmur was among hem comunly.
No wonder is; for to the peples ecre
Ther com no word, but that thay mortherid were.
For which, wher as his peple therbyfore
Had loved him wel, the sclaunder of his diffame
Made hem that thay him hatede therfore;
To ben a mordrer is an hateful name.
But natheles, for ernest or for game,
He of his cruel purpos nolde stente,
To tempt his wyf was set al his entente.
Whan that his doughter twelf yer was of age,
He to the court of Rome, in suche wise
Enformed of his wille, sent his message,
Comaundyng hem, such bulles to devyse,
As to his cruel purpos may suffise,
How that the pope, as for his peples reste,
Bad him to wedde another, if him leste.

I say, he bad, thay schulde countrefete
The popes bulles, makyng mencioun
That he hath leve his firste wyf to lete,
As by the popes dispensacioun,
To stynte rancour and discencioun
Bitwix his peple and him; thus sayd the bulle,
The which thay han publisshid atte fulle.

The rude poepel, as it no wonder is,
Wende ful wel that it had be right so.
But whan these tydynges come to Grisildis,
I deeme that hir herte was ful wo;
But sche y-like sad for evermo
Disposid was, this humble creature,
Thadversite of fortun al tendure;
Abydyng ever his lust and his plesaunce,
To whom that sche was give, hert and al,
As to hir verray worldly suffisaunce.
But schortly if I this story telle schal,

This marquys writen hath in special
A letter, in which he schewith his entent,
And secretly he to Boloyne it sent.
To th'erl of Panyk, which that hadde tho
Weddid his suster, prayd he specially
To brynge hom agein his children tuo
In honurable estaat al openly.
But oon thing he him prayde outerly,
That he to no wight, though men wold enquere,
Schuld not tellen whos children thay were,
But say the mayde schuld i-weddid be
Unto the markys of Saluce anoon.
And as this eorl was prayd, so dede he,
For at day set he on his way is goon
Toward Saluce, and lordes many oon
In riche array, this mayden for to guyde,
Her yonge brother rydyng by hir syde.

Arrayed was toward hir mariage
This freisshe may al ful of gemmes clere;
Hir brother, which that seven yer was of age,
Arrayed eek ful freissh in his manere;
And thus in gret noblesse and with glad chere
Toward Saluces schapyng her journay,
Fro day to day thay ryden in her way.

INCIPIT PARS QUINTA.

Among al this, after his wikked usage,
This marquis yit his wif to tempte more
To the uttrest proef of hir corrage,
Fully to han experiens and lore,
If that sche were as stedefast as byfore,
He on a day in open audience
Ful boystrously hath sayd hir this senteuce.

"Certes, Grisildes, I had y-nough plesaunce
To have yow to my wif, for your goodnesse,
And for youre trouthe, and for your obeissaunce,

Nought for your lignage, ne for your richesse;
But now know I in verray sothfastnesse,
That in gret lordschip, if I wel avyse,
Ther is gret servitude in sondry wyse;
  I may not do, as every ploughman may;
My pocple me constreignith for to take
Another wyf, and cryen day by day;
And eek the pope, rancour for to slake,
Consentith it, that dar I undertake;
And trewely, thus moche I wol yow say,
My newe wif is comyng by the way.
  "Be strong of hert, and voyde anoon hir place,
And thilke dower that ye broughten me
Tak it agayn, I graunt it of my grace.
Retourneth to your fadres hous," quod he,
"No man may alway have prosperite.
With even hert I rede yow endure
The strok of fortune or of adventure."
  And sche agayn answerd in pacience:
"My lord," quod sche, "I wot, and wist alway,
How that betwixe your magnificence
And my poverte no wight can ne may
Make comparisoun, it is no nay;
I ne held me never digne in no manere
To ben your wyf, ne yit your chamberere.
  "And in this hous, ther ye me lady made,
(The highe God take I for my witnesse,
And al so wisly he my soule glade)
I never huld me lady ne maistresse,
But humble servaunt to your worthinesse,
And ever schal, whil that my lyf may dure,
Aboven every worldly creature.
  "That ye so longe of your benignite
Han holden me in honour and nobleye,
Wher as I was not worthy for to be,
That thonk I God and yow, to whom I preye
For-yeld it yow! Ther is no more to seye.

Unto my fader gladly wil I wende,
And with him duelle unto my lyves ende.
"Ther I was fostred as a child ful smal,
Til I be deed my lyf ther wil I lede,
A widow clene in body, hert, and al;
For sith I gaf to yow my maydenhede,
And am your trewe wyf, it is no drede,
God schilde such a lordes wyf to take
Another man to housbond or to make.

"And of your newe wif, God of his grace
So graunte yow wele and prosperite;
For I wol gladly yelden hir my place,
In which that I was blisful wont to be.
For sith it liketh yow, my lord," quod sche,
"That whilom were al myn hertes reste,
That I schal gon, I wil go whan yow leste.

"But ther as ye profre me such dowayre
As I ferst brought, it is wel in my mynde,
It were my wrecchid clothes, no thing faire,
The whiche to me were hard now for to fynde.
O goode God! how gentil and how kynde
Ye semed by your speche and your visage,
That day that maked was our mariage!

"But soth is sayd, algate I fynd it trewe,
For in effect it proved is on me,
Love is nought old as whan that it is newe.
But certes, lord, for noon adversite
To deyen in the caas, it schal not be
That ever in word or werk I schal repente
That I yow gaf myn hert in hol ententc.

"My lord, ye wot that in my fadres place
Ye dede me strippe out of my pore wede,
And richely me cladden of your grace;
To yow brought I nought elles out of drede,
But faith, and nakednesse, and maydenhede;
And her agayn my clothyng I restore,
And eek my weddyng ryng for evermore.

"The remenant of your jewels redy be
Within your chambur dar I saufly sayn.
Naked out of my fadres hous," quod sche,
"I com, and naked moot I torne agayn.
Al your pleisauns wold I fulfille fayn;
But yit I hope it be not youre entent,
That I smocless out of your paleys went.
"Ye couthe not doon so dishonest a thing,
That thilke wombe, in which your children leye,
Schulde byforn the poeple, in my walkyng,
He seye al bare: wherfore I yow pray
Let me not lik a worm go by the way;
Remembre yow, myn oughne lord so deore,
I was your wyf, though I unworthy were.
"Wherfor, in guerdoun of my maydenhede,
Which that I brought and nought agayn I bere,
As vouchethsauf to geve me to my meede
But such a smok as I was wont to were,
That I therwith may wrye the wombe of here
That was your wif; and here take I my leve
Of yow, myn oughne lord, lest I yow greve."
"The smok," quod he, "that thou hast on thy bak,
Let it be stille, and ber it forth with the."
But wel unnethes thilke word he spak,
But went his way for routhe and for pite.
Byforn the folk hirselven strippith sche,
And in hir smok, with heed and foot al bare,
Toward hir faderhouse forth is sche fare.

The folk hir folwen wepyng in hir weye,
And fortune ay thay cursen as thay goon;
But sche fro wepyng kept hir eyen dreye,
Ne in this tyme word ne spak sche noon.
Hir fader, that this tyding herd anoon,
Cursed the day and tyme, that nature
Schoop him to ben a lyves creature.

For out of doute this olde pore man
Was ever in suspect of hir mariage;

For ever he deemed, sith that it bigan,
That whan the lord fulfilled had his corrage,
Him wolde think that it were disparnge
To his estate, so lowe for to light,
And voyden hire as sone as ever he might.
  Agayns his doughter hastily goth he;
For he by noyse of folk knew hir comyng;
And with hir olde cote, as it might be,
He covered hir ful sor'wfully wepyng;
But on hir body might he it nought bringe,
For rude was the cloth, and mor of age
By dayes fele[1] than at hir mariage.
  Thus with hir fader for a certeyn space
Dwellith this flour of wifly pacience,
That neyther by her wordes ne by hir face,
Byforn the folk, nor eck in her absence,
Ne schewed sche that hir was doon offence,
Ne of hir highe astaat no remembraunce
Ne hadde sche, as by hir countenaunce.
  No wonder is, for in hir gret estate
Hir gost was ever in playn humilite;
Ne tender mouth, noon herte delicate,
Ne pompe, ne semblant of realte;
But ful of pacient benignite,
Discrete, and prideles, ay honurable,
And to hir housbond ever meke and stable.
  Men speke of Job, and most for his humblesse,
As clerkes, whan hem lust, can wel endite,
Namely of men, but as in sothfastnesse,
Though clerkes prayse wommen but a lite,
Ther can no man in humblesse him acquyte
As wommen can, ne can be half so trewe
As wommen ben, but it be falle of newe.

---

[1] *Fele* is the Anglo-Saxon for *many*; modern German, *viel*, pronounced *fel*.

PARS SEXTA.

Fro Boloyne is this erl of Panik y-come,
Of which the fame up-sprong to more and lasse,
And to the peoples eeres allo and some
Was couth eek, that a newe marquisesse
He with him brought, in such pomp and richesse,
That never was ther seyn with mannes ye
So noble array in al West Lombardye.
  The marquys, which that schoop and knew al this,
Er that this erl was come, sent his messnge
For thilke[1] cely pore Grisildis;
And sche with humble hert and glad visage,
Not with no swollen hert in hir corrage,
Cam at his hest, and on hir knees hir sette,
And reverently and wyfly sche him grette.
  "Grisild," quod he, "my wil is outrely,
This mayden, that schal weddid be to me,
Receyved be to morwe as really
As it possible is in myn hous to be;
And eek that every wight in his degre
Have his estaat in sittyng and servyse,
In high plesaunce, as I can devyse.
  "I have no womman suffisant certeyne
The chambres for tarray in ordinance
After my lust, and therfor wold I feyne,
That thin were al such maner governaunce;
Thow knowest eek of al my plesaunce;
Though thyn array be badde, and ille byseye;
Do thou thy dever atte leste weye."
  "Nought oonly, lord, that I am glad," quod sche,
"To don your lust, but I desire also
Yow for to serve and plese in my degre,
Withoute feyntyng, and schal evermo;
Ne never for no wele, ne for no wo,

---

[1] The final *e* has been added to *thilk*, as more correct, grammatically, and necessary for the metre.

Ne schal the gost withinne myn herte stente
To love yow best with al my trewe entent."
And with that word sche gan the hous to dight,
And tables for to sette, and beddes make,
And peyned hir to doon al that sche might,
Preying the chamberers for Goddes sake
To hasten hem, and faste swepe and schake;
And sche the moste servisable of alle
Hath every chamber arrayed, and his halle.
  Abouten undern[1] gan this lord alight,
That with him brought these noble children tweye;
For which the peple ran to se that sight
Of her array, so richely biseye.
And than at erst amonges hem thay seye,
That Walter was no fool, though that him lest
To chaunge his wyf; for it was for the best.
  For sche is fairer, as thay demen alle,
Than is Grisild, and more tender of age,
And fairer fruyt bitwen hem schulde falle,
And more plesaunt for hir high lynage;
Hir brother eck so fair was of visage,
That hem to seen the peple hath caught plesaunce,
Comending now the marquis governaunce.
  O stormy peple, unsad and ever untrewe,
And undiscret, and chaunging as a fane,
Delytyng ever in rombel that is newe,
For lik the moone ay wax ye and wane!
Ay ful of clappyng, dere y-nough a jane,[2]
Youre doom is fals, your constaunce yvel previth;
A ful gret fool is he that on yow leevith.
  Thus sayde sand folke in that citee,
Whan that the peeple gased up and doun;
For thay were glad right for the novelte,
To have a newe lady of her toun.

[1] *Undern* — the third hour of the day, i. e. nine o'clock
[2] *Jane* is a small coin of Genoa (Janua). The meaning is, Your praise is dear enough at a farthing.

No more of this now make I mencioun,
But to Grisildes agayn wol I me dresse,
And telle hir constance, and her busynesse.
Ful busy was Grisild in every thing,
That to the feste was appertinent;
Right nought was sche abaissht of hir clothing,
Though it were ruyde, and som del eek to-rent;
But with glad cheer to the gate is sche went,
With other folk, to greete the marquisesse,
And after that doth forth her busynesse.
With so glad chier his gestes sche receyveth,
And so conuyngly everich in his degre,
That no defaute no man aparceyveth,
But ay thay wondren what sche mighte be,
That in so pover array was for to so,
And couthe such honour and reverence,
And worthily thay prayse hir prudence.
In all this mene while sche ne stent,
This mayde and eek hir brother to comende
With al hir hert in ful buxom entent,
So wel, that no man couthe hir pris amende;
But atte last whan that these lordes wende
To sitte doun to mete, he gan to calle
Grisild, as sche was busy in his halle.
"Grisyld," quod he, as it were in his play,
"How likith the my wif and hir beaute?"
"Right wel, my lord," quod sche, "for in good fay,
A fairer saugh I never noon than sche.
I pray to God, give hir prosperite;
And so hope I, that he wol to yow sende
Plesaunce y-nough unto your lyves ende.
"On thing warn I yow and bischc also,
That ye ne prike with no tormentynge
This tendre mayden, as ye have do mo;[1]

[1] For *ms*. Tyrwhitt says, This is one of the most licentious corruptions of orthography that I remember to have seen in Chaucer.

For sche is fostrid in hir norischinge
More tendrely, and to my supposynge
Sche couthe not adversite endure,
As couthe a pore fostrid creature."
 And whan this Walter saugh hir pacience,
Hir glade cheer, and no malice at al,
And he so oft had doon to hir offence,
And sche ay sad and constant as a wal,
Continuyng ever hir innocence over al,
This sturdy marquys gan his herte dresse
To rewen upon hir wyfly stedefastnesse.
 "This is y-nough, Grisilde myn!" quod he,
"Be now no more agast, no yvel apayed.
I have thy faith and thy benignite,
As wel as ever womman was, assayed
In gret estate, and propreliche arrayed;
Now knowe I, dere wyf, thy stedefastnesse."
And hir in armes took, and gan hir kesse.
 And sche for wonder took of it no keepe;
Sche herde not what thing he to hir sayde,
Sche ferd as sche had stert out of a sleepe,
Til sche out of hir masidnesse abrayde.
"Grisild," quod he, "by God that for us deyde,
Thou art my wyf, ne noon other I have,
Ne never had, as God my soule save.
 "This is my doughter, which thou hast supposed
To be my wif; that other faithfully
Schal be myn heir, as I have ay purposed;
Thow bar hem in thy body trewely.
At Boloyne have I kept hem prively;
Tak hem agayn, for now maistow not seye,
That thou hast lorn noon of thy children tweye.
 "And folk, that other weyes han seyd of me,
I warn hem wel, that I have doon this deede
For no malice, ne for no cruelte,
But for t'assaye in the thy wommanhede;
And not to slen my children, God forbede!

But for to kepe hem prively and stille,
Til I thy purpos knewe and al thy wil."
  Whan sche this herd, aswoned doun sche fallith
For pitous joy, and after her swownyng
Sche bothe hir yonge children to hir callith,
And in hir armes pitously wepyng
Embraseth hem, and tenderly kissyng,
Ful lik a moder with hir salte teris
Sche bathis bothe hir visage and hir ceris.
  O, such a pitous thing it was to see
Her swownyng, and hir humble vois to heere!
"*Graunt mercy*, lord, God thank it yow," quod sche,
"That ye han saved me my children deere.
Now rek I never to be deed right heere,
Sith I stond in your love and in your grace,
No fors of deth, ne whan my spirit pace.
  "O tender deere yonge children myne,
Youre woful moder wende stedefastly,
That cruel houndes or som foul vermyne
Had eten yow; but God of his mercy,
And your benigne fader tenderly
Hath doon yow kepe!" And in that same stounde
Al sodeinly sche swapped doun to grounde.
  And in hir swough so sadly holdith sche
Hir children tuo, whan sche gan hem tembrace,
That with gret sleight and gret difficulte
The children from her arm they gonne arace.
O! many a teer on many a pitous face
Doun ran of hem that stooden hir bisyde,
Unnethe aboute hir mighte thay abyde.
  Walter hir gladith, and hir sorwe slakith,
Sche rysith up abaisshed from hir traunce,
And every wight hir joy and feste makith,
Til sche hath caught agayn her continaunce.
Wauter hir doth so faithfully plesaunce,
That it was daynte for to see the cheere
Bitwix hem tuo, now thay be met in feere.

These ladys, whan that thay her tyme say,
Han taken hir, and into chambre goon,
And strippe hir out of hir rude array,
And in a cloth of gold that brighte schon,
With a coroun of many a riche stoon
Upon hir heed, thay into halle hir brought,
And ther sche was honoured as hir ought.
  Thus hath this pitous day a blisful ende;
For every man and womman doth his might
This day in mirth and revel to despende,
Til on the welken schon the sterres bright;
For more solempne in every mannes sight.
This feste was, and gretter of costage,
Than was the revel of hir mariage.
  Ful many a yer in heigh prosperite
Lyven these tuo in concord and in rest,
And richeliche his doughter maried he
Unto a lord, oon of the worthiest
Of al Ytaile, and thanne in pees and rest
His wyves fader in his court he kepith,
Til that the soule out of his body crepith.
  His sone succedith in his heritage,
In rest and pees, after his fader day;
And fortunat was eek in mariage,
Al put he not his wyf in gret assay.
This world is not so strong, it is no nay,
As it hath ben in olde tymes yore,
And herknith, what this auctor saith therfore.
  This story is sayd, not for that wyves scholde
Folwe Grisild, as in humilite,
For it were importable, though thay wolde;
But for that every wight in his degre
Schulde be constant in adversite,
As was Grisild; therfore Petrark writeth
This story, which with high stile he enditeth.
  For sith a womman was so pacient
Unto a mortal man, wel more us oughte

Receyven al in gre that God us sent.
For gret skil is he prove that he wroughte,
But he ne temptith no man that he boughte,
As saith seint Jame, if ye his pistil rede;
He provith folk al day, it is no drede;
  And suffrith us, as for our exercise,
With scharpe scourges of adversite
Ful ofte to be bete in sondry wise;
Nought for to knowe oure wille, for certes he,
Er we were born, knew al our freltc;
And for oure best is al his governaunce;
Let us thanne lyve in vertuous suffraunce.
  But oo word, lordes, herkneth er I go:
It were ful hard to fynde now a dayes
As Grisildes in al a toun thre or tuo;
For if that thay were put to such assayes,
The gold of hem hath now so badde alayes
With bras, that though the coyn be fair at ye,
  wolde rather brest in tuo than plye.
For which heer, for the wyves love of Bathe, —
Hos lyf and alle of hir secte God meyntene
Ihigh maistry, and elles were it scathe, —
Iil with lusty herte freisch and grene,
S. yow a song to glade yow, I wene;
A: lat us stynt of cruestful matiere.
Henith my song, that saith in this manere.

L'ENVOYE DE CHAUCER.[1]

Grip is deed, and eck hir pacience,
And the at oones buried in Itayle;
For iche I crye in open audience,
No wlid man so hardy be to assayle
His w²s pacience, in hope to fynde
Grisilt, for in certeyn he schal faylo.

---

[1] In the ...ye, Chaucer seems to indemnify himself for his patient adoption of P...rch in the foregoing tale, by giving the reins to his characteristic ...nd irony.

O noble wyves, ful of heigh prudence,
Let noon humilite your tonges nayle;
Ne lat no clerk have cause or diligence
To write of yow a story of such mervaylo,
As of Grisildes pacient and kynde,
Lest Chichivache[1] yow swolwe in hir entraile.
Folwith ecco, that holdith no silence,
But ever answereth at the countretayle;
Beth nought bydaffed for your innocence,
But scharply tak on yow the governayle;
Empryntith wel this lessoun on your mynde,
For comun profyt, sith it may avayle.
Ye archewyves, stondith at defens,
Syn ye ben stroug, as is a greet chamayle,
Ne suffre not that men yow don offens.
And slendre wyves, felle as in batnyle,
Beth egre as is a tyger yond in Inde;
Ay clappith as a mylle, I yow counsaile.
Ne drede hem not, do hem no reverence,
For though thin housbond armed be in mayle,
The arwes of thy crabbid eloquence
Schal perse his brest, and eek his adventayle:
In gelousy I rede eek thou him bynde,
And thou schalt make him couche as doth a quayle.
If thou be fair, ther folk ben in presence
Schew thou thy visage and thin apparaile;
If thou be foul, be fre of thy despeuse,
To gete the frendes do ay thy travayle;
Be ay of chier as light as lef on lynde,
And let hem care and wepe, and wryng and wayle.

[1] The allusion is to the subject of an old ballad. It is a kind of Pageant, in which two beasts are introduced, called *Bycorne* and *Chichevache*. The former is supposed to feed upon obedient husbands, and the latter upon patient wives; and the humour of the piece consists in representing Bycorne as pampered with a superfluity of food, and Chichevache as half-starved. The name Chichevache is French, *vacca parca*. — T.

III.

STEPHEN HAWES.
(15. Cent.)

"The only writer deserving the name of a poet in the reign of Henry the Seventh is Stephen Hawes. He flourished about the close of the fifteenth century and was a native of Suffolk.... His capital performance is a Poem entitled 'The Passetyme of Plesure or the History of Grande Amoure and la Bel Pucel, contayning the knowledge of the seven Sciences, and the course of man's lyfe in this worlde.' It is dedicated to the King Henry VII. Neither the year of his birth nor of his death is known."

        WARTON "History of English Poetry."

THE PASTIME OF PLESURE.

TO THE READER

Sithe that all meune for the most part by a naturall inclination, desire rather to spend their dayes in plesure and delectable pastimes, then in paineful studyes and tedious labours. And yet nevertheles by the secrete inspiracion of Almighty God (all men in general) so insaciately thirsteth for the knowledge of wisdome and learnyng, that some for very earnest desire therof (thoughe nature grudgeth) cease not to spend their dayes and houres, with suche cōtinuall and importunate travayle in sekynge the same, that havyng no regarde to the over pressyng of Nature, in searchynge with all diligence for the true vaiue of knowledge, do sodainely bryng forth their owne confusion. Some contrariwise (whom nature to muche ruleth) beyng discomforted wyth painefull and tedious study, rather chose to be drowned in the stinkyng floude of ignoraunce, thē wyth so muche sweate and paynes, to sayle (wyth a by wynde) into the plesaunt handle of wisdome and science, which thing considered (most gentle reader) I offer here unto the for thy better instruction this little volume, conteynynge and treatyng upon the seven liberall sciences, and the whole course of man's life, firste compiled and

devised by Stephen Hawes gentleman, grome of the
chamber to the famous Prynce and seconde Salomon,
kynge Henrye the seventh. A man (as by his worckes
appeareth) of a plesaunte wytte, and singuler learnynge,
wherin thou shalt finde at one tyme, wisdome and
learnyng, with myrthe and solace. So that herein thou
mayest easelye fynde (as it were in pastyme) wythout
offence of nature that thyng, and in short space, whiche
many great clarkes wythout great paynes and travayle,
and long continuaunce of time heretofore coulde never
obteyne nor get, which as it was firste entituled by the
Avcthoure, to be the Pastime of Plesure, and under
the same title so dedicated to the sayed worthye Prynce,
by the Aucthoure therof: so shalt thou good reader
wyth deliberate readyng therof, fynde it not onely the
Pastyme of Plesure, but also of profite.

Farewel.

TO THE HIGH AND MIGHTY
PRINCE,

HENRY THE SEVENTH,

BY THE GRACE OF GOD,
KYNG OF ENGLANDE AND OF FRAUNCE,
LORDE OF IRELANDE, &c.

Right mighty prince, and redoubted soverayn
Sayling forthe well, in the shyp of grace
Over the waves of this life uncertayne,
Ryght towarde heaven, to have dwellyng place
Grace dothe you guyde, in every doubtfull case
Your governaunce, doth ever more eschewe
The synne of slouthe, enemy to vertue.

Grace stirreth well, the grace of God is great
Whych you hath brought to your ryall se,
And in your ryght it hath you surely sette
Above us all, to have the soveraintie:
Whose worthy power, and regall dygnitie
All our rancour, and our debate gan cease
And hath us brought, both welthe, rest, and peace.

From whom dyscendeth, by the ryghtful lyne
Noble prynce Henry, to succede the crowne
That in his youth, doth so clearely shyne
In euery vertue, casting the vyce adowne:
He shall of fame, attayne the hye renowne
No doubte but grace, shall hym well enclose
Whych by true ryght, sprang of the red rose.

Your noble grace, and excellent hycnes
For to accepte I beseche ryght humbly,
Thys little boke, opprest wyth rudenes
Without rethoryke, or colour crafty:
Nothynge I am experte in poetry,
As the monke of Bury, floure of eloquence
Which was in the time of great excellence,

Of your predecessour, the. V. king Henry,
Unto whose grace, he dyd present
Ryght famous bokes, of parfit memory:
Of hys faynyng, wyth termes cloquent.
Whose fatall ficcions, are yet permanent.
Grounded on reason, wyth cloudy fygures
He cloked the truth of al his scriptures.

The light of trouth, I lacke cunnyng to cloke
To drawe a curtayne, I dare not to presume
Nor hyde my matter, with a misty smoke
My rudenes cunnyng, dothe so sore consume
Yet as I may, I shall blowe out a fume
To hyde my mynde, underneth a fable
By covert coloure, well and probable.

Besechyng your grace to pardon mine ignoraunce,
Whiche this fayned fable, to eschue idlenes,
Have so compiled, nowe without doubtance
For to present, to your hye worthines
To folowe the trace, and all the perfitenes
Of my master Lydgate, with due exercise
Suche fayned tales, I do fynde and devise.

For under a coloure, a truthe may arise
As was the guise, in olde antiquityo
Of tho poetes olde, a tale to surmise
To cloke the trouthe, of their infirmitye
Or yet on joye to haue moralitye
I me excuse, if by negligence
That I do offende, for lacke of science.

Your graces most bounden seruaunt, Stephen Hawes, one of the gromes of your maiesties chamber, tho. xxi. yeare of your prosperous raygne.

HOWE GRAUND AMOUR WALKED IN A MEDOWE, AND MET WITH
FAME, ENVIRONED WITH TONGUES OF FIRE.

CHAP. I.

When Phœbus entred was, in Geminy
Shinyng aboue, in his fayre golde spere
And horned Dyane, then but one degre
In the Crabbe had entred, fayre and cleare
When that Aurora, did well appeare
In the depured ayre, and cruddy firmament
Forthe then I walked, without impediment

In to a medowe bothe gaye and glorious,
Whiche Flora depainted with many a colour
Like a place of pleasure most solacious
Encensyng out, the aromatike odoure
Of Zepherus breathe, whiche that every floure
Throughe his fume, dothe alwaie engender.
So as I went among the floures tender

By sodaine chaunce, a faire pathe I founde
On whiche I loked, and right oft I mused
And then all about, I behelde the grounde
With the faire pathe, whiche I sawe so used
My chaunce or fortune, I nothing refused
But in the pathe, forth I went a pace
To knowe whither, and unto what place

It woulde me bryng, by any similitude
So forth I went, were it ryght or wrong
Tyll that I sawe, of royall pulcritude
Before my face an ymage fayre and strong
With two fayre handes, stretched out along
Unto two hye wayes, there in particion
And in the right hande was this description:

This is the strayght waye of contemplacion
Unto the ioyfull tower perdurable
Who that wyll walke, unto that mancion
He must forsake, all thynges variable
With the vayne glory, so muche deceyvable
And though the way, be hard and daungerous
The last ende thereof shal be ryght precious.

And in the other hande ryght fayre written was
This is the waye, of worldly dignitye
Of the active lyfe, who wyll in it passe
Unto the tower of fayre dame Beautye
Fame shal tell hym, of the way in certaintye
Unto La bell Pucell, the fayre lady excellent
Above all other in cleare beauty splendent

I behelde ryght well, bothe the wayes twayne
And mused oft, whyche was best to take:
The one was sharpe, the other was more plaine
And unto my selfe, I began to make
A sodayne argument, for I myght not slake
Of my great musyng, of this royall ymage
And of these two wayes, so much in usage

For thys goodly picture was in altitude,
Nyne fote and more, of fayre marble stone
Ryght well favored, and of great attribute,
Thoughe it were made full many yeres agone.
Thus stode I musynge, my selfe all alone
By right long tyme; but at the last I went
The actyve way, with all my whole enteut.

Thus all alone I began to travayle
Forthe on my waye by long continuaunce;
But often times, I had great marvayle
Of the by pathes so full of plesaunce,
Whiche for to take, I had great doubtaunce
But evermore, as nere as I myght
I toke the waye, whiche went before me right

And at the laste, when Phebus in the west
Gan to avayle with all his beames merye,
When cleare Dyana in the fayre southest
Gan for to ryse, lightyng our emispery
With clowdes cleare wythout the stormy pery,
Me thought afarre, I had a vysyon
Of a picture, of marveylous facyon.

To whiche I went, without lenger delaye
Beholdyng well, the right faire portrayture
Made of fine copper, shynyng faire and gaye
Full well truely, accordiug to mesure
And, as I thought, nine fote of stature;
Yet in the breast with letters fayre and blewe
Was written a sentence, olde and true:

This is the waye, and the sytuacion
Unto the toure, of famous Doctrine,
Who that will learne, must be ruled by Reason
And with all his diligence he must encline
Slouthe to eschue, and for to determine
And set his hert to be intelligible
To a willyng herte is nought impossible

Beside the ymage I adowne me sette
After my laboure, my selfe to repose,
Till at the last, with a gasping nette
Slouth my head caught, with his whole purpose
It vayled not, the bodyc for to dispose
Againste the heade, when it is applied,
The heade must rule, it can not be denied

Thus as I satte in deadly slomber
Of a great horne, I hearde a royall blast,
With which I awoke, and had a great wonder
From whence it came; it made me sore agast,
I loked about, the night was well nere past
And fayre golden Phebus in the morow graye
With clowdes redde began to breake the daye.

I sawe come ridyng in a valey farre
A goodly ladye, environned about
With tongues of fire, as bright as any starre
That fiery flambes, enseused al way out
Whiche I behelde, and was in great doubt,
Her palfrey swift, rennyng as the winde
With two white greyhoūds, that were not behind.

When that these greyhoundes had me so espied
With faunyng chere of great humilitie
In goodly haste, they fast unto me hied;
I mused why, and wherfore it shoulde be,
But I welcomed them, in every degree;
They leaped oft, and were of me right faine,
I suffred them, and cherished them againe.

Their collers were of golde and of tyssue fine
Wherin their names appeared by scripture
Of dyamondes that clerely do shine;
The letters were grauen fayre and pure
To reade their names, I did my busye cure:
The one was Gouernaunce, the other named Grace,
Then was I gladde of all this sodayne cace

And then the ladye, with fiery flambe
Of brennyng tongues, was in my presence
Upon her palfrey, whiche had unto name
Pegase the swifte, so faire in excellence
Whiche sometime longed with his preminence
To kyng Percius, the sonne of Jupiter
On whom he rode by the worlde so farre.

To me she saied, she marueyled muche why
That her greyhoundes shewed me that fauoure;
What was my name, she asked me truely.
To whom I saied: it was La Graunde Amoure
Desechyng you to be to me succoure
To the tower of Doctrine, and also me tell
Your proper name, and where you do dwell.

My name, quod she, in all the world is knowen;
I clipped Fame in every region,
For I my horne in sundrye wise haue blowen
After the deathe of many a champion
And with my tongues have made aye mencion
Of their great actes, agayne to revive
In flamyng tongues, for to abide on live.

It was the custome of olde antiquitye
When the golden world, had domination
And nature highe in her aucthoritie
More stronger had her operation
Then she hath nowe in her digression;
The people then did all their busye payne,
After their death in fame to liue agayne.

Recorde of Saturne, the first kyng of Crete,
Whiche in his youth throughe his diligence
Founde first plowing of the landes swete
And after this by his great sapience
For the commen profite and beneuolence
Of all metalles, he made diuision
One from an other, by good provision.

And then also, as some poetes fayne,
He founde shotyng, and drawyng of the bowe;
Yet as of that, I am nothynge certaine,
But for his cunnynge of hye degre and lowe
He was well beloved, as I do well knowe
Throughe whose laboure and aye busy cure
His fame shall live, and shall right long endure.

In whose time raigned also in Thessayle,
A parte of Grece, the kyng Melizyus
That was right strong and fierce in battaile,
By whose laboure, as the storye sheweth vs
He brake first horses, wilde and rigorious,
Teachyng his men, on them right wel to ryde
And he him solfo did first the horse bestryde.

Also Mynerve, the right hardy goddese,
In the same time of so byghe renowne,
Vainquished Pallas by her great worthines
And first made harneys, to laye his pride adowne,
Whose great defence in every realme and towne
Was spredde about for her hye chyualrye,
Whiche by her harneys wanne the victorye.

Dothe not remayne yet in remembraunce
The famous actes of the noble Hercules,
That so many monsters put to utteraunce
By his great wisdome and hye prowes?
As the recule of Troye beareth good witnes
That in his time he would no battayle take
But for the wealthe of the commens sake.

Thus the whole mindes were ever fixt and set
Of noble men, in olde time to deuise
Suche thinges as were to the comen profite;
For in that time, suche was their goodly guise,
That after death their fame shoulde arise
For to endure and abide in mynde,
As yet in bokes we maye them written fynde.

O ye estates, surmountyng in noblenes,
Remembre well the noble paynyms all,
Howe by their labour they wanne the highnes
Of worthy fame, to raygue memoriall,
And them applyed, ever in speciall
Thinges to practise, whiche should profite be
To the comen wealth and their heires in fee.

OF THE SWETE REPORT OF FAME OF THE FAIRE LADY LA BEL PUCEL IN THE TOWER OF MUSIKE.

CHAP. II.

And after this Fame gan to expresse
Of jeopardous waye to the tower perillous
And of the beautye, and the semelinesse
Of La bel Pucell, so gaye and glorious,
That dwelled in the tower so marueylous,
Unto which might come no maner of creature
But by great laboure and hard adventure.

For by the waye there lye in waite
Gyantes great, disfigured of nature,
That all devoureth by their euil conceite,
Against whose strêgth there may no man endure;
They are so huge and strong out of measure
With many serpentes, foule and odious
In sundry likenesse, blacke and tedious.

But beyonde them, a great sea there is
Beyoude whiche sea, there is a goodly land
Most full of fruite, replete with joye and blisse,
Of right fine golde appeareth all the sande
In this faire realme, where the tower doth stand,
Made all of golde, enameled aboute
With noble stories, whiche do appeare without.

In whiche dwelleth by great aucthorityc
Of La bel Pucell, whiche is so fayre and bryght,
To whom in beautye no peare I can see,
For lyke as Phebus above all starres in lyght
When that he is in his spere aryght
Dothe excede with his beames clenre,
So dothe her beauty above other appeare

She is bothe good, aye wise and vertuous
And also discended of a noble lyne,
Ityche, comely, ryght meke, and bounteous,
All maner vertues in her clearly shine,
No vyce of her maye ryght longe domyne;
And I dame Fame in euery nacion
Of her do make the same relation.

Her swete report so my hart set on fyre
With brennyng love, most hote and feruent,
That her to see I had great desyre,
Saiynge to Fame: O ladye excellent,
I have determined in my iudgement
For La bel Pucell, the most fayre ladye,
To passe the waye of so great jeopardye.

You shall, quod Fame, attayne the victory,
If you wyll do, as I shal to you say,
And all my lesson retayne in memory:
To the tower of Doctrine ye shall take your waye,
You are now wythin a dayes iourney;
Both these greyhoundes shal kepe you company;
Loke that you cherishe them full gentely.

And Countenaunce, the goodly portres,
Shall let you in full well and nobly,
And also shewe you of the perfectnes
Of all the seven sciences ryght notably.
There in your mynd you may ententifely
Unto dame Doctrine geve perfite audience
Whiche shall enfourme you in every science.

Farewell, she sayed, I may not nowe abide!
Walke on your way with all your whole delite
To the tower of Doctrine at this morowe tide;
Ye shall to morowe, of it haue a syght.
Kepe on your waye nowe before you ryght;
For I must hence, to specifye the dedes
Of their worthines accordyng to their medes.

And with that she did from me departe
Upon her stede, swifter then the wynde.
When she was gone full wofull was my hart,
With inward trouble oppressed was my mynde;
Yet were the greyhoundes, left with me behind
Whiche did me comforte in my great vyage
To the tower of Doctrine, with their fawning courage.

So forthe I went, tossynge on my brayne,
Greatly musynge, ouer hyll and vale.
The way was troublous, and ey nothing playne,
Tyll at the laste I came to a dale
Beholdyng Phebus, declinyng lowe and pale;
With my greyhoundes in the fayre twy light
I sate me downe, for to rest me all nyght.

Slouthe vpon me so fast began to crepe,
That of fyne force I downe me layed
Upon an hyll, with my greyhoundes to slepe. &c. &c.

IV.

SIR THOMAS MORE.

1480—1535.

"Of the works of Sir Thomas More it was necessary to give a specimen, both because our language was then in a great degree formed and settled, and because it appears from Ben Jonson, that his works were considered as models of pure and elegant style."

JOHNSON's History of the English Language.

THE DESCRIPCION
OF
RICHARD THE THIRDE.

RICHARDE, the thirde sonne of Richarde, Duke of York, was in witte and courage egall with his two brothers, in bodye and prowesse farre vnder them bothe, little of stature, ill fetured of limmes, croke backed, his left shoulder much higher than his right, hard fauoured of visage, and such as is in states called warlye, in other menne otherwise, he was malicious, wrathfull, enuious, and from afore his birth, euer frowarde. It is for trouth reported, that the duches his mother had so much a doo in her trauaile, that shee coulde not bee deliuered of hym vncutte: and that hee came into the worlde with the feete forwarde, as menne bee borne outwarde, and (as the fame runneth) also not vntothed, whither menne of hatred reporte abouc the trouthe, or elles that nature chaunged her course in hys beginninge, whiche in the course of his lyfe many thinges vnnaturallye committed. None euill captaine was hee in the warre, as to whiche his disposicion was more metely then for peace. Sundrye victories hadde hee, and sommetime ouerthrowes, but neuer in defaulte as for his owno parsone, either of

hardinesse or polytike order, free was hee called of
dyspence, and sommewhat aboue hys power liberall,
with large giftes bee get him vnstedfaste frendeshippe,
for whiche hee was fain to pil and spoyle in other
places, and get him stedfast hatred. Hee was close
and secrete, a deepe dissimuler, lowlye of counteynaunce,
arrogant of heart, outwardly coumpinable where he in-
wardely hated, not letting to kisse whome hee thoughte
to kyll: dispitious and cruell, not for euill will alway,
but after for ambicion, and either for the suretie or
encrease of his estate. Frende and foo was muche
what indifferent, where his aduauntage grew, he spared
no mans deathe, whose life withstoode his purpose.
He slewe with his owne handes king Henry the sixt,
being prisoner in the Tower, as menne constantly saye,
and that without commaundement or knoweledge of the
king, whiche woulde vndoubtedly yf he had entended
that thinge, haue appointed that boocherly office, to
some other then his owne borne brother.

Somme wise menne also weene, that his drift
couertly conuayde, lacked not in helping furth his
brother of Clarence to his death: whiche hee resisted
openly, howbeit somwhat (as menne deme) more faintly
then he that wer hartely minded to his welth. And
they that thus deme, think that he long time in king
Edwardes life, forethought to be king in that case the
king his brother (whose life hee looked that euill dyete
shoulde shorten) shoulde happen to decease (as in dede
he did) while his children wer yonge. And thei deme,
that for thys intente he was gladde of his brothers

death the duke of Clarence, whose life must nedes haue hindered hym so entendynge, whither the same duke of Clarence hadde kepte him true to his nephew the yonge king, or enterprised to be kyng himselfe. But of al this pointe, is there no certaintie, and whoso diuineth vppon coniectures, maye as wel shote to farre as to short. Howbeit this haue I by credible informacion learned, that the selfe nighte in whiche kynge Edwarde died, one Mystlebrooke longe ere mornynge, came in greate haste to the house of one Pottyer dwellyng in Reddecrosse strete without Crepulgate: and when he was with hastye rappyng quickly letten in, hee shewed vnto Pottyer that kynge Edwarde was departed. By my trouthe manne quod Pottyer then wyll my mayster the duke of Gloucester bee kynge. What cause hee hadde soo to thynke harde it is to saye, whyther hee being toward him, anye thinge knewe that hee suche thynge purposed, or otherwyse had anye inkelynge thereof: for hee was not likelye to speake it of noughte.

But nowe to returne to the course of this hystorye, were it that the duke of Gloucester hadde of old foreminded this conclusion, or was nowe at erste thereunto moued, and putte in hope by the occasion of the tender age of the younge princes, his nepheues (as opportunitye and lykelyhoode of spede, putteth a manne in courage of that hee neuer entended) certayn is it that hee contriued theyr destruccion, with the vsurpacion of the regal dignitye vppon hymselfe. And for as muche as hee well wiste and holpe to mayntayn, a long con-

tinued grudge and hearte brennynge betwene the quenes
kinred and the kinges blood cyther partye enuying
others authoritye, he nowe thought that their deuision
shoulde bee (as it was in dede) a fortherlye begynnynge
to the pursuite of his intente, and a sure ground for the
foundacion of al his building yf he might firste vnder
the pretext of reuengynge of olde displeasure, abuse
the auger and ygnoraunce of the tone partie, to the
destruccion of the tother: and then wynne to his purpose as manye as he coulde· and those that coulde not
be wonne, might be loste ere they looked therefore.
For of one thynge was hee certayne, that if his entente
were perceiued, he shold soone haue made peace
betwene the bothe parties, with his owne bloude.
Kynge Edwarde in his life, albeit that this discen-
cion beetwene hys frendes sommewhat yrked hym: yet
in his good health he sommewhat the lesse regarded it,
because hee thought whatsoeuer busines shoulde falle
betwene them, hymselfe should alwaye bee hable to
rule bothe the parties.
But in his last sicknesse, when hee receiued his
naturall strengthe soo sore enfebled, that hee dyspayred
all recouerye, then hee consyderynge the youthe of his
chyldren, albeit hee nothynge lesse mistrusted then
that that happened, yet well forseynge that manye
harmes myghte growe by theyr debate, whyle the
youth of hys children shoulde lacke discrecion of themself and good counsayle of their frendes, of whiche
either party shold counsayle for their owne commodity
and rather by pleasaunte aduyse too wynne themselfe

fauour, than by profitable aduertisemente to do the children good, he called some of them before him that were at variaunce, and in especyall the lorde marques Dorsette the quenes sonne by her fyrst housebande, and Richarde the lorde Hastynges, a noble man, than lorde chaumberlayne agayne whome the quene specially grudged, for the great fauoure the kyng bare hym, and also for that shee thoughte hym secretely familyer with the kynge in wanton coumpanye. Her kynred also bare hym sore, as well for that the kynge hadde made hym captayne of Calyce (whiche office the lorde Ryuers, brother to the quene, claimed of the kinges former promyse) as for diuerse other great giftes which hee receyued, that they loked for. When these lordes with diuerse other of bothe the parties were comme in presence, the kynge liftinge vppe himselfe and vndersette with pillowes, as it is reported on this wyse sayd vnto them, My lordes, my dere kinsmenne and alies, in what plighte I lye you see, and I feele. By whiche the lesse whyle I looke to lyue with you, the more depelye am I moued to care in what case I leaue you, for such as I leaue you, suche bee my children lyke to fynde you. Whiche if they shoulde (that Godde forbydde) fynde you at varyaunce, myght happe to fall themselfe at warre ere their discrecion woulde serue to sette you at peace. Ye se their youthe, of whiche I recken the ouely suretie to reste in youre concord. For it suffiseth not that al you loue them, yf eche of you hate other. If they wer menne, your faithfulnesse happelye woulde suffise. But childehood must be maintained by mens authoritye, and slipper youth vnder-propped with elder counsayle, which neither they can haue, but ye geue it, nor ye geue it, if ye gree not. For what eche laboureth to breake that the other maketh, and for hatred of ech of others parson, impugneth eche others counsayle, there must it nedes bee long ere anye good conclusion goe forwarde. And also while either partye laboureth to be chiefe, flattery shall haue more place then plaine and faithfull aduyse, of whyche muste needes ensue the euyll bringing vppe of the prynce, whose mynd in tender youth infect, shal redily fal to mischief and riot, and drawe down with this noble realme to ruine, but if grace turn him to wisdom: which if God send, then thei that by euill menes before pleased hym best, shal after fall farthest out of fauour, so that euer at length ouill driftes dreue to nought, and good plain wayes prosper. Great variaunce hath ther long bene betwene you, not alway for great causes. Sometime a thing right wel intended, our misconstruccion turneth vnto worse or a smal displeasure done vs, eyther our owne affeccion or euil tongues agreueth. But this wote I well ye neuer had so great cause of hatred, as ye haue of loue. That we be al men, that we be christen men, this shall I leaue for prechers to tel you (and yet I wote nere whither any prechers wordes ought more to moue you, then his that is by and by gooying to the place that thei all preache of). But this shal I desire you to remember, that the one parte of you is of my bloode, the other of myne alies, and eche of yow with other, eyther of kinred or affinitie, whiche spirytuall kynred of affynyty, if the sacramentes of Christes churche, beare that weyghte with vs that woulde Godde thei did, shoulde no lesse moue vs to charitye, then the respecte of fleshlye consanguinitye. Oure Lorde forbydde, that you loue together the worse, for the selfe cause that you ought to loue the better. And yet that happeneth. And no where fynde wee so deadlye debate, as amonge them, whyche by nature and lawe moste oughte to agree together. Suche a pestilente serpente is ambicion and desyre of vaine glorye and soueraintye, whiche amonge states where he once entreth crepeth foorth so farre, tyll with denision and variaunce hee turneth all to mischiefe. Firste longing to be nexte the best, afterwarde egall with the beste, and at laste chiefe and aboue the beste. Of which immoderate appetite of woorship, of thereby of debate and disscncion what losse, what sorowe, what trouble hathe within these fewe yeares growen in this realme, I praye Godde as wel forgeate as wee well remember.

Whiche thinges yf I coulde as well haue forescne, as I haue with my more payne then pleasure proued, by Goddes blessed Ladie (that was euer his othe) I woulde neuer haue won the courtesye of mennes knees, with the losse of soo many heades. But sithen thynges passed cannot be gaine called, muche oughte wee the more beware, by what occasion we haue taken soo greate hurte afore, that we efte soones fall not in that occasion agayne. Nowe be those griefes passed, and

all is (Godde be thanked) quiete, and likelie righte
wel to prosper in wealthfull peace vnder youre coseyns
my children, if Godde sende them life and you loue.
Of whiche twoo thinges, the lesse losse wer they by
whome thoughe Godde dydde hys pleasure, yet shoulde
the realme alway finde kinges and paraduenture as
good kinges. But yf you among youre selfe in a
childes reygne fall at debate, many a good man shall
perish and happely he to, and ye to, ere thys land
finde peace again. Wherfore in these laste wordes that
euer I looke to speak with you: I exhort you and
require you al, for the loue that you haue euer borne
to me, for the loue that I haue euer born to you, for
the loue that our Lord beareth to vs all, from this time
forwarde, all grieues forgotten, eche of you loue other.
Whiche I verelye truste you will, if ye any thing
earthly regard, either Godde or your king, affinitie or
kinred, this realme, your owne countrey, or your owne
surety. And therewithal the king no longer onduring
to sitte vp, laide him down on his right side, his face
towarde them: and none was there present that coulde
refrain from weping. But the lordes recomforting him
with as good wordes as they could, and answering for
the time as thei thought to stand with his pleasure,
there in his presence (as by their wordes appered) ech
forgaue other, and ioyned their hands together, when
(as it after appeared by their dedes) their hearts wer
far a sonder. As sone as the king was departed, the
noble prince his sonne drew toward London, which at
the time of his decease, kept his houshold at Ludlow

in Wales. Which countrey being far of from the law and recourse to iustice, was begon to be farre oute of good wyll and waxen wild, robbers and riuers walking at libertie vncorrected. And for this encheason the prince was in the life of his father sente thither, to the end that the authoritie of his presence should refraine euill disposed parsons fro the boldness of their former outerages, to the gouernaunce and ordering of this yong prince at his sending thyther, was there appointed Sir Anthony Woduille lord Riuers and brother vnto the quene, a right honourable man, as valiaunte of hande as politike in counsnyle. Adioyned wer there vnto him other of the same partie, and in effect euery one as he was nerest of kin vnto the quene, so was planted next about the prince. That drifte by the queue not vnwisely deuised, whereby her bloode mighte of youth be rooted in the princes fauor, the duke of Gloucester turned vnto their destruccion, and vpon that grounde set the foundacion of all his vnhappy building. For whom soeuer he perceiued, either at variance with them, or bearing himself their fauor, hee brake vnto them, som by mouth, som by writing and secret messengers, that it neyther was reason nor in any wise to be suffered, that the yong king their master and kinsmanne, shoold bee in the handes and custodye of his mothers kinred, sequestred in maner from theyr compani and attendance, of which cueri one ought him as faithful scruice as they, and manye of them far more honorable part of kin then his mothers side: whose blood (quod he) sauing the kinges pleasure, was

ful vnmetely to be matched with his: whiche nowe to
be as who say remoued from the kyng, and the lesse
noble to be left aboute him, is (quod he) neither
honorable to hys magestie, nor vnto vs, and also to his
grace no surety to haue the mightiest of his frendes
from him, and vnto vs no little ieopardy, to suffer our
welproued euill willers, to grow in ouergret authoritie
with the prince in youth, namely which is lighte of
beliefe and sone perswaded. Ye remember I trow king
Edward himself, albeit he was a manne of age and of
discrecion, yet was he in manye thynges ruled by the
bende, more then stode either with his honour, or our
profite, or with the commoditie of any manne els, except onely the immoderate aduauncement of them selfe.
Whiche whither they sorer thirsted after their owne
weale, or our woe, it wer hard I wene to gesse. And
if some folkes frendship had not holden better place
with the king, then any respect of kinred, thei might
peraduenture easily haue be trapped and brought to
confusion somme of vs ere this. Why not as easily as
they haue done some other alreadye, as neere of his
royal bloode as we. But our Lord hath wrought his
wil, and thanke be to his grace that peril is paste.
Howe be it as great is growing, yf wee suffer this
yonge kyng in our enemyes hande, whiche without his
wyttyng, might abuse the name of his commaundement,
to ani of our vndoing, which thyng God and good
prouision forbyd. Of which good prouision none of us
hath any thing the lesse nede, for the late made
attonementes, in whiche the kinges pleasure hadde more

place then the parties willes. Nor none of vs I beleue is so vnwyse, ouersone to truste a newe frende made of an olde foe, or to think that an houerly kindnes, sodainely contract in one houre continued, yet scant a fortnight, shold be deper setled in their stomackes: then a long accustomed malice many yeres rooted.

With these wordes and writynges and suche other, the duke of Gloucester sone set a fyre, them that were of themself othe to kindle, and in especiall twayne, Edwarde duke of Buckingham, and Richarde lorde of Hastinges and chaumberlayn, both men of honour and of great power. The tone by longe succession from his ancestrie, the tother by his office and the kinges fauor. These two not bearing eche to other so muche loue, as hatred bothe vnto the quenes parte: in thys poynt accorded together wyth the duke of Gloucester, that they wolde vtterlye amoue fro the kinges companye, all his mothers frendes, vnder the name of their enemyes. Vpon this concluded, the duke of Gloucester vnderstandyng, that the lordes whiche at that tyme were aboute the kyng, entended to bryng him vppe to his coronacion, accoumpanied with suche power of their frendes, that it shoulde bee harde for hym to brynge his purpose to passe, without the gathering and great assemble of people and in maner of open warre, wherof the ende he wiste was doubtuous, and in which the kyng being on their side, his part should haue the face and name of a rebellion: he secretly therefore by diuers meanes, caused the quene to be perswaded and brought in the mynd, that it neither wer nede, and also shold be ieopardous, the king to come vp strong. For where as nowe euery lorde loued other, and none other thing studyed vppon, but aboute the coronacion and honoure of the king: if the lordes of her kinred shold assemble in the kinges name muche people, thei should geue the lordes atwixte whome and them hadde bene sommetyme debate, to feare and suspecte, leste they shoulde gather thys people, not for the kynges sauegarde whome no manne empugned, but for theyr destruccion, hauying more regarde to their olde variaunce, then their newe attonement. For whiche cause thei shoulde assemble on the other partie muche people agayne for their defence, whose power she wyste wel farre stretched. And thus should all the realme fall on a rore. And of al the hurte that therof should ensue, which was likely not to be litle, and the most harme there like to fal wher she lest would, all the worlde woulde put her and her kinred in the wyght, and say that thei had vnwyselye and vntrewlye also, broken the amitie and peace that the kyng her husband so prudentelye made, betwene hys kinne and hers in his death bed, and whiche the other party faithfully obserued.

The quene being in this wise perswaded, suche woorde sente vnto her sonne, and vnto her brother being aboute the kynge, and ouer that the duke of Gloucester hymselfe and other lordes the chiefe of hys bende, wrote vnto the kynge soo reuerentelye, and to the queenes frendes, there soo louyngelye, that they nothynge earthelye mystrustynge, broughte the kynge vppe in greate haste, not in good spede, with a sober coumpanye. Nowe was the king in his waye to London gone, from Northampton, when these dukes of Gloucester and Buckyngham came thither. Where remained behynd, the lorde Ryuers the kynges vncle, entendyng on the morowe to folow the kynge, and bee with hym at Stonye Stratford miles thence, earely or hee departed. So was there made that nyghte muche frendely chere betwene these dukes and the lorde Riuers a greate while. But incontinente after that they were oppenlye with greate courtesye departed, and the lorde Riuers lodged, the dukes secretelye with a fewe of their moste priuye frendes, sette them downe in counsayle, wherin they spent a great parte of the nyght. And at their risinge in the dawnyng of the day, thei sent about priuily to their seruantes in their innes and lodgynges about, geuinge them commaundemente to make them selfe shortely readye, for their lordes wer to horsebackward. Vppon whiche messages, manye of their folke were attendaunt, when manye of the lorde Riuers seruantes were vnreadye. Now hadde these dukes taken also into their custodye the kayes of the inne, that none shoulde passe foorth without theyr licence.

And ouer this in the byghe waye towarde Stonye Stratforde where the kynge laye, they hadde beestowed certayne of theyr folke, that shoulde send backe agayne, and compell to retourne, anye manne that were gotten oute of Northampton toward Stonye Stratforde, tyll they should gene other lycence. For as muche as the dukes themselfe entended for the shewe of theire dylygence, to bee the fyrste that shoulde that daye attende vppon the kynges highnesse oute of that towne: thus bare they folke in hande. But when the lorde Ryuers vnderstode the gates closed, and the wayes on euerye side besette, neyther hys seruauntes nor hymself suffered to go oute, parceiuyng well so greate a thyng without his knowledge not begun for noughte, comparyng this maner present with this last nightes chere, in so few houres so gret a chaunge marueylouslye misliked. How be it sithe hee coulde not geat awaye, and keepe himselfe close, hee woulde not, leste he shoulde seeme to hyde himselfe for some secret feare of hys owne faulte, whereof he saw no such cause in hym self: he determined vppon the suretie of his own conscience, to goo boldelye to them, and inquire what thys matter myghte meane. Whome as soone as they sawe, they beganne to quarrell with hym, and saye, that hee intended to sette distaunce beetweene the kynge and them, and to brynge them to confusion, but it shoulde not lye in hys power. And when hee beganne (as hee was a very well spoken manne) in goodly wise to excuse himself, they taryed not the ende of his aunswere, but shortely tooke him and putte him in warde, and that done, foorthwyth wente to horsebacke, and tooke the waye to Stonye Stratforde. Where they founde the kinge with his companie readye to leape on horsebacke, and departe forwarde, to leaue that lodging for them, because it was to streighte for bothe coumpanies. And as sone as they came in his

presence, they lighte adowne with all their companie
aboute them. To whome the duke of Buckingham
stide, goe afore gentlemenne and yeomen, kepe your
rovmes. And thus in goodly arraye, thei came to the
kinge, and on theiro knees in very humble wise, salued
his grace; whiche receyued them in very ioyous and
amiable maner, nothynge earthlye knowing nor mis-
trustinge as yet. But euen by and by in his presence,
they piked a quarell to the lorde Richarde Graye, the
kynges other brother by his mother, sayinge that hee
with the lorde marques his brother and the lorde Riuers
his vncle, hadde coumpassed to rule the kinge and the
realme, and to sette variaunce among the states, and
to subdewe and destroye the noble blood of the realm.
Toward the accoumplishinge whereof, they sayde that
the lorde Marques hadde entered into the Tower of
London, and thence taken out the kinges treasor, and
sent menne to the sea. All whiche thinge these dukes
wiste well were done for good purposes and necessari
by the whole counsaile at London, sauing that sommewhat thei must sai. Vnto whiche woordes, the king
aunswered, what my brother Marques hath done I cannot saie. But in good faith I dare well aunswere for
myne vncle Riuers and my brother here, that thei be
innocent of any such matters. Ye my liege quod the
duke of Buckingham thei haue kepte theire dealing in
these matters farre fro the knowledge of your good
grace. And foorthwith thei arrested the lord Richarde
and Sir Thomas Waughan knighte, in the kinges presence, and broughte the king and all backe vnto

Northampton, where they tooke againe further counsaile. And there they sent awaie from the kinge whom it pleased them, and sette newe seruantes aboute him, suche as lyked better them than him. At whiche dealinge hee wepte and was nothing contente, but it booted not. And at dyner the duke of Gloucester sonte a dishe from his owne table to the lord Riuers, prayinge him to be of good chere, all should be well inough. And he thanked the duke, and prayed the messenger to beare it to his nephewe the lord Richard with the same message for his comfort, who he thought had more nede of comfort, as one to whom such aduersitie was straunge. But himself had been al his dayes in vre therewith, and therfore coulde beare it the better. But for al this coumfortable courtesye of the duke of Gloucester he sent the lorde Riuers and the lord Richarde with Sir Thomas Vaughan into the Northe countrey into diuers places to prison, and afterward al to Pomfrait, where they were in conclusion beheaded.

V.

EDMUND SPENSER.

1553—1599.

"The noblest allegorical poem in our own language — indeed, the noblest allegorical poem in the world — is Spenser's 'Faerie Queene;' at the same time it is probable, that if it had not been allegorical at all, it would have been a more felicitous and attractive work of imagination."

J. WORDSWORTH in his "Lectures on Poetry."

"It would be superfluous to speak in praise of SPENSER. With Chaucer, with Shakespeare and with Milton he ranks in the first class of our poets."

R. SOUTHEY.

THE FAERIE QUEENE.

BOOK I. CANTO I.

*The patron of true Holinesse
Foule Errour doth defeate;
Hypocrisie, him to entrappe,
Doth to his home entreate.*

I.

A gentle knight was pricking on the plaine,
Ycladd in mightie armes and silver shielde,
Wherein old dints of deepe woundes did remaine,
The cruel markes of many' a bloody fielde;
Yet armes till that time did he never wield;
His angry steede did chide his foming bitt,
As much disdayning to the curbe to yield:
Full iolly knight he seemd, and faire did sitt,
As one for knightly giusts and fierce encounters fitt.

II.

And on his brest a bloodie crosse he bore,
The deare remembrance of his dying Lord,
For whose sweete sake that glorious badge he wore,
And dead, as living, ever him ador'd:
Upon his shield the like was also scor'd,
For soveraine hope, which in his helpe he had.
Right, faithfull, true he was in deede and word;
But of his cheere did seeme too solemne sad;
Yet nothing did he dread, but ever was ydrad.

III.

Upon a great adventure he was bond,
That greatest Gloriana to him gave,
(That greatest glorious Queene of Faery lond)
To winne him worshippe, and her grace to have,
Which of all earthly things he most did crave.
And ever as he rode, his hart did earne
To prove his puissance in battell brave
Upon his foe, and his new force to learne;
Upon his foe, a dragon horrible and stearne.

IV.

A lovely ladie rode him faire beside
Upon a lowly asse more white then snow;
Yet she much whiter; but the same did hide
Under a vele, that wimpled was full low;
And over all a blacke stole shee did throw,
As one that inly mournd; so was she sad,
And heavie sate upon her palfrey slow;
Seemed in heart some hidden care she had;
And by her in a line a milke-white lambe she lad.

V.

So pure and innocent, as that same lambe,
She was in life and every vertuous lore,
And by descent from royall lynage came
Of ancient kinges and queenes, that had of yore
Their scepters stretcht from east to westerne shore,
And all the world in their subjection held;
Till that infernal feend with foule uprore
Forwasted all their land, and them expeld;
Whom to avenge, she had this knight from far compeld.

VI.

Behind her farre away a dwarfe did lag,
That lasie seemd, in being ever last,
Or wearied with bearing of her bag
Of needments at his backe. Thus as they past,

The day with cloudes was suddeine overcast,
And angry Iove an hideous storme of raine
Did poure into his lemans lap so fast,
That everie wight to shrowd it did constrain;
And this faire couple eke to shroud themselves were fain.

VII.
Enforst to seeke some covert nigh at hand,
A shadie grove not farr away they spide,
That promist ayde the tempest to withstand;
Whose loftie trees, yclad with sommers pride
Did spred so broad, that heavens light did hide,
Not perceable with power of any starr;
And all within were pathes and allcies wide,
With footing worne, and leading inward farr:
Faire harbour that them seems; so in they entred ar.

VIII.
And foorth they passe, with pleasure forward led,
Ioying to heare the birdes sweete harmony,
Which therein shrouded from the tempest dred,
Seemd in their song to scorne the cruell sky.
Much can they praise the trees so straight and hy:
The sayling pine, the cedar proud and tall;
The vine-propp elme, the poplar never dry;
The builder oake, sole king of forrests all;
The aspine good for staves, the cypresse funerall;

IX.
The laurell, meed of mightie conquerours
And poets sage; the firre that weepeth still;
The willow, worne of forlorne paramours;
The eugh, obedient to the benders will;
The birch for shaftes, the sallow for the mill;
The mirrhe sweete-bleeding in the bitter wound;
The warlike beech, the ash for nothing ill;
The fruitful olive, and the platane round;
The carver holme, the maple, seldom inward sound.

X.

Led with delight, they thus beguile the way,
Untill the blustring storme is overblowne;
When, weening to returne, whence they did stray,
They cannot finde that path, which first was showne,
But wander too and fro in waies unknowne,
Furthest from end then, when they neerest weene,
That makes them doubt their wits be not their owne.
So many paths, so many turnings seene,
That which of them to take in diverse doubt they been.

XI.

At last resolving forward still to fare,
Till that some end they finde, or in or out,
That path they take, that beaten seemd most bare,
And like to lead the labyrinth about;
Which when by tract they hunted had throughout,
At length it brought them to a hollowe cave
Amid the thickest woods. The champion stout
Eftsoones dismounted from his courser brave,
And to the dwarfe awhile his needlesse spere he gave.

XII.

"Be well aware," quoth then that ladie milde,
"Least suddaine mischiefe ye too rash provoke:
The danger hid, the place unknowne and wilde,
Breedes dreadfull doubts: oft fire is without smoke,
And perill without show; therefore your stroke,
Sir Knight, with-hold, till further tryall made."
"Ah, Ladie," sayd he, "shame were to revoke
The forward footing for an hidden shade:
Vertue gives her selfe light through darknesse for to wade."

XIII.

"Yea, but," quoth she, "the perill of this place
I better wot then you: Though nowe too late
To wish you backe returne with foule disgrace,
Yet wisedome warnes, whilest foot is in the gate,

To stay the steppe, ere forced to retrate.
This is the Wandring Wood, this Errours Den,
A monster vile, whom God and man does hate:
Therefore I read beware." "Fly, fly," quoth then
The fearefull dwarfe; "this is'no place for living men."

XIV.

But, full of fire and greedy hardiment,
The youthfull knight could not for ought be staide;
But forth unto the darksome hole he went,
And looked in: his glistring armor made
A litle glooming light, much like a shade;
By which he saw the ugly monster plaine:
Halfe like a serpent horribly displaide,
But th' other halfe did womans shape retaine,
Most lothsom, filthie, foule, and full of vile disdaine.

XV.

And, as she lay upon the durtie ground,
Her huge long taile her den all overspred,
Yet was in knots and many boughtes upwound,
Pointed with mortall sting; of her there bred
A thousand yong ones, which she dayly fed,
Sucking upon her poisnous dugs; each one
Of sundrie shapes, yet all ill-favored:
Soone as that uncouth light upon them shone,
Into her mouth they crept, and suddain all were gone.

XVI.

Their dam upstart out of her den effraide,
And rushed forth, hurling her hideous taile
About her cursed head; whose folds displaid
Were stretcht now forth at length without entraile.
She lookt about, and seeing one in mayle,
Armed to point, sought backe to turne againe;
For light she hated as the deadly bale,
Ay wont in desert darknes to remaine,
Where plain none might her see, nor she see any plaine.

XVII.

Which when the valiant Elfe perceiv'd, he lept
As lyon fierce upon the flying pray,
And with his trenchand blade her boldly kept
From turning backe, and forced her to stay:
Therewith enrag'd she loudly gan to bray,
And turning fierce her speckled taile advaunst,
Threatning her angrie sting, him to dismay;
Who, nought aghast, his mightie hand enhaunst;
The stroke down from her head unto her shoulder glaunst.

XVIII.

Much daunted with that dint her sence was dazd;
Yet kindling rage her selfe she gathered round,
And all attonce her beastly bodie raizd
With doubled forces high above the ground:
Tho, wrapping up her wrethed sterne arownd,
Lept fierce upon his shield, and her huge traine
All suddenly about his body wound,
That hand or foot to stirr he strove in vaine.
God helpe the man so wrapt in Errours endlesse traine!

XIX.

His lady, sad to see his sore constraint,
Cride out, "Now, now, Sir Knight, shew what ye bee;
Add faith unto your force, and be not faint;
Strangle her, els she sure will strangle thee."
That when he heard, in great perplexitie,
His gall did grate for griefe and high disdaine;
And, knitting all his force, got one hand free,
Wherewith he grypt her gorge with so great paine,
That soone to loose her wicked bands did her constraine.

XX.

Therewith she spewd out of her filthie maw
A floud of poyson horrible and blacke,
Full of great lumps of flesh and gobbets raw,
Which stunk so vildly, that it forst him slacke

His grasping hold, and from her turne him backe:
Her vomit full of bookes and papers was,
With loathly frogs and toades, which eyes did lacke,
And creeping sought way in the weedy gras,
Her filthie parbreake all the place defiled has.

XII.

As when old father Nilus gins to swell
With timely pride above the Aegyptian vale,
His fattie waves doe fertile slime outwell,
And overflow each plaine and lowly dale;
But, when his later spring gins to avale,
Huge heapes of mudd he leaves, wherin there breed
Ten thousand kindes of creatures, partly male
And partly female, of his fruitful seed:
Such ugly monstrous shapes elswhere may no man reed.

XLII.

The same so sore annoyed has the knight,
That, wel-nigh choked with the deadly stinke,
His forces faile, ne can no leager fight.
Whose corage when the feend perceivd to shrinke,
She poured forth out of her hellish sinke
Her fruitfull cursed spawne of serpents small,
(Deformed monsters, fowle, and blacke as inke,)
Which swarming all about his legs did crall,
And him encombred sore, but could not hurt at all.

XLIII.

As gentle shepheard in sweete eventide,
When ruddy Phebus gins to welke in west,
High on an hill, his flocke to vewen wide,
Markes which doe byte their hasty supper best;
A cloud of cumbrous gnattes doe him molest,
All striving to infixe their feeble stinges,
That from their noyance he no where can rest,
But with his clownish hands their tender wings
He brusheth oft, and oft doth mar their murmurings:

Five Centuries. 1

XXIV.

Thus ill bestedd, and fearefull more of shame
Then of the certeine perill he stood in,
Halfe furious unto his foe he came,
Resolvd in minde all suddenly to win,
Or soone to lose, before he once would lin;
And stroke at her with more then manly force,
That from her body, full of filthie sin,
He raft her hatefull heade without remorse;
A streame of cole-black blood forth gushed from her corse.

XXV.

Her scattred brood, soone as their parent deare
They saw so rudely falling to the ground,
Groning full deadly all with troublous feare
Gathred themselves about her body round,
Weening their wonted entrance to have found
At her wide mouth; but, being there withstood,
They flocked all about her bleeding wound,
And sucked up their dying mothers bloud,
Making her death their life, and eke her hurt their good.

XXVI.

That détestable sight him much amazde,
To see th' unkindly impes, of heaven accurst,
Devoure their dam; on whom while so he gazde,
Having all satisfide their bloudy thurst,
Their bellies swolne he saw with fulnesse burst,
And bowels gushing forth: well worthy end
Of such, as drunke her life the which them nurst.
Now needeth him no lenger labour spend,
His foes have slaine themselves, with whom he should con-
    tend.

XXVII.

His lady seeing all, that chaunst, from farre,
Approcht in hast to greet his victorie,
And saide: "Faire knight, borne under happie starre,
Who see your vanquisht foes before you lye;

Well worthie be you of that armory,
Wherein ye have great glory wonne this day,
And proov'd your strength on a strong enimie,
Your first adventure; many, such I pray,
And henceforth ever wish that like succeed it may!"

XXVIII.

Then mounted he upon his steede againe,
And with the lady backward sought to wend:
That path he kept, which beaten was most plaine,
Ne ever would to any by-way bend;
But still did follow one unto the end,
The which at last out of the wood them brought.
So forward on his way (with God to frend)
He passed forth, and new adventure sought;
Long way he traveiled, before he heard of ought.

XXIX.

At length they chaunst to meet upon the way
An aged sire, in long blacke weedes yclad,
His feete all bare, his beard all hoarie gray,
And by his belt his booke he hanging had;
Sober he seemde, and very sagely sad;
And to the ground his eyes were lowly bent,
Simple in shew, and voide of malice bad;
And all the way he prayed, as he went,
And often knockt his brest, as one that did repent.

XXX.

He faire the knight saluted, louting low,
Who faire him quited, as that courteous was;
And after asked him, if he did know
Of straunge adventures, which abroad did pas.
"Ah! my dear sonne," quoth he, "how should, alas!
Silly old man, that lives in hidden cell,
Bidding his beades all day for his trespás,
Tydings of warre and worldly trouble tell?
With holy father sits not with such thinges to mell.

XXXI.

"But if of daunger, which hereby doth dwell,
And homebredd evil ye desire to heare,
Of a straunge man I can you tidings tell,
That wasteth all this countrie farre and neare."
"Of such," saide he, "I chiefly doe inquere;
And shall thee well rewarde to shew the place,
In which that wicked wight his dayes doth weare:
For to all knighthood it is foule disgrace,
That such a cursed creature lives so long a space."

XXXII.

"Far hence," quoth he, "in wastful wildernesse
His dwelling is, by which no living wight
May ever passe, but thorough great distresse."
"Now," saide the ladie, "draweth toward night;
And well I wote, that of your later fight
Ye all forwearied be; for what so strong,
But, wanting rest, will also want of might?
The sunne, that measures heaven all day long,
At night doth baite his steedes the ocean waves emong.

XXXIII.

"Then with the sunne take, sir, your timely rest,
And with new day new worke at once begin;
Untroubled night, they say, gives counsell best."
"Right well, Sir Knight, ye have advised bin,"
Quoth then that aged man; "the way to win
Is wisely to advise. Now day is spent:
Therefore with me ye may take up your in
For this same night." The knight was well content:
So with that godly father to his home they went.

XXXIV.

A little lowly hermitage it was,
Downe in a dale, hard by a forest's side,
Far from resort of people, that did pas
In traveill to and froe: a little wyde

There was an holy chappell edifyde,
Wherein the hermite dewly wont to say
His holy things each morne and eventyde:
Thereby a christall streame did gently play,
Which from a sacred fountaine welled forth alway.

XXXV.
Arrived there, the litle house they fill,
Ne looke for entertainement, where none was;
Rest is their feast, and all thinges at their will:
The noblest mind the best contentment has.
With faire discourse the evening so they pas;
For that olde man of pleasing wordes had store,
And well could file his tongue, as smooth as glas:
He told of saintes and popes, and evermore
He strowd an Ave-Mary after and before.

XXXVI.
The drouping night thus creepeth on them fast;
And the sad humor loading their eye-liddes,
As messenger of Morpheus, on them cast
Sweet slombring deaw, the which to sleep them biddes.
Unto their lodgings then his guestes he riddes,
Where when all drownd in deadly sleepe he findes,
He to his studie goes; and there amiddes
His magick bookes, and artes of sundrie kindes,
He seeks out mighty charmes to trouble sleepy minds.

BOOK II. CANTO IX.

*The House of Temperaunce, in which
Doth sober Alma dwell,
Besieged of many foes, whom straunge-
er knightes to flight compell.*

I.
Of all Gods workes, which doe this worlde adorne,
There is no one more faire and excellent
Then is mans body, both for powre and forme,
Whiles it is kept in sober government;

But none then it more fowle and indecent,
Distempred through misrule and passions bace;
It grows a monster, and incontinent .
Doth lose his dignity and native grace.
Behold, who list, both one and other in this place.

II.

After the Paynim brethren conquer'd were,
The Briton prince recov'ring his stolne sword,
And Guyon his lost shield, they both yfere
Forth passed on their way in fayre accord,
Till him the prince with gentle court did bord;
"Sir knight, mote I of you this court'sy read,
To weet why on your shield, so goodly scord,
Beare ye the picture of that ladies head!
Full lively is the semblaunt, though the substance dead."

III.

"Fayre sir," sayd he, "if in that picture dead
Such life ye read, and vertue in vaine shew;
What mote ye weene, if the trew lively-head
Of that most glorious visage he did vew!
But yf the beauty of her mind ye knew,
That is, her bounty, and imperiall powre,
Thousand times fairer then her mortall hew,
O! how great wonder would your thoughts devoure,
And infinite desire into your spirite poure!

IV.

"She is the mighty Queene of Faëry,
Whose faire retraitt I in my shield doe beare;
Shee is the flowre of grace and chastity,
Throughout the world renowmed far and neare,
My life, my liege, my soveraine, my deare,
Whose glory shineth as the morning starre,
And with her light the earth enlumines cleare;
Far reach her mercies, and her praises farre,
As well in state of peace, as puissaunce in warre."

V.

"Thrise happy man," said then the Briton knight,
"Whom gracious lott and thy great valiaunce
Have made thee soldier of that princesse bright,
Which with her bounty and glad countenaunce
Doth blesse her servaunts, and them high advaunce!
How may straunge knight hope ever to aspire,
By faithfull service and meete amenaunce
Unto such blisse? sufficient were that hire
For losse of thousand lives, to die at her desire."

VI.

Said Guyon: "Noble lord, what meed so great,
Or grace of earthly prince so soveraine,
But by your wondrous worth and warlike feat
Ye well may hope, and easely attaine?
But were your will her sold to entertaine,
And numbred be mongst Knights of Maydenhed,
Great guerdon, well I wote, should you remaine,
And in her favor high bee reckoned,
As Arthegall and Sophy now beene honored."

VII.

"Certes," then said the prince, "I God avow,
That sith I armes and knighthood first did plight,
My whole desire hath beene, and yet is now,
To serve that queene with al my powre and might.
Now hath the sunne with his lamp-burning light
Walkt round about the world, and I no lesse,
Sith of that goddesse I have sought tho sight,
Yet no where can her find: such happinesse
Heven doth to me envy and fortune favourlesse."

VIII.

"Fortune, the foe of famous chevisaunce,
Seldom," said Guyon, "yields to vertue aide,
But in her way throwes mischiefe and mischaunce,
Whereby her course is stopt and passage staid.

But you, faire sir, be not herewith dismaid,
But constant keepe the way in which ye stand;
Which were it not that I am els delaid
With hard adventure, which I have in hand,
I labour would to guide you through al Faery-laud."

IX.

"Gramercy, sir," said he; "but mote I weete
What straunge adventure doe ye now pursew?
Perhaps my succour or advizement meete
Mote stead you much your purpose to subdew."
Then gan Sir Guyon all the story shew
Of false Acrasia, and her wicked wiles;
Which to avenge, the palmer him forth drew
From Faery court. So talked they, the whiles
They wasted had much way, and measurd many miles.

X.

And now faire Phoebus gan decline in haste
His weary wagon to the westerne vale,
Whenas they spide a goodly castle, plaste
Foreby a river in a pleasaunt dale;
Which choosing for that evenings hospitale,
They thether marcht: but when they came in sight,
And from their sweaty coursers did avale,
They found the gates fast barred long ere night,
And every loup fast lockt, as fearing foes despight.

XI.

Which when they saw, they weened fowle reproch
Was to them doen, their entraunce to forestall;
Till that the squire gan nigher to approch,
And wind his horne under the castle wall,
That with the noise it shooke as it would fall.
Eftsoones forth looked from the highest spire
The watch, and lowd unto the knights did call,
To weete what they so rudely did require?
Who gently answered, they entraunce did desire.

XII.

"Fly, fly, good knights," said he, "fly fast away,
If that your lives ye love, as meete ye should!
Fly fast, and save yourselves from neare decay;
Here may ye not have entraunce, though we would.
We would and would againe, if that we could;
But thousand enemies about us rave,
And with long siege us in this castle hould;
Seven yeares this wize they us besieged have,
And many good knights slaine that have us sought to save."

XIII.

Thus as he spoke, loe! with outragious cry
A thousand villeins rownd about them swarmd
Out of the rockes and caves adioyning nye;
Vile caitive wretches, ragged, rude, deformd,
All threatning death, all in straunge manner armd;
Some with unweldy clubs, some with long speares,
Some rusty knives, some staves in fier warmd:
Sterne was their looke, like wild amazed steares,
Staring with hollow eies and stiff upstanding heares.

XIV.

Fiersly at first those knights they did assayle,
And drove them to recoile: but, when againe
They gave fresh charge, their forces gan to fayle,
Unhable their encounter to sustaine;
For with much puissaunce and impetuous maine
Those champions broke on them, that forst them fly,
Like scattered sheepe, whenas the shepherds swaine
A lion and a tigre doth espye
With greedy pace forth rushing from the forest nye.

XV.

A while they fled, but soon retournd againe
With greater fury then before was found;
And evermore their cruell capitaine
Sought with his raskall routs t'enclose them rownd,

And overronne to tread them to the grownd:
But soone the knights with their bright-burning blades
Broke their rude troupes, and orders did confownd,
Hewing and slashing at their idle shades;
For though they bodies seem, yet substaunce from them fades.

XVI.

As when a swarme of gnats at eventide
Out of the fennes of Allan doe arise,
Their murmuring small trompetts sownden wide,
Whiles in the aire their clustring army flies,
That as a cloud doth seeme to dim the skies;
Ne man nor beast may rest or take repast
For their sharpe wounds and noyous iniuries,
Till the fierce northerne wind with blustring blast
Doth blow them quite away, and in the ocean cast:

XVII.

Thus when they had that troublous rout disperst,
Unto the castle gate they come againe,
And entraunce crav'd, which was denied erst.
Now when report of that their perlous paine,
And combrous conflict which they did sustaine,
Came to the ladies eare which there did dwell,
Shee forth issdwed with a goodly traine
Of squires and ladies equipaged well,
And entertained them right fairely, as befell.

XVIII.

Alma she called was; a virgin bright,
That had not yet felt Cupides wanton rage;
Yet was shee woo'd of many a gentle knight,
And many a lord of noble parentage,
That sought with her to lincke in marriage:
For shee was faire, as faire mote ever bee,
And in the flowre now of her freshest age;
Yet full of grace and goodly modestee,
That even heven reioyced her sweete face to see.

XIX.

In robe of lilly white she was arayd,
That from her shoulder to her heele downe raught;
The traine whereof loose far behind her strayd,
Braunched with gold and perle most richly wrought,
And borne of two faire damsels which were taught
That service well: her yellow golden heare
Was trimly woven, and in tresses wrought,
Ne other tire she on her head did weare,
But crowned with a garland of sweete rosiere.

XX.

Goodly shee entertaind those noble knights,
And brought them up into her castle hall;
Where gentle court and gracious delight
Shee to them made, with mildnesse virginall,
Shewing herselfe both wise and liberall.
There when they rested had a season dew,
They her besought of favour speciall
Of that faire castle to affoord them vew:
Shee graunted; and, them leading forth, the same did shew.

XXI.

First she them led up to the castle wall,
That was so high as foe might not it clime
And all so faire and fensible withall;
Not built of bricke, ne yet of stone and lime,
But of thing like to that Ægyptian slime,
Whereof king Nine whilome built Babell towre;
But, O great pitty! that no lenger time
So goodly workmanship should not endure!
Soone it must turne to earth; no earthly thing is sure.

XXII.

The frame thereof seemd partly circulare,
And part triangulare: O worke divine!
Those two the first and last proportions are;
The one imperfect, mortall, fœminine;

Th' other immortall, porfect, masculine;
And twixt them both a quadrate was the base,
Proportiond equally by seven and nine;
Nine was the circle sett in heavens place:
All which compacted, made a goodly diapase.

XXIII.

Therein two gates were placed seemly well:
The one before, by which all in did pas,
Did th' other far in workmanship excell;
For not of wood, nor of enduring bras,
But of more worthy substance fram'd it was:
Doubly disparted, it did locke and close,
That, when it locked, none might thorough pas,
And, when it opened, no man might it close;
Still opened to their friendes, and closed to their foes.

XXIV.

Of hewen stone the porch was fayrely wrought,
Stone more of valew, and more smooth and fine,
Then iett or marble far from Ireland brought;
Over the which was cast a wandring vine,
Enchaced with a wanton yvie twine:
And over it a fayre portcullis hong,
Which to the gate directly did incline
With comely compasse and compacture strong,
Nether unseemly short, nor yet exceeding long.

XXV.

Within the barbican a porter sate,
Day and night duely keeping watch and ward;
Nor wight nor word mote passe out of the gate,
But in good order, and with dew regard;
Utterers of secrets he from thence debard,
Bablers of folly, and blazers of cryme:
His larum-bell might lowd and wyde be hard
When cause requyrd, but never out of time;
Early and late it rong, at evening and at prime.

XXVI.

And rownd about the porch on every syde
Twise sixteene warders satt, all armed bright
In glistring steele, and strongly fortifyde;
Tall yeomen seemed they and of great might,
And were enraunged ready still for fight.
By them as Alma passed with her guestes,
They did obeysaunce, as beseemed right.
And then againe retourned to their restes:
The porter eke to her did lout with humble gestes.

XXVII.

Thence she them brought into a stately hall,
Wherein were many tables fayre dispred,
And ready dight with drapets festivall,
Against the vianndes should be ministred.
At th' upper end there sate, yclad in red
Downe to the ground, a comely personage,
That in his hand a white rod menaged;
He steward was, hight Diet; rype of age,
And in demeanure sober and in counsell sage.

XXVIII.

And through the hall there walked to and fro
A iolly yeoman, marshall of the same,
Whose name was Appetite; he did bestow
Both guestes and meate, whenever in they came,
And knew them how to order without blame,
As him the steward badd. They both attone
Did dewty to their lady, as became;
Who, passing by, forth ledd her guestes anone
Into the kitchin rowme, ne spard for nicenesse none.

XXIX.

It was a vaut ybuilt for great dispence,
With many raunges reard along the wall,
And one great chimney, whose long tonnell thence
The smoke forth threw: and in the midst of all

There placed was a caudron wido and tall
Upon a mightie fornace, burning whott,
More whott then Aetn', or flaming Mongiball;
For day and night it brent, ne ceased not,
So long as any thing it in the caudron gott.

XXX.

But to delay the heat, least by mischaunce
It might breake out and set the whole on fyre,
There added was by goodly ordinaunce
An huge great payre of bellowes, which did styre
Continually, and cooling breath inspyre.
About the caudron many cookes accoyld
With hookes and ladles, as need did requyre;
The whyles the viaundes in the vessell boyld,
They did about their businesse sweat, and sorely toyld.

XXXI.

The maister cooke was cald Concoction;
A carefull man, and full of comely guyse;
The kitchin clerke, that hight Digestion,
Did order all th' achátes in seemely wise,
And set them forth, as well he could devise.
The rest had severall offices assynd;
Some to remove the scum as it did rise;
Others to beare the same away did mynd;
And others it to use according to his kynd.

XXXII.

But all the liquour, which was fowle and waste,
Not good nor serviceable elles for ought,
They in another great rownd vessell plaste,
Till by a conduit pipe it thence were brought;
And all the rest, that noyous was and nought,
By secret wayes, that none might it espy,
Was close convaid, and to the backgate brought,
That cleped was Port Esquiline, whereby
It was avoided quite, and throwne out privily.

XXXIII.

Which goodly order and great workmans skill
Whenas those knights beheld, with rare delight
And gazing wonder they their mindes did fill;
For never had they seene so straunge a sight.
Thence backe againe faire Alma led them right,
And soone into a goodly parlour brought,
That was with royall arras richly dight,
In which was nothing pourtrahed nor wrought;
Not wrought nor pourtrahed, but easie to be thought:

XXXIV.

And in the midst thereof upon the floure
A lovely bevy of faire ladies sate,
Courted of many a iolly paramoure,
The which them did in modest wise amate,
And each one sought his lady to aggrate:
And eke emongst them little Cupid playd
His wanton sportes, being retourned late
From his fierce warres, and having from him layd
His cruell bow, wherewith he thousands hath dismayd.

XXXV.

Diverse delights they fownd themselves to please;
Some song in sweet consórt; some laught for ioy;
Some plaid with strawes; some ydly satt at ease;
But other some could not abide to toy,
All pleasaunce was to them griefe and annoy;
This frownd; that faund; the third for shame did blush;
Another seemd envious, or coy;
Another in her teeth did gnaw a rush;
But at these straungers presence every one did hush.

XXXVI.

Soone as the gracious Alma came in place,
They all attonce out of their seates arose,
And to her homage made with humble grace;
Whom when the knights beheld, they gan dispose

Themselves to court, and each a damzell chose:
The prince by chaunce did on a lady light,
That was right faire and fresh as morning rose,
But somwhat sad and solemne eke in sight,
As if some pensive thought constraind her gentle spright.

XXXVII.

In a long purple pall, whose skirt with gold
Was fretted all about, she was arayd;
And in her haud a poplar braunch did hold,
To whom the prince in courteous maner sayd:
"Gentle Madáme, why beene ye thus dismayd,
And your faire beautie doe with sadnes spill?
Lives any that you hath this ill apayd?
Or doen you love, or doen you lack your will?
Whatever bec the cause, it sure bescemes you ill."

XXXVIII.

"Fayre sir," said she, halfe in disdaineful wise,
"How is it that this word in me ye blame,
And in yourselfe doe not tho same advise?
Him ill beseemes anothers fault to name,
That may unwares be blotted with the same:
Pensive I yeeld I am, and sad in mind,
Through great desire of glory and of fame;
Ne ought I weene are ye therein behynd,
That have twelve months sought one, yet no where can
  her find."

XXXIX.

The prince was inly moved at her speach,
Well weeting trew what she had rashly told;
Yet with faire semblaunt sought to hyde the breach,
Which chaunge of colour did perforce unfold,
Now seeming flaming whott, now stony cold:
Tho, turning soft aside, he did inquyre
What wight she was that poplar braunch did hold:
It answered was, her name was Prays-desire,
That by well doing sought to honour to aspyre.

XL.

The whiles the Faery knight did entertaine
Another damsell of that gentle crew,
That was right fayre and modest of demayne,
But that too oft she chaung'd her native hew:
Straunge was her tyre, and all her garment blew,
Close rownd about her tuckt with many a plight;
Upon her fist the bird which shonneth vew
And keeps in coverts close from living wight,
Did sitt, as yet ashamd how rude Pan did her dight.

XLI.

So long as Guyon with her communed,
Unto the grownd she cast her modest eye,
And ever and anone with rosy red
The bashfull blood her snowy cheekes did dye,
That her became as polisht yvory,
Which cunning craftesman hand hath overlayd
With fayre vermilion or pure castory.
Great wonder had the knight to see the mayd
So straungely passioned, and to her gently said,

XLII.

"Fayre damzell, seemeth by your troubled cheare,
That either me too bold ye weene, this wise
You to molest, or other ill to feare
That in the secret of your hart close lyes,
From whence it doth, as cloud from sea, aryse:
If it be I, of pardon I you pray;
But, if ought else that I mote not devyse,
I will, if please you it discure, assay
To ease you of that ill, so wisely as I may."

XLIII.

She answerd nought, but more abasht for shame
Held downe her head, the whiles her lovely face
The flashing blood with blushing did inflame,
And the strong passion mard her modest grace,

That Guyon mervayld at her uncouth cace;
Till Alma him bespake; "Why wonder yee,
Faire sir, at that which ye so much embrace?
She is the fountaine of your modestee;
You shamefast are, but Shamefastnes itselfe is shee."

XLIV.

Thereat the Elfe did blush in privitee,
And turnd his face away; but she the same
Dissembled faire, and faynd to oversee.
Thus they awhile with court and goodly game
Themselves did solace each one with his dame,
Till that great lady thence away them sought
To vew her castles other wondrous frame:
Up to a stately turret she them brought,
Ascending by ten steps of alabaster wrought.

XLV.

That turrets frame most admirable was,
Like highest heaven compassed around,
And lifted high above this earthly masse,
Which it survewd, as hils doen lower ground:
But not on ground mote like to this be found;
Not that, which antique Cadmus whylome built
In Thebes, which Alexander did confound;
Nor that proud towre of Troy, though richly guilt,
From which young Hectors blood by cruell Greekes was spilt.

XLVI.

The roofe hereof was arched over head,
And deckt with flowres and herbars daintily;
Two goodly beacons, set in watches stead,
Therein gave light, and flamd continually:
For they of living fire most subtilly
Were made, and set in silver sockets bright,
Cover'd with lids deviz'd of substance sly,
That readily they shut and open might.
O, who can tell the prayses of that makers might!

XLVII.

Ne can I tell, ne can I stay to tell,
This parts great workemanship and wondrous powre,
That all this other worldes worke doth excell,
And likest is unto that heavenly towre
That God hath built for his owne blessed bowre.
Therein were divers rowmes, and divers stages;
But three the chiefest and of greatest powre,
In which there dwelt three honorable sages,
The wisest men, I weene, that lived in their ages.

XLVIII.

Not he, whom Greece, the nourse of all good arts,
By Phœbus doome the wisest thought alive,
Might be compar'd to these by many parts:
Nor that sage Pylian syre, which did survive
Three ages, such as mortall men contrive,
By whose advise old Priams cittie fell,
With these in praise of pollicies mote strive.
These three in these three rowmes did sondry dwell,
And counselled faire Alma how to governe well.

XLIX.

The first of them could things to come foresee;
The next could of thinges present best advize;
The third things past could keep in memoree:
So that no time nor reason could arize,
But that the same could one of these comprize.
Forthy the first did in the forepart sit,
That nought mote hinder his quicke preiudize;
He had a sharpe foresight and working wit
That never idle was, ne once would rest a whit.

L.

His chamber was dispainted all within
With sondry colours, in the which were writ
Infinite shapes of thinges dispersed thin;
Some such as in the world were never yit,

Ne can devized be of mortall wit;
Some daily seene and knowen by their names,
Such as in idle fantasies do flit:
Infernall hags, centaurs, feendes, hippodames,
Apes, lyons, aegles, owles, fooles, lovers, children, dames.

LI.

And all the chamber filled was with flyes
Which buzzed all about, and made such sound
That they encombred all mens eares and eyes;
Like many swarmes of bees assembled round,
After their hives with honny do abound.
All those were idle thoughtes and fantasies,
Devices, dreames, opinions unsound,
Shewes, visions, sooth-sayes, and prophesies;
And all that fained is, as leasings, tales, and lies.

LII.

Emongst them all sate he which wonned there,
That hight Phantastes by his nature trew;
A man of yeares yet fresh, as mote appere,
Of swarth complexion, and of crabbed hew,
That him full of melancholy did shew;
Bent hollow beetle browes, sharpe staring eyes
That mad or foolish seemd: one by his vew
Mote deeme him borne with ill-disposed skyes,
When oblique Saturne sate in th' house of agonyes.

LIII.

Whom Alma having shewed to her guestes,
Thence brought them to the second rowme, whose wals
Were painted faire with memorable gestes
Of famous wisards; and with picturals
Of magistrates, of courts, of tribunals,
Of commen wealthes, of states, of pollicy,
Of lawes, of iudgementes, and of decretals,
All artes, all science, all philosophy,
And all that in the world was ay thought wittily.

LIV.

Of those that rowme was full; and them among
There sate a man of ripe and perfect age,
Who did them meditate all his life long,
That through continuall practise and uságe
He now was growne right wise and woudrous sage;
Great plesure had those straunger knightes to see
His goodly reason and grave personage,
That his disciples both desyrd to bee:
But Alma thence them led to th' hindmost rowme of three.

LV.

That chamber seemed ruinous and old,
And therefore was removed far behind,
Yet were the wals, that did the same uphold,
Right firme and strong, though somwhat they declind;
And therein sat an old old man, halfe blind,
And all decrepit in his feeble corse,
Yet lively vigour rested in his mind,
And recompenst them with a better scorse:
Weake body well is chang'd for minds redoubled forse.

LVI.

This man of infinite remembraunce was,
And things foregone through many ages held,
Which he recorded still as they did pas,
Ne suffred them to perish through long eld,
As all things els the which this world doth weld;
But laid them up in his immortall scrine,
Where they for ever incorrupted dweld.
The warres he well remembred of king Ninc,
Of old Assaracus, and Inachus divine.

LVII.

The yeares of Nestor nothing were to his,
Ne yet Mathusalem, though longest liv'd;
For he remembred both their infancis:
Ne wonder then if that he were depriv'd

Of native strength now that he them surviv'd.
His chamber all was hangd about with rolls
And old recórds from auncient times derivd,
Some made in books, some in long parchment scrolls,
That were all worm-eaten and full of canker holes.

LVIII.

Amidst them all he in a chaire was sett,
Tossing and turning them withouten end;
But for he was unhable them to fett,
A little boy did on him still attend
To reach, whenever he for ought did send;
And oft when thinges were lost, or laid amis,
That boy them sought and unto him did lend:
Therefore he Anamnestes cleped is;
And that old man Eumnestes, by their propertis.

LIX.

The knightes there entring did him reverence dew,
And wondred at his endlesse exercise.
Then as they gan his library to vew,
And antique regesters for to avise,
There chaunced to the princes hand to rize
An auncient booke, hight *Briton Moniments*,
That of this lands first conquest did devize,
And old division into regiments,
Till it reduced was to one mans governements.

LX.

Sir Guyon chaunst eke on another booke,
That hight *Antiquitee of Faery Lond*:
In which whenas he greedily did looke,
Th' ofspring of Elves and Faryes there he fond,
As it delivered was from hond to hond:
Whereat they, burning both with fervent fire
Their countreys auncestry to understond,
Crav'd leave of Alma and that aged sire
To read those bookes; who gladly graunted their desire.

CANTO X.

**A chronicle of Briton kings,
From Brute to Uthers rayne;**
. . . .

I.

Who now shall give unto me words and sound
Equall unto this haughty enterprise?
Or who shall lend me wings, with which from ground
My lowly verse may loftily arise,
And lift itselfe unto the highest skyes?
More ample spirit than hetherto was wount
Here needes me, whiles the famous auncestryes
Of my most dreadred soveraigne I recount,
By which all earthly princes she doth far surmount.

II.

No under sunne that shines so wide and faire,
Whence all that lives does borrow life and light,
Lives ought that to her linage may compaire;
Which though from earth it be derived right,
Yet doth itselfe stretch forth to hevens hight,
And all the world with wonder overspred;
A labor huge, exceeding far my might!
How shall fraile pen, with fear disparaged,
Conceive such soveraine glory and great bountyhed?

III.

Argument worthy of Mæonian quill;
Or rather worthy of great Phoebus rote,
Whereon the ruines of great Ossa hill,
And triumphes of Phlegræan Iove, he wrote,
That all the gods admird his lofty note.
But, if some relish of that hevenly lay
His learned daughters would to me report
To decke my song withall, I would assay
Thy name, O soveraine Queene, to blazon far away.

IV.

Thy name, O soveraine Queene, thy realm, and race,
From this renowmed prince derived arre,
Who mightily upheld that royall mace
Which now thou bear'st, to thee descended farre
From mighty kings and conquerours in warre,
Thy fathers and great grandfathers of old,
Whose noble deeds above the northern starre
Immortall Fame for ever hath enrold;
As in that old mans booke they were in order told.

V.

The land which warlike Britons now possesse,
And therein have their mighty empire raysd,
In antique times was salvage wildernesse,
Unpeopled, unmannurd, unprovd, unprayed;
Ne was it island then, ne was it paysd
Amid the ocean waves, ne was it sought
Of merchants farre for profits therein praysd;
But was all desolate, and of some thought
By sea to have bene from the Celticke mayn-land brought.

VI.

Ne did it then deserve a name to have,
Till that the venturous mariner that way
Learning his ship from those white rocks to save,
Which all along the southerne sea-coast lay
Threatning unheedy wrecke and rash decay,
For saftёty that same his sea-marke made,
And nam'd it ALBION; but later day,
Finding in it fit ports for fishers trade,
Gan more the same frequent, and further to invade.

VII.

But far in land a salvage nation dwelt
Of hideous giaunts, and halfe-beastly men,
That never tasted grace, nor goodnes felt;
But wild like beastes lurking in loathsome den,

And flying fast as roebucke through the fen,
All naked without shame or care of cold,
By hunting and by spoiling liveden;
Of stature huge, and eke of corage bold,
That sonnes of men amazd their sternesse to behold.

VIII.

But whence they sprong, or how they were begott,
Uneath is to assure; uneath to wene
That monstrous error which doth some assott,
That Dioclesians fifty daughters shene
Into this land by chaunce have driven bene;
Where, companing with feends and filthy sprights
Through vaine illusion of their lust unclene,
They brought forth geaunts, and such dreadful wights
As far exceeded men in their immeasurd mights.

IX.

They held this land, and with their filthinesse
Polluted this same gentle soyle long time;
That their owne mother loathd their beastliuesse,
And gan abhorre her broods unkindly crime,
All were they borne of her owne native slime:
Until that Brutus, anciently deriv'd
From roiall stocke of old Assaracs line,
Driven by fatall error here arriv'd,
And them of their unjust possession depriv'd.

X.

But ere he had established his throne,
And spred his empire to the utmost shore,
He fought great batteils with his salvage fone;
In which he them defeated evermore,
And many giaunts left on grouing flore,
That well can witnes yet unto this day
The westerne Hogh, besprincled with the gore
Of mighty Goëmot, whome in stout fray
Corineus conquered, and cruelly did slay.

XI.

And eke that ample pitt, yet far renownd
For the large leape which Debon did compell
Coulin to make, being eight lugs of grownd,
Into the which retourning backe he fell;
But those three monstrous stones doe most excell,
Which that huge sonne of hideous Albion,
Whose father Hercules in Fraunce did quell,
Great Godmer threw, in fierce contention,
At bold Canutus; but of him was slaine anon.

XII.

In meed of these great conquests by them gott,
Corineus had that province utmost west
To him assigned for his worthy lott,
Which of his name and memorable gest
He called Cornwaile, yet so called best:
And Debons shayre was, that is Devonshyre;
But Canute had his portion from the rest,
The which he cald Canutium, for his hyre;
Now Cantium, which Kent we comenly inquyre.

XIII.

Thus Brute this realme unto his rule subdewd,
And raigned long in great felicity,
Lov'd of his freends, and of his foes eschewd:
He left three sonnes, his famous progeny,
Borne of fayre Inogene of Italy;
Mongst whom he parted his imperiall state,
And Locrine left chiefe lord of Britany.
At last ripe age bad him surrender late
His life, and long good fortune, unto finall fate.

XIV.

Locrine was left the soveraine lord of all;
But Albanact had all the northerne part,
Which of himselfe Albania he did call;
And Camber did possesse the westerne quart,

Which Severne now from Logris doth depart:
And each his portion peaceably enioyd,
Ne was there outward breach, nor grudge in hart,
That once their quiet government annoyd;
But each his paynes to others profit still employd.

XV.

Untill a nation straung, with visage swart
And corage fierce that all men did affray,
Which through the world then swarmd in every part,
And overflowd all countries far away,
Like Noyes great flood, with their impórtune sway,
This land invaded with like violence,
And did themselves through all the north display:
Untill that Locrine for his realmes defence,
Did head against them make and strong munificence.

XVI.

He them encountred, a confused rout,
Foreby the river that whylóme was hight
The ancient Abus, where with courage stout
He them defeated in victorious fight,
And chaste so fiercely after fearefull flight,
That forst their chiefetain, for his safeties sake,
(Their chiefetain Humber named was aright,)
Unto the mighty streame him to betake,
Where he an end of batteill and of life did make.

XVII.

The king retourned proud of victory
And insolent wox through unwonted ease,
That shortly he forgot the ieopardy,
Which in his land he lately did appease,
And fell to vaine voluptuous disease:
He lov'd faire Ladie Estrild, leudly lov'd,
Whose wanton pleasures him too much did please,
That quite his hart from Guendolene remov'd,
From Guendolene his wife, though alwaies faithful prov'd.

XVIII.

The noble daughter of Corinēus
Would not endure to bee so vile disdaind,
But, gathering force and corage valorous,
Encountred him in batteill well ordaind,
In which him vanquisht she to fly constraind;
But she so fast pursewd, that him she tooke
And threw in bands, where he till death remaind;
Als his faire leman flying through a brooke
She overhent, nought moved with her piteous looke.

XIX.

But both herselfe, and eke her daughter deare
Begotten by her kingly paramoure,
The faire Sabrina, almost dead with feare,
She there attached, far from all succoùre:
The one she slew in that impatient stoure;
But the sad virgin innocent of all
Adowne the rolling river she did poure,
Which of her name now Severne men do call:
Such was the end that to disloyall love did fall.

XX.

Then for her sonne, which she to Locrin bore,
(Madan was young, unmeet the rule to sway,)
In her owne hand the crowne she kept in store,
Till ryper years he raught and stronger stay;
During which time her powre she did display
Through all this realme, the glory of her sex,
And first taught men a woman to obay;
But, when her sonne to mans estate did wex,
She it surrendred, ne her selfe would lenger vex.

XXI.

Tho Madan raignd, unworthie of his race;
For with all shame that sacred throne he fild.
Next Memprise, as unworthy of that place,
In which being consorted with Manild,

For thirst of single kingdom him he kild.
But Ebranck salved both their infamies
With noble deedes, and warreyd on Brunchild
In Henault, where yet of his victories
Brave moniments remaine, which yet that land envies.

XXII.
An happy man in his first dayes he was,
And happy father of faire progeny:
For all so many weekes, as the yeare has,
So many children he did multiply;
Of which were twentie sonnes, which did apply
Their mindes to prayse and chevalrous desyre:
Those germans did subdew all Germany,
Of whom it hight; but in the end their syre
With foule repulse from Fraunce was forced to retyre.

XXIII.
Which blott his sonne succeeding in his seat,
The second Brute, the second both in name
And eke in semblaunce of his puissaunce great,
Right well recur'd, and did away that blame
With recompence of everlasting fame:
He with his victour sword first opened
The bowels of wide Fraunce, a forlorne dame,
And taught her first how to be conquered;
Since which with sondrie spoiles she hath been ransacked.

XXIV.
Let Scaldis tell, and let tell Hania,
And let the marsh of Esthambruges tell,
What colour were their waters that same day,
And all the moore twixt Elversham and Dell,
With blood of Henalois which therein fell.
How of that day did sad Brunchildis see
The *greene shield* dyde in dolorous vermell?
That not *scuith guiridh* it mote seeme to bee,
But rather y *scuith gogh*, signe of sad crueltee.

XXV.

His sonne king Leill, by fathers labour long,
Enioyd an heritage of lasting peace,
And built Cairleill, and built Cairleon strong.
Next Huddibras his realme did not encrease,
But taught the land from wearie wars to cease.
Whose footsteps Bladud following, in artes
Exceld at Athens all the learned preace,
From whence he brought them to these salvage parts,
And with sweet science mollifide their stubborne harts.

XXVI.

Ensample of his wondrous faculty,
Behold the boyling baths at Cairdabon,
Which seeth with secret fire eternally,
And in their entrailles, full of quick brimstón,
Nourish the flames which they are warmd upon,
That to their people wealth they forth do well,
And health to every forreyne nation:
Yet he at last, contending to excell
The reach of men, through flight into fond mischief fell.

XXVII.

Next him king Leyr in happie peace long raynd,
But had no issue male him to succeed,
But three faire daughters, which were well uptraind
In all that seemed fitt for kingly seed;
Mongst whom his realme he equally decreed
To have divided: tho, when feeble age
Nigh to his utmost date he saw proceed,
He cald his daughters, and with speeches sage
Inquyrd, which of them most did love her parentage?

XXVIII.

The eldest Gonorill gan to protest,
That she much more than her owne life him lov'd;
And Regan greater love to him profest
Then all the world, whenever it were proov'd;

But Cordeill said she loved him as behoov'd;
Whose simple answere, wanting colours fayre
To paint it forth, him to displeasaunce moov'd,
That in his crown he counted her no hayre,
But twixt the other twain his kingdom whole did shayre.

XXIX.

So wedded th' one to Maglan king of Scottes,
And th' other to the king of Cambria,
And twixt them shayrd his realme by equall lottes;
But, without dowre, the wise Cordelia
Was sent to Aganip of Celtica.
Their aged syre, thus eased of his crowne,
A private life ledd in Albania
With Gonorill, long had in great renowne,
That nought him griev'd to beene from rule deposed downe.

XXX.

But true it is that, when the oyle is spent
The light goes out, and wecke is throwne away;
So, when he had resignd his regiment,
His daughter gan despise his drouping day,
And wearie wax of his continuall stay:
Tho to his daughter Regan he repayrd,
Who him at first well used every way;
But, when of his departure she despayrd,
Her bountie she abated, and his cheare empayrd.

XXXI.

The wretched man gan then avise too late,
That love is not where most it is profest;
Too truely tryde in his extremest state!
At last, resolv'd likewise to prove the rest,
He to Cordelia himselfe addrest,
Who with entyre affection him receav'd,
As for her syre and king her seemed best;
And after all an army strong she leav'd,
To war on those which him had of his realme bereav'd.

XXXII.

So to his crowne she him restord againe;
In which he dyde, made ripe for death by eld,
And after wild it should to her remaine:
Who peaceably the same long time did weld,
And all mens harts in dew obedience held:
Till that her sisters children, woxen strong,
Through proud ambition against her rebeld,
And overcommen kept in prison long,
Till weary of that wretched life herselfe she hong.

XXXIII.

Then gan the bloody brethren both to raine:
But fierce Cundah gan shortly to envy
His brother Morgan, prickt with proud disdaine
To have a pere in part of soverainty;
And, kindling coles of cruell enmity,
Raisd warre, and him in batteill overthrew;
Whence as he to those woody hilles did fly,
Which hight of him Glamorgan, there him slew:
Then did he raigne alone, when he none equal knew.

XXXIV.

His sonne Rivall' his dead rowme did supply,
In whose sad time blood did from heaven rayne.
Next great Gurgustus, then faire Cœcily,
In constant peace their kingdomes did contayne,
After whom Lago and Kinmarke did rayne,
And Gorbogud, till far in years he grew;
Then his ambitious sonnes unto them twayne
Arraught the rule, and from their father drew;
Stout Ferrex and sterne Porrex him in prison threw.

XXXV.

But O! the greedy thirst of royall crowne,
That knowes no kinred, nor regardes no right,
Stird Porrex up to put his brother downe;
Who, unto him assembling forreigne might,

Made warre on him, and fell himselfe in fight:
Whose death t' avenge, his mother mercilesse,
Most mercilesse of women, Wyden hight,
Her other sonne fast sleeping did oppresse,
And with most cruell hand him murdred pittilesse.

XXXVI.

Here ended Brutus sacred progeny,
Which had seven hundred years this sceptre borne
With high renowme and great felicity:
The noble braunch from th' antique stocke was torne
Through discord, and the roiall throne forlorne.
Thenceforth this realme was into factions rent,
Whilest each of Brutus boasted to be borne,
That in the end was left no moniment
Of Brutus, nor of Britons glorie auncient.

XXXVII.

Then up arose a man of matchlesse might,
And wondrous wit to menage high affayres,
Who, stird with pitty of the stressed plight
Of this sad realme, cut into sondry shayres
By such as claymd themselves Brutes rightfull hayres,
Gathered the princes of the people loose
To taken counsell of their common cares;
Who, with his wisedom won, him streight did choose
Their king, and swore him fealty to win or loose.

XXXVIII.

Then made he head against his enimies,
And Ymner slew of Logris miscreate;
Then Ruddoc and proud Stater, both allyes,
This of Albany newly nominate,
And that of Cambry king confirmed late,
He overthrew through his owne valiaunce,
Whose countries he reduc'd to quiet state,
And shortly brought to civile governaunce,
Now one, which earst were many made through variaunce.

XXXIX.

Then made he sacred lawes, which some men say
Were unto him reveald in vision;
By which he freed the traveilers high-way,
The churches part, and ploughmans portion,
Restraining stealth and strong extortion;
The gracious Numa of great Britany:
For, till his dayes, the chiefe dominion
By strength was wielded without pollicy:
Therefore he first wore crowne of gold for dignity.

XL.

Donwallo dyde, (for what may live for ay?)
And left two sonnes, of peareleше prowesse both,
That sacked Rome too dearely did assay,
The recompence of their periúred oth;
And ransackt Greece wel tryde, when they were wroth,
Besides subiected France and Germany,
Which yet their praises speake, all be they loth,
And inly tremble at the memory
Of Brennus and Belinus, kinges of Britany.

XLI.

Next them did Gurgunt, great Belinus sonne,
In rule succeede, and eke in fathers praise;
He Easterland subdewd, and Denmarke wonne,
And of them both did foy and tribute raise,
The which was dew in his dead fathers daies.
He also gave to fugitives of Spayne,
Whom he at sea found wandring from their waies,
A scate in Ireland safely to remayne,
Which they should hold of him as subiect to Britáyne.

XLII.

After him raigned Guitheline his hayre,
The iustest man and trewest in his daies,
Who had to wife Dame Mertia the fayre,
A woman worthy of immortall praise,

Which for this realme found many goodly layes,
And wholesome statutes to her husband brought;
Her many deemd to have beene of the Fayes,
As was Aegerié that Numa tought:
Those yet of her be Mertian lawes both nam'd and thought.

XLIII.

Her sonne Sifillus after her did rayne;
And then Kimarus; and then Danius:
Next whom Morindus did the crowne sustayne;
Who, had he not with wrath outrageous
And cruell rancour dim'd his valorous
And mightie deedes, should matched have the best
As well in that same field victorious
Against the forreine Morands he exprest;
Yet lives his memorie, though carcase sleepe in rest.

XLIV.

Five sonnes he left begotten of one wife,
All which successively by turnes did rayne:
First Gorboman, a man of virtuous life;
Next Archigald, who for his proud disdayne
Deposed was from princedome soverayne,
And pitteous Elidure put in his sted;
Who shortly it to him restord agayne,
Till by his death he it recovered;
But Peridure and Vigent him disthronized:

XLV.

In wretched prison long he did remaine,
Till they out-raigned had their utmost date,
And then therein resoized was againe,
And ruled long with honorable state,
Till he surrendred realme and life to fate.
Then all the sonnes of these five brethren raynd
By dew successe, and all their nephewes late;
Even thrise eleven descents the crowne retaynd,
Till aged Hely by dew heritage it gaynd.

XLVI.

He had two sonnes, whose eldest, called Lud,
Left of his life most famous memory,
And endlesse moniments of his great good:
The ruin'd wals he did rædifye
Of Troynovant, gainst force of enimy,
And built that gate which of his name is hight,
By which he lyes entombed solemnly:
He left two sonnes, too young to rule aright,
Androgeus and Tenantius, pictures of his might.

XLVII.

Whilst they were young, Cassibalane their eme
Was by the people chosen in their sted,
Who on him tooke the roiall diademe,
And goodly well long time it governed;
Till the prowde Romanes him disquieted,
And warlike Cæsar, tempted with the name
Of this sweet island never conquered,
And envying the Britons blazed fame,
(O hideous hunger of dominion!) hether came.

XLVIII.

Yet twise they were repulsed backe againe,
And twise renforst backe to their ships to fly;
The whiles with blood they all the shore did staine,
And the gray ocean into purple dy:
Ne had they footing found at last perdie,
Had not Androgeus, false to native soyle,
And envious of uncles soveraintie,
Betrayd his country unto forreine spoyle.
Nought els but treason from the first this land did foyle!

XLIX.

So by him Cæsar got the victory,
Through great bloodshed and many a sad assay,
In which himselfe was charged heavily
Of hardy Nennius, whom he yet did slay,

But lost his sword, yet to be seene this day.
Thenceforth this land was tributarie made
T' ambitious Rome, and did their rule obay,
Till Arthur all that reckoning defrayd:
Yet oft the Briton kings against them strongly swayd.

L.

Next him Tenantius raignd; then Kimbeline,
What time th' Eternall Lord in fleshly slime
Enwombed was, from wretched Adams line
To purge away the guilt of sinful crime.
O joyous memorie of happy time,
That heavenly grace so plenteously displayd!
O too high ditty for my simple rime! —
Soone after this the Romanes him warrayd;
For that their tribute he refusd to let be payd.

LI.

Good Claudius, that next was emperour,
An army brought, and with him batteile fought,
In which the king was by a treachetour
Disguised slaine, ere any thereof thought:
Yet ceased not the bloody fight for ought:
For Arvirage his brothers place supplyde
Both in his armes and crowne, and by that draught
Did drive the Romans to the weaker syde,
That they to peace agreed. So all was pacifyde.

LII.

Was never king more highly magnifide,
Nor dredd of Romanes, then was Arvirage;
For which the emperour to him allide
His daughter Genuiss' in marriage:
Yet shortly he renounst the vassallage
Of Rome againe, who hether hastly sent
Vespasian, that with great spoile and rage
Forwasted all, till Genuissa gent
Persuaded him to ceasse, and her lord to relent.

LIII.

He dide; and him succeeded Marius,
Who ioyd his dayes in great tranquillity.
Then Coyll; and after him good Lucius,
That first received Christianity,
The sacred pledge of Christes Evangely,
Yet true it is, that long before that day
Hither came Ioseph of Arimathy,
Who brought with him the Holy Grayle, (they say,)
And preacht the truth; but since it greatly did decay.

LIV.

This good king shortly without issew dide,
Whereof great trouble in the kingdome grew,
That did herselfe in sondry parts divide,
And with her powre her owne selfe overthrew,
Whilest Romanes daily did the weake subdew:
Which seeing, stout Bunduca up arose,
And taking armes the Britons to her drew;
With whom she marched straight against her foes,
And them unwares besides the Severne did enclose.

LV.

There she with them a cruell batteill tryde,
Not with so good successe as shee deserv'd;
By reason that the captaines on her syde,
Corrupted by Paulinus, from her swerv'd:
Yet such, as were through former flight preserv'd,
Gathering againe, her host she did renew,
And with fresh corage on the victor servd:
But being all defeated, save a few,
Rather than fly, or be captiv'd herselfe she slew.

LVI.

O famous moniment of womens prayse!
Matchable either to Semiramis,
Whom antique history so high doth rayse,
Or to Hypsiphil', or to Thomiris:

Her host two hundred thousand numbred is,
Who, whiles good fortune favoured her might
Triumphed oft against her enemis;
And yet, though overcome in haplesse fight,
Shee triumphed on death, in enemies despight.

LVII.

Her reliques Fulgent having gathered,
Fought with Severus, and him overthrew;
Yet in the chace was slaine of them that fled;
So made them victors whome he did subdew.
Then gan Carausius tirannize anew,
And gainst the Romanes bent their proper powre;
But him Allectus treacherously slew,
And tooke on him the robe of emperoure;
Nath'lesse the same enioyed but short happy howre.

LVIII.

For Asclepiodate him overcame,
And left inglorious on the vanquisht playne,
Without or robe or rag to hide his shame;
Then afterwards he in his stead did raigne.
But shortly was by Coyll in batteill slaine,
Who after long debate, since Lucies tyme,
Was of the Britons first crownd soveraine:
Then gan this realme renew her passed prime:
He of his name Coylchester built of stone and lime.

LIX.

Which when the Romanes heard, they hether sent
Constantius, a man of mickle might,
With whome king Coyll made an agreëment,
And to him gave for wife his daughter bright,
Faire Helena, the fairest living wight,
Who in all godly thewes and goodly praise
Did far excell, but was most famous hight
For skil in musieke of all in her daies,
As well in curious instruments as cunning laies:

LX.

Of whome he did great Constantine begett,
Who afterward was emperour of Rome;
To which whiles absent he his mind did sett,
Octavius here lept into his roome,
And it usurped by unrighteous doome:
But he his title justifide by might,
Slaying Traherne, and having overcome
The Romane legion in dreadfull fight:
So settled he his kingdome, and confirmd his right:

LXI.

But, wanting yssew male, his daughter deare
He gave in wedlocke to Maximian,
And him with her made of his kingdome heyre,
Who soone by meanes thereof the empire wan,
Till murdred by the freends of Gratian.
Then gan the Hunnes and Picts invade this land,
During the raigne of Maximinian;
Who dying left none heire them to withstand:
But that they overran all parts with easy hand.

LXII.

The weary Britons, whose war-hable youth
Was by Maximian lately ledd away,
With wretched miseryes and woefull ruth
Were to those pagans made an open pray,
And daily spectacle of sad decay:
Whome Romane warres, which now fowr hundred yeares
And more had wasted could no whit dismay;
Til, by consent of Commons and of Peares,
They crownd the second Constantine with ioyous teares.

LXIII.

Who having oft in batteill vanquished
Those spoylefull Picts, and swarming Easterlings,
Long time in peace his realme established,
Yet oft annoyd with sondry bordragings

Of neighbour Scots and forrein scatterlings,
With which the world did in those dayes abound.
Which to outbarre, with painefull pyonings
From sea to sea he heapt a mighty mound,
Which from Alcluid to Panwelt did that border bownd.

LXIV.

Three sonnes he dying left, all under age,
By meanes whereof their uncle Vortigere
Usurpt the crowne during their pupillage;
Which th' infants tutors gathering to feare,
Them closely into Armorick did beare:
For dread of whom, and for those Picts annoyes,
He sent to Germany straunge aid to reare;
From whence eftsoones arrived here three boyes
Of Saxons, whom he for his safety imployes.

LXV.

Two brethren were their capitayns, which hight
Hengist and Horsus, well approv'd in warre,
And both of them men of renowmed might;
Who making vantage of their civile jarre,
And of those forreyners which came from farre,
Grew great, and got large portions of land,
That in the realme ere long they stronger arre
Then they which sought at first their helping hand,
And Vortiger enforst the kingdome to aband.

LXVI.

But, by the helpe of Vortimere his sonne,
He is againe unto his rule restord;
And Hengist, seeming sad for that was donne,
Received is to grace and new accord,
Through his faire daughters face and flattring word.
Soone after which, three hundred lords he slew
Of British blood, all sitting at his bord;
Whose dolefull moniments who list to rew,
Th' eternall marks of treason may at Stonheng vew.

LXVII.

By this the sonnes of Constantine, which fled,
Ambrose and Uther, did ripe yeares attayne,
And, here arriving, strongly challenged
The crowne which Vortiger did long detayne:
Who, flying from his guilt, by them was slayne;
And Hengist eke soone brought to shamefull death.
Thenceforth Aurelius peaceably did rayne,
Till that through poyson stopped was his breath;
So now entombed lies at Stoneheng by the heath.

LXVIII.

After him Uther, which Pendragon hight,
Succeeding — There abruptly it did end,
Without full point, or other cesure right;
As if the rest some wicked hand did rend,
Or th' author selfe could not at least attend
To finish it: that so untimely breach
The prince himselfe halfe seemed to offend;
Yet secret pleasure did offence empeach,
And wonder of antiquity long stopt his speach.

LXIX.

At last, quite ravisht with delight to heare
The royall ofspring of his native land,
Cryde out; "Deare countrey! O how dearely deare
Ought thy remembraunce and perpetuall band
Be to thy foster child, that from thy hand
Did commun breath and nouriture receave!
How brutish is it not to understand
How much to her we owe, that all us gave;
That gave unto us all whatever good we have!"

VI.

BEN JONSON.
1554—1637.

"It is a small disparagement to BEN JONSON, to say that he stands second only to so wonderful a man as Shakspeare. And we think that, on the whole, he must be held (in the Drama) to occupy the second place. The Palm should always be given to originality; and amongst the contemporaries of Shakspeare Jonson was the most original."

"Jonson stood alone. His course lay aside that of Shakspeare, not in his track. He took his way on a far lower level, it is true, yet on a way he had himself discovered. He borrowed help, indeed, not infrequently from his friends the ancients and illuminated his subjects with their thoughts; but so far as regards the style or constitution of his plays, Jonson was decidedly original. He owed as little to his contemporaries as to the English poets who preceded him, as Shakspear himself."

Barry Cornwall in his "Memoir of the Life and Writings of B. J."

THE ALCHEMIST.
A COMEDY.

THE ARGUMENT.

T he Sickness hot, a Master quit, for fear,
H is House in Town, and left one Servant there.
E ase him corrupted, and gave means to know

A Cheater and his Punk; who, now brought low,
L eaving their narrow Practice, were become
C os'ners at large; and only wanting some
H ouse to set up, with him they here contract,
E ach for a Share, and all begin to act:
M uch Company they draw, and much abuse,
I n casting Figures, telling Fortunes, News,
S elling of Flies, flat Bawd'ry, with the Stone,
T ill it, and they, and all in Fume are gone.

PROLOGUE.

Fortune, that favours Fools, these two short Hours
  We wish away, both for your sakes and ours,
Judging Spectators; and desire in place,
  To th' Author Justice, to our selves but Grace.
Our Scene is LONDON, 'cause we would make known,
  No Countries Mirth is better than our own:
No Clime breeds better Matter for your Whore,
  Bawd, Squire, Impostor, many Persons more,
Whose Manners, now call'd Humours, feed the Stage;
  And which have still been Subject for the Rage

Or Spleen of Comick Writers. Tho' this Pen
  Did never aim to grieve, but better Men;
Howe'er the Age he lives in doth endure
  The Vices that she breeds, above their Cure.
But when the wholesome Remedies are sweet,
  And in their working Gain and Profit meet,
He hopes to find no Spirit so much diseas'd,
  But will with such fair Correctives be pleas'd;
For here he doth not fear who can apply.
If there be any that will sit so nigh
Unto the Stream to look what it doth run,
  They shall find things, they'ld think, or wish, were done;
They are so natural Follies, but so shown,
  As even the Doers may see, and yet not own.

THE PERSONS OF THE PLAY.

SUBTLE, the Alchemist.
FACE, the House-keeper.
DOL. COMMON, their Colleague.
DAPPER, a Clerk.
DRUGGER, a Tobacco-man.
LOVE-WIT, Master of the House.
EPICURE MAMMON, a Knight.
SURLEY, a Gamester.
TRIBULATION, a Pastor of Amsterdam.
ANANIAS, a Deacon there.
KASTRILL, the angry Boy.
DA. PLIANT, his Sister, a Widow.

    Neighbours, Officers, Mutes.
    The Scene, LONDON.

ACT I. SCENE I.

Face, Subtle, Dol. Common.

Believ't, I will. *Sub.* Thy worst. If..t at thee.
  Dol. Ha' you your Wits? Why Gentlemen! for Love——
  Fac. Sirrah, I'll strip you.—*Sub.* What to do? lick Figs
Out at my —— *Fac.* Rogue, Rogue, out of all your sleights.
  Dol. Nay, look ye, Sovereign, General, are you Madmen?
  Sub. O, let the wild Sheep loose. I'll Gum your Silks
With good Strong-water, an' you come.
  Dol. Will you have
The Neighbours hear you? Will you betray all?
Heark, I hear some body. *Fac.* Sirrah—*Sub.* I shall mar
All that the Taylor has made, if you approach.
  Fac. You most notorious Whelp, you Insolent Slave,
Dare you do this? *Sub.* Yes faith, yes faith. *Fac.* Why, who
Am I, my Mungril? who am I? *Sub.* I'll tell you,
Since you know not your self — *Fac.* Speak lower, Rogue.
  Sub. Yes, You were once (time's not long past) the good,
Honest, plain Livery-three-pound-thrum, that kept
Your Masters Worships House here in the *Friers*,
For the Vacations — *Fac.* Will you be so loud?
  Sub. Since, by my means, translated Suburb-Captain.
  Fac. By your means, Doctor Dog?
  Sub. Within Man's memory,
All this I speak of. *Fac.* Why, I pray you, have I
Been countenanc'd by you, or you by me?
Do but collect, Sir, where I met you first.
  Sub. I do not hear well. *Fac.* Not of this, I think it.
But I shall put you in mind, Sir; at *Pie-corner*,
Taking your meal of Steam in, from Cook Stalls;
Where, like the Father of Hunger, you did walk
Piteously costive, with your pinch'd horn-nose,

And your Complexion of the *Roman* Wash,
Stuck full of black and melancholick Worms,
Like Powder-corns shot at th' *Artillery-yard.*
   Sub. I wish you could advance your Voice a little.
   Fac. When you went pinn'd up in the several Rags
Yo' had rak'd and pick'd from Dunghills, before Day;
Your Feet in mouldy Slippers, for your Kibes
A Felt of Rug, and a thin threddcn Cloke,
That scarce would cover your no-Buttocks — —
   Sub. So, Sir!
   Fac. When all your *Alchemy,* and your *Algebra,*
Your *Minerals, Vegetals,* and *Animals,*
Your Conjuring, Coz'ning, and your dozen of Trades,
Could not relieve your Corps with so much Linnen
Would make you Tinder, but to see a Fire;
I ga' you Count'nance, Credit for your Coals,
Your Stills, your Glasses, your Materials;
Built you a Fornace, drew you Customers,
Advanc'd all your black Arts; lent you, beside,
A House to practise in — *Sub.* Your Master's House?
   Fac. Where you have studied the more thriving Skill
Of Bawd'ry since. *Sub.* Yes, in your Master's House.
You and the Rats here kept Possession.
Make it not strange. I know yo' were one could keep
The Buttry-hatch still lock'd, and save the Chippings,
Sell the Dole-Beer to *Aquavitæ*-men,
The which, together with your *Christmass* Vails
At *Post and Pair,* your letting out of Counters,
Made you a pretty Stock, some twenty Marks,
And gave you credit to converse with Cobwebs,
Here, since your Mistris Death hath broke up House.
   Fac. You might talk softlier, Rascal. *Sub.* No, you *Scarabe,*
I'll thunder you in Pieces! I will teach you
How to beware to tempt a Fury again,
That carries Tempest in his Hand and Voice.
   Fac. The Place has made you valiant.
   Sub. No, your Clothes.

Thou Vermin, have I ta'ne thee out of Dung,
So poor, so wretched, when no living Thing
Would keep thee Company, but a Spider, or worse?
Rais'd thee from Brooms, and Dust, and Watring Pots?
Sublim'd thee, and *exalted* thee, and *fix'd* thee
I' the *third Region*, call'd our *State of Grace?*
Wrought thee to *Spirit*, to *Quintessence*, with pains
Would twice have won me the *Philosopher's Work?*
Put thee in Words and Fashion, made thee fit
For more than ordinary Fellowships?
Giv'n thee thy Oaths, thy quarrelling Dimensions?
Thy Rules to cheat at Horse-race, Cock-pit, Cards,
Dice, or whatever gallant Tincture else?
Made thee a Second in mine own great Art?
And have I this for Thanks? Do you rebel?
Do you fly out i' the *Projection?*
Would you be gone now?
    Dol. Gentlemen, what mean you?
Will you mar all?   *Sub.* Slave, thou had'st no Name —
    Dol. Will you undo your selves with civil War?
    Sub. Never been known, past *Equi clibanum*,
The heat of Horse-dung, under Ground, in Cellars,
Or an Ale house darker than deaf *John's;* been lost
To all Mankind, but Laundresses and Tapsters,
Had not I been.
    Dol. Do you know who hears you, Sovereign?
    Fac. Sirrah ——
    Dol. Nay, General, I thought you were civil ——
    Fac. I shall turn desperate, if you grow thus loud.
    Sub. And hang thy self, I care not.
    Fac. Hang thee, Colliar,
And all thy Pots and Pans, in Picture, I will,
Since thou hast mov'd me ——
    Dol. (O, this I'll orethrow all.)
    Fac. Write thee up Bawd in *Paul's*, have all thy Tricks
Of coz'ning with a hollow Coal, Dust, Scrapings,
Searching for things lost with a Sieve and Shears,

Erecting *Figures* in your Rows of Houses,
And taking in of Shadows with a Glass,
Told in Red Letters; and a Face cut for thee,
Worse than *Gamaliel Ratsey's*. *Dol.* Are you sound?
Ha' you your Senses, Masters? *Fac.* I will have
A Book, but barely reckoning thy Impostures,
Shall prove a true *Philosopher's Stone*, to Printers.
   Sub. Away, you Trencher-Rascal.
   Fac. Out, you Dog-leach,
The Vomit of all Prisons — *Dol.* Will you be
Your own Destructions, Gentlemen? Still spew'd out
For lying too heavy o' the Basket.
   Sub. Cheater. *Fac.* Bawd.
   Sub. Cow-herd. *Fac.* Conjurer. *Sub.* Cut-purse.
   Fac. Witch. *Dol.* O me!
We are ruin'd! lost! Ha' you no more regard
To your Reputations? Where's your Judgment? 'Slight,
Have yet some Care of me, o' your Republick —
   Fac. Away this Brach. I'll bring the Rogue, within
The Statute of *Sorcery, Tricesimo tertio*
Of *Harry* the Eighth: I, and (perhaps) thy Neck
Within a Noose, for laundring Gold, and barbing it.
   Dol. You'll bring your Head within a Cockscomb, will
you?   [*She catches out* Face's *Sword, and breaks* Subtle's *Glass.*
And you, Sir, with your *Menstrue*, gather it up.
'Sdeath, you abominable pair of Stinkards,
Leave off your Barking, and grow one again,
Or, by the Light that shines, I'll cut your Throats.
I'll not be made a Prey unto the Marshal,
For ne'er a snarling Dog-bolt o' you both.
Ha' you together cozen'd all this while,
And all the World? and shall it now be said,
Yo' have made most courteous shift to cozen your selves?
You will accuse him? You will bring him in
Within the *Statute*? Who shall take your Word?
A whorson, upstart, *Apocryphal* Captain,

Whom not a Puritan in *Black-Friers* will trust
So much as for a Feather! And you too
Will give the Cause, forsooth? You will insult,
And claim a Primacy in the Divisions?
You must be Chief? As if you only had
The Powder to project with, and the Work
Were not begun out of Equality?
The Venture *Tripartite!* All Things in common?
Without Priority? 'Sdeath, you perpetual Curs,
Fall to your Couples again, and cozen kindly,
And heartily and lovingly as you should,
And lose not the Beginning of a *Term*,
Or, by this Hand, I shall grow factious too,
And take my part, and quit you. *Fac.* 'Tis his fault,
He ever murmurs, and objects his Pains,
And says, the weight of all lies upon him.
 Sub. Why, so it does. *Dol.* How does it? Do not we
Sustain our Parts? *Sub.* Yes, but they are not equal.
 Dol. Why, if your Part exceed to Day, I hope
Ours may to morrow match it. *Sub.* I, they may.
 Dol. May, murmuring Mastiff! I and do. Death on me!
Help me to throttle him. *Sub.* Dorothee, Mrs. *Dorothee*,
'Ods precious, I'll do any thing. What do you mean?
 Dol. Because o' your *Fermentation* and *Cibation!*
 Sub. Not I, by Heaven ——
 Dol. Your *Sol* and *Luna* — help me.
 Sub. Would I were hang'd then. I'll conform myself.
 Dol. Will you, Sir? Do so then, and quickly swear.
 Sub. What shall I swear?
 Dol. To leave your Faction, Sir,
And labour kindly in the common Work.
 Sub. Let me not breathe, if I meant ought beside.
I only us'd those Speeches as a Spur
To him. *Dol.* I hope we need no Spurs, Sir. Do we?
 Fac. 'Slid, prove to-day who shall shark best.
 Sub. Agreed.
 Dol. Yes, and work close and friendly.

Sub. 'Slight, the Knot
Shall grow the stronger for this Breach with me.
 Dol. Why, so, my good Baboons! Shall we go make
A sort of sober, scurvy, precise Neighbours,
(That scarce have smil'd twice sin' the King came in)
A Feast of Laughter at our Follies? Rascals,
Would run themselves from breath, to see me ride,
Or you t' have but a Hole to thrust your Heads in,
For which you should pay Ear-rent? No, agree.
And may *Don Provost* ride a feasting long,
In his old Velvet Jerkin and stain'd Scarfs,
(My noble Sovereign, and worthy General)
Ere we contribute a new Crewel Garter
To his most worsted Worship. *Sub.* Royal *Doll!*
Spoken like *Claridiana* and thy self.
 Fac. For which, at Supper, thou shalt sit in triumph,
And not be styl'd *Dol Common*, but *Dol Proper*,
Dol Singular. The longest Cut, at Night,
Shall draw thee for his *Dol Particular*.
 Sub. Who's that? one Rings. To the Windo', *Dol*.
Pray Heav'n,
The Master do not trouble us this Quarter.
 Fac. O, fear not him! While there dies one a Week
O' the Plague, he's safe, from thinking toward *London*.
Beside, he's busie at his Hop-yards now:
I had a Letter from him: If he do,
He'll send such word, for airing o' the House,
As you shall have sufficient time to quit it:
Tho' we break up a Fortnight, 'tis no matter.
 Sub. Who is it, *Dol?*
 Dol. A fine young Quodling. *Fac.* O,
My Lawyers Clerk, I lighted on last Night
In *Holborn*, at the *Dagger*. He would have
(I told you of him) a Familiar,
To rifle with at Horses and win Cups.
 Dol. O, let him in.
 Sub. Stay. Who shall do't? *Fac.* Get you

Your Robes on, I will meet him, as going out.
Dol. And what shall I do? *Fac.* Not be seen, away.
Seem you very reserv'd?
Sub. Enough. *Fac.* God b' w' you, Sir.
I pray you let him know that I was here.
His Name is *Dapper.* I would gladly have staid but —

SCENE II.

Dapper, Face, Subtle.

Dap. Captain, I am here.
Fac. Who's that? He's come, I think, Doctor.
Good faith, Sir, I was going away. *Dap.* In a truth,
I am very sorry, Captain. *Fac.* But I thought
Sure I should meet you. *Dap.* I, I am very glad.
I had a scurvy Writ or two to make,
And I had lent my Watch last Night to one
That dines to day at the Sheriffs, and so was robb'd
Of my pass-time. Is this the Cunning-man?
Fac. This is his Worship. *Dap.* Is he a Doctor?
Fac. Yes.
Dap. And ha' you broke with him, Captain?
Fac. I. *Dap.* And how?
Fac. Faith, he does make the Matter, Sir, so dainty,
I know not what to say — *Dap.* Not so, good Captain.
Fac. Would I were fairly rid on't, believe me.
Dap. Nay, now you grieve me, Sir. Why should you wish so?
I dare assure you, I'll not be ungrateful.
Fac. I cannot think you will, Sir. But the Law
Is such a thing —— And then he says, *Read's* Matter
Falling so lately — *Dap. Read?* He was an Ass,
And dealt, Sir, with a Fool. *Fac.* It was a Clerk, Sir.
Dap. A Clerk?
Fac. Nay, hear me, Sir, you know the Law
Better, I think — *Dap.* I should, Sir, and the Danger.
You know, I shew'd the *Statute* to you? *Fac.* You did so.

Dap. And I will tell then? By this Hand of Flesh,
Would it might never write good Court-hand more,
If I discover. What do you think of me,
That I am a *Chiause?*
    Fac. What's that? *Dap.* The *Turk* was, here —
As one would say, Do you think I am a *Turk?*
    Fac. I'll tell the Doctor so.
    Dap. Do, good sweet Captain.
    Fac. Come, noble Doctor, pray thee let's prevail;
This is the Gentleman, and he is no *Chiause.*
    Sub. Captain, I have return'd you all my Answer.
I would do much, Sir, for your Love — But this
I neither may nor can. *Fac.* Tut, do not say so.
You deal now with a noble Fellow, Doctor,
One that will thank you richly, and h'is no *Chiause:*
Let that, Sir, move you.
    Sub. Pray you, forbear — *Fac.* He has
Four Angels here — *Sub.* You do me wrong, good Sir.
    Fac. Doctor, wherein? To tempt you with these Spirits?
    Sub. To tempt my Art, and Love, Sir, to my Peril.
'Fore Heav'n, I scarce can think you are my Friend,
That so would draw me to apparent danger.
    Fac I draw you? A Horse draw you, and a Halter,
You, and your Flies together —— *Dap.* Nay, good Captain.
    Fac. That know no difference of Men.
    Sub. Good Words, Sir.
    Fac. Good Deeds, Sir, Doctor Dogs-meat.
'Slight, I bring you
No cheating *Clim o' the Cloughs,* or *Claribels,*
That look as big as *Five-and-fifty,* and *Flush,*
And spit out Secrets like hot Custard —— *Dap.* Captain.
    Fac. Nor any melancholick Under scribe
Shall tell the *Vicar;* but a special Genteel,
That is the Heir to Forty Marks a Year,
Consorts with the small Poets of the time,
Is the sole Hope of his old Grand-mother,
That knows the Law, and writes you six fair Hands,

Is a fine Clerk, and has his Cyph'ring perfect,
Will take his Oath o' the *Greek Xenophon*,
If need be, in his Pocket; and can court
His Mistris out of *Ovid*. *Dap.* Nay, dear Captain.
    Fac. Did you not tell me so? *Dap.* Yes, but I'ld ha' you
Use Master Doctor with some more respect.
    Fac. Hang him, proud Stag, with his broad Velvet Head.
But for your sake, I'ld choak, ere I would change
An Article of Breath with such a Puckfoist ——
Come, let's be gone. *Sub.* Pray you le' me speak with you.
    Dap. His Worship calls you, Captain. *Fac.* I am sorry
I e'er embark'd my self in such a Business.
    Dap. Nay, good Sir, he did call you.
    Fac. Will he take then?
    Sub. First, hear me —
    Fac. Not a Syllable, 'less you take,
    Sub. Pray ye, Sir ——
    Fac. Upon no Terms, but an *Assumpsit.*
    Sub. Your Humour must be Law.   [*He takes Money.*
    Fac. Why now, Sir, talk!
Now I dare hear you with mine Honour. Speak.
So may this Gentleman too.
    Sub. Why, Sir — *Fac.* No whispering.
    Sub. 'Fore Heaven, you do not apprehend the Loss
You do your self in this. *Fac.* Wherein? For what?
    Sub. Marry, to be so importunate for one,
That, when he has it, will undo you all?
He'll win up all the Mony i' the Town.
    Fac. How?
    Sub. Yes, and blow up Gamester after Gamester,
As they do Crackers in a Puppet-Play.
If I do give him a *Familiar*,
Give you him all you play for; never set him:
For he will have it. *Fac.* You are mistaken, Doctor.
Why, he does ask one but for Cups and Horses,
A rifling *Fly;* none o' your great *Familiars.*
    Dap. Yes Captain, I would have it for all Games.

Sub. I told you so. *Fac.* 'Slight, that's a new Business!
I understood you, a tame Bird, to fly
Twice in a Term, or so, on *Friday* Nights,
When you had left the Office, for a Nag
Of forty or fifty Shillings. *Dap.* I, tis true, Sir;
But I do think now I shall leave the Law,
And therefore — *Fac.* Why, this changes quite the Case!
Do' you think that I dare move him?
Dap. If you please, Sir;
All's one to him, I see. *Fac.* What! for that Mony?
I cannot with my Conscience: Nor should you
Make the Request, methinks. *Dap.* No, Sir, I mean
To add Consideration. *Fac.* Why then, Sir,
I'll try. Say that it were for all Games, Doctor?
Sub. I say then, not a Mouth shall eat for him
At any Ordinary, but o' the Score,
That is a Gaming Mouth, conceive me. *Fac.* Indeed!
Sub. He'll draw you all the Treasure of the Realm,
If it be set him. *Fac.* Speak you this from Art?
Sub. I, Sir, and Reason too, the Ground of Art.
He is o' the only best Complexion,
The Queen of *Fairy* loves. *Fac.* What! is he?
Sub. Peace.
He'll over-bear you. Sir, should she but see him —
Fac. What? *Sub.* Do not you tell him.
Fac. Will he win at Cards too?
Sub. The Spirits of dead *Holland*, living *Isaac*,
You'ld swear, were in him; such a vigorous Luck
As cannot be resisted. 'Slight, he'll put
Six o' your Gallants to a Cloak, indeed.
Fac. A strange Success, that some Man shall be born to!
Sub. He hears you, Man ——
Dap. Sir, I'll not be ingrateful.
Fac. Faith I have Confidence in his good Nature:
You hear, he says he will not be ingrateful.
Sub. Why, as you please; my Venture follows yours.
Fac. Troth, do it, Doctor; think him trusty, and make him.

He may make us both happy in an Hour;
Win some five thousand Pound, and send us two o' it.
  Dap. Believe it, and I will, Sir. *Fac.* And you shall, Sir
You have heard all?
  Dap. No, what was't? Nothing, I, Sir.
  Fac. Nothing? [Face *takes him aside.*
  Dap. A little, Sir. *Fac.* Well, a rare Star
Reign'd at your birth.
  Dap. At mine Sir? No. *Fac.* The Doctor
Swears that you are ——
  Sub. Nay, Captain, you'll tell all now.
  Fac. Allied to the Queen of *Fairy.*
  Dap. Who? that I am?
Believe it, no such matter —— *Fac.* Yes, and that
Yo' were born with a Cawl o' your Head.
  Dap. Who says so? *Fac.* Come,
You know it wel enough, tho' you dissemble it.
  Dap. I-fac, I do not; You are mistaken. *Fac.* How!
Swear by your fic? and in a thing so known
Unto the Docto'? How shall we, Sir, trust you
I' the other mater? Can we ever think,
When you have won five or six thousand Pound,
You'll send us shares in't by this rate? *Dap.* By *Jove*, Sir,
I'll win ten thousand Pound, and send you half.
I-fac's no Oath *Sub.* No, no, he did but jest.
  Fac. Go to Go thank the Doctor. He's your Friend,
To take it so. *Dap.* I thank his Worship. *Fac.* So!
Another Angl! *Dap.* Must I? *Fac.* Must you? 'Slight,
What else is Thanks? Will you be trivial? Doctor,
When must he come for his *Familiar?*
  Dap. Shal I not ha' it with me? *Sub.* O, good Sir!
There must. World of Ceremonies pass,
You must b bath'd and fumigated first;
Besides, th Queen of *Fairy* does not rise
Till it be Non. *Fac.* Not, if she danc'd, to Night.
  Sub. Ad she must bless it. *Fac.* Did you never see
Her Royal Grace yet? *Dap.* Whom? your Aunt of *Fairy?*

Sub. Not since she kist him in the Cradle, Captain;
I can resolve you that. *Fac.* Well, see her Grace,
Whate'er it cost you, for a thing that I know.
It will be somewhat hard to compass; but
However, see her. You are made, believe it,
If you can see her. Her Grace is a lone Woman,
And very rich; and if she take a Phant'sie,
She will do strange things. See her at any Hand.
'Slid, she may hap to leave you all she has!
It is the Doctor's fear. *Dap.* How will't be done?
   Fac. Let me alone, take you no thought. Do you
But say to me, Captain: I'll see her Grace.
   Dap. I'll see her Grace. *Fac.* Enough.
   Sub. Who's there? [*One knocks without.*
Anon. (Conduct him forth by the back way;
Sir, against one a Clock prepare your self:
Till when you must be fasting; only take
Three drops of Vinegar in at your Nose,
Two at your Mouth, and one at either Ear;
Then bath your Finger's ends, and wash your Eyes,
To sharpen your five Senses, and cry *Hum*
Thrice, and then *Buz* as often; and then come
   Fac. Can you remember this? *Dap.* I warant you.
   Fac. Well then, away. 'Tis but your bestowing
Some twenty Nobles 'mong her Graces Servans,
And put on a clean Shirt. You do not know
What grace her Grace may do in clean Linnen.

SCENE III.

Subtle, Drugger, Face.

   Sub. Come in! (Good Wives, I pray you forbear me now;
Troth I can do you no good till Afternoon.)
What is your Name, say you? *Abel Drugger?*
   Dru. Yes, Sir.
   Sub. A Seller of Tobacco? *Dru.* Yes, Sir. *Sub.* Umh.
Free of the *Grocers?* *Dru.* I, an't please you.

Sub. Well —
Your Business, *Abel?* *Dru.* This, an't please your Worship:
I am a young Beginner, and am building
Of a new Shop, an't like your Worship, just
At corner of a Street: (Here's the Plot on't)
And I would know by Art, Sir, of your Worship,
Which way I should make my Door, by *Necromancy*,
And where my Shelves; and which should be for Boxes,
And which for Pots. I would be glad to thrive, Sir.
And I was wish'd to your Worship by a Gentleman,
One Captain *Face*, that says you know Mens *Planets*,
And their good *Angels*, and their bad. *Sub.* I do,
If I do see 'em —— *Fac.* What! my honest *Abel?*
Thou art well met here. *Dru.* Troth, Sir, I was speaking,
Just as your Worship came here, of your Worship.
I pray you speak for me to Master Doctor.
    Fac. He shall do any thing. Doctor, do you hear?
This is my Friend, *Abel*, an honest Fellow;
He lets me have good Tobacco, and he does not
Sophisticate it with Sack-lees or Oil,
Nor washes it in Muscadel and Grains,
Nor buries it in Gravel, under Ground,
Wrapp'd up in greasie Leather, or piss'd Clouts:
But keeps it in fine Lilly-pots, that open'd,
Smell like Conserve of Roses, or *French* Beans.
He has his Maple Block, his silver Tongs,
Winchester Pipes, and Fire of Juniper,
A neat, spruce, honest Fellow, and no Goldsmith.
    Sub. H' is a fortunate Fellow, that I am sure on —
    Fac. Already, Sir, ha' you found it? Lo' thee, *Abel!*
    Sub. And in right way to'ward Riches ——
    Fac. Sir. *Sub.* This Summer
He will be of the Cloathing of his Company,
And next Spring call'd to the Scarlet; spend what he can.
    Fac. What, and so little Beard? *Sub.* You must think,
He may have a Receit to make Hair come:
But he'll be wise, preserve his Youth, and fine for't;

His Fortune looks for him another way.
 Fac. 'Slid, Doctor, how canst thou know this so soon?
I am amus'd at that! *Sub.* By a Rule, Captain,
In *Metaposcopy*, which I do work by;
A certain Star i' the Forehead, which you see not.
Your Chestnut, or your Olive-colour'd Face
Do's never fail: and your long Ear doth promise.
I knew't, by certain Spots too, in his Teeth,
And on the Nail of his *Mercurial* Finger.
 Fac. Which Finger's that? *Sub.* His little Finger. Look!
Yo' were born upon a Wednesday?
 Dru. Yes indeed, Sir.
 Sub. The Thumb, in *Chiromancy*, we give *Venus*;
The Fore-finger, to *Jove;* the midst, to *Saturn;*
The Ring, to *Sol;* the least, to *Mercury:*
Who was the Lord, Sir, of his *Horoscope*,
His *House of Life* being *Libra;* which fore-shew'd
He should be a Merchant, and should Trade with Ballance.
 Fac. Why, this is strange? I'st not, honest *Nab?*
 Sub. There is a Ship, now coming from *Ormus*,
That shall yield him such a Commodity
Of Drugs — This is the West, and this the South?
 Dru. Yes, Sir. *Sub.* And those are your two sides?
 Dru. I, Sir.
 Sub. Make me your Door, then, South; your Broad-side,
  West:
And, on the East-side of your Shop, aloft,
Write *Mathlai, Tarmiel*, and *Baraborat;*
Upon the North-part, *Rael, Velel, Thiel.*
They are the Names of those *Mercurial* Spirits,
That do fright Flies from Boxes. *Dru.* Yes, Sir. *Sub.* And
Beneath your Threshold, bury me a Load-stone
To draw in Gallants, that wear Spurs. The rest,
They'll seem to follow. *Fac.* That's a Secret, *Nab!*.
 Sub. And on your Stall a Puppet, with a Vice,
And a Court-*fucus* to call City-dames.
You shall deal much with *Minerals. Dru.* Sir, I have

At home, already —— *Sub.* I, I know, you have *Arsnike*,
Vitriol, Sal-tartre, Argale, Alkaly,
Cinoper: I know all. This Fellow, Captain,
Will come, in time, to be a great Distiller,
And give a Say (I will not say directly,
But very fair) at the *Philosopher's Stone.*
    Fac. Why, how now, *Abel!* is this true? *Dru.* Good Captain,
What must I give? *Fac.* Nay, I'll not counsel thee.
Thou hear'st what Wealth (he says, spend what thou canst)
Th'art like to come too. *Dru.* I would gi' him a Crown.
    Fac. A Crown! and toward such a Fortune? Heart,
Thou shalt rather gi' him thy Shop. No Gold about thee?
    Dru. Yes, I have a *Portague*, I ha' kept this half Year.
    Fac. Out on thee, *Nab.* 'Slight, there was not such an Offer;
'Shalt keep't no longer, I'll gi' it him for thee?
Doctor, *Nab* prays your Worship to drink this, and Swears
He will appear more grateful, as your Skill
Do's raise him in the World. *Dru.* I would intreat
Another Favour of his Worship. *Fac.* What is't, *Nab?*
    Dru. But, to look over, Sir, my *Almanack*,
And cross out my ill-days, that I may neither
Bargain, nor trust upon them. *Fac.* That he shall, *Nab.*
Leave it, it shall be done, 'gainst Afternoon.
    Sub. And a direction for his Shelves. *Fac.* Now, *Nab?*
Art thou well pleas'd, *Nab? Dru.* 'Thank, Sir, both your Worships.
    Fac. Away!
Why, now you smoky persecuter of Nature!
Now do you see, that something's to be done,
Beside your Beech-coal, and your cor'sive Waters,
Your Crosslets, Crucibles, and Cucurbites?
You must have Stuff, brought home to you, to work on?
And, yet, you think, I am at no expence,
In searching out these Veins, then following 'em,
Then trying 'em out. 'Fore God, my Intelligence,

Cost me more Money, than my share oft comes too,
In these rare Works. *Sub.* You 'are pleasant, Sir. How now?

SCENE IV.

Face, Dol, Subtle.

Fac. What says my dainty *Dolkin?* *Dol.* Yonder Fish-wife
Will not away. And there's your Giantess,
The Bawd of *Lambeth.* *Sub.* Heart, I cannot speak with 'em.
Dol. Not afore Night, I' have told 'em, in a Voice,
Thorough the Trunk, like one of your *Familiars.*
But I have spied Sir *Epicure Mammon* — *Sub.* Where?
Dol. Coming along, at far end of the Lane,
Slow of his Feet, but earnest of his Tongue,
To one that's with him. *Sub.* Face, go you, and shift.
Dol, You must presently make ready, too ——
Dol. Why, what's the matter? *Sub.* O, I did look for him
With the Suns rising: 'Marvel, he could sleep!
This is the Day I am to perfect for him
The *Magisterium,* our *great Work,* the *Stone:*
And yield it, made into his Hands: of which,
He has, this Month, talk'd, as he were possess'd.
And now he's dealing pieces on't away,
Me-thinks I see him entring Ordinaries,
Dispensing for the Pox, and Plaguy Houses,
Reaching his Dose, walking *Moore-fields* for Lepers,
And offering Citizens-wives Pomander-bracelets,
As his Preservative, made of the *Elixir;*
Searching the Spittle, to make old Bawds young?
And the High-ways, for Beggars, to make rich:
I see no end of his Labours. He will make
Nature asham'd of her long sleep: when Art,
Who's but a Step-dame, shall do more than she,
In her best love to Mankind, ever could?
If his Dream last, he'll turn the Age to Gold.

ACT II. SCENE I.

Mammon, Surly.

Come on, Sir! Now, you set your Foot on Shore
In *novo Orbe;* here's the rich *Peru:*
And there within, Sir, are the Golden Mines,
Great *Solomon's Ophir!* He was Sailing to't,
Three Years, but we have reach'd it in ten Months.
This is the Day, wherein, to all my Friends,
I will pronounce the happy Word: *Be Rich!*
This Day you shall be *spectatissimi.*
You shall no more deal with the hollow Dye,
Or the frail Card. No more be at Charge of keeping
The Livery-punk, for the young Heir, that must
Seal, at all Hours, in his Shirt. No more,
If he deny, ha' him beaten to't, as he is
That brings him the Commodity. No more
Shall thirst of Sattin, or the Covetous hunger
Of Velvet Entrails, for a rude-spun Cloke,
To be displaid at *Madam Augusta's,* make
The Sons of *Sword,* and *Hazzard* fall before
The Golden Calf, and on their Knees, whole Nights,
Commit Idolatry with Wine, and Trumpets:
Or go a feasting, after Drum and Ensign.
No more of this. You shall start up young *Vicerois,*
And have your Punques, and Punquetees, my *Surly.*
And unto thee, I speak it first: *Be Rich!*
Where is my *Subtle?* there? Within
    hough! *Sur.* Within, Sir.
He'll come to you, by and by.
    Mam. That's his Fire-drake,
His Lungs, his *Zephyrus,* be that puffs his Coals,
Till he firk Nature up, in her own Center.
You are not faithful, Sir. This Night, I'll change
All, that is Metal, in thy House, to Gold.

And, early in the Morning, will I send
To all the Plumbers, and the Pewterers,
And Buy their Tin, and Lead up: and to *Lothbury*,
For all the Copper. *Sur.* What, and turn that too?
   Mam. Yes, and I'll purchase *Devonshire*, and *Cornwall*,
And make them perfect *Indies!* You admire now?
   Sur. No, faith. *Mam.* But when you see the effects of the
      great Medicine,
Of which one part projected on a hundred
Of *Mercury*, or *Venus*, or the *Moon*,
Shall turn it to as many of the *Sun;*
Nay, to a thousand, so *ad infinitum:*
You will believe me. *Sur.* Yes, when I see't, I will.
But, if my Eyes do cozen me so (and I
Giving 'em no occasion) sure I'll have
A Whore, shall p... 'em out, next Day. *Mam.* Ha! Why?
Do you think, I fable with you? I assure you,
He that has once the *Flower of the Sun*,
The perfect *Ruby*, which we call *Elixir*,
Not only can do that, but by it's Vertue,
Can confer Honour, Love, Respect, long Life,
Give Safety, Valour, yea, and Victory,
To whom he will. In eight and twenty Days,
I'll make an old Man of Fourscore a Child.
   Sur. No doubt, he's that already. *Mam.* Nay, I mean,
Restore his Years, renew him, like an Eagle,
To the fifth Age; make him get Sons and Daughters,
Young Giants; as our *Philosophers* have done
(The antient *Patriarchs* afore the Flood)
But taking, once a Week, on a Knive's Point,
The quantity of a Grain of Mustard of it:
Become stout *Marses*, and beget young *Cupids*.
   Sur. The decay'd *Vestals* of *Pickt-hatch* would thank you,
That keep the Fire a-live, there. *Mam.* 'Tis the secret
Of Nature, naturiz'd 'gainst all Infections,
Cures all Diseases, coming of all Causes;
A Month's Grief in a Day; a Years in twelve:

And, of what Age soever, in a Month.
Past all the Doses of your drugging Doctors.
I'll undertake, withal, to fright the Plague
Out o' the Kingdom, in three Months. *Sur.* And I'll
Be bound, the Players shall Sing your Praises, then,
Without their Poets. *Mam.* Sir, I'll do't. Mean time,
I'll give away so much unto my Man,
Shall serve th' whole City, with Preservative,
Weekly; each House his Dose, and at the rate —
   Sur. As he that built the Water-work, do's with Water?
   Mam. You are incredulous. *Sur.* Faith, I have a Humour,
I would not willingly be gull'd. Your *Stone*
Cannot transmute me. *Mam. Pertinax Surly,*
Will you believe Antiquity? Records?
I'll shew you a Book, where *Moses,* and his Sister,
And *Solomon* have written of the Art;
I, and a Treatise penn'd by *Adam. Sur.* How!
   Mam. O' the *Philosopher's Stone,* and in high *Dutch.*
   Sur. Did *Adam* write, Sir, in high *Dutch?* *Mam.* He did:
Which proves it was the Primitive Tongue. *Sur.* What
     Paper?
   Mam. On Cedar Board. *Sur.* O that, indeed (they say)
Will last 'gainst Worms. *Mam.* 'Tis like your *Irish* Wood,
'Gainst Cob-webs. I have a piece of *Jason's* Fleece, too,
Which was no other than a Book of *Alchemy.*
Writ in large Sheep-skin, a good fat Ram-vellum.
Such was *Pythagoras's* Thigh, *Pandora's* Tub;
And, all that Fable of *Medea's* Charms,
The manner of our Work: The Bulls, our Furnace,
Still breathing Fire: our *Argent-vive,* the Dragon:
The Dragons Teeth, *Mercury* Sublimate,
That keeps the whiteness, hardness, and the biting;
And they are gather'd into *Jason's* Helm,
(Th' *Alembick*) and then sow'd in *Mars* his Field,
And thence sublim'd so often, till they are fix'd.
Both this, th' *Hesperian* Garden, *Cadmus* Story,
Jove's Shower, the Boon of *Midas, Argus* Eyes,

Boccace his *Demogorgon*, thousands more,
All abstract Riddles of our *Stone*. How now?

SCENE II.
Mammon, Face, Surly.

Mam. Do we succeed? Is our Day come? and hold's it?
Fac. The Evening will set red upon you, Sir;
You have colour for it, Crimson: the red *Ferment*
Has done his Office. Three Hours hence, prepare you
To see Projection. *Mam.* Pertinax, my *Surly*,
Again, I say to thee, aloud, *Be Rich*,
This Day, thou shalt have Ingots: and, to Morrow,
Give Lords th' affront. Is it, my *Zephyrus*, right?
Blushes the *Bolts-head*? *Fac.* Like a Wench with Child, Sir,
That were, but now, discover'd to her Master.
Mam. Excellent witty, *Lungs*! My only Care is,
Where to get Stuff enough, to Project on,
This Town will not half serve me. *Fac.* No, Sir? Buy
The covering off o' Churches. *Mam.* That's true. *Fac.* Yes,
Let 'em stand bare, as do their Auditory.
Or cap 'em, new, with Shingles. *Mam.* No good Thatch:
Thatch will lye light upo' the Rafters, *Lungs*.
Lungs, I will manumit thee, from the Furnace;
I will restore thee thy Complexion, *Puffe*,
Lost in the Embers; and repair this Brain,
Hurt wi' the Fume o' the Metals. *Fac.* I have blown, Sir,
Hard for your Worship; thrown by many a Coal,
When 'twas not Beech; weigh'd those I put in, just,
To keep your heat still even; These Bleard Eyes
Have wak'd, to read your several Colours, Sir:
Of the *pale Citron*, the *green Lyon*, the *Crow*,
The *Peacock's Tail*, the *plumed Swan*. *Mam.* And lastly,
Thou hast descryed the *Flower*, the *Sanguis Agni!*
Fac. Yes, Sir. *Mam.* Where's Master? *Fac.* At's Prayers,
Sir, he
Good Man, he's doing his Devotions,

For the Success. *Mam. Lungs*, I will set a Period
To all thy Labours: Thou shalt be the Master
Of my *Seraglio. Fac.* Good, Sir. *Mam.* But do you hear?
I'll geld you, *Lungs. Fac.* Yes, Sir. *Mam.* For I do mean
To have a List of Wives and Concubines,
Equal with *Solomon*, who had the *Stone*
Alike with me: and I will make me a Back
With the *Elixir*, that shall be as tough
As *Hercules*, to encounter Fifty a Night.
Th'art sure thou saw'st it *Blood? Fac.* Both *Blood* and *Spirit*,
    Sir.
  Mam. I will have all my Beds, blown up; not stuft:
Down is too hard. And then, mine Oval Room
Fill'd with such Pictures as *Tiberius* took
From *Elephantis*, and dull *Aretine*
But coldly imitated. Then, my Glasses
Cut in more subtil Angles, to disperse,
And multiply the Figures, as I walk
Naked between my *Succubæ*. My Mists
I'll have of Perfume, vapor'd 'bout the Room,
To lose our selves in; and my Baths, like Pits
To fall into: from whence we will come forth,
And rowl us dry in Gossamour and Roses.
(Is it arriv'd at *Ruby?*) —— Where I spy
A wealthy Citizen, or rich Lawyer,
Have a sublim'd pure Wife, unto that Fellow
I'll send a thousand Pound, to be my Cuckold.
  Fac. And I shall carry it? *Mam.* No, I'll ha' no Bawds,
But Fathers and Mothers. They will do it best,
Best of all others. And my Flatterers
Shall be the pure, and gravest of Divines,
That I can get for Money. My meet Fools,
Eloquent Burgesses, and then my Poets
The same that writ so subtily of the *Fart;*
Whom I will entertain still for that Subject.
The few that would give out themselves, to be
Court and Town-stallions, and, each where, belye

Ladies, who are known most Innocent, for them;
Those will I beg, to make me *Eunuchs* of:
And they shall fan me with Ten Estrich Tails
A piece, made in a Plume, to gather-Wind.
We will be brave, *Puffe*, now we ha' the *Medicine*.
My Meat shall all come in in *Indian* Shells,
Dishes of Agat set in Gold, and studded
With Emeralds, Saphirs, Hyacinchs, and Rubies.
The Tongues of Carps, Dormise, and Camels Heels,
Boil'd i' the Spirit of *Sol*, and dissolv'd Pearl,
(*Apicius* Diet 'gainst the *Epilepsie*)
And I will eat these Broaths with Spoons of Amber,
Headed with Diamant, and Carbuncle.
My Foot-boy shall eat Pheasants, calver'd Salmons,
Knots, Godwits, Lampreys: I my self will have
The Beards of Barbels serv'd, in stead of Sallads;
Oil'd Mushromes; and the swelling unctuous Paps
Of a fat pregnant Sow, newly cut off,
Drest with an exquisite, and poynant Sauce;
For which, I'll say unto my Cook, There's Gold,
Go forth, and be a Knight. *Fac.* Sir, I'll go look
A little, how it heightens. *Mam.* Do. My Shirts
I'll have of Taffata-sarsnet, soft and light
As Cob-webs; and for all my other Rayment,
It shall be such as might provoke the *Persian*,
Were he to teach the World Riot anew.
My Gloves of Fishes, and Birds-skin, perfum'd
With Gums of *Paradise*, and Eastern Air ——
   Sur. And do' you think to have the *Stone*, with this?
   Mam. No, I do think t' have all this, with the *Stone*.
   Sur. Why, I have heard, he must be *homo frugi*,
A Pious, Holy, and Religious Man,
One free from mortal Sin, a very Virgin.
   Mam. That makes it, Sir, he is so. But I Buy it.
My Venture brings it me. He, honest Wretch,
A notable, superstitious, good Soul,
Has worn his Knees bare, and his Slippers bald,

With Prayer and Fasting for it: and, Sir, let him
Do it alone, for me, still. Here he comes.
Not a prophane Word, afore him: 'Tis Poyson.

SCENE III.
Mammon, Subtle, Surly, Face.

Mam. Good Morrow, Father. *Sub.* Gentle Son, good
    Morrow,
And to your Friend there. What is he, is with you?
    Mam. An Heretick, that I did bring along,
In hope, Sir, to convert him. *Sub.* Son, I doubt
Yo'are covetous, that thus you meet your time
I' the just Point: prevent your Day, at Morning.
This argues something, worthy of a Fear
Of importune and carnal Appetite:
Take heed, do you not cause the Blessing to leave you
With your ungovern'd haste. I should be sorry
To see my Labours, now e'en at perfection,
Got by long watching, and large patience,
Not prosper, where my Love and Zeal hath plac'd 'em.
Which (Heaven I call to witness, with your self,
T'o whom I have pour'd my Thoughts) in all my Ends,
Have look'd no way, but unto publick Good,
To pious Uses, and dear Charity,
Now grown a Prodigy with Men. Wherein
If you, my Son, should now prevaricate,
And, to your own particular Lusts, employ
So Great and Catholick a Bliss, be sure,
A Curse will follow, yea, and overtake
Your subtle and most secret way. *Mam.* I know, Sir,
You shall not need to fear me. I but come,
To ha' you confute this Gentleman. *Sur.* Who is,
Indeed, Sir, somewhat caustive of belief
Toward your *Stone;* would not be gull'd. *Sub.* Well, Son,
All that I can convince him in, is this,
The work is done: Bright *Sol* is in his *Robe.*

We have a *Med'cine* of the *triple Soul*,
The *glorified Spirit*. Thanks be to Heaven,
And make us worthy of it. ULEN SPIEGEL.
  Fac. Anon, Sir. *Sub.* Look well to the Register,
And let your heat still lessen by degrees,
To the *Aludels*. *Fac.* Yes, Sir. *Sub.* Did you look
O' the *Bolts-head* yet? *Fac.* Which? on *D.* Sir? *Sub.* 1.
What's the Complexion? *Fac.* Whitish. *Sub.* Infuse Vinegar,
To draw his *volatile substance*, and his *Tincture*:
And let the Water in *Glass E.* be *feltred*,
And put into the *Gripes Egg*. Lute him well;
And leave him clos'd in *Balneo*. *Fac.* I will, Sir.
  Sur. What a brave Language here is? next to Canting?
  Sub. I' have another work, you never saw, Son,
That three Days since past the *Philosopher's Wheel*,
In the lent heat of *Athanor*; and's become
Sulphur o' Nature. *Mam.* But 'tis for me? *Sub.* What need
    you?
You have enough, in that is perfect. *Mam.* O, but ——
  Sub. Why, this is covetise! *Mam.* No, I assure you,
I shall employ it all in pious uses,
Founding of Colleges, and *Grammar* Schools,
Marrying young Virgins, building Hospitals,
And now, and then, a Church. *Sub.* How now? *Fac.* Sir,
    please you,
Shall I not change the *feltre?* *Sub.* Marry, yes,
And bring me the Complexion of *Glass B.*
  Mam. Ha' you another? *Sub.* Yes, Son, were I assur'd
Your piety were firm, we would not want
The means to glorifie it. But I hope the best:
I mean to tinct *C.* in *Sand-heat*, to Morrow,
And give him *Imbibition*. *Mam.* Of white Oil?
  Sub. No, Sir, of red. *F.* is come over the *Helm* too,
I thank my Maker, in S. *Maries Bath*,
And shews *Lac Virginis*. Blessed be Heaven.
I sent you of his *fæces* there *calcin'd*.
Out of that *Calx*, I' ha' won the *Salt of Mercury*.

Mam. By powring on your *rectified water?*
Sub. Yes, and *reverberating* in *Athanor.*
How now? What colour says it? *Fac.* The ground black, Sir.
  Mam. That's your *Crowes head?*
  Sur. Your *Cocks-comb's,* is't not?
  Sub. No, 'tis not perfect, would it were the *Crow.*
That work wants something. *Sur.* (O, look'd for this.
The Hay is a pitching.) *Sub.* Are you sure, you loos'd 'em
I'their own *menstrue? Fac.* Yes, Sir, and then married 'em
And put them in a *Bolts-head,* nipp'd to *digestion,*
According as you bade me, when I set
The *Liquor of Mars to Circulation,*
In the same heat. *Sub.* The Process, then, was right.
  Fac. Yes, by the token, Sir, the *Retort* brake,
And what was sav'd, was put into the *Pellicane,*
And Sign'd with *Hermes' Seal. Sub.* I think 'twas so.
We should have a new *Amalgama.* (*Sur.* O, this Ferret
Is rank as any Pole-cat.) *Sub.* But I care not.
Let him e'en dye; we have enough beside,
In *Embrion.* H. ha's his *white-shirt* on? *Fac.* Yes, Sir,
He's ripe for *inceration:* He stands warm,
In his *Ash-Fire.* I would not, you should let
Any die now, if I might counsel, Sir,
For lucks sake to the rest. It is not good.
  Mam. He says right. *Sur.* I, are you bolted?
  Fac. Nay, I know't, Sir,
I have seen th' ill Fortune. What is some three Ounces
Of fresh *materials? Mam.* Is't no more? *Fac.* No more, Sir,
Of Gold, t' *Amalgame,* with some six of *Mercury.*
  Mam. Away, here's Mony. What will serve?
  Fac. Ask him, Sir.
  Mam. How much? *Sub.* Give him Nine Pound: you may
    gi' him Ten.
  Sur. Yes. T'wenty, and be Cozen'd, do. *Mam.* There 'tis.
  Sub. This needs not. But that you will have it so,
To see conclusions of all; for two
Of our inferiour Works, are at *fixation.*

A third is in *ascension*. Go your ways.
Ha' you set the Oil of *Luna* in *Kemia?*
  Fac. Yes, Sir.   *Sub.* And the *Philosopher's* Vinegar.
  Fac. I.
  Sur. We shall have a Sallad.   *Mam.* When do you make
    Projection?
  Sub. Son, be not hasty, I *exalt* our *Med'cine*,
By hanging him in *Balneo vaporoso*,
And giving him solution; then *congeal* him;
For look how oft I iterate the Work,
So many times I add unto his Vertue.
As, if at first one Ounce convert a hundred,
After his second loose, he'll turn a thousand,
His third solution, ten; his fourth a hundred,
After his fifth, a thousand thousand Ounces
Of any imperfect Metal, into pure
Silver or Gold, in all Examinations,
As good as any of the natural Mine.
Get you your Stuff here against Afternoon,
Your Brass, your Pewter, and your Andirons.
  Mam. Not those of Iron?
  Sub. Yes, you may bring them too.
We'll change all Metals.   *Sur.* I believe you in that.
  Mam. Then I may send my Spits?
  Sub. Yes, and your Racks.
  Sur. And Dripping-pans, and Pot-hangers, and Hooks?
Shall he not?   *Sub.* If he please.   *Sur.* To be an Ass.
  Sub. How, Sir!
  Mam. This Gent'man you must bear withal:
I told you, he had no Faith.   *Sur.* And a little Hope, Sir;
But much less Charity, should I gull my self.
  Sub. Why, what have you observ'd, Sir, in our Art,
Seems so impossible?   *Sur.* But your whole Work, no more.
That you should hatch Gold in a Furnace, Sir,
As they do Eggs in *Egypt!*   *Sub.* Sir, do you
Believe that Eggs are hatch'd so?   *Sur.* If I should?
  Sub. Why, I think that the greater Miracle.

No Egg but differs from a Chicken more
Than Metals in themselves. *Sur.* That cannot be.
The Egg's ordain'd by Nature to that end,
And is a Chicken in *Potentia*.
    Sub. The same we say of Lead, and other Metals,
Which would be Gold, if they had time. *Mam.* And that
Our Art doth further. *Sub.* I, for 'twere absurd
To think that Nature in the Earth bred Gold
Perfect i' the instant. Something went before.
There must be remote Matter. *Sur.* I, what is that?
    Sub. Marry, we say —— *Mam.* 1, now it heats: stand
        Father,
Pound him to Dust —— *Sub.* It is, of the one part,
A humid Exhalation, which we call
Materia liquida, or the *unctuous Water;*
On the other part, a certain crass and viscous
Portion of Earth; both which concorporate
Do make the Elementary Matter of Gold;
Which is not yet *propria materia,*
But commune to all Metals, and all Stones.
For, where it is forsaken of that moisture,
And hath more driness, it becomes a Stone;
Where it retains more of the humid fatness,
It turns to *Sulphur*, or to *Quicksilver,*
Who are the Parents of all other *Metals*.
Nor can this remote Matter suddenly
Progress so from extreme unto extreme,
As to grow Gold, and leap o'er all the Means.
Nature doth first beget th' imperfect, then
Proceeds she to the Perfect. Of that airy
And oily Water, *Mercury* is engendred;
Sulphur o' the fat and earthly part; the one
(Which is the last) supplying the place of Male,
The other of Female, in all Metals.
Some do believe that *Hermaphrodeity*,
That both do act and suffer. But these two
Make the rest ductile, malleable, extensive.

And even in Gold they are; for we do find
Seeds of them, by our Fire, and Gold in them,
And can produce the *species* of each Metal
More perfect thence, than Nature doth in Earth.
Beside, who doth not see, in daily practice,
Art can beget Bees, Hornets, Beetles, Wasps,
Out of the Carcasses and Dung of Creatures;
Yea, Scorpions of an Herb, being rightly plac'd?
And these are living Creatures, far more perfect
And excellent than Metals. *Mam.* Well said, *Father!*
Nay, if he take you in Hand, Sir, with an *Argument*,
He'll bray you in a Mortar. *Sur.* Pray you, Sir, stay.
Rather then I'll be bray'd, Sir, I'll believe
That *Alchemy* is a pretty kind of Game,
Somewhat like Tricks o'the Cards, to cheat a Man
With charming. *Sub.* Sir?
   Sur. What else are all your Terms,
Whereon no one o'your Writers 'grees with other?
Of your *Elixir*, your *Lac virginis*,
Your *Stone*, your *Med'cine*, and your *Chrysosperme*,
Your *Sal*, your *Sulphur*, and your *Mercury*,
Your *Oil of Height*, your *Tree of Life*, your *Blood*,
Your *Marchesite*, your *Tutie*, your *Magnesia*,
Your *Toade*, your *Crow*, your *Dragon*, and your *Panthar*,
Your *Sun*, your *Moon*, your *Firmament*, your *Adrop*,
Your *Lato*, *Azoch*, *Zernich*, *Chibrit*, *Heautarit*.
And then your *Red Man*, and your *White-Woman*,
With all your *Broths*, your *Menstrues*, and *Materials*,
Of *Piss* and *Egg-shels*, *Womens Terms*, *Man's Blood*,
Hair o' th' Head, *burnt Clouts*, *Chalk*, *Merds*, and *Clay*,
Powder of Bones, *Scalings of Iron*, *Glass*,
And Worlds of other strange *Ingredients*,
Would burst a Man to name? *Sub.* And *all these*, nam'd,
Intending but one thing; which Art our Writers
Us'd to obscure their Art. *Mam.* Sir, so I told him,
Because the simple Idiot should not learn it,
And make it vulgar. *Sub.* Was not all the *Knowledge*

Of the *Egyptians* writ in mystick *Symbols?*
Speak not the *Scriptures* oft in *Parables?*
Are not the choicest *Fables* of the *Poets,*
That were the *Fountains* and first *Springs of Wisdom,*
Wrapt in perplext *Allegories?* *Mam.* I urg'd that,
And clear'd to him, that *Sysiphus* was damn'd
To roll the ceasless Stone, only because
He *would* have ours *common.* Who is this? [*Doll is seen.*
God's precious. — What do you mean? Go in, *good Lady,*
Let me intreat you. Where's this Varlet? *Fac.* Sir?
 Sub. You very Knave! do you use me thus?
 Fac. Wherein, Sir?
 Sub. Go in, and see, you Traitor. Go.
 Mam. Who is it, Sir?
 Sub. Nothing, Sir: Nothing.
 Mam. What's the matter, good Sir?
I have not seen you thus distemper'd? Who is't?
 Sub. All Arts have still had, Sir, their *Adversaries;*
But ours the *most ignorant.* What now? [*Face returns.*
 Fac. 'Twas not my Fault, Sir; she would speak with you.
 Sub. Would she, Sir? Follow me.
 Mam. Stay, *Lungs.* *Fac.* I dare not, Sir.
 Mam. How! Pray thee stay.
 Fac. She's mad, Sir, and sent hither——
 Mam. Stay Man, what is she! *Fac.* A Lord's Sister, Sir.
(He'll be mad too. *Mam.* I warrant thee.)
Why sent hither?
 Fac. Sir, to be cur'd. *Sur.* Why Rascal!
 Fac. Loe you. Here, Sir. [*He goes out.*
 Mam. 'Fore God, a *Bradamante,* a brave Piece.
 Sur. Heart, this is a Bawdy-house! I'll be burnt else.
 Mam. O, by this Light, no. Do not wrong him. He's
Too scrupulous that way. It is his Vice.
No, he's a rare Physician, do him right,
An excellent *Paracelsian,* and has done
Strange Cures with *Mineral Physick.* He deals all
With Spirits, he. He will not hear a Word

Of *Galen*, or his tedious *Recipe's.*
How now, *Lungs!* [*Face again.*
   Fac. Softly, Sir, speak softly. I meant
To ha' told your Worship all. This must not hear.
   Mam. No, he will not be gull'd: let him alone.
   Fac. Y'are very right, Sir, she is a most rare *Scholar*,
And is gone mad with studying *Braughton's Works.*
If you but name a Word touching the *Hebrew*,
She falls into her Fit, and will discourse
So learnedly of *Genoalogies*,
As you would run mad too, to hear her, Sir.
   Mam. How might one do t' have Conference with her,
     Lungs?
   Fac. O, divers have run mad upon the conference,
I do not know, Sir: I am sent in haste,
To fetch a Viol. *Sur.* Be not gull'd, Sir *Mammon.*
   Mam. Wherein? Pray ye, be patient.
   Sur. Yes, as you are,
And trust confederate Knaves, and Bawds, and Whores.
   Mam. You are too foul, believe it. Come here, *Ulen*,
One word. *Fac.* I dare not, in good faith.
   Mam. Stay, Knave.
   Fac. H' is extream angry that you saw her, Sir.
   Mam. Drink that. What is she when she's out of her Fit?
   Fac. O, the most affablest creature, Sir! so merry!
So pleasant! she'll mount you up, like *Quick-silver*,
Over the Helm; and *circulate*, like *Oil*,
A very *Vegetal*, Discourse of *State*,
Of *Mathematicks*, *Bawdry*, any thing ⸺
   Mam. Is she no ways accessible? no means,
No trick to give a Man a taste of her ⸺ wit ⸺
Or so? — U l e n. *Fac.* I'll come to you again, Sir.
   Mam. Surly, I did not think, one o' your breeding
Would traduce Personages of worth. *Sur.* Sir *Epicure*,
Your friend to use: yet, still, loth to be gull'd.
I do not like your *Philosophical* Bawds.
Their *Stone* is Letchery enough to pay for,

Without this Bait. *Mam.* 'Heart, you abuse your self. —
I know the Lady, and her Friends, and Means,
The Original of this Disaster. Her Brother
Has told me all. *Sur.* And yet you ne'er saw her
Till now? *Mam.* O, yes, but I forgot. I have (believe it)
One o' the treacherousest memories, I do think,
Of all Mankind. *Sur.* What call you her Brother?
   Mam. My Lord ——
He wi' not have his Name known, now I think on't.
   Sur. A very treacherous Memory! *Mam.* O my faith.
   Sur. Tut. If you ha' it not about you, pass it,
Till we meet next. *Mam.* Nay, by this hand, 'tis true.
He's one I honour, and my Noble Friend,
And I respect his House. *Sur.* Heart, can it be,
That a grave Sir, a rich, that has no need,
A wise Sir, too, at other times, should thus
With his own Oaths, and Arguments, make hard means
To gull himself? And this be your *Elixir,*
Your *lapis mineralis,* and your *lunary,*
Give me your honest trick, yet, at *Primero,*
Or *Gleek;* and take your *lutum sapientis,*
Your *menstruum simplex:* I'll have Gold before you,
And with less Danger of the *Quicksilver,*
Or the hot *Sulphur.*
   Fac. Here's one from Captain *Face,* Sir?   [*To* Surley.
Desires you to meet him i' the *Temple-Church,*
Some half hour hence, and upon earnest Business.
Sir, if you please to quit us, now; and come
                        [*He whispers* Mammon.
Again within two Hours, you shall have
My Master busie examining o' the Works;
And I will steal you unto the Party,
That you may see her converse. Sir, shall I say,
You'll meet the Captain's Worship? *Sur.* I will.
But, by Attorney, and to a second Purpose.
Now, I am sure, it is a Bawdy-house;
I'll swear it, were the Marshal here to thank me:

The naming this Commander doth confirm it.
Don Face! why, h' is the most authentick Dealer
I' these Commodities! The *Superintendent*
To all the quainter Traffickers in Town.
He is the *Visitor*, and does appoint,
Who lies with whom, and at what Hour; what Price;
Which Gown; and in what Smock; what Fall; what Tyre.
Him will I prove, by a third Person to find
The Subtilties of this dark *Labyrinth:*
Which, if I do discover, dear Sir *Mammon*,
You'll give your poor Friend leave, tho' no *Philosopher*,
To laugh: for you that are, 'tis thought, shall weep.
  Fac. Sir, he does pray, you'll not forget.
  Sur. I will not, Sir.
Sir *Epicure*, I shall leave you?
  Mam. I follow you, straight.
  Fac. But do so, good Sir, to avoid Suspicion,
This Gent'man has a par'lous Head.
  Mam. But wilt thou, U L ᴇ N,
Be constant to thy Promise? *Fac.* As my Life, Sir.
  Mam. And wilt thou insinuate what I am? and praise me?
And say, I am a noble Fellow? *Fac.* O what else, Sir.
And that you'll make her royal, with the *Stone*,
An Empress; and your self King of *Bantam*.
  Mam. Wilt thou do this?
  Fac. Will I, Sir? *Mam. Lungs*, my *Lungs!*
I love thee. *Fac.* Send your Stuff, Sir, that my Master
May busie himself about projection.
  Mam. Th' hast witch'd me, Rogue? Take, go.
  Fac. Your Jack, and all, Sir.
  Mam. Thou art a Villain — I will send my Jack,
And the Weights too. Slave, I could bite thine Ear.
Away, thou dost not care for me. *Fac.* Not I, Sir?
  Mam. Come, I was born to make thee, my good Weasel,
Set thee on a Bench, and ha' thee twirl a Chain
With the best Lord's Vermine of 'em all. *Fac.* Away Sir.
  Mam. A *Count*, nay, a *Count-Palatine* ——

Fac. Good, Sir, go.
Mam. Shall not advance thee better: no, nor faster.

SCENE IV.

Subtle, Face, Dol.

Sub. Has he bit? Has he bit?
Fac. And swallow'd too, my *Subtle.*
I ha' giv'n him Line, and now he plays, yfaith.
Sub. And shall we twitch him?
Fac. Thorow both the Gills.
A Wench is a rare bait, with which a man
No sooner's taken, but he straight firks mad.
Sub. Dol, my Lord *Wha'ts'kums* Sister, you must now
Bear your self STATELICH. *Dol.* O let me alone.
I'll not forget my Race, I warrant you
I'll keep my Distance, laugh and talk aloud;
Have all the tricks of a proud scurvy Lady,
And be as rude as her Woman. *Fac.* Well said, *Sanguine.*
Sub. But will he send his Andirons?
Fac. His Jack too;
And's Iron shooing-Horn: I ha' spoken to him. Well,
I must not lose my wary Gamster, yonder.
Sub. O *Monsieur Caution,* that will not be gull'd?
Fac. I, if I can strike a fine hook into him, now,
The *Temple*-Church, there I have cast mine Angle.
Well, pray for me, I'll about it.
Sub. What more Gudgeons! [*One knocks.*
Dol, scout, scout; 'way, *Face,* you must go to the door.
'Pray God it may be my *Anabaptist.* Who is't, *Dol!*
Dol. I know him not. He looks like a Goldend-man.
Sub. Gods-so! 'tis he, he said he would send.
What call you him?
The *sanctified Elder,* that should deal
For *Mammon*'s Jack and Andirons! Let him in.
Stay, help me off, first with my Gown. Away
Madam, to your withdrawing Chamber. Now,

In a new tune, new gesture, but old Language.
This fellow is sent from one negotiates with me
About the *Stone* too; for the *holy Brethren*,
Of *Amsterdam*, the *exil'd Saints*: that hope
To raise their *Discipline* by it. I must use him
In some strange Fashion, now to make him admire me.

SCENE V.

Subtle, Face, Ananias.

Sub. Where is my Drudge? *Fac.* Sir.
Sub. Take away the *Recipient*,
And rectifie your *Menstrue* from the *Phlegma*.
Then pour it o' the *Sol*, in the *Cucurbite*,
And let 'em macerate together. *Fac.* Yes, Sir.
And save the Ground? *Sub.* No. *Terra damnata*
Must not have entrance in the *work*. Who are you?
 Ana. A *faithful Brother*, if it please you.
 Sub. What's that?
A *Lullianist?* a *Ripley? Filius artis?*
Can you *sublime* and *dulcifie? calcine?*
Know you the *Sapor Pontick? Sapor Styptick?*
Or what is *homogene*, or *heterogene?*
 Ana. I understand no *Heathen* Language, truly.
 Sub. Heathen, you *Knipper-Doling?* Is *Ars Sacra*,
Or *Chrysopœia*, or *Spagyrica*,
Or the *Pamphysick*, or *Panarchick* Knowledge,
A *Heathen* Language? *Ana. Heathen Greek!*
I take it. *Sub.* How? *Heathen Greek?*
 Ana. All's *Heathen* but the *Hebrew*.
 Sub. Sirrah, my Varlet, stand you forth, and speak to him.
Like a *Philosopher:* Answer i' the language.
Name the Vexations, and the Martyrizations
Of Metals in the Work. *Fac.* Sir, *Putrefaction*,
Solution, Ablution, Sublimation,
Cohobation, Calcination, Ceration, and
Fixation. *Sub.* This is *Heathen Greek*, to you now?

And whence comes *Vivification?* *Fac.* After *Mortification.*
Sub. What's *Cohobation.* *Fac.* 'Tis the pouring on
Your *Aqua Regis,* and then drawing him off,
To the *Trine Circle* of the seven *Spheres.*
Sub. What's the proper Passion of Metals?
Fac. Malleation.
Sub. What's your *ultimum supplicium auri?*
Fac. Antimonium.
Sub. This's *Heathen Greek* to you? And what's your *Mercury?*
Fac. A very fugitive, he will be gone, Sir.
Sub. How know you him? *Fac.* By his *Viscosity,*
His *Oleosity,* and his *Suscitability.*
Sub. How do you *sublime* him?
Fac. With the *Calce* of Egg-shells,
White Marble, *Chalk.* *Sub.* Your *Magisterium,* now?
What's that? *Fac.* Shifting, Sir, your Elements,
Dry into cold, cold into moist, moist into hot, hot into dry.
Sub. This's *Heathen Greek* to you still?
Your *Lapis Philosophicus?* *Fac.* 'Tis a *Stone,* and not
A *Stone;* a *Spirit,* a *Soul,* and a *Body:*
Which if you do *dissolve,* it is *dissolv'd;*
If you *coagulate,* it is *coagulated;*
If you make it to *fly,* it *flieth.* *Sub.* Enough.
This's *Heathen Greek* to you? What are you, Sir?
Ana. Please you, a Servant of the *Exil'd Brethren,*
That deal with Widows, and with Orphans Goods;
And make a just account unto the *Saints:*
A *Deacon.* *Sub.* O, you are sent from Master *Wholsome,*
Your *Teacher?* *Ana.* From *Tribulation Wholsome,*
Our very zealous *Pastor.* *Sub.* Good. I have
Some Orphans Goods to come here.
Ana. Of what kind, Sir?
Sub. Pewter, and Brass, Andirons, and Kitchenware,
Metals, that we must use our Med'cine on:
Wherein the *Brethren* may have a penn'orth,

For ready money. *Ana.* Were the Orphans Parents
Sincere *Professors?*
    Sub. Why do you ask? *Ana.* Because
We then are to deal justly, and give (in truth)
Their utmost value. *Sub.* 'Slid, you'ld cozen else,
And if their Parents were not of the *faithful?*
I will not trust you, now I think on't,
'Till I ha' talk'd with your *Pastor.* Ha' you brought money
To buy more Coals?
    Ana. No surely. *Sub.* No? How so?
    Ana. The *Brethren* bid me say to you, Sir,
Surely, they will not venture any more,
Till they have seen *Projection.*
    Sub. How! *Ana.* You have had,
For the Instruments, as Bricks and Lome, and Glasses,
Already thirty pound; and for Materials,
They say, some ninety more: And they have heard since,
That one at *Heidelberg,* made it of an Egg,
And a small Paper of Pindust.
    Sub. What's your Name?
    Ana. My Name is *Ananias.*
    Sub. Out, the Varlet
That cozen'd the *Apostles!* Hence, away,
Flee *Mischief;* had your *holy Consistory*
No Name to send me, of another Sound,
Than wicked *Ananias?* send your *Elders*
Hither, to make atonement for you, quickly,
And gi' me satisfaction; or out goes
The fire: and down th' *Alembicks,* and the fornace.
Piger Henricus, or what not. Thou wretch,
Both *Sericon,* and *Bufo,* shall be lost,
Tell 'em. All hope of rooting out the *Bishops,*
Or th' *Antichristian Hierarchy* shall perish,
If they stay threescore Minutes. The *Aqueity,*
Terreity, and *Sulphureity*
Shall run together again, and all be annull'd,
'Thou wicked *Ananias.* This will fetch 'em,

And make 'em haste towards their gulling more.
A man must deal like a rough Nurse, and fright
Those that are froward to an appetite.

SCENE VI.

Face, Subtle, Drugger.

Fac. H'is busie with his Spirits, but we'll upon him.
Sub. How now! What mates? What Baiards ha' we here?
Fac. I told you, he would be furious. Sir, here's *Nab*,
Has brought you another piece of Gold to look on:
(We must appease him. Give it me) and prays you,
You would devise (what is it *Nab?*) *Dru.* A sign, Sir.
Fac. I, a good lucky one, a thriving Sign, Doctor.
Sub. I was devising now.
Fac. ('Slight, do not say so,
He will repent he ga' you any more.)
What say you to his *Constellation,* Doctor?
The *Ballance?*
Sub. No, that way is stale, and common.
A Townsman born in *Taurus,* gives the Bull;
Or the Bull's-head: In *Aries,* the Ram.
A poor device. No, I will have his Name
Form'd in some mystick Character; whose *Radii,*
Striking the Senses of the Passers by,
Shall, by a virtual influence, breed affections,
That may result upon the Party owns it:
As thus —— *Fac. Nab!*
Sub. He shall have a Bell, that's *Abel;*
And by it standing one whose Name is *Dee,*
In a Rug Gown; there's *D,* and *Rug,* that's *Drug!*
And right anenst him a Dog snarling *Er;*
There's *Drugger, Abel Drugger.* That's his Sign.
And here's now *Mystery,* and *Hieroglyphick!*
Fac. Abel, thou art made.
Dru. I do thank his Worship.
Fac. Six o' thy Legs more will not do it, *Nab.*

He has brought you a Pipe of *Tobacco*, Doctor.
 Dru. Yes, Sir:
I have another thing I would impart ——
 Fac. Out with it, *Nab.*
 Dru. Sir, there is lodg'd, hard by me
A rich young Widow — *Fac.* Good? a *bona roba?*
 Dru. But Nineteen at the most.
 Fac. Very good, *Abel.*
 Dru. Marry, sh'is not in fashion yet; she wears
A hood; but 't stands acop. *Fac.* No matter, *Abel.*
 Dru. And I do now and then give her a *fucus* —
 Fac. What! dost thou deal, *Nab?*
 Sub. I did tell you, Captain.
 Dru. And Physick too sometime, Sir: for which she
  trusts me
With all her Mind. She's come here of purpose
T'o learn the Fashion.
 Fac. Good (his match too!) on, *Nab.*
 Dru. And she does strangely long to know her fortune.
 Fac. Gods lid, *Nab,* send her to the Doctor hither.
 Dru. Yes, I have spoke to her of his Worship already:
But she's afraid it will be blown abroad,
And hurt her Marriage. *Fac.* Hurt it? 'Tis the way
To heal it, if 'twere hurt; to make it more
Follow'd and sought: *Nab,* Thou shalt tell her this;
She'll be more known, more talk'd of; and your Widows
Are ne'er of any Price till they be famous;
Their Honour is the Multitude of Suitors:
Send her, it may be thy good fortune. What?
Thou dost not know. *Dru.* No, Sir, she'll never marry
Under a Knight. Her Brother has made a Vow.
 Fac. What, and dost thou despair, my little *Nab,*
Knowing what the Doctor has set down for thee,
And seeing so many of the City dubb'd?
One Glass o' thy water, with a *Madam,* I know
Will have it done, *Nab.* What's her Brother? a Knight?
 Dru. No, Sir, a Gentleman newly warm in his land, Sir,

Scarce cold in his one and twenty, that does govern
His Sister here; and is a Man himself
Of some three thousand a year, and is come up
To learn to quarrel, and to live by his Wits,
And will go down again and die i' the Country.
    Fac. How! to quarrel?
    Dru. Yes, Sir, to carry Quarrels,
As Gallants do, to manage 'em by Line.
    Fuc. 'Slid, *Nab!* The Doctor is the only Man
In *Christendom* for him. He has made a Table,
With *Mathematical* Demonstrations,
Touching the Art of Quarrels. He will give him
An Instrument to quarrel by. Go, bring 'em both,
Him and his Sister. And, for thee, with her
The Doctor happ'ly may persuade. Go to.
'Shat give his Worship a new Damask Suit
Upon the Premisses.
    Sub. O good Captain. *Fac.* He shall,
He is the honestest fellow, Doctor. Stay not,
No Offers, bring the Damask, and the Parties.
    Dru. I'll try my Power, Sir.
    Fac. And thy will too, *Nab.*
    Sub. 'Tis good *Tobacco*, this! what is't an Ounce?
    Fuc. He'll send you a Pound, Doctor.
    Sub. O, no. *Fuc.* He will do't,
It is the goodest Soul: *Abel,* about it.
(Thou shalt know more anon. Away, be gone.)
A miserable Rogue, and lives with Cheese,
And has the Worms. That was the Cause indeed
Why he came now. He dealt with me in private,
To get a Med'cine for 'em.
    Sub. And shall, Sir. This works.
    Fac. A wife, a wife for one on'us, my dear *Subtle:*
We'll e'en draw Lots, and he that fails, shall have
The more in Goods, the other has in Tail.
    Sub. Rather the less. For she may be so light
She may want Grains.

Fac. I, or be such a Burden
A Man would scarce endure her for the whole.
   Sub. Faith, best let's see her first, and then determine.
   Fac. Content. But *Dol* must ha' no breath on't.
   Sub. Mum.
Away, you to your *Surly* yonder, catch him.
   Fac. Pray God I ha' not staid too long.
   Sub. I fear it.

ACT III. SCENE I.

Tribulation, Ananias.

   Tri. These Chastisements are common to the Saints,
And such Rebukes we of the *Separation*
Must bear, with willing shoulders, as the trials
Sent forth to tempt our frailties.
   Ana. In pure Zeal
I do not like the Man: He is a *Heathen*,
And speaks the Language of *Canaan*, truly.
   Tri. I think him a prophane Person indeed.
   Ana. He bears
The visible mark of the Beast in his fore-head.
And for his *Stone*, it is a Work of Darkness,
And with *Philosophy* blinds the Eyes of man.
   Tri. Good Brother, we must bend unto all means
That may give furtherance to the *holy Cause*.
   Ana. Which his cannot: The *sanctified Cause*
Should have a *sanctified Course*.
   Tri. Not always necessary:
The Children of Perdition are oft times
Made Instruments even of the greatest Works.
Beside, we should give somewhat to Man's nature,
The place he lives in, still about the Fire,
And fume of Metals, that intoxicate
The brain of man, and make him prone to passion.
Where have you greater Atheists than your Cooks?

Or more prophane or cholerick, than your Glassmen?
More Antichristian than your Bell-founders?
What makes the Devil so devilish, I would ask you,
Sathan, our common Enemy, but his being
Perpetually about the Fire, and boiling
Brimstone and *Arsnick?* We must give, I say,
Unto the Motives, and the stirrers up
Of Humours in the Blood. It may be so.
When as the Work is done, the *Stone* is made,
This heat of his may turn into a Zeal,
And stand up for the beauteous Discipline,
Against the menstruous Cloth, and Rag of *Rome*.
We must await his calling, and the coming
Of the good Spirit. You did fault t' upbraid him
With the *Brethrens* blessing of *Heidelberg*, weighing
What need we have to hasten on the Work,
For the restoring of the *silenc'a Saints*,
Which ne'er will be, but by the *Philosopher's Stone*.
And so a learned Elder, one of *Scotland*,
Assur'd me; *Aurum potabile* being
The only Med'cine, for the civil Magistrate,
T' incline him to a feeling of the Cause;
And must be daily us'd in the Disease.

 Ana. I have not edified more, truly, by Man;
Not since the beautiful light first shone on me:
And I am sad my Zeal hath so offended.
 Tri. Let us call on him then.
 Ana. The motion's good,
And of the Spirit; I will knock first: Peace be within.

SCENE II.

Subtle, Tribulation, Ananias.

 Sub. O 'are you come? 'Twas time. Your threescore minutes
Were at last thread, you see; and down had gone
Furnus acediæ, Turris circulatorius:

Lembek, Bolts-head, Retort, and *Pellicane*
Had all been Cinders. Wicked *Ananias!*
Art thou returned? Nay then it goes down yet.
    Tri. Sir, be appeas'd, he is come to humble
Himself in Spirit, and to ask your Patience,
If too much Zeal hath carried him aside
From the due path. *Sub.* Why, this doth qualifie!
    Tri. The *Brethren* had no Purpose, verily,
To give you the least Grievance: but are ready
To lend their willing Hands to any project
The Spirit and you direct.
    Sub. This qualifies more!
    Tri. And for the Orphans Goods, let them be valu'd,
Or what is needful else to the holy Work,
It shall be numbred; here, by me, the *Saints*
Throw down their Purse before you.
    Sub. This qualifies most!
Why, thus it should be, now you understand.
Have I discours'd so unto you of our *Stones*
And of the good that it shall bring your Cause?
Shew'd you (beside the main of hiring Forces
Abroad, drawing the *Hollanders,* your Friends,
From th' *Indies,* to serve you, with all their Fleet)
That ev'n the med'cinal use should make you a Faction,
And Party in the Realm? As put the Case,
That some great man in State, he have the Gout,
Why, you but send three drops of your *Elixir,*
You help him straight: there you have made a Friend.
Another has the Palsie, or the Dropsie,
He takes of your incombustible stuff,
He's young again: there you have made a friend.
A Lady that is past the feat of Body,
Tho' not of mind, and hath her face decay'd
Beyond all cure of Paintings, you restore
With the Oil of *Talck;* there you have made a friend:
And all her friends. A Lord that is a *Leper,*
A Knight that has the Bone-ach, or a Squire

That hath both these, you make 'em smooth and sound,
With a bare *fricace* of your Med'cine: still
You increase your friends.
  Tri. I, 'tis very pregnant.
    Sub. And then the turning of this Lawyer's Pewter
To Plate at *Christmas* ——
    Ana. Christ-tide, I pray you.
 Sub. Yet, *Ananias!*
  Ana. I have done. *Sub.* Or changing
His parcel gilt to massie Gold. You cannot
But raise your friends. Withal, to be of Power
To pay an Army in the Field, to buy
The King of *France* out of his Realms, or *Spain*
Out of the *Indies.* What can you not do.
Against Lords spiritual and temporal,
That shall oppone you? *Tri.* Verily, 'tis true.
We may be temporal Lords ourselves, I take it.
    Sub. You may be any thing, and leave off to make
Long winded Exercises, or suck up
Your ha, and hum, in a tune. I not deny,
But such as are not grac'd in a State,
May, for their Ends, be adverse in Religion,
And get a tune to call the Flock together:
For (to say sooth) a tune does much with women,
And other phlegmatick People; it is your Bell.
  Ana. Bells are prophane: a tune may be religious.
  Sub. No warning with you? Then farewel my Patience.
'Slight, it shall down: I will not be thus tortur'd.
  Tri. I pray you, Sir.
  Sub. All shall perish. I have spoke it.
    Tri. Let me find Grace, Sir, in your eyes; the man
He stands corrected: neither did his zeal
(But as your self) allow a tune somewhere;
Which now being to'ard the Stone, we shall not need.
    Sub. No, nor your holy Vizard, to win Widows
To give you Legacies; or make zealous Wives
To rob their husbands for the *Common Cause:*

Nor take the start of Bonds broke but one day;
And say, *they were forfeited by Providence.*
Nor shall you need o'er Night to eat huge Meals,
To celebrate your next Day's Fast the better:
The whilst the *Brethren* and the *Sisters* humbled,
Abate the stiffness of the Flesh. Nor cast
Before your hungry Hearers scrupulous Bones;
As whether a Christian may hawk or hunt,
Or whether *Matrons of the holy Assembly*
May lay their Hair out, or wear Doublets;
Or have that Idol Starch about their Linnen.
 Ana. It is indeed an Idol.
 Tri. Mind him not, Sir.
I do command thee, Spirit (of zeal, but trouble)
To Peace within him. Pray you, Sir, go on.
 Sub. Nor shall you need to libel 'gainst the *Prelates*,
And shorten so your Ears against the hearing
Of the next wire-drawn Grace. Nor of necessity
Rail against Plays, to please the Alderman,
Whose daily Custard you devour. Nor lie
With zealous Rage till you are hoarse. Not one
Of these so singular Arts. Nor call your selves
By Names of *Tribulation, Persecution,*
Restraint, Long-Patience, and such like affected
By the whole family, or wood of you,
Only for Glory, and to catch the Ear
Of the *Disciple.* *Tri.* Truly, Sir, they are
Ways that the *Godly Brethren* have invented
For Propagation of the *Glorious Cause,*
As very notable Means, and whereby also
Themselves grow soon, and profitably famous.
 Sub. O, but the *Stone,* all's idle to't! nothing!
The Art of Angels, Nature's Miracle,
The Divine Secret that doth fly in Clouds
From *East* to *West;* and whose Tradition
Is not from Men, but Spirits.
 Ana. I hate *Traditions:*

I do not trust them —— *Tri.* Peace.
  Ana. They are *Popish* all.
I will not peace. I will not —— *Tri. Ananias.*
  Ana. Please the prophane, to grieve the godly, I may not.
  Sub. Well, *Ananias*, thou shalt over-come.
  Tri. It is an ignorant Zeal that haunts him, Sir.
But truly, else, a very faithful *Brother*,
A Botcher: and a Man, by Revelation,
That hath a competent knowledge of the Truth.
  Sub. Has he a competent Sum there i' the Bag
To buy the Goods within? I am made Guardian,
And must, for Charity and Conscience sake,
Now see the most be made for my poor Orphan:
Tho' I desire the *Brethren* too, good Gainers;
There they are within. When you have view'd, and bought 'em,
And tane the Inventory of what they are,
They are ready for *Projection;* there's no more
To do: Cast on the *Med'cine,* so much Silver
As there is Tin there, so much Gold as Brass,
I'll gi'it you in by Weight. *Tri.* But how long time,
Sir, must the *Saints* expect yet? *Sub.* Let me see,
How's the Moon now? Eight, nine, ten days hence,
He will be *Silver Potate;* then three days
Before he *Citronise:* some fifteen days
The *Magisterium* will be perfected.
  Ana. About the second Day of the third Week,
In the ninth Month? *Sub.* Yes, my good *Ananias.*
  Tri. What will the Orphans Goods arise to, think you?
  Sub. Some hundred Marks, as much as fill'd three Cars,
Unladed now: you'll make six Millions of 'em.
But I must ha' more Coals laid in.
  Tri. How? *Sub.* Another Load,
And then we have finish'd. We must now increase
Our Fire to *Ignis ardens,* we are past
Fimus equinus, Balnei Cineres,
And all those lenter heats. If the holy Purse

Should with this draught fall low, and that the Saints
Do need a present Sum, I have a trick
To melt the Pewter, you shall buy now, instantly,
And with a Tincture make you as good *Dutch* Dollars
As any are in *Holland*. *Tri.* Can you so?
   Sub. I, and shall 'bide the third Examination.
   Ana. It will be joyful Tidings to the *Brethren*.
   Sub. But you must carry it secret. *Tri.* I, but stay,
This Act of coining, is it lawful? *Ana.* Lawful?
We know no Magistrate. Or, if we did,
This's foreign Coin.
   Sub. It is no coining, Sir.
It is but casting. *Tri.* Ha? you distinguish well.
Casting of money may be lawful. *Ana.* 'Tis, Sir.
   Tri. Truly, I take it so.
   Sub. There's no scruple,
Sir, to be made of it; believe *Ananias:*
This Case of Conscience he is studied in.
   Tri. I'll make a question of it to the *Brethren*.
   Ana. The *Brethren* shall approve it lawful, doubt not.
Where shall it be done?
   Sub. For that we'll talk anon.   [*Knock without.*
There's some to speak with me. Go in, I pray you,
And view the Parcels. That's the Inventory.
I'll come to you straight. Who is it? *Face!* Appear.

SCENE III.

Subtle, Face, Dol.

   Sub. How now, Good Prize?
   Fac. Good Pox! Yond' caustive Cheater
Never came on. *Sub.* How then?
   Fac. I ha' walk'd the round
Till now, and no such thing.
   Sub. And ha' you quit him?
   Fac. Quit him? an hell would quit him too, he were happy.
'Slight would you have me stalk like a Mill-Jade,

All day, for one that will not yield us Grains?
I know him of old. *Sub.* O but to ha' gull'd him,
Had been a Maistry. *Fac.* Let him go, black Boy,
And turn thee, that some fresh News may possess thee.
A noble *Count*, a *Don* of *Spain*, my dear
Delicious Compeer, and my Party-bawd,
Who is come hither, private for his Conscience,
And brought Munition with him, six great Sloops,
Bigger than three *Dutch* Hoys, beside round Trunks,
Furnish'd with Pistolets, and Pieces of Eight,
Will straight be here, my Rogue, to have thy Bath,
('That is the Colour) and to make his Battry
Upon our *Dol*, our Castle, our Cinque-Port,
Our *Dover* Pier, or what thou wilt. Where is she?
She must prepare Perfumes, delicate Linnen,
The Bath in chief, a Banquet, and her Wit,
Where is the *Doxy?* *Sub.* I'll send her to thee:
And but dispatch my Brace of little *John Leydens*,
And come again my self. *Fac.* Are they within then?
   Sub. Numbring the Sum. *Fac.* How much?
   Sub. A hundred Marks, Boy.
   Fac. Why, this's a lucky day! Ten Pounds of *Mammon!*
Three o' my Clark! A Portague o' my Grocer!
This o' the *Brethren!* beside Reversions,
And States to come i' the Widow, and my *Count?*
My share to day will not be bought for forty——
   Dol. What?
   Fac. Pounds, dainty *Dorothee*, art thou so near?
   Dol. Yes, say Lord General, how fares our Camp?
   Fac. As with the few that had intrench'd themselves
Safe, by their Discipline, against a World, *Dol*,
And laugh'd within those Trenches, and grew fat
With thinking on the Booties, *Dol*, brought in
Daily by their small Parties. This dear hour
A doughty *Don* is taken with my *Dol;*
And thou maist make his Ransom what thou wilt,
My *Donsabel!* He shall be brought here fetter'd

With thy fair Looks before he sees thee; and thrown
In a Down-bed, as dark as any Dungeon,
Where thou shalt keep him waking with thy Drum;
Thy Drum, my *Dol;* thy Drum; till he be tame,
As the poor Black-Birds were i' the great Frost,
Or Bees are with a Bason; and so hive him
I' the Swan-skin Coverlid, and Cambrick Sheets,
Till he work Honey and Wax, my little *God's-gift.*
 Dol. What is he, General? *Fac.* An *Adalantado,*
A *Grande,* Girl. Was not my *Dapper* here yet?
 Dol. No. *Fac.* Nor my *Drugger?*
 Dol. Neither. *Fac.* A Pox on 'em,
They are so long a furnishing! Such Stinkards
Would not be seen upon these festival days.
How now! ha' you done?
 Sub. Done. They are gone. The Sum
Is here in bank, my *Face.* I would we knew
Another Chapman now would buy them out-right.
 Fac. 'Slid, *Nab* shall do't against he ha' the Widow,
To furnish Houshold. *Sub.* Excellent well thought on.
Pray God he come. *Fac.* I pray he keep away
Till our new Business be o'er past. *Sub.* But, *Face,*
How cam'st thou by this secret *Don? Fac.* A Spirit
Brought me th' Intelligence in a Paper here,
As I was conjuring yonder in my Circle
For *Surly,* I ha' my Flies abroad. Your Bath
Is famous, *Subtle,* by my means. Sweet *Dol,*
He will come here in a hir'd Coach, obscure,
And our own Coach-man, whom I have sent as Guide,
No Creature else. Who's that?   [*One knocks.*
 Sub. It is not he!
 Fac. O, no, not yet this Hour.
 Sub. Who is't? *Dol.* Dapper,
Your Clerk. *Fac.* God's will then, *Queen of Fairy,*
On with your Tyre; and Doctor with your Robes.
Let's dispatch him for God's sake. *Sub.* 'Twill be long.
 Fac. I warrant you, take but the *Cues* I give you,

It shall be brief enough. 'Slight, here are more!
Abel, and I think the angry Boy, the Heir,
That fain would quarrel.
    Sub. And the Widow? *Fac.* No,
Not that I see. Away. O Sir, you are welcome.

SCENE IV.

Face, Dapper, Drugger, Kastril.

Fac. The Doctor is within moving for you;
(I have had the most to do to win him to it)
He swears you'll be the Dearling of the Dice:
He never heard her Highness doat till now (he says)
Your Aunt has given you the most gracious Words
That can be thought on. *Dap.* Shall I see her Grace?
    Fac. See her, and kiss her too. What, honest *Nab?*
Ha'st brought the Damask? *Nab.* No, Sir, here's *Tobacco.*
    Fac. 'Tis well done, *Nab:* Thou'lt bring the Damask too?
    Dru. Yes, here's the Gentleman, Captain, Master *Kastril*,
I have brought to see the Doctor.
    Fac. Where's the Widow?
    Dru. Sir, as he likes, his Sister (he says) shall come.
    Fac. O, is it so? Good time. Is your Name *Kastril*, Sir?
    Kas. I, and the best of the *Kastrils*, I'ld be sorry else,
By fifteen hundred a Year. Where is the Doctor?
My mad Tobacco-Boy, here, tells me of one
That can do things. Has he any Skill? *Fac.* Wherein, Sir?
    Kas. To carry a Business, manage a Quarrel fairly,
Upon fit terms. *Fac.* It seems, Sir, yo'are but young
About the Town, that can make that a Question.
    Kas. Sir, not so young, but I have heard some Speech
Of the angry Boys, and seen 'em take Tobacco;
And in his Shop: And I can take it too.
And I would fain be one of 'em, and go down
And practise i' the Country. *Fac.* Sir, for the *Duello*,
The Doctor, I assure you, shall inform you,
To the least shadow of a Hair: and shew you

An Instrument he has of his own making,
Wherewith no sooner shall you make report
Of any Quarrel, but he will take the height on't
Most instantly, and tell in what degree
Of Safety it lies in, or Mortality.
And how it may be born, whether in a *Right Line*,
Or a *Half Circle*, or may else be cast
Into an *Angle blunt*, if not *acute:*
All this he will demonstrate. And then, Rules
To give and take the Lie by. *Kas.* How? to take it?
   Fac. Yes, in *Oblique* he'll shew you, or in *Circle*,
But never in *Diameter.* The whole Town
Study his *Theorems*, and dispute them ordinarily
At the eating *Academies.* *Kas.* But does he teach
Living by the Wits too? *Fac.* Any thing whatever.
You cannot think that Subtilty but he reads it.
He made me a Captain. I was a stark Pimp,
Just o' your standing, 'fore I met with him:
It i' not two Months since. I'll tell you his Method:
First, he will enter you at some Ordinary.
   Kas. No, I'll not come there. You shall pardon me.
   Fac. For why, Sir?
   Kas. There's gaming there, and Tricks.
   Fac. Why, would you be
A Gallant, and not game? *Kas.* I, 'twill spend a Man.
   Fac. Spend you? It will repair you when you are spent.
How do they live by their Wits there, that have vented
Six times your Fortunes?
   Kas. What, three thousand a Year!
   Fac. I, forty thousand.
   Kas. Are there such? *Fac.* I, Sir,
And Gallants yet. Here's a young Gentleman,
Is born to nothing, forty Marks a Year,
Which I count nothing. He is to be initiated,
And have a *Fly* o' the Doctor. He will win you
By unresistable luck, within this Fortnight,
Enough to buy a *Barony.* They will set him

THE ALCHEMIST.

Upmost at the Groom-Porters all the *Christmas!*
And for the whole Year through at every place
Where there is Play, present him with the Chair;
The best Attendance, the best Drink; sometimes
Two Glasses of *Canary*, and pay nothing;
The purest Linnen, and the sharpest Knife,
The Partridge next his Trencher; and somewhere
The dainty Bed, in private with the dainty.
You shall ha' your Ordinaries bid for him,
As Play-Houses for a Poet; and the Master
Pray him aloud to name what Dish he affects,
Which must be butter'd Shrimps; and those that drink
To no Mouth else, will drink to his, as being
The goodly *President* Mouth of all the Board.
   Kas. Do you not gull one?
   Fac. 'Od's my life! Do you think it?
You shall have a cast Commander, (can but get
In credit with a Glover, or a Spurrier,
For some two pair of either's Ware, aforehand)
Will, by most swift Posts dealing with him,
Arrive at competent means to keep himself,
His Punk, and naked Boy, in excellent fashion,
And be admir'd for't. *Kas.* Will the Doctor teach this?
   Fac. He will do more, Sir, when your Land is gone.
(As Men of Spirit hate to keep Earth long)
In a Vacation, when small Money is stirring,
And Ordinaries suspended till the Term,
He'll shew a Perspective, where on one side
You shall behold the Faces and the Persons
Of all sufficient young Heirs in Town,
Whose Bonds are currant for Commodity;
On th' other side, the Merchant's Forms, and others,
That without help of any second Broker,
(Who would expect a Share) will trust such Parcels.
In the third Square, the very Street, and Sign
Where the Commodity dwells, and does but wait
To be delivered, be it Pepper, Soap,

Hops, or Tobacco, Oat-meal, Woad, or Cheeses.
All which you may so handle, to enjoy
To your own use, and never stand oblig'd.
    Kas. I'faith! Is he such a Fellow?
    Fac. Why, *Nab* here knows him.
And then for making Matches for rich Widows,
Young Gentlewomen, Heirs, the fortunat'st Man!
He's sent to, far and near, all over *England*,
To have his Counsel, and to know their Fortunes.
    Kas. God's will, my Suster shall see him.
    Fac. I'll tell you, Sir,
What he did tell me of *Nab*. It's a strange thing!
(By the way, you must eat no Cheese, *Nab*, it breeds Melan-
    choly:
And that same Melancholy breeds Worms) but pass it,
He told me, honest *Nab* here was ne'er at Tavern,
But once in's life! *Dru.* Truth, and no more I was not.
    Fac. And then he was so sick ——
    Dru. Could he tell you that too?
    Fac. How should I know it?
    Dru. In troth we had been a shooting,
And had a piece of fat Ram-mutton to supper,
That lay so heavy o' my Stomach ——
    Fac. And he has no Head
To bear any Wine; for what with the Noise o' the Fidlers,
And care of his Shop, for he dares keep no Servants ——
    Dru. My head did so ake ——
    Fac. As he was fain to be brought home,
The Doctor told me. And then a good *Old Woman* ——
    Dru. (Yes, faith, she dwells in *Sea-coal-lane*,) did
    cure me,
With sodden Ale, and Pellitory o' the Wall:
Cost me but Two-pence. I had another Sickness
Was worse than that. *Fac.* I, that was with the Grief
Thou took'st for being sess'd at Eighteen-pence,
For the Water-Work. *Dru.* In truth, and it was like
T'have cost me almost my Life. *Fac.* Thy Hair went off?

Dru. Yes, 't was done for spight.
Fac. Nay, so says the Doctor.
    Kas. Pray thee, Tobacco-boy, go fetch my Suster,
I'll see this learned Boy before I go:
And so shall she. *Fac.* Sir, he is busie now:
But if you have a Sister to fetch hither,
Perhaps your own Pains may command her sooner;
And he by that time will be free. *Kas.* I go.
    Fac. *Drugger*, she's thine: the Damask. (*Subtle* and I must
        wrestle for her.) Come on, Master *Dapper*.
You see how I turn Clients here away,
To give your Cause dispatch. Ha' you perform'd
The Ceremonies were enjoin'd you?
    Dap. Yes, o' the Vinegar
And the clean Shirt.
    Fac. 'Tis well: that Shirt may do you
More worship than you think. Your Aunt's afire,
But that she will not shew it, t' have a sight on you.
Ha' you provided for her Grace's Servants?
    Dap. Yes, here are six score *Edward*'s Shillings.
    Fac. Good.
    Dap. And an old *Harry*'s Sovereign. *Fac.* Very good.
    Dap. And three *James* Shillings, and an *Elizabeth* Groat,
Just twenty Nobles. *Fac.* O, you are too just.
I would you had had the other Noble in *Maries*.
    Dap. I have some *Philip* and *Maries*. *Fac.* I, those same
Are best of all. Where are they? Hark, the Doctor.

SCENE V.

Subtle, Face, Dapper, Dol.

    Subtle *disguis'd like a Priest of* Fairy.
  Sub. Is yet her Graces Cousin come? *Fac.* He is come.
  Sub. And is he fasting? *Fac.* Yes.
  Sub. And hath he cry'd *Hum?*
  Fac. Thrice, you must answer. *Dap.* Thrice.

Sub. And as oft *Buz?*
Fac. If you have, say.   *Dap.* I have.   *Sub.* Then, to her
   Cuz,
Hoping that he hath Vinegar'd his Senses,
As he was bid, the *Fairy Queen* dispenses,
By me, this Robe, the Petticoat of *Fortune;*
Which that he straight put on, she doth importune.
And though to *Fortune* near be her Petticoat,
Yet nearer is her Smock, the Queen doth note:
And therefore, even of that a piece she hath sent,
Which, being a Child, to wrap him in was rent;
And prays him for a Scarf he now will wear it
(With as much Love as then her *Grace* did tear it)
About his Eyes, to shew he is fortunate.
                    [*They blind him with a Rag.*
And, trusting unto her to make his State,
He'll throw away all worldly Pelf about him;
Which that he will perform, she doth not doubt him.
   Fac. She need not doubt him, Sir. Alas, he has nothing,
But what he will part withal as willingly,
Upon her *Graces* word ('Throw away your Purse.)
As she would ask it: (Handkerchiefs and all)
She cannot bid that thing, but he'll obey.
(If you have a Ring about you, cast it off,
Or a silver Seal at your Wrist; her *Grace* will send
Her *Fairies* here to search you, therefore deal
Directly with her *Highness.* If they find
That you conceal a Mite, you are undone.)
                    [*He throws away, as they bid him.*
   Dap. Truly, there's all.
   Fac. All what?   *Dap.* My Money, truly.
   Fac. Keep nothing that is transitory about you.
(Bid *Dol* play Musick.) Look, the *Elves* are come
To pinch you, if you tell not truth. Advise you.
          [*Dol enters with a Cittern; they pinch him.*
   Dap. O, I have a Paper with a Spur-ryal in't.
   Fac. Ti, ti.

They knew't, they say. *Sub.* Ti, ti, ti, ti, he has more yet.
Fac. Ti, ti, ti, ti. I' the t' other Pocket?
Sub. Titi, titi, titi, titi.
They must pinch him, or he will never confess, they say.
Dap. O, o.
Fac. Nay, pray you hold. He is her *Graces* Nephew.
Ti, ti, ti? What care you? Good faith, you shall care.
Deal plainly, Sir, and shame the *Fairies*. Shew
You are an Innocent.
Dap. By this good Light, I ha' nothing.
Sub. Ti, ti, ti, ti, to, ta. He does equivocate, she says.
Ti, ti do ti, ti ti do, ti da; and swears by the Light when he is
    blinded.
Dap. By this good Dark, I ha' nothing but a Half-Crown
Of Gold, about my Wrist, that my Love gave me;
And a Leaden Heart I wore sin' she forsook me.
Fac. I thought 'twas something. And would you incur
Your Aunts displeasure for these Trifles? Come,
I had rather you had thrown away twenty Half-crowns.
You may wear your Leaden Heart still. How now?
Sub. What News, *Dol*?
Dol. Yonder's your Knight, Sir *Mammon*.
Fac. Gods lid, we never thought of him till now.
Where is he? *Dol.* Here hard by. H's at the Door.
Sub. And you are not ready now? *Dol.* Get his Suit.
He must be sent back. *Fac.* O, by no means.
What shall we do with this same Puffing here,
Now he's o' the Spit?
Sub. Why, lay him back a while,
With some Device. Ti, ti, ti, ti, ti, ti, Would her *Grace* speak
    with me?
I come. Help, *Dol.* *Fac.* Who's there? Sir *Epicure*,
    [*He speaks through the Key-hole, the other knocking.*
My Master's i' the way. Please you to walk
Three or four Turns, but till his back be turn'd,
And I am for you. Quickly, *Dol.* *Sub.* Her *Grace*
Commends her kindly to you, Master *Dapper.*

Dap. I long to see her *Grace.* *Sub.* She now is set
At Dinner in her Bed, and has sent you
From her own private Trencher a dead Mouse,
And a piece of Gingerbread, to be merry withal,
And stay your Stomach, lest you faint with fasting:
Yet if you could hold out till she saw you (she says)
It would be better for you. *Fac.* Sir, he shall
Hold out, and 'twere this two Hours, for her *Highness;*
I can assure you that. We will not lose
All we ha' done —— *Sub.* He must not see, nor speak
To any body, till then. *Fac.* For that we'll put, Sir,
A Stay in's Mouth. *Sub.* Of what? *Fac.* Of Gingerbread.
Make you it fit. He that hath pleas'd her *Grace*
Thus far, shall not now crinkle for a little.
Gape, Sir, and let him fit you. *Sub.* Where shall we now
Bestow him? *Dol.* I' the Privy. *Sub.* Come along, Sir,
I now must shew you *Fortune*'s Privy Lodgings.
    Fac. Are they perfum'd, and his Bath ready? *Sub.* All.
Only the Fumigation's somewhat strong.
    Fac. Sir *Epicure,* I am yours, Sir, by and by.

ACT IV. SCENE I.

Face, Mammon, Dol.

O Sir, yo' are come i' the only finest time? ——
  Mam. Where's Master?
  Fac. Now preparing for Projection, Sir.
Your Stuff will b' all chang'd shortly.
  Mam. Into Gold?
  Fac. To Gold and Silver, Sir. *Mam.* Silver I care
    not for.
  Fac. Yes, Sir, a little to give Beggars.
  Mam. Where's the Lady?
  Fac. At hand here. I ha' told her such brave things
    o' you,

Touching your Bounty, and your noble Spirit —
Mam. Hast thou?
Fac. As she is almost in her Fit to see you.
But, good Sir, no *Divinity* i' your Conference,
For fear of putting her in rage — *Mam.* I warrant thee.
Fac. Six Men will not hold her down. And then
If the old Man should hear or see you —— *Mam.* Fear not.
Fac. The very House, Sir, would run mad. You know it,
How scrupulous he is, and violent,
'Gainst the least act of Sin. *Physick,* or *Mathematicks,*
Poetry, State, or *Bawd'ry* (as I told you)
She will endure, and never startle: But
No word of Controversie. *Mam.* I am school'd, good ULEN.
Fac. And you must praise her House, remember that,
And her Nobility. *Mam.* Let me alone:
No *Herald,* nor no *Antiquary, Lungs,*
Shall do it better. Go. *Fac.* Why, this is yet
A kind of modern Happiness, to have
Dol Common for a great Lady. *Mam.* Now, *Epicure,*
Heighten thy self, talk to her, all in Gold;
Rain her as many Showers as *Jove* did Drops
Unto his *Danae!* Shew the *God* a Miser,
Compar'd with *Mammon.* What? the *Stone* will do't.
She shall feel Gold, taste Gold, hear Gold, sleep Gold:
Nay, we will *concumbere* Gold. I will be puissant,
And mighty in my talk to her. Here she comes.
Fac. To him, *Dol,* suckle him. — This is the noble Knight,
I told your Ladyship —— *Mam.* Madam, with your pardon,
I kiss your Vesture. *Dol.* Sir, I were uncivil
If I would suffer that; my Lip to you, Sir.
Mam. I hope my Lord your Brother be in health, Lady.
Dol. My Lord, my Brother is, though I no Lady, Sir.
Fac. (Well said, my *Guiny*-bird.)
Mam. Right noble Madam ——
Fac. (O, we shall have most fierce Idolatry.)
Mam. 'Tis your Prerogative.
Dol. Rather your Courtesie.

Mam. Were there nought else t'enlarge your Vertues
    to me,
These Answers speak your Breeding and your Blood.
    Dol. Blood we boast none, Sir, a poor Barons Daughter.
    Mam. Poor! and gat you? Prophane not. Had your
        father
Slept all the happy remnant of my Life
After that Act, lien but there still, and panted,
H' had done enough to make himself, his Issue,
And his Posterity noble. *Dol.* Sir, although
We may be said to want the Gilt and Trapings,
The Dress of Honour, yet we strive to keep
The Seeds and the Materials. *Mam.* I do see
The old Ingredient, Vertue, was not lost,
Nor the Drug Money us'd to make your Compound.
There is a strange Nobility i' your Eye,
This Lip, that Chin! Methinks you do resemble
One o' the *Austriack* Princes. *Fac.* Very like,
Her Father was an *Irish* Costarmonger.
    Mam. The House of *Valois* just had such a Nose,
And such a Forehead yet the *Medici*
Of *Florence* boast. *Dol.* Troth, and I have been lik'ned
To all these Princes. *Fac.* I'll be sworn, I heard it.
    Mam. I know not how! it is not any one,
But e'n the very choice of all their Features.
    Fac. I'll in, and laugh. *Mam.* A certain Toach, or Air,
That sparkles a Divinity, beyond
An earthly Beauty! *Dol.* O, you play the Courtier.
    Mam. Good Lady, gi' me leave ——
    Dol. In faith, I may not,
To mock me, Sir. *Mam.* To burn in this sweet Flame;
The *Phœnix* never knew a nobler Death.
    Dol. Nay, now you court the Courtier, and destroy
What you would build. This Art, Sir, i' your words,
Calls your whole Faith in question. *Mam.* By my Soul ——
    Dol. Nay Oaths are made o' the same air, Sir.
    Mam. Nature

Never bestow'd upon Mortality
A more unblam'd, a more harmonious Feature:
She play'd the Step-dame in all Faces else.
Sweet Madam, le' me be particular ——
    Dol. Particular, Sir? I pray you, know your Distance.
    Mam. In no ill sense, sweet Lady, but to ask
How you fair Graces pass the Hours? I see
Yo' are lodg'd here, i' the House of a rare Man,
An excellent Artist; but what's that to you?
    Dol. Yes, Sir; I study here the *Mathematicks*,
And *Distillation*. *Mam.* O, cry you pardon.
He's a Divine Instructor, can extract
The Souls of all things by his Art; call all
The Vertues, and the Miracles of the Sun,
Into a temperate Furnace; teach dull Nature
What her own Forces are. A Man, the Emp'ror
Has courted, above *Kelley;* sent his Medals
And Chains, t' invite him.
    Dol. I, and for his Physick, Sir ——
    Mam. Above the Art of *Æsculapius*,
That drew the Envy of the Thunderer!
I know all this, and more. *Dol.* Troth, I am taken, Sir,
Whole with these Studies, that contemplate Nature.
    Mam. It is a noble Humour; but this Form
Was not intended to so dark a use.
Had you been crooked, foul, of some course Mold,
A Cloyster had done well; but such a Feature
That might stand up the Glory of a Kingdom,
To live Recluse, is a meer *Solœcism*,
Though in a Nunnery. It must not be.
I muse, my Lord your Brother will permit it!
You should spend half my Land first, were I he.
Does not this Diamant better on my Finger,
Than i' the Quarry? *Dol.* Yes. *Mam.* Why, you are
    like it.
You were created, Lady, for the Light!
Here, you shall wear it; take it, the first Pledge

Of what I speak, to bind you to believe me.
Dol. In Chains of Adamant?
Mam. Yes, the strongest Bands.
And take a Secret too. Here, by your Side,
Doth stand, this Hour, the happiest Man in *Europe.*
Dol. You are contented, Sir? *Mam.* Nay, in true being,
The Envy of Princes and the Fear of States.
Dol. Say you so, Sir *Epicure!*
Mam. Yes, and thou shalt prove it,
Daughter of Honour. I have cast mine Eye
Upon thy Form, and I will rear this Beauty
Above all Styles. *Dol.* You mean no Treason, Sir!
Mam. No, I will take away that Jealousie.
I am the Lord of the *Philosopher's Stone,*
And thou the Lady. *Dol.* How, Sir! ha' you that?
Mam. I am the Master of the *Mastery.*
This day the good old Wretch here o' the House
Has made it for us. Now he's at *Projection.*
Think there thy first Wish now; let me hear it,
And it shall rain into thy Lap, no Shower,
But Floods of Gold, whole Cataracts, a Deluge,
To get a Nation on thee. *Dol.* You are pleas'd, Sir,
To work on the Ambition of our Sex.
Mam. I'm pleas'd the Glory of her Sex should know,
This Nook, here, of the *Friers* is no Climate
For her to live obscurely in, to learn
Physick and Surgery, for the Constables Wife
Of some odd Hundred in *Essex:* but come forth,
And taste the Air of Palaces; eat, drink
The Toils of *Emp'ricks,* and their boasted Practice;
Tincture of Pearl, and Corral, Gold and Amber;
Be seen at Feasts and Triumphs; have it ask'd,
What Miracle she is? Set all the Eyes
Of Court afire, like a Burning-glass,
And work 'em into Cinders, when the Jewels
Of twenty Stars adorn thee, and the Light
Strikes out the Stars; that when thy Name is mention'd,

Queens may look pale; and we but shewing our Love,
Nero's Poppæa may be lost in Story!
Thus will we have it. *Dol.* I could well consent, Sir.
But, in a Monarchy, how will this be?
The Prince will soon take notice, and both seise
You and your *Stone*, it being a Wealth unfit
For any private Subject. *Mam.* If he knew it.
 Dol. Your self do boast it, Sir. *Mam.* To thee, my
  Life.
 Dol. O, but beware, Sir! You may come to end
The remnant of your Days in a loath'd Prison,
By speaking of it. *Mam.* 'Tis no idle fear:
We'll therefore go withal, my Girl, and live
In a Free State, where we will eat our Mullets,
Sous'd in High-Country Wines, sup Pheasants Eggs,
And have our Cockles, boil'd in Silver Shels,
Our Shrimps to swim again, as when they liv'd,
In a rare Butter, made of Dolphins Milk,
Whose Cream does look like Opals; and with these
Delicate Meats set our selves high for Pleasure,
And take us down again, and then renew
Our Youth and Strength, with drinking the *Elixir*,
And so enjoy a Perpetuity
Of Life and Lust. And thou shalt ha' thy Wardrobe
Richer than *Nature's*, still to change thy self,
And vary oftner, for thy Pride, than she,
Or *Art*, her wise and almost-equal Servant.
 Fac. Sir, you are too loud, I hear you ev'ry word
Into the Laboratory. Some fitter place:
The Garden, or great Chamber above. How like you her?
 Mam. Excellent *Lungs!* There's for thee.
 Fac. But do you hear?
Good Sir, beware, no mention of the *Rabbins*.
 Mam. We think not on 'em.
 Fac. O, it is well, Sir. *Subtle!*

SCENE II.

Face, Subtle, Kastril, Dame Pliant.

Fac. Dost thou not laugh?
Sub. Yes. Are they gone? *Fac.* All's clear.
Sub. The Widow is come.
Fac. And your quarrelling Disciple?
Sub. I. *Fac.* I must to my Captainship again then.
Sub. Stay, bring 'em in first.
Fac. So I meant. What is she?
A *Bony-bell? Sub.* I know not. *Fac.* We'll draw Lots,
You'll stand to that?
Sub. What else? *Fac.* O, for a Suit,
To fall now like a Curtain, flap. *Sub.* To th' Door, Man!
Fac. You'll have the first Kiss, 'cause I am not ready.
Sub. Yes, and perhaps hit you thro' both the Nostrils.
Fac. Who would you speak with?
Kas. Where's the Captain? *Fac.* Gone, Sir,
About some Business.
Kas. Gone? *Fac.* He'll return straight.
But Master Doctor, his Lieutenant, is here.
Sub. Come near, my worshipful Boy, my *Terræ Fili,*
That is, my Boy of Land; make thy Approaches:
Welcome: I know thy Lust, and thy Desires,
And I will serve and satisfie 'em. Begin,
Charge me from thence, or thence, or in this Line;
Here is my Center; ground thy Quarrel. *Kas.* You lie.
Sub. How, Child of Wrath and Anger! the loud Lie?
For what, my sudden Boy? *Kas.* Nay, that look you to,
I am afore-hand. *Sub.* O, this's no true *Grammar,*
And as ill *Logick!* You must render Causes, Child,
Your first and second *Intentions,* know your *Canons,*
And your *Divisions, Moods, Degrees,* and *Differences,*
Your *Predicaments, Substance,* and *Accident,*
Series *extern* and *intern,* with their *Causes,*
Efficient, Material, Formal, Final,
And ha' your *Elements* perfect — *Kas.* What is this!

The angry Tongue he talks in? *Sub.* That *false Precept*
Of being before-hand, has deceiv'd a number,
And made 'em enter Quarrels, often-times,
Before they were aware; and afterward,
Against their Wills. *Kas.* How must I do then, Sir?
  Sub. I cry this Lady mercy: She should first
Have been saluted. I do call you Lady,
Because you are to be one, ere't be long,
My soft and buxom Widow. [*He kisses her.*
  Kas. Is she, i' faith?
  Sub. Yes, or my Art is an egregious Liar.
  Kas. How know you?
  Sub. By inspection on her Forehead,
And subtlety of her Lip, which must be tasted
Often, to make a Judgment. 'Slight, she melts
  [*He kisses her again.*
Like a *Myrabolane!* Here is yet a Line,
In *Rivo Frontis*, tells me, he is no Knight.
  Pli. What is he then, Sir? *Sub.* Let me see your Hand.
O, your *Linea Fortunæ* makes it plain;
And *Stella* here, in *Monte Veneris;*
But most of all, *junctura annularis.*
He is a Soldier, or a Man of Art, Lady;
But shall have some great Honour shortly. *Pli.* Brother,
He's a rare Man, believe me! *Kas.* Hold your peace.
Here comes the t'other rare Man. 'Save you, *Captain.*
  Fac. Good Master *Kastril*, is this your Sister? *Kas.*
    I, Sir.
Please to kiss her, and be proud to know her.
  Fac. I shall be proud to know you, Lady. *Pli.* Brother,
He calls me Lady too. *Kas.* I, peace. I heard it.
  Fac. The *Count* is come.
  Sub. Where is he? *Fac.* At the Door.
  Sub. Why, you must entertain him. *Fac.* What'll you do
With these the while?
  Sub. Why, have 'em up, and shew 'em
Some fustian Book, or the dark Glass. *Fac.* 'Fore God,

She is a delicate Dab chick! I must have her.
   Sub. Must you? I, if your Fortune will, you must.
Come, Sir, the Captain will come to us presently;
I'll ha' you to my Chamber of *Demonstrations,*
Where I'll shew you both the *Grammar* and *Logick,*
And *Rhetorick* of Quarrelling; my whole Method
Drawn out in Tables; and my Instrument,
That hath the several Scales upou't, shall make you
Able to quarrel, at a Straws-breadth by Moon-light.
And, Lady, I'll have you look in a Glass,
Some half an hour, but to clear your Eye-sight,
Against you see your Fortune; which is greater
Than I may judge upon the sudden, trust me.

SCENE III.

Face, Subtle, Surly.

   Fac. Where are you, Doctor?
   Sub. I'll come to you presently.
   Fac. I will ha' this same Widow, now I ha' seen her,
On any Composition. *Sub.* What do you say?
   Fac. Ha' you dispos'd of them? *Sub.* I ha' sent 'em *up.*
   Fac. Subtle, In troth, I needs must have this *Widow.*
   Sub. Is that the matter?
   Fac. Nay, but hear me. *Sub.* Go to,
If you rebel once, *Dol* shall know it all.
Therefore be quiet, and obey your Chance.
   Fac. Nay, thou art so violent now — Do but *conceive:*
Thou art old, and canst not serve ——
   Sub. Who, cannot I?
'Slight, I will serve her with thee, for a — *Fac.* Nay,
But understand: I'll gi' you Composition.
   Sub. I will not treat with thee: What, sell my Fortune?
'Tis better than my Birth-right. Do not murmur.
Win her, and carry her. If you grumble, *Dol*
Knows it directly. *Fac.* Well, Sir, I am silent.
Will you go help to fetch in *Don* in state?

Sub. I follow you, Sir; We must keep *Face* in awe,
Or he will over-look us like a Tyrant.
Brain of a Taylor! Who comes here? *Don John?*
                         [*Surly like a Spaniard.*
Sur. Sennores, beso las manos a vuestras mercedes.
Sub. Would you had stoop'd a little and kist our *anos.*
Fac. Peace, *Subtle.* *Sub.* Stab me; I shall never hold,
  man.
He looks in that deep Ruff, like a Head in a Platter,
Serv'd in by a short Cloke upon two Tressils.
  Fac. Or, what do you say to a Collar of Brawn, cut down
Beneath the Souse, and wriggled with a Knife?
  Sub. 'Slud, he does look too fat to be a *Spaniard.*
  Fac. Perhaps some *Fleming,* or some *Hollander* got him
In d' *Alva's* time; *Count Egmont's* Bastard. *Sub. Don,*
Your scurvy yellow *Madrid* Face is welcome.
  Sur. Gratia. *Sub.* He speaks out of a Fortification.
Pray God, he ha' no Squibs in those deep Sets.
  Sur. Por dios, Sennores, muy linda casa!
  Sub. What says he? *Fac.* Praises the House, I think,
I know no more but's Action. *Sub.* Yes, the *Casa,*
My precious *Diego,* will prove fair enough
To cozen you in. Do you mark? You shall
Be cozen'd, *Diego.* *Fac.* Cozen'd do you say?
My worthy *Donzel* cozen'd. *Sur. Entiendo.*
  Sub. Do you intend it? So do we, dear *Don.*
Have you brought Pistolets, or Portagues,
My solemn *Don?* Dost thou feel any? *Fac.* Full.
                         [*He feels his Pockets.*
  Sub. You shall be emptied, *Don,* pumped and drawn
Dry, as they say. *Fac.* Milked, in troth, sweet *Don.*
  Sub. See all the Monsters; the great Lion of all, *Don.*
  Sur. Con licentia, se puede ver a esta Sennora?
  Sub. What talks he now?
  Fac. O'the *Sennora.* *Sub.* O, *Don.*
That is the Lioness, which you shall see
Also, my *Don.* *Fac.* 'Slid, *Subtle,* how shall we do?

Sub. For what?
Fac. Why, *Dol's* employ'd, you know. *Sub.* That's true.
'Fore Heaven, I know not: He must stay, that's all.
Fac. Stay? That he must not by no means.
Sub. No! Why?
Fac. Unless you'll mar all, 'Slight, he'll suspect it:
And then he will not pay, not half so well.
This is a travell'd Punk-master, and do's know
All the Delays; a notable hot Rascal,
And looks already rampant. *Sub.* 'Sdeath, and *Mummon*
Must not be troubled. *Fac. Mummon*, in no case.
Sub. What shall we do then?
Fac. Think: you must be sudden.
Sur. Entiendo, qua la Sennora es tan hermosa, que codicio tan a ver la, como la bien aventuranza de mi vida.
Fac. Mi vida? 'Slid, *Subtle*, he puts me in mind o' the Widow.
What dost thou say to draw her to't? ha?
And tell her it is her Fortune? All our Venture
Now lies upon't. It is but one Man more,
Which on's chance to have her: and beside
There is no Maidenhead to be fear'd or lost;
What dost thou think on't, *Subtle?*
Sub. Who, I? Why —
Fac. The Credit of our House too is engag'd.
Sub. You made me an offer for my Share ere-while,
What wilt thou gi' me, i' faith? *Fac.* O, by that Light
I'll not buy now. You know your doom to me.
E'en take your Lot, obey your Chance, Sir; win her,
And wear her out for me.
Sub. 'Slight, I'll not work her then.
Fac. It is the *Common Cause;* therefore bethink you.
Dol else must know it, as you said. *Sub.* I care not.
Sur. Sennores, por que se tarda tanta?
Sub. Faith, I am not fit, I am old.
Fac. That's now no Reason, Sir.

Sur. Puede ser, de hazer burla de mi amor.
Fac. You hear the *Don* too? By this Air I call
And loose the Hinges, *Dol. Sub.* A Plague of Hell —
 Fac. Will you then do? *Sub.* Yo' are a *terrible Rogue,*
I'll think of this. Will you, Sir, call the Widow?
 Fac. Yes, and I'll take her too, with all her Faults,
Now I do think on't better. *Sub.* With all my heart, Sir:
Am I discharg'd o'the Lot? *Fac.* As you please.
 Sub. Hands.
 Fac. Remember now, that upon any Change,
You never claim her.
 Sub. Much good Joy, and Health to you, Sir.
Marry a Whore? *Fate,* let me wed a Witch first.
 Sur. Por estas honrada's barbas —
 Sub. He swears by his Beard.
Dispatch, and call the Brother too.
 Sur. Tiengo duda, Sennores,
Que no me hogan alguna traycion.
 Sub. How, issue on? Yes, præsto Sennor. Please you
Enthratha the *Chambrata,* worthy *Don ?*
Where if you please the *Fates,* in your *Bathada,*
You shall be soak'd, and stroak'd, and tub'd, and rub'd,
And scrub'd, and fub'd, dear *Don,* before you go.
You shall in faith, my scurvy Baboon *Don,*
Be curried, claw'd, and flaw'd, and taw'd, indeed.
I will the heartlier go about it now,
And make the Widow a Punck so much the sooner,
To be reveng'd on this impetuous *Face;*
The quickly doing of it, is the grace.

SCENE IV.

Face, Kastril, Da. Pliant, Subtle, Surly.

 Fac. Come, Lady: I knew the Doctor would not leave,
T'ill he had found the very nick of her Fortune.
 Kas. To be a *Countess,* say you? A *Spanish Countess,* Sir?
 Pli. Why, is that better than an *English Countess?*

Fac. Better? 'Slight, make you that a Question, Lady?
Kas. Nay, she is a Fool, Captain, you must pardon her.
Fac. Ask from your Courtier, to your Inns of Courtman,
To your meer Millener; they will tell you all,
Your Spanish Gennet is the best Horse; your *Spanish*
Stoup is the best Garb; your *Spanish* Beard
Is the best Cut; your *Spanish* Ruffs are the best
Wear, your *Spanish Pavin* the best Dance;
Your *Spanish* Titillation in a Glove
The best Perfume. And for your *Spanish* Pike,
And *Spanish* Blade, let your poor Captain speak.
Here comes the Doctor. *Sub.* My most honour'd Lady,
(For so I am now to style you, having found
By this my *Scheme*, you are to undergo
An honourable Fortune, very shortly)
What will you say now, if some —
   Fac. I had told her all, Sir;
And her right worshipful Brother here, that she shall be
A *Countess*; do not delay 'em, Sir: a *Spanish Countess.*
   Sub. Still, my scarce worshipful Captain, you can keep
No Secret. Well, since he has told you, Madam,
Do you forgive him, and I do.
   Kas. She shall do that, Sir,
I'll look to't, 'tis my Charge.
   Sub. Well then: Nought rests
But that she fit her Love now to her Fortune.
   Pli. Truly I shall never brook a *Spaniard.* *Sub.* No?
   Pli. Never sin' *Eighty-eight* could I abide 'em,
And that was some three year afore I was born, in truth.
   Sub. Come, you must love him, or be miserable;
Chuse which you will.
   Fac. By this good Rush, persuade her,
She will cry Strawberries else, within this Twelve-month.
   Sub. Nay, Shads and Mackarel, which is worse.
   Fac. Indeed, Sir?
   Kas. God's lid, you shall love him, or I'll kick you.
   Pli. Why?

I'll do as you will ha' me, Brother. *Kas.* Do,
Or by this Hand I'll maul you. *Fac.* Nay, good Sir,
Be not so fierce. *Sub.* No, my enraged Child,
She will be rul'd. What, when she comes to taste
The Pleasure of a Countess! to be courted —
Fac. And kist, and ruffled! *Sub.* I, behind the Hangings.
Fac. And then come forth in Pomp!
Fac. Of keeping all th' Idolaters o' the Chamber
Barer to her, than at their Prayers! *Sub.* Is serv'd
Upon the Knee! *Fac.* And has her Pages, Ushers,
Footmen, and Coaches —
Sub. Her six Mares — *Fac.* Nay, eight!
Sub. To hurry her through *London*, to th' *Exchange*,
Bet'lem, the *China-house* — *Fac.* Yes, and have
The Citizens gape at her, and praise her Tires!
And my Lords Goose-turd Bands, that rides with her!
Kas. Most brave! By this Hand, you are not my Sister,
If you refuse. *Pli.* I will not refuse, Brother.
*Sub. Que es esto, Sennores, que non se venga?
Esta tardanza me mata!* *Fac.* Is it the *Count* come?
The Doctor knew he would be here, by his Art.
Sub. Es gallanta Madama, Don! gallantissima!
*Sur. Por todos los dios-es, la mas acabada
Hermosura, que he visto en mi vida!*
Fac. Is't not a gallant Language that they speak?
Kas. An admirable Language! Is't not *French*?
Fac. No, *Spanish*, Sir. *Kas.* It goes like Law-*French*,
And that, they say, is the Courtliest Language. *Fac.* List, Sir.
*Sur. El Sol ha perdido su lumbre, con el
Resplendor, que trae esta dama. Valga me dios!*
Fac. He admires your Sister.
Kas. Must not she make Curt'sie?
Sub. 'Ods will, she must go to him, Man, and kiss him!
It is the *Spanish* Fashion for the Women,
To make first Court. *Fac.* 'Tis true he tells you, Sir:
His Art knows all. *Sur. Por que no se acude?*
Kas. He speaks to her, I think. *Fac.* That he does, Sir.

250   BEN JONSON.

Sur. Por el amor de dios, que es esto, que se tarda?
Kas. Nay, sco: she will not understand him! Gull.
Noddy. *Pli.* What say you, Brother? *Kas.* Ass, Sister,
Go kuss him, as the cunning Man would ha' you,
I'll thrust a Pin i' your Buttocks else. *Fac.* O, no Sir.
Sur. Sennora mia, mi persona muy indigna esta
Allegar a tanta Hermosura.
Fac. Does he not use her bravely? *Kas.* Bravely, i' faith!
Fac. Nay, he will use her better. *Kas.* Do you think so?
Sur. Sennora, si sera servida, entremus.
Kas. Where does he carry her?
Fac. Into the Garden, Sir;
Take you no thought: I must interpret for her.
Sub. Give *Dol* the Word. Come, my fierce Child, advance.
We'll to our quarrelling Lesson again. *Kas.* Agreed,
I love a *Spanish* Boy with all my Heart.
Sub. Nay, and by this means, Sir, you shall be Brother
To a great *Count.* *Kas.* I, I knew that at first.
This Match will advance the House of the *Kastrils.*
Sub. 'Pray God your Sister prove but pliant.
Kas. Why,
Her name is so, by her other Husband. *Sub.* How!
Kas. The Widow *Pliant.* Knew you not that?
Sub. No faith, Sir:
Yet, by erection of her Figure, I guest it.
Come, let's go practise. *Kas.* Yes, but do you think, Doctor,
I e'er shall quarrel well? *Sub.* I warrant you.

SCENE V.

Dol, Mammon, Face, Subtle.

Dol. For, after Alexander's Death — [*In her fit of talking.*
Mam. Good Lady ---
Dol. That Perdiccas and Antigonus were slain,
The two that stood, Seleuc', and Ptolmee ——
Mam. Madam. *Dol.* Made up the two *Legs*, and the fourth
  Beast,

That was Gog-north, and Egypt-south: which after
Was call'd Gog-Iron leg, and South Iron-leg — Mam. La —
Dol. *And then Gog-horned. So was Egypt, too.*
Then Egypt clay-leg, and Gog clay-leg——
Mam. Sweet Madam.
Dol. *And last Gog-dust, and Egypt dust, which fall*
In the last Link of the fourth Chain. And these
Be Stars in Story, which none see or look at ——
Mam. What shall I do? Dol. *For, as he says, except*
We call the Rabbins, and the Heathen Greeks ——
Mam. Dear Lady! Dol. *To come from* Salem, *and from* Athens,
And teach the People of great Britain
Fac. What's the Matter, Sir?
Dol. *To speak the Tongue of* Eber, *and* Javan — Mam. O
She's in her fit. Dol. *We shall know nothing*— Fac. Death, Sir,
We are undone. Dol. *Where then a learned Linguist*
Shall see the ancient us'd communion
Of Vowels and Consonants — Fac. My Master will hear!
Dol. *A Wisdom, which* Pythagoras *held most high* —
Mam. Sweet honourable Lady. Dol. *To comprize*
All sounds of Voyces, in few Marks of Letters ——
Fac. Nay, you must never hope to lay her now.
Dol. *And so we may arrive by* Talmud *Skill,*
And prophane Greek, *to raise the building up*
Of Helens *House against the* Ismaelite,
King of Thogarma, *and his* Habergions
Brimstony, blue, and fiery; and the Force
Of King Abaddon, *and the Beast of* Cittim;
Which Rabbi David Kimchi, Onkelos,
And Aben Ezra do interpret Rome.
Fac. How did you put her into 't? Mam. Alas, I talk'd
Of a fifth *Monarchy* I would erect, [*They speak together.*
With the *Philosophers* (by chance) and she
Falls on the other four straight. Fac. Out of *Broughton!*
I told you so. 'Slid stop her Mouth. Mam. Is 't best?
Fac. She'll never leave else. If the old Man hear her,
We are but *fæces*, Ashes. Sub. What's to do there?

Fac. O, we are lost. Now she hears him, she is quiet.
Mam. Where shall I hide me?
     [*Upon* Subtle's *entry they disperse.*
 Sub. How! what sight is here!
Close deeds of Darkness, and that shun the light!
Bring him again. Who is he? what, my Son!
O, I have liv'd too long. *Mam.* Nay, good dear Father,
There was no unchaste purpose. *Sub.* Not? and flee me
When I come in? *Mam.* That was my Error. *Sub.* Error?
Guilt, guilt, my Son. Give it the right name. No marvel,
If I found check in our *great work* within,
When such affairs as these were managing!
 Mam. Why, have you so?
 Sub. It has stood still this half Hour:
And all the rest of our *less Works* gone back.
Where is the Instrument of Wickedness,
My lewd false Drudge? *Mam.* Nay, good Sir! blame not him!
Believe me, 'twas against his will, or knowledge.
I saw her by chance. *Sub.* Will you commit more sin
T' excuse a Varlet? *Mam.* By my hope 'tis true, Sir.
 Sub. Nay, then I wonder less, if you, for whom
The blessing was prepar'd, would so tempt Heaven:
And lose your Fortunes. *Mam.* Why Sir?
 Sub. This 'll retard
The *work,* a Month at least. *Mam.* Why, if it do,
What remedy? but think it not, good Father:
Our Purposes were honest. *Sub.* As they were,
So the Reward will prove. How now! Aye me.
God, and all Saints be good to us. What's that?
     [*A great Crack and Noise within.*
 Fac. O Sir, we are defeated! all the *Works*
Are flown *in fumo:* every Glass is burst.
Fornace, and all rent down! as if a bolt
Of Thunder had been driven through the House.
Retorts, Receivers, Pellicanes, Bolt-heads,
All struck in shivers! Help, good Sir! alas,
     [Subtle *falls down as in a swoon.*

Coldness and death invades him. Nay, Sir *Mammon*,
Do the fair office of a Man! You stand,
As you were readier to depart than he.
Who's there? My Lord her Brother is come.
 Mam. Ha, *Lungs!*
 Fac. His Coach is at the Door. Avoid his sight,
For he's as furious as his Sister is mad.   [*One knocks.*
 Mam. Alas!
 Fac. My Brain is quite undone with the fume, Sir.
I ne'er must hope to be mine own Man again.
 Mam. Is all lost, *Lungs?* Will nothing be preserv'd,
Of all our cost? *Fac.* Faith very little, Sir.
A Peck of Coals, or so, which is cold comfort, Sir.
 Mam. O my voluptuous mind! I am justly punish'd.
 Fac. And so am I, Sir.
 Mam. Cast from all my Hopes ——
 Fac. Nay, certainties, Sir.
 Mam. By mine own base affections.
 Sub. O, the curst Fruits of Vice and Lust!
       [*Subtle seems to come to himself.*
 Mam. Good Fatler,
It was my Sin. Forg've it. *Sub.* Hangs my Roof
Over us still, and wil not fall, O justice,
Upon us, for this wicked Man! *Fac.* Nay, look, Sir,
You grieve him now with staying in his sight:
Good Sir, the noble Man will come too, and take you,
And that may breed a Tragedy. *Mam.* I'll go.
 Fac. I, and repent it home, Sir. It may be,
For some good Penance you may ha't yet,
A hundred Pound to the Box at *Bet'lem* —— *Mam.* Yes.
 Fac. For the restoring such as ha' their Wits.
 Mam. I'll do't.
 Fac. I'll send one to you to receive it. *Mam.* Do.
Is no *projection* left? *Fac.* All flown, or stinks, Sir.
 Mam. Will nought be sav'd, that's good for Med'cine,
  think'st thou?
 Fac. I cannot tell, Sir. There will be, perhaps,

Something, about the scraping of the Shardes,
Will cure the Itch, tho' not your itch of mind, Sir.
It shall be sav'd for you, and sent home. Good Sir,
This way, for fear the Lord should meet you. *Sub. Face.*
    Fac. I. *Sub.* Is he gone? *Fac.* Yes, and as heavily
As all the Gold he hop'd for, were in his Blood.
Let us be light though. *Sub.* I, as Balls, and bound
And hit our Heads against the Roof for joy:
There's so much of our care now cast away.
    Fac. Now to our *Don.*
    Sub. Yes, your young widow, by this time
Is made a *Countess, Face:* Sh' has been in travail
Of a young Heir for you.
    Fac. Good, Sir. *Sub.* Off with your case,
And greet her kindly, as a Bridegroom should,
After these common hazards. *Fac.* Very well, Sir.
Will you go fetch *Don Diego* off, the while?
    Sub. And fetch him over too, if you'll be pleas'd, Sir:
Would *Dol* were in her Place, to pick his Pockets now.
    Fac. Why, you can do it as well, if you would set to't.
I pray you prove your Vertue. *Sub.* For your sake, Sir.

SCENE VI.

Surly, Da. Pliant, Subtle, Face.

    Sur. Lady, you see into what Hands you are faln:
'Mongst what a nest of Villains! and how near
Your Honour was t' have catch'd a certain clap
(Thro' your credulity) had I but been
So punctually forward, as place, time,
And other Circumstances would ha' made a Man:
For yo' are a handsome Woman, would you were wise too.
I am a Gentleman come here disguised,
Only to find the Knaveries of this *Ciadel*,
And where I might ha' wrong'd your honour, and ha' not,
I claim some Interest in your Love. You are,
They say, a widow, rich: and I an a Batchellor,

Worth nought; your Fortunes may make me a Man,
As mine ha' preserv'd you a Woman. Think upon it,
And whether I have deserv'd you, or no.
    Pli. I will, Sir.
    Sur. And for these Houshold-rogues, let me alone,
To treat with them.
    Sub. How doth my noble *Diego?*
And my dear Madam *Countess?* Hath the *Count*
Been courteous, Lady? liberal? and open?
Donsel, methinks you look melancholick,
After your Bussiness, and scurvy! Truely,
I do not like the dullness of your Eye,
It hath a heavy cast ....

. . . .
Be lighter, I will make your Pockets so.
                                  [*He falls to picking of them.*
    Sur. Will you, *Don* Bawd, and pick-purse? How now!
Reel you?
Stand up, Sir, you shall find since I am so heavy,
I'll gi' you equal weight. *Sub.* Help, murder!
    Sur. No, Sir. There's no such thing intended. A good Cart,
And a clean Whip shall ease you of that fear.
I am the *Spanish Don*, that should be cozened.
Do you see? cozened? where's your Captain *Face?*
That Parcel-broker, and whole bawd, all Raskal.
    Fac. How, *Surly! Sur.* O, make your approach, good Captain.
I have found from whence your Copper Rings and Spoons
Come, now, wherewith you cheat abroad in Taverns.
'Twas here you learn'd t'anoint your Boot with Brimstone,
Then rub Mens Gold on't, for a kind of Touch,
And say 'twas naught, when you had chang'd the Colour,
That you might ha't for nothing. And this Doctor,
Your sooty, smoky-bearded compeer, he
Will close you so much Gold, in a Bolts-head,
And, on a turn, convey (i'the stead) another

With *sublim'd Mercury*, that shall burst i' the heat,
And fly out all *in fumo?* Then weeps *Mammon:*
Then swoons his Worship. Or, he is the *Faustus,*
That casteth Figures, and can Conjure, cures
Plagues, Piles, and Pox, by the *Ephemerides,*
And holds Intelligence with all the Bawds,
And Midwives of three Shires? while you send in —
Captain, (what is he gone?) Dam'sels with Child,
Wives that are barren, or the waiting Maid
With the Green Sickness? Nay, Sir, you must tarry,
Tho' he be scap'd, and answer by the Ears, Sir.

SCENE VII.

Face, Kastril, Surly, Subtle, Drugger, Ananias, Dame Pliant, Dol.

 Fac. Why, now's the time, if ever you will quarrel
Well (as they say) and be a true-born Child.
The Doctor, and your Sister both are abus'd.
 Kas. Where is he? which is he? he is a Slave
What e'er he is, and the Son of a ...... Are you
The Man, Sir, I would know? *Sur.* I should be loth, Sir,
To confess so much. *Kas.* Then you lie i' your Throat.
 Sur. How?
 Fac. A very errant Rogue, Sir, and a cheater,
Employ'd here by another Conjurer,
That does not love the Doctor, and would cross him,
If he knew how — *Sur.* Sir, you are abus'd. *Kas.* You lye:
And 'tis no matter. *Fac.* Well said, Sir. He is
The impudent'st Raskal —
 Sur. You are indeed. Will you hear me, Sir?
 Fac. By no means: Bid him be gone. *Kas.* Be gone, Sir,
  quickly.
 Sur. This's strange! Lady, do you inform your Brother.
 Fac. There is not such a foist in all the Town,
The Doctor had him presently: and finds yet,
The *Spanish Count* will come here. Bear up, *Subtle.*

Sub. Yes, Sir, he must appear within this hour
Fac. And yet this Rogue will come in a disguise,
By the Temptation of another Spirit,
To trouble our Art, tho' he could not hurt it. *Kas.* I,
I know — Away, you talk like a foolish Mauther.
Sur. Sir, all is truth, she says. *Fac.* Do not believe him, Sir.
He is the lying'st Swabber! Come your ways, Sir.
Sur. You are valiant out of Company. *Kas.* Yes, How
then, Sir?
Fac. Nay, here's an honest Fellow too, that knows him,
And all his Tricks. (Make good what I say, *Abel*)
This cheater would ha' cozen'd thee o' the Widow.
He owes this honest *Drugger*, here, seven Pound,
He has had on him, in two-penny' or the of *Tobacco*.
Dru. Yes, Sir. And he has damn'd himself three Terms to
pay me.
Fac. And what does he owe for *Lotium?* *Dr.* Thirty
Shillings, Sir.
And for six *Syringes.* *Sur.* *Hydra* of Villany!
Fac. Nay, Sir, you must quarrel him out o' the House.
Kas. I will, — Sir, if you get not out o' Doors, you lye:
And you are a Pimp. *Sur.* Why, this is Madness, Sir,
Not Valor in you: I must laugh at this.
Kas. It is my Humour: you are a Pimp, and a Trig,
And an *Amadis de Gaule*, or a *Don Quixot.*
Dru. Or a Knight o' the *curious Coxcomb.* Do you see?
Ana. Peace to the Houshold. *Kas.* I'll keep Peace for no
Man.
Ana. Casting of Dollers is concluded lawful.
Kas. Is he the Constable? *Sub.* Peace, *Ananias.* *Fac.*
No, Sir.
Kas. Then you are an *Otter*, and a *Shad*, a *Whit*,
A very *Tim.* *Sur.* You'll hear me, Sir? *Kas.* I will not.
Ana. What is the Motive? *Sub.* Zeal in the young Gentleman,
Against his *Spanish* Slops —— *Ana.* They are Prophane,
Lewd, Superstitious, and Idolatrous Breeches.

Sur. New Raskals! *Kas.* Will you be gone. Sir? *Ana.*
Avoid, *Satan.*
Thou art not of the Light. That Ruff of Pride,
About thy Neck, betrays thee: 'and is the same
With that which the unclean Birds, in *seventy seven*,
Were seen to prank it with, on divers Coasts.
Thou look'st like *Anti-christ*, in the lewd Hat.
Sur. I must give way. *Kas.* Be gone, Sir. *Sur.* But I'll take
A course with you — *Ana.* Depart, proud *Spanish* Fiend.
Sur. Captain, and Doctor — *Ana.* Child of Perdition.
Kas. Hence, Sir.
Did I not quarrel bravely? *Fac.* Yes, indeed, Sir.
Kas. Nay, an' I give my mind to't, I shall do't.
Fac. O, you must follow, Sir, and threaten him tame.
He'll turn again else. *Kas.* I'll return him then.
Fac. Drugger, this Rogue prevented us, for thee:
We had determin'd that thou should'st ha' come,
In a *Spanish* Suit, and ha' carry'd her so; and he
A brokerly Slave, goes, puts it on himself.
Hast' brought the Damask? *Dru.* Yes, Sir. *Fac.* Thou must
borrow
A *Spanish* Suit. Hast thou no credit with the Players?
Dru. Yes, Sir: did you never see me play the Fool?
Fac. I know not, *Nab*; thou shalt, if I can help it.
Hieronymo's old Cloak, Ruff, and Hat will serve,
 [Subtle *hath whispered with him this while.*
I'll tell thee more when thou bring'st 'em. *Ana.* Sir, I know
The *Spaniard* hates the *Brethren*, and hath Spies
Upon their Actions: and that this was one
I make no scruple. But the holy Synod
Have been in Prayer, and Meditation for it.
And 'tis reveal'd no less to them than me,
That casting of Money is most lawful. *Sub.* True:
But here I cannot do it; if the House
Shou'd chance to be suspected, all would out,
And we be lock'd up in the *Tower* for ever,
To make Gold there (for th' State) never come out:

And then are you defeated. *Ana.* I will tell
This to the *Elders*, and the weaker *Brethren*,
That the whole Company of the *Separation*
May join in humble Prayer again. (*Sub.* And Fasting)
    Ana. Yea, for some fitter Place. The Peace of Mind
Rest with these Walls. *Sub.* Thanks, courteous *Ananias.*
    Fac. What did he come for? *Sub.* About casting Dollers,
Presently out of hand. And so I told him,
A *Spanish* Minister came here to Spie,
Against the faithful —— *Fac.* I conceive. Come *Subtle,*
Thou art so down upon the least Disaster!
How wouldst tho' ha' done, if I had not helpt thee out?
    Sub. I thank thee, *Face,* for the angry Boy, i-faith.
    Fac. Who would ha' lookt it should ha' been that Raskal
Surly? He had dy'd his Beard and all. Well, Sir,
Here's Damask come to make you a Suit. *Sub.* Where's
    Drugger?
    Fac. He's gone to borrow me a *Spanish* Habit;
I'll be the *Count,* now. *Sub.* But where's the Widow?
    Fac. Within, with my Lord's Sister: Madam *Dol*
Is entertaining her. *Sub.* By your favour, *Face,*
Now she is honest I will stand again.
    Fac. You will not offer it? *Sub.* Why? *Fac.* Stand to
    your Word
Or —— here comes *Dol.* She knows —— *Sub.* Yo'are tyrannous still.
    Fac. Strict for my Right. How now, *Dol?* Hast' told her,
The *Spanish Count* will come? *Dol.* Yes, but another is come,
You little look'd for! *Fac.* Who's that? *Dol.* Your Master:
The Master of the House. *Sub.* How, *Dol! Fac.* She lies,
This is some Trick. Come, leave your Quiblins, *Dorothee.*
    Dol. Look out and see. *Sub.* Art thou in earnest? *Dol.*
    'Slight.
Forty o' the Neighbours are about him, talking.
    Fac. 'Tis he, by this good Day. *Dol.* 'Twill prove ill Day
For some on us. *Fac.* We are undone, and taken.
    Dol. Lost, I'm afraid. *Sub.* You said he would not come,

While there died one a Week, within the Liberties.
Fac. No: 'twas within the Walls. *Sub.* Was't so? Cry'you
  mercy.
I thought the Liberties. What shall we do now, *Face?*
Fac. Be silent: not a word, if he call or knock,
I'll into mine old shape again and meet him,
Of *Jeremy*, the Butler. I' the mean time,
Do you two pack up all the Goods, and purchase,
That we can carry i' the two Trunks. I'll keep him
Off for to Day, if I cannot longer: and then
At Night, I'll ship you both away to *Ratcliff*,
Where we'll meet to Morrow, and there we'll share.
Let *Mammon's* Brass and Pewter keep the Cellar;
We'll have another time for that. But, *Dol*,
'Pr'y thee go heat a little Water quickly,
Subtle must shave me. All my Captain's Beard
Must off, to make me appear smooth *Jeremy*.
You'll do't? *Sub.* Yes, I'll shave you, as well as I can.
  Fac. And not cut my Throat, but trim me? *Sub.* You shall
    see, Sir.

ACT V. SCENE I.

Love-Wit, Neighbours.

Lov. Has there been such resort, say you? *Neighb.* 1. Daily,
  Sir.
Neighb. 2. And Nightly, too. *Neighb.* 3. I, some as brave as
  Lords.
Neighb. 4. Ladies, and Gentlewomen. *Neighb.* 5. Citizens
  Wives.
Neighb. 1. And Knights. *Neighb.* 6. In Coaches.
Neighb. 2. Yes, and Oyster-women.
Neighb. 1. Beside other Gallants. *Neighb.* 3. Sailors Wives.
Neighb. 4. *Tobacco-men*. *Neighb.* 5. Another *Pimlico!*
Lov. What should my Knave advance,
To draw this Company? He hung out no Banners
Of a strange Calf, with five Legs, to be seen?

Or a huge Lobster, with six Claws? *Neighb.* 6. No, Sir.
Neighb. 3. We had gone in then, Sir. *Lov.* He has no Gift
Of teaching i' the Nose, that e'er I knew of.
You saw no Bills set up that promis'd Cure
Of Agues, or the Tooth-ach? *Neighb.* 2. No such thing, Sir.
Lov. Nor heard a Drum strook, for Baboons, or Puppets?
Neighb. 5. Neither, Sir.
Lov. What Device should he bring forth now?
I love a teeming Wit as I love my Nourishment:
'Pray God he ha' not kept such open House,
That he hath sold my Hangings, and my Bedding:
I left him nothing else: If he have eat 'em,
A Plague o' the Mouth, say I: Sure he has got
Some bawdy Pictures, to call this ging;
The Frier, and the Nun; or the new *Motion*
Of the Knights Courses, covering the Parsons Mare;
The Boy of six Year old, with the great Thing:
Or't may be, he has the Fleas that run at Tilt,
Upon a Table, or some Dog to dance?
When saw you him? *Nei.* 1. Who, Sir, *Jeremy?*
Neighb. 2. *Jeremy* Butler?
We saw him not this Month. *Lov.* How!
Neighb. 4. Not these five Weeks, Sir.
Neighb. 6. These six Weeks, at the least.
Lov. Yo' amaze me, Neighbours!
Neighb. 5. Sure, if your Worship know not where he is,
He's slipt away. *Neighb.* 6. Pray God, he be not made away.
                                                    [*He knocks.*
Lov. Ha? It's no time to question, then. *Neighb.* 6. About
Some three Weeks since, I heard a doleful Cry,
As I sate up, a mending my Wives Stockings.
Lov. This's strange! that none will answer!
Didst thou hear
A Cry, saist thou? *Neighb.* 6. Yes, Sir, like unto a Man
That had been strangled an Hour, and could not speak.
Neighb. 2. I heard it too, just this Day three Weeks, at
        Two a' Clock

Next Morning. *Lov.* These be Miracles, or you make 'em so!
A Man an Hour strangled, and could not speak,
And both you heard him cry? *Neighb.* 3. Yes, downward, Sir.
    Lov. Thou art a wise Fellow: Give me thy Hand I pray thee.
What Trade art thou on?
    Neighb. 3. A Smith, an't please your Worship.
    Lov. A Smith? Then lend me thy help to get this Door open.
    Neighb. 3. That I will presently, Sir, but fetch my Tools —
    Neighb. 1. Sir, best to knock again, afore you break it.

SCENE II.

Love-wit, Face, Neighbours.

    Lov. I will. *Fac.* What mean you, Sir? *Neighb.* 1, 2, 4. O, here's *Jeremy!*
    Fac. Good Sir, come from the Door.
    Lov. Why! what's the matter?
    Fac. Yet farther, you are too near yet.
    Lov. I' the name of Wonder! What means the Fellow?
    Fac. The House, Sir, has been visited.
    Lov. What? with the Plague? stand thou then farther.
    Fac. No, Sir, I had it not. *Lov.* Who had it then? I left
None else, but thee, i' the House! *Fac.* Yes, Sir, my Fellow,
The Cat, that kept the Buttery, had it on her
A Week before I spied it: but I got her
Convey'd away, i' the Night. And so I shut
The House up for a Month ——
    Lov. How! *Fac.* Purposing then, Sir,
T'have burnt Rose-vinegar, Treacle, and Tar,
And ha' made it sweet, that you should ne'er ha' known it;
Because I knew the News would but afflict you, Sir.
    Lov. Breathe less, and farther off. Why this is stranger!
The Neighbours tell me all, here, that the Doors
Have still been open — *Fac.* How, Sir!
    Lov. Gallants, Men, and Women,

And of all sorts, tag-rag, been seen to flock here
In threaves, these ten Weeks, as to a second *Hogs-den*,
In Days of *Pimlico*, and *Eye-bright!* *Fac.* Sir,
Their Wisdoms will not say so! *Lov.* To Day, they speak
Of Coaches, and Gallants; one in a *French* hood,
Went in, they tell me: and another was seen
In a Velvet Gown at the Window! divers more
Pass in and out! *Fac.* They did pass thro' the Doors then,
Or Walls, I assure their Eye-sights, and their Spectacles;
For here, Sir, are the Keys: and here have been,
In this my Pocket, now above twenty Days!
And for before, I kept the Fort alone there.
But that 'tis yet not deep i'the Afternoon,
I should believe my Neighbours had seen double
Thro' the Black-pot, and made these Apparitions!
For, on my Faith to your Worship, for these three Weeks,
And upwards, the Door has not been open'd. *Lov.* Strange!
   Neighb. 1. Good faith, I think I saw a Coach! *Neighb.* 2. And
      I too,
I'd ha' been sworn! *Lov.* Do you but think it now?
And but one Coach? *Neighb.* 4. We cannot tell, Sir: *Jeremy*
Is a very honest Fellow. *Fac.* Did you see me at all?
   Neighb. 1. No; that we are sure on. *Neighb.* 2. I'll be sworn
      o' that.
   Lov. Fine Rogues to have your Testimonies built on!
   Neighb. 3. Is *Jeremy* come? *Neighb.* 1. O, yes, you may leave
      your Tools,
We were deceiv'd, he says. *Neighb.* 2. He has had the
      Keys:
And the Door has been shut these three Weeks. *Neighb.* 3.
      Like enough.
   Lov. Peace, and get hence, you Changelings. *Fac. Surly*
      come!
And *Mammon* made acquainted? They'll tell all.
(How shall I beat them off? What shall I do?)
Nothing's more wretched than a guilty Conscience.

SCENE III.

Surly, Mammon, Love-wit, Face, Neighbours, Kastril, Ananias, Tribulation, Dapper, Subtle.

Sur. No, Sir, he was a great Physician. This,
It was no Bawdy-house: but a meer *Chancel.*
You knew the Lord, and his Sister. *Mam.* Nay, good *Surly.*
Sur. The happy Word, *Be Rich* — *Mam.* Play not the Tyran —
Sur. Should be to day pronounc'd to all your Friends.
And where be your Andirons now? and your brass Pots,
That should ha'been golden Flaggons, and great Wedges?
  Mam. Let me but breathe. What! they ha' shut their Doors,
Me thinks! *Sur.* I, now 'tis Holy-day with them.
  Mam. Rogues,
Cozeners, Impostors, Bawds. *Fac.* What mean you, Sir?
  [*Mammon and* Surly *knock.*
  Mam. To enter if we can. *Fac.* Another Man's House?
Here is the Owner, Sir. Turn you to him,
And speak your Business. *Mam.* Are you, Sir, the Owner?
  Lov. Yes, Sir.
  Mam. And are those Knaves within your Cheaters!
  Lov. What Knaves, what Cheaters? *Mam.* Subtle, and his *Lungs.*
  Fac. The Gentleman is distracted, Sir! No Lungs,
Nor Lights ha' been seen here these three Weeks, Sir,
Within these Doors, upon my Word! *Sur.* Your Word,
Groom arrogant? *Fac.* Yes, Sir, I am the House-keeper,
And know the Keys ha' not been out o' my Hands.
  Sur. This's a new *Face.*
  Fac. You do mistake the House, Sir!
What Sign was't at? *Sur.* You Raskal! This is one
O' the Confederacy. Come, let's get Officers,
And force the Door. *Lov.* 'Pray you stay, Gentlemen.
  Sur. No, Sir, we'll come with warrant.
  Mam. I, and then
We shall ha' your Doors open. *Lov.* What means this?

Fac. I cannot tell, Sir.
Neighb. 1. These are two o' the Gallants,
That we do think we saw. *Fac.* Two of the Fools?
You talk as idly as they. Good-faith, Sir,
I think the *Moon* has cras'd 'em all! (O me,
The angry Boy come too? He'll make a noise,
And ne'er away till he have betray'd us all.)
    Kas. What Rogues, Bawds, Slaves, you'll open the Door
        anon,   [*Kastril knocks.*
Punk, Cockatrice, my Suster. By this light
I'll fetch the Marshal to you. You are a Wh...,
To keep your Castle ——
    Fac. Who would you speak with, Sir?
    Kas. The Bawdy Doctor, and the cozening Captain,
And Pus my Suster. *Lov.* This is something, sure!
    Fac. Upon my trust, the Doors were never open, Sir.
    Kas. I have heard all their Tricks told me twice over,
By the fat Knight, and the lean Gentleman.
    Lov. Here comes another. *Fac. Ananias* too?
And his *Pastor? Tri.* The Doors are shut against us.
                                          [*They beat too at the Door.*
    Ana. Come forth, you Seed of Sulphur, Sons of Fire,
Your stench is broke forth: Abomination
Is in the House. *Kas.* I, my Suster's there. *Ana.* The Place,
It is become a Cage of unclean Birds.
    Kas. Yes, I will fetch the Scavenger and the Constable.
    Tri. You shall do well.
    Ana. We'll join to weed them out.
    Kas. You will not come then? Punk, device my Suster!
    Ana. Call her not Sister. She's a Harlot, verily.
    Kas. I'll raise the Street.
    Lov. Good Gentlemen, a Word.
    Ana. Satan avoid, and hinder not our Zeal.
    Lov. The World's turn'd *Bet'lem.*
    Fac. These are all broke loose,
Out of St. *Kather'nes* where they use to keep
The better sort of Mad-folks. *Neighb.* 1. All these Persons

We saw go in and out here. *Neighb.* 2. Yes, indeed, Sir.
Neighb. 3. These were the Parties. *Fac.* Peace, you Drun-
kards. Sir,
I wonder at it! Please you to give me leave
To touch the Door, I'll try an' the Lock be chang'd.
    Lov. It mazes me! *Fac.* Good faith, Sir, I believe
There's no such thing. 'Tis all *deceptio visus.*
Would I could get him away.   [Dapper *cries out within.*
    Dap. Master Captain, Master Doctor. *Lov.* Who's that?
Fac. (Our Clerk within, that I forgot!) I know not, Sir.
Dap. For God's sake, when will her Grace be at leisure?
Fac. Ha!
Illusions, some Spirit o' the Air: (his Gag is melted,
And now he sets out the Throat.) *Dap.* I'm almost stifled —
    Fac. (Would you were altogether.)
    Lov. 'Tis i' the House.
Ha! List. *Fac.* Believe it, Sir, i' the Air!
    Lov. Peace, you —
    Dap. Mine Aunts *Grace* does not use me well.
    Sub. You Fool,
Peace, you 'll mar all.
    Fac. Or you will else, you Rogue.
    Lov. O, is it so? Then you converse with Spirits!
Come Sir. No more o' your Tricks, good *Jeremy,*
The truth, the shortest way. *Fac.* Dismiss this Rabble, Sir.
What shall I do? I am catch'd.
    Lov. Good Neighbours,
I thank you all. You may depart. Come, Sir.
You know that I am an indulgent Master:
And therefore conceal nothing. What's your Med'cine,
To draw so many several sorts of wild Fowl?
    Fac. Sir, you were wont to affect Mirth and Wit:
(But here's no place to talk on't i' the Street.)
Give me but leave to make the best of my Fortune,
And only pardon me the Abuse of your House:
It's all I beg. I'll help you to a Widow,
In recompence, that you shall give me Thanks for,

Will make you seven Years younger, and a rich one.
'Tis but your putting on a *Spanish* Cloak.
I have her within. You need not fear the House,
It was not visited. *Lov.* But by me, who came
Sooner than you expected. *Fac.* It is true, Sir.
'Pray you forgive me.
   Lov. Let's see your Widow.

SCENE IV.

Subtle, Face, Dapper, Dol.

  Sub. How! ha' you eaten your Gag?
  Dap. Yes faith, it crumbled
Away i' my Mouth.
  Sub. You ha' spoil'd all then. *Dap.* No,
I hope my Aunt of *Fairy* will forgive me.
  Sub. Your Aunt's a gracious Lady: but in troth
You were to blame. *Dap.* The fume did over-come me,
And I did do't to stay my Stomach. 'Pray you
So satisfie her Grace. Here comes the Captain.
  Fac. How now! Is his Mouth down?
  Sub. I! he has spoken!
  Fac. (A Pox, I heard him, and you too.) He's undone then.
(I have been fain to say, the House is haunted
With Spirits, to keep Churle back.
  Sub. And hast thou done it?
  Fac. Sure, for this night.
  Sub. Why, then triumph and sing
Of *Face* so famous, the precious King
Of present wits. *Fac.* Did you not hear the coil,
About the Door? *Sub.* Yes, and I dwindled with it.)
  Fac. Shew him his Aunt, and let him be dispatch'd:
I'll send her to you. *Sub.* Well Sir, your Aunt her *Grace*,
Will give you Audience presently, on my sute,
And the Captain's word, that you did not eat your Gag
In any Contempt of her *Highness*.
  Dap. Not I, in troth, Sir.   [Dol *like the Queen of* Fairy.

Sub. Here she is come. Down o' your Knees and wriggle:
She has a stately Presence. Good, Yet nearer
And bid, God save you. *Dap.* Madam.
Sub. And your Aunt.
Dap. And my most gracious Aunt, God save your *Grace.*
Dol. Nephew, we thought to have been angry with you,
But that sweet Face of yours hath turn'd the Tide,
And made it flow with joy, that ebb'd of Love.
Arise, and touch our Velvet Gown. *Sub.* The Skirts,
And kiss 'em. So. *Dol.* Let me now stroke that Head:
*Much, Nephew, shalt thou win; much shalt thou spend;
Much shalt thou give away; much shalt thou lend!*
Sub. (I, much indeed.) Why do you not thank her Grace?
Dap. I cannot speak for joy.
Sub. See, the kind wretch!
Your *Graces* Kinsman right. *Dol.* Give me the *Bird.*
Here is your *Fly* in a Purse, about your Neck, Cousin,
Wear it, and feed it about this Day sev'night,
On your right Wrist — *Sub.* Open a Vein with a Pin,
And let it suck but once a week; till then,
You must not look on't. *Dol.* No: And, Kinsman,
Bear your self worthy of the Blood you come on.
Sub. Her Grace would ha' you eat no more *Woolsack* Pies,
Nor *Dagger* Frume'ty. *Dol.* Nor break his fast,
In *Heaven* and *Hell.* *Sub.* She's with you every where!
Nor play with Costar-mongers, at *mum-chance, tray-trip.*
God make you rich, (when as your Aunt has done it:) but keep
The gallant'st Company, and the best Games —— *Dap.* Yes,
Sir.
Sub. Gleek and *Primero:* and what you get, be true to us.
Dap. By this Hand, I will.
Sub. You may bring's a thousand Pound
Before to morrow night, (if but three thousand
Be stirring) an' you will. *Dap.* I swear, I will then.
Sub. Your *Grace* will command him no more Duties?
Dol. No:
But come, and see me often. I may chance

To leave him three or four hundred Chests of Treasure,
Add some twelve thousand Acres of *Fairy* Land,
If he game well, and comely, with good Gamesters.
  Sub. There's a kind Aunt! kiss her departing part.
But you must sell your forty Mark a Year, now.
  Dap. I, Sir, I mean. *Sub.* Or, gi't away: Pox on't.
  Dap. I'll gi't mine Aunt. I'll go and fetch the Writings.
  Sub. 'Tis well, away. *Fac.* Where's *Subtle?*
  Sub. Here. What News?
  Fac. Drugger is at the Door, go take his Sute,
And bid him fetch a Parson, presently:
Say, he shall marry the Widow. Thou shalt spend
A hundred Pound by the service! Now Queen *Dol.*
Ha' you pack'd up all? *Dol.* Yes. And how do you like
The Lady *Pliant?* *Dol.* A good dull innocent.
  Sub. Here's your *Hieronimo's* Cloke, and Hat.
  Fac. Give me 'em. *Sub.* And the Ruff too?
  Fac. Yes, I'll come to you presently.
  Sub. Now he is gone about his Project, *Dol*,
I told you of, for the Widow. *Dol.* 'Tis direct
Against our Articles. *Sub.* Well, we'll fit him, wench.
Hast thou gull'd her of her jewels, or her Bracelets?
  Dol. No, but I will do't. *Sub.* Soon at Night, my *Dolly*,
When we are shipt, and all our Goods aboard,
East-ward for *Ratcliff;* we will turn our course
To *Brainford*, westward, if thou saist the word,
And take our leaves of this o'er-weening Raskal,
This peremptory *Face.* *Dol.* Content, I am weary of him.
  Sub. Thou hast cause, when the slave will run a wiving,
    Dol,
Against the Instrument that was drawn between us.
  Dol. I'll pluck his Bird as bare as I can. *Sub.* Yes, tell her,
She must by any means address some Present
To th' cunning Man; make him amends for wronging
His art with her Suspicion; send a Ring,
Or Chain of Pearl; she will be tortur'd else
Extremely in her sleep, say: and ha' strange things

Come to her. Wilt thou? *Dol.* Yes. *Sub.* My fine Flitter-
 mouse,
My Bird o' the night, we'll tickle it at the *Pigeons*,
When we have all, and may unlock the Trunks,
And say: this's mine, and thine; and thine and mine.
 [*They kiss.*
 Fac. What now, a billing? *Sub.* Yes, a little exalted
In the good Passage of our Stock affairs.
 Fac. Drugger has brought his Parson; take him in, *Subtle*,
And send *Nab* back again to wash his Face.
 Sub. I will: and shave himself. *Fac.* If you can get him.
 Dol. You are hot upon it, *Face*, what e'er it is!
 Fac. A trick that *Dol* shall spend Ten Pound a Month by.
Is he gone? *Sub.* The Chaplain waits you i' the Hall, Sir.
 Fac. I'll go bestow him. *Dol.* He'll now marry her, in-
 stantly.
 Sub. He cannot, yet, he is not ready. Dear *Dol*,
Cozen her all thou canst. To deceive him
Is no deceit, but justice, that would break
Such an inextricable tye as ours was.
 Dol. Let me alone to fit him. *Fac.* Come, my ventures,
You ha' packt up all? Where be the Trunks? Bring forth.
 Sub. Here. *Fac.* Let's see 'em. Where's the Money?
 Sub. Here.
The *Brethrens* money, this. *Druggers* and *Dappers*,
What Paper's that? *Dol.* The jewel of the waiting Maids,
That stole it from her Lady, to know certain ——
 Fac. If she should have Precedence of her Mistris?
 Dol. Yes.
 Fac. What Box is that? *Sub.* The Fish-wives Rings, I
 think.
And th' Ale wives single money. Is't not *Dol?*
 Dol. Yes: and the whistle, that the Sailor's Wife
Brought you to know an' her Husband were with *Ward*.
 Fac. We'll wet it to morrow, and our Silver-beakers,
And Tavern Cups. Where be the *French* Petticoats,
And Girdles, and Hangers? *Sub.* Here i' the Trunk,

And the Bolts of Lawn. *Fac.* Is *Druggers* Damask there?
And the *Tobacco?* *Sub.* Yes. *Fac.* Give me the Keys.
    Dol. Why you the Keys! *Sub.* No matter, *Dol:* because
We shall not open 'em, before he comes.
    Fac. 'Tis true, you shall not open them, indeed:
Nor have 'em forth. Do you see? Not forth, *Doll Dol.* No!
    Fac. No, my Smock-rampant. The right is, my Master
Knows all, has pardon'd me, and he will keep 'em;
Doctor, 'tis true (you look) for all your Figures:
I sent for him, indeed. Wherefore, good Partners,
Both he, and she, be satisfied: for here
Determines the *Indenture tripartite*,
'Twixt *Subtle*, *Dol* and *Face*. All I can do
Is to help you over the Wall, o' the back side;
Or lend you a Sheet to save your Velvet Gown, *Dol*.
Here will be Officers presently, bethink you,
Of some course suddainly to scape the Dock;
For thither you'll come else. Hark you, Thunder.
                                                   [*Some knock.*
    Sub. You are a precious Fiend! *Off.* Open the Door.
    Fac. Dol, I am sorry for thee i' faith. But hearst thou?
It shall go hard, but I will place thee somewhere:
Thou shalt ha' my Letter to Mistris *Amo. Dol.* Hang you ——
    Fac. Or Madam *Cæsarean. Dol.* Pox upon you, Rogue,
Would I had but time to beat thee. *Fac. Subtle*,
Let's know where you set up next: I'll send you
A Customer, now and then, for old Acquaintance:
What new course ha' you? *Sub.* Rogue, I'll hang my self,
That I may walk a greater Devil than thou,
And haunt thee i' the Flock-Bed, and the Buttery.

SCENE V.

Love-wit, Officers, Mammon, Surly, Face, Kastril, Ananias,
        Tribulation, Drugger, Da. Pliant.

    What do you mean, my Masters? *Mam.* Open your Door,
Cheaters, Bawds, Conjurers! *Off.* Or we'll break it open.

Lov. What Warrant have you? *Off.* Warrant enough, Sir, *doubt not.*
If you'll not open it — *Lov.* Is there an Officer there?
Off. Yes, two or three for failing. *Lov.* Have but patience,
And I will open it straight. *Fac.* Sir, ha' you done?
Is it a Marriage? perfect? *Lov.* Yes, my Brain.
Fac. Off with your Ruff, and Cloke then; be your self, Sir.
Sur. Down with the Door. *Kas.* 'Slight, ding it open.
Lov. Hold,
Hold, Gentlemen, what means this violence?
Mam. Where is this Colliar? *Sur.* And my Captain *Face?*
Mam. Those Day-Owls. *Sur.* That are birding in Mens Purses.
Mam. Madam *Suppository.* *Kas.* *Dozey*, my Sister.
Ana. Locusts
Of the foul Pit. *Tri.* Prophane as *Bel* and the *Dragon.*
Ana. Worse than the Grashoppers, or the Lice of *Egypt.*
Lov. Good Gentlemen, hear me. Are you Officers,
And cannot stay this Violence? *Off.* Keep the Peace.
Lov. Gentlemen, what is the Matter? Whom do you seek?
Mam. The *Chimical* Cozener. *Sur.* And the Captain Pander.
Kas. The *Nun* my Suster. *Mam.* Madam *Rabbi.*
Ana. Scorpions,
And Caterpillars. *Lov.* Fewer at once, I pray you.
Off. One after another, Gentlemen, I charge you,
By vertue of my staff —— *Ana.* They are the vessels
Of Pride, Lust, and the Cart. *Lov.* Good Zeal, lie still,
A little while. *Tri.* Peace, Deacon *Ananias.*
Lov. The House is mine here, and the Doors are open:
If there be any such Persons you seek for,
Use your Authority, search on o' God's Name.
I am but newly come to Town, and finding
This tumult 'bout my Door (to tell you true)
It somewhat maz'd me; till my Man, here, (fearing
My more displeasure) told me he had done

Somewhat an insolent part, let out my House
(Belike, presuming on my known aversion
From any Air o' the Town, while there was Sickness)
To a Doctor, and a Captain: who, what they are,
Or where they be, he knows not. *Mam.* Are they gone?
[*They enter.*
    Lov. You may go in and search, Sir. Here, I find
The empty walls worse than I left 'em, smok'd,
A few crack'd Pots, and Glasses, and a Fornace;
The Ceiling fill'd with *Poesies* of the Candle:
And, *Madam*, with a *Dildo*, writ o' the Walls.
Only one Gentlewoman, I met here,
That is within, that said she was a Widow ——
    Kas. I, that's my Suster. I'll go thump her. Where is she?
    Lov. And should ha' married a *Spanish Count*, but he,
When he came to't, neglected her so grosly,
That I, a widower, am gone through with her.
    Sur. How! Have I lost her then?
    Lov. Were you the *Don*, Sir?
Good faith, now, she do's blame yo' extremely, and says
You swore, and told her, you had tane the pains
To dye your Beard, and umbre o'er your Face,
Borrow'd a Sute, and Ruff, all for her love;
And then did nothing. What an Over-sight,
And want of putting forward, Sir, was this!
Well fare an old Harquebuzier, yet,
Could prime his Powder, and give fire, and hit,
All in a twinckling. *Mam.* The whole nest are fled!
    Lov. What sort of Birds were they?
[*Mammon comes forth.*
    Mam. A kind of Choughs,
Or thievish Daws, Sir, that have pickt my Purse
Of eight-score and ten pounds, within these five Weeks,
Beside my first Materials; and my Goods,
That lie i' the Cellar; which I am glad they ha' left.
I may have home yet. *Lov.* Think you so, Sir? *Mam.* I.
    Lov. By order of Law, Sir, but not otherwise.

Mam. Not mine own stuff? *Lov.* Sir, I can take no
   knowledge,
That they are yours but by publick means.
If you can bring Certificate, that you were gull'd of 'em,
Or any formal Writ out of a Court,
That you did cozen your self, I will not hold them.
  Mam. I'll rather lose 'em. *Lov.* That you shall not, Sir,
By me, in troth. Upon these terms they are yours.
What should they ha' been, Sir, turn'd into Gold all?
  Mam. No.
I cannot tell. It may be they should. What then?
  Lov. What a great loss in Hope have you sustained?
  Mam. Not I, the Commonwealth has. *Fac.* I, he would
   ha' built
The City new; and made a Ditch about it
Of Silver, should have run with Cream from *Hogsden;*
That every Sunday in *Moorfields*, the Younkers,
And Tits, and Tom-boys should have fed on, *gratis.*
  Mam. I will go mount a Turnip-cart, and preach
The end o' the world, within these two months. *Surly,*
What! in a dream? *Sur.* Must I needs cheat my self,
With that foolish vice of Honesty!
Come, let us go, and hearken out the Rogues.
That *Face* I'll mark for mine, if e'er I meet him.
  Fac. If I can hear of him, Sir, I'll bring you word
Unto yourLodgings; for in troth, they were strangers
To me, I thought 'em honest, as my self, Sir. [*They come forth.*
  Tri. 'Tis well, the *Saints* shall not lose all yet. Go,
And get some Carts—— *Lov.* For what, my zealous Friends?
  Ana. To bear away the portion of the righteous
Out of this Den of Thieves. *Lov.* What is that portion?
  Ana. The Goods, sometimes the Orphans, that the *Brethren*
Bought with their Silver Pence. *Lov.* What, those i' the
   Cellar,
The Knight Sir *Mammon* claims? *Ana.* I do defie
The wicked *Mammon,* so do all the *Brethren.*
Thou prophane Man, I ask thee, with what conscience

Thou canst advance that Idol against us,
That have the Seal?   Were not the Shillings numbred,
That made the Pounds?   Were not the Pounds told out,
Upon the second day of the fourth week,
In the eighth month, upon the Table dormant,
The Year of the last patience of the *Saints*,
Six hundred and ten?
   Lov.   Mine earnest vehement Botcher,
And *Deacon* also, I cannot dispute with you;
But if you get you not away the sooner,
I shall confute you with a Cudgel. *Ana.* Sir.
   Tri. Be patient, *Ananias.*   *Ana.* I am strong,
And will stand up, well girt, against an Host,
That threaten *God* in exile.   *Lov.* I shall send you
To *Amsterdam* to your Cellar.   *Ana.* I will pray there,
Against thy House: may Dogs defile thy Walls,
And Wasps, and Hornets breed beneath thy Roof,
This seat of falshood, and this cave of coz'nage.
   Lov. Another too?   *Dru.* Not I Sir, I am no Brother.
                       [*Drugger enters, and he beats him away.*
   Lov. Away you *Harry Nicholas*, do you talk?
   Fac. No, this was *Abel Drugger.*   Good Sir, Go.
                                             [*To the Parson.*
And satisfie him; tell him, all is done:
He staid too long a washing of his Face.
The Doctor, he shall hear of him at *Westchester;*
And of the Captain, tell him, at *Yarmouth,* or
Some good Port-town else, lying for a wind.
If you get off the angry Child, now, Sir ——
   Kas. Come on, you yew, you have match'd most sweetly,
       ha' you not?   [*To his Sister.*
Did not I say, I would never ha' you tupt
But by a dubb'd Boy, to make you a Lady *Tom!*
'Slight, you are a Mammet! O I could touse you, now.
Death, mun'you marry with a Pox?   *Lov.* You lye, Boy!
As sound as you and I am afore-hand with you. *Kas.* Anon?
   Lov. Come, will you quarrel? I will seize you, Sirrah.

Why do you not buckle to your Tools? *Kas.* Gods light!
This is a fine old Boy, as ere I saw!
 Lov. What, do you change your Copy, now? Proceed,
Here stands my Dove: stoop at her if you dare.
 Kas. 'Slight, I must love him! I cannot chuse, i' faith!
And I should be hang'd for't. Suster, I protest,
I honour thee for this match. *Lov.* O, do you so, Sir.
 Kas. Yes, an' thou canst take *Tobacco*, and drink, old Boy,
I'll give her five hundred Pound more to her marriage,
Than her own State. *Lov.* Fill a Pipe-full, *Jeremy.*
 Fac. Yes, but go in, and take it, Sir. *Lov.* We will.
I will be rul'd by thee in any thing, *Jeremy.*
 Kas. 'Slight, thou art not hide-bound! thou art a *Jovy*' Boy!
Come let's in. I pry'thee, and take our whiffs.
 Lov. Whiff in with your Sister, brother Boy. That Master
That had receiv'd such happiness by a Servant,
In such a Widow, and with so much Wealth,
Were very ungrateful, if he would not be
A little indulgent to that Servants wit,
And help his Fortune, though with some small strain
Of his own Candor. Therefore, Gentlemen,
And kind Spectators, if I have out-stript
An old Mans gravity, or strict Canon, think
What a young Wife, and a good Brain may do:
Stretch ages truth sometimes, and crack it too.
Speak for thy self, Knave. *Fac.* So I will, Sir. Gentlemen,
My part a little fell in this last *Scene*,
Yet 'twas *decorum*. And though I am clean
Got off from *Subtle*, *Surly*, *Mammon*, *Dol*,
Hot *Ananias*, *Dapper*, *Drugger*, all
With whom I traded; yet I put my self
On you, that are my Country: and this Pelf,
Which I have got, if you do quit me, rests
To feast you often, and invite new Guests.

VII.

JOHN LOCKE.
1632—1704.

"LOCKE is one of the greatest philosophers and *most powerful writers* that ever adorned this country, celebrated not only by his wisdom, but by his piety and virtue, by his love of truth and diligence in the pursuit of it, and by a noble ardour in defence of the civil and religious rights of mankind. He possessed a noble and lofty mind, superior to prejudice and capable, by its native energy, of exploring the truth, even in the regions of the intellectual world before unknown; his judgement was accurate and profound, his imagination vigorous, as he was well furnished with the ornaments of elegant learning."

The (London) Cyclopædia.
Vol. XXI.

SOME OF LOCKE'S
THOUGHTS CONCERNING EDUCATION.

"A sound Mind in a sound Body"—is a short, but full Description of a happy State in this World. He that has these two, has little more to wish for; and he that wants either of them, will be but little the better for any thing else. Mens Happiness or Misery is most part of their own making. He, whose Mind directs not wisely, will never take the right Way; and he, whose Body is crazy and feeble, will never be able to advance in it. I confess, there are some Men's Constitutions of Body and Mind so vigorous, and well framed by Nature, that they need not much Assistance from others; but by the Strength of their natural Genius, they are from their Cradles carried towards what is excellent; and by the Privilege of their happy Constitutions, are able to do Wonders. But Examples of this Kind are but few; and I think I may say, that of all the Men we meet with, nine Parts of ten are what they are, good or evil, useful or not, by their Education. 'Tis that which makes the great Difference in Mankind. The little, or almost insensible Impressions on our tender Infancies, have very important and lasting Consequences: And there it is, as in the Fountains of some Rivers, where a gentle Application of the Hand turns the flexible Waters into Channels, that make them take quite contrary Courses; and by this little Direction given them at first in the Source, they receive different Tendencies, and arrive at last at very remote and distant Places.

Health. — I imagine the Minds of Children as easily turned this or that way, as Water itself; and though this be the principal Part, and our main Care should be about the Inside, yet the Clay Cottage is not to be neglected. I shall therefore begin with the Case, and consider first the *Health* of the Body, as that which perhaps you may rather expect from that Study I have been thought more peculiarly to have applied myself to; and that also which will be soonest dispatched, as lying, if I guess not amiss, in a very little Compass.

How necessary *Health* is to our Business and Happiness; and how requisite a strong Constitution, able to endure Hardships and Fatigue, is to one that will make any Figure in the World, is too obvious to need any Proof.

The Consideration I shall here have of *Health*, shall be, not what a Physician ought to do with a sick or crazy Child, but what the Parents, without the Help of Physick, should do for the *Preservation and Improvement of an healthy*, or at least *not sickly Constitution* in their Children: And this perhaps might be all dispatched in this one short Rule, *viz.* That Gentlemen should use their Children as the honest Farmers and substantial Yeomen do theirs. But because the Mothers possibly may think this a little too hard, and the Fathers too short, I shall explain myself more particularly; only laying down this as a general and certain Observation for the Women to consider, *viz.* That most Children's Constitutions are either spoiled, or at least harmed, by *Cockering* and *Tenderness.*

Warmth. — The first Thing to be taken care of, is, that Children be not too *warmly clad or covered*, Winter or Summer. The Face, when we are born, is no less tender than any other Part of the Body. 'Tis Use alone hardens it, and makes it more able to endure the Cold: And therefore the *Scythian* Philosopher gave a very significant Answer to the *Athenian*, who wondered how he could go naked in Frost and Snow. *How*, said the *Scythian*, *can you endure your Face exposed to the sharp Winter Air? My Face is used to it,* said the *Athenian*. *Think me all Face*, replied the *Scythian*. Our Bodies will endure any thing, that from the Beginning they are accustomed to.

Give me Leave therefore to advise you, not to fence too carefully against the Cold of this our Climate. There are those in *England*, who wear the same Clothes Winter and Summer, and that without any Inconvenience, or more Sense of Cold than others find. But if the Mother will needs have an Allowance for Frost and Snow, for fear of Harm, and the Father for fear of Censure, be sure let not his Winter-Clothing be too warm: And amongst other Things, remember, that when Nature has so well covered his Head with Hair, and strengthened it with a Year or two's Age, that he can run about by Day without a Cap, it is best that by Night a Child should also lie without one; there being nothing that more exposes to Headach, Colds, Catarrhs, Coughs, and several other Diseases, than keeping the *Head warm*.

I have said *He* here, because the principal Aim of my Discourse is, how a young Gentleman should be brought up from his Infancy, which, in all Things, will not so perfectly suit the Education of *Daughters;* though where the Difference of Sex requires different Treatment, it will be no hard Matter to distinguish.

Swimming. — I shall not need here to mention *Swimming*, when he is of an Age able to learn, and has any one to teach him. 'Tis that saves many a Man's Life; and the *Romans* thought it so necessary, that they ranked it with Letters; and it was the common Phrase to mark one ill-educated, and good for nothing, that he had neither learnt to read nor to swim. *Nec literas didicit, nec natare.* But besides the gaining a Skill which may serve him at need, the Advantages to Health, by often *bathing in cold Water*, during the Heat of Summer, are so many, that I think nothing need to be said to encourage it, provided this one Caution be used, That he never go into the Water, when Exercise has at all warmed him, or left any Emotion in his Blood or Pulse.

Air. — Another Thing that is of great Advantage to every one's Health, but especially Children's, is, to be much in the *open Air*, and very little as may be by the Fire, even in Winter. By this he will accustom himself also to Heat and Cold, Shine and Rain; all which, if a Man's Body will not endure, it will serve him to very little Purpose in this World; and when he is grown up, it is too late to begin to use him to it. It must be got early, and by Degrees. Thus the Body may be brought to bear almost any thing. If I should advise him to play in the *Wind and Sun without a Hut*, I doubt whether it could be borne. There would a thousand Objections be made against it, which at last would amount to no more in Truth, than being Sunburnt. And if my young Master be to be kept always in the Shade, and never exposed to the Sun and Wind, for fear of his Complexion, it may be a good Way to make him a *Beau*, but not a Man of Business. And altho' greater Regard be to be had to Beauty in the Daughters, yet I will take the Liberty to say, that the more they are in the *Air*, without Prejudice to their Faces, the stronger and healthier they will be; and the nearer they come to the Hardships of their Brothers in their Education, the greater Advantage will they receive from it all the remaining Part of their Lives.

Habits. — Playing in the *open Air* has but this one Danger in it, that I know; and that is, that when he is hot with running up and down, he should sit or lie down on the cold or moist Earth. This I grant; and drinking cold Drink, when they are hot with Labour or Exercise, brings more People to the Grave, or to the Brink of it, by Fevers and other Diseases, than any thing I know. These Mischiefs are easily enough prevented whilst he is little, being then seldom out of Sight. And if, during his Childhood, he be constantly and rigorously kept from sitting on the Ground, or drinking any cold Liquor, whilst he is hot, the Custom of forbearing, grown into *Habit*, will help much to preserve him, when he is no longer under his Maid's or Tutor's Eye. This is all I think can be done in the Case: For, as Years increase, Liberty must come with them; and in a great many Things he must be trusted to his own Conduct, since there cannot always be a Guard upon him, except what you have put into his own Mind by good Principles, and established Habits, which is the best and surest, and therefore most to be taken Care of: For, from repeated Cautions and Rules, ever so often inculcated, you are not to expect any thing either in this, or any other Case, farther than Practice has established them into Habits.

Clothes. — One thing the Mention of the Girls brings into my Mind, which must not be forgot; and that is, that your Son's *Clothes* be *never* made *strait*, especially about the Breast. Let Nature have Scope to fashion the Body as she thinks best. She works of herself a great deal better and exacter than we can direct her: And if Women were themselves to frame the Bodies of their Children in their Wombs, as they often endeavour to mend their Shapes when they are out, we should as certainly have no perfect Children born, as we have few well-shaped that are *strait-laced*, or much tampered with. This Consideration should, methinks, keep busy People (I will not say ignorant

Nurses and Bodice-makers) from medling in a Matter they understand not; and they should be afraid to put Nature out of her Way in fashioning the Parts, when they know not how the least and meanest is made: And yet I have seen so many Instances of Children receiving great Harm from *strait-lacing*, that I cannot but conclude there are other Creatures, as well as Monkeys, who, little wiser than they, destroy their young ones by senseless Fondness, and too much embracing.

Narrow Breasts, short and stinking Breath, ill Lungs, and Crookedness, are the natural and almost constant Effects of *hard Bodice*, and *Clothes that pinch*. That Way of making slender Waists and fine Shapes, serves but the more effectually to spoil them. Nor can there indeed but be Disproportion in the Parts, when the Nourishment prepared in the several Offices of the Body cannot be distributed as Nature designs. And therefore what Wonder is it, if, it being laid where it can, on some Part not so *braced*, it often makes a Shoulder or a Hip higher or bigger than its just Proportion? 'Tis generally known, that the Women of *China*, (imagining I know not what Kind of Beauty in it) by bracing and binding them hard from their Infancy, have very little Feet. I saw lately a Pair of *China* Shoes, which I was told were for a grown Woman: They were so exceedingly disproportioned to the Feet of one of the same Age amongst us, that they would scarce have been big enough for one of our little Girls. Besides this, 'tis observed, that their Women are also very little, and short-lived; whereas the Men are of the ordinary Stature of other Men, and live to a proportionable Age. These Defects in the Female Sex of that Country, are, by some, imputed to the unreasonable Binding of their Feet, whereby the free Circulation of the Blood is hindered, and the Growth and Health of the whole Body suffers. And how often do we see, that some small Part of the Foot being injured by a Wrench or a Blow, the whole Leg or Thigh thereby loses its Strength and Nourishment, and dwindles away? How much greater Inconveniencies may we expect, when the *Thorax*, wherein is placed the Heart and Seat of Life, is unnaturally *compressed*, and hindered from its due Expansion?

Diet. — As for his *Diet*, it ought to be very *plain* and simple; and if I might advise, Flesh should be forborn as long as he is in Coats, or at least 'till he is two or three Years old. But whatever Advantage this may be to his present and future Health and Strength, I fear it will hardly be consented to by Parents, misled by the Custom of eating too much Flesh themselves, who will be apt to think their Children, as they do themselves, in Danger to be starved, if they have not Flesh at least twice a Day. This I am sure, Children would breed their Teeth with much less Danger, be freer from Diseases whilst they were little, and lay the Foundations of an healthy and strong Constitution much surer, if they were not crammed so much as they are by fond Mothers and foolish Servants, and were kept wholly from Flesh, the first three or four Years of their Lives.

But if my young Master must needs have Flesh, let it be but once a Day, and of one Sort at a Meal. Plain Beef, Mutton, Veal, etc. without other Sauce than Hunger, is best; and great Care should be used, that he eat *Bread* plentifully, both alone and with every thing else; and whatever he eats that is solid, make him chew it well. We *English* are often negligent herein; from whence follow Indigestion, and other great Inconveniencies.

For *Breakfast* and *Supper*, *Milk*, *Milk-Pottage*, *Water-Gruel*, *Flummery*, and twenty other Things, that we are wont to make in *England*, are very fit for Children; only, in all these, let Care be taken that they be plain, and without much Mixture, and very sparingly seasoned with Sugar, or rather none at all; especially all *Spice*, and other Things that may heat the Blood, are carefully to be avoided. Be sparing also of *Salt* in the seasoning of all his Victuals, and use him not to high-seasoned Meats. Our Palates grow into a Relish and Liking of the Seasoning and Cookery, which by Custom they are set to; and an over-much Use of Salt, besides that it occasions Thirst, and over-much Drinking, has other ill Effects upon the Body. I should think, that a good Piece of well-made and well-baked *brown Bread*, sometimes with, and sometimes without *Butter* or *Cheese*, would be often the best Breakfast for my young Master. I am sure it is as wholesome, and will make him as strong a Man as greater Delicacies; and if he be used to it, it will be as pleasant to him. If he at any Time calls for Victuals between Meals, use him to nothing but dry *Bread*. If he be hungry more than wanton, *Bread* alone will down; and if he be not hungry, it is not fit he should eat. By this you will obtain two good Effects. 1. That by Custom he will come to be in Love with *Bread;* for, as I said, our Palates and Stomachs too are pleased with the Things we are used to. Another Good you will gain hereby is, That you will not teach him to eat more nor oftener than Nature requires. I do not think that all People's Appetites are alike; some have naturally stronger, and some weaker Stomachs. But this I think, that many are made *Gormands* and *Gluttons* by Custom, that were not so by Nature: And I see, in some Countries, Men as lusty and strong, that eat but two Meals a Day, as others that have set their Stomachs by a constant Usage, like Larums, to call on them for four or five. The *Romans* usually fasted 'till Supper, the only set Meal, even of those who ate more than once a Day; and those who used Breakfasts, as some did at eight, some at ten, others at twelve of the Clock, and some later, neither eat Flesh nor had any Thing made ready for them. *Augustus*, when the greatest Monarch on the Earth, tells us, he took a Bit of dry Bread in his Chariot. And *Seneca*, giving an Account how he managed himself, even when he was old, and his Age permitted Indulgence, says, That he used to eat a Piece of dry Bread for his Dinner, without the Formality of sitting to it, though his Estate would as well have paid for a better Meal, (had Health required it) as any Subject's in *England*, were it doubled. The Masters of the World were bred up with this spare Diet; and the young Gentlemen of *Rome* felt no Want of Strength or Spirit, because they eat but once a Day. Or, if it happened by Chance, that any one could not fast so long as till Supper, their only set Meal, he took nothing but a Bit of dry Bread, or at most a few Raisins, or some such slight Thing with it, to stay his Stomach. This Part of Temperance was found so necessary both for Health and Business, that the Custom of only one Meal a Day held out against that prevailing Luxury, which their Eastern Conquests and Spoils had brought in amongst them; and those who had given up their old frugal Eating, and made Feasts, yet began them not till the Evening. And more than one set Meal a Day was thought so monstrous, that it was a Reproach as low down as *Cæsar's* Time, to make an Entertainment, or sit down to a full Table, till towards Sun-set; and therefore, if it would not be thought too severe, I should judge it most convenient, that my young Master should have nothing but *Bread* too for *Breakfast*. You cannot imagine of what Force Custom is; and I impute a great Part of our Diseases in *England*, to our eating too much *Flesh*, and too little *Bread*.

His *Drink* should be only small Beer; and that too he should never be suffered to have between Meals, but after he had eat a Piece of Bread. The Reasons, why I say this, are these.

1. More Fevers and Surfeits are got by Peoples drinking when they are hot, than by any one Thing

I know. Therefore, if by Play he be hot and dry, Bread will ill go down; and so if he cannot have *Drink*, but upon that Condition, he will be forced to forbear; for, if he be very hot, he should by no Means *drink;* at least a good Piece of Bread first to be eaten, will gain Time to warm the Beer *Blood-hot*, which then he may drink safely. If he be very dry, it will go down so warmed, and quench his Thirst better; and if he will not drink it so warmed, abstaining will not hurt him. Besides, this will teach him to forbear, which is an Habit of greatest Use for Health of Body and Mind too.

2. *Habits.* — Not being permitted to *drink* without eating, will prevent the Custom of having the Cup often at his Nose; a dangerous Beginning, and Preparation to *Good-Fellowship*. Men often bring habitual Hunger and Thirst on themselves by Custom. And if you please to try, you may, though he be weaned from it, bring him by Use to such a Necessity again of *Drinking* in the Night, that he will not be able to sleep without it, it being the Lullaby used by Nurses, to still crying Children. I believe, Mothers generally find some Difficulty to wean their Children from *drinking* in the Night, when they first take them home. Believe it, Custom prevails as much by Day as by Night; and you may, if you please, bring any one to be thirsty every Hour.

I once lived in a House, where, to appease a froward Child, they gave him *Drink* as often as he cried; so that he was constantly bibbing: And, though he could not speak, yet he drank more in twenty-four Hours, than I did. Try it when you please, you may with Small, as well as with Strong Beer, drink yourself into a Drought. The great Thing to be minded in Education, is, what *Habits* you settle; and therefore in this, as all other Things, do not begin to make any Thing *customary*, the Practice whereof you would not have continue, and increase. It is convenient, for Health and Sobriety, to *drink* no more than natural Thirst requires; and he that eats not salt Meats, nor drinks strong Drink, will seldom thirst between Meals, unless he has been accustomed to such unseasonable *Drinking*.

Above all, take great Care that he seldom, if ever, taste any *Wine* or *strong Drink*.

Fruit. — *Fruit* makes one of the most difficult Chapters in the Government of Health, especially that of Children. Our first Parents ventured *Paradise* for it; and it is no Wonder our Children cannot stand the Temptation, though it cost them their Health. The Regulation of this cannot come under any one general Rule; for I am by no Means of their Mind, who would keep Children almost wholely upon *Fruit*, as a Thing totally unwholesome for them: By which strict Way, they make them but the more ravenous after it, and to eat good or bad, ripe or unripe, all that they can get, whenever they come at it. *Melons*, *Peaches*, most Sorts of *Plums*, and all Sort of *Grapes* in *England*, I think Children should be *wholely kept from*, as having a very tempting Taste, in a very unwholesome Juice; so that, if it were possible, they should never so much as see them, or know there were any such Thing. But *Strawberries*, *Cherries*, *Gooseberries*, or *Currants*, when thorough ripe, I think may be pretty safely allowed them, and that with a very liberal Hand, if they be eaten with these Cautions: 1. Not after Meals, as we usually do, when the Stomach is already full of other Food: But I think they should be eaten rather before or between Meals, and Children should have them for their Breakfasts. 2. Bread eaten with them. 3. Perfectly ripe. If they are thus eaten, I imagine them rather conducing, than hurtful to our Health. *Summer-Fruits*, being suited to the hot Season of the Year they come in, refresh our Stomachs, languishing and fainting under it; and therefore I should not be altogether so strict in this Point, as some are to their Children; who being kept so very short, instead of a moderate Quantity of well-chosen *Fruit*, which being allowed them, would content them, whenever they can get loose, or bribe a Servant to supply them, satisfy their Longing with any Trash they can get, and eat to a Surfeit.

Apples and *Pears* too, which are thorough ripe, and have been gathered some Time, I think may be safely eaten at any Time, and in pretty large Quantities; especially *Apples*, which never did any Body Hurt, that I have heard, after *October*.

Fruits also dryed without Sugar, I think very wholesome. But *Sweetmeats* of all Kinds are to be avoided; which, whether they do more Harm to the Maker or Eater, is not easy to tell. This I am sure, it is one of the most inconvenient Ways of Expence that Vanity hath yet found out; and so I leave them to the Ladies.

Sleep. — Of all that looks soft and effeminate, nothing is more to be indulged Children, than *Sleep.* In this alone they are to be permitted to have their full Satisfaction; nothing contributing more to the Growth and Health of Children, than *Sleep.* All that is to be regulated in it, is, in what Part of the twenty-four Hours they should take it; which will easily be resolved, by only saying, that it is of great Use to accustom them to rise early in the Morning. It is best so to do, for Health; and he that, from his Childhood, has, by a settled Custom, made *rising betimes* easy and familiar to him, will not, when he is a Man, waste the best and most useful Part of his Life in Drowziness, and lying a Bed. If Children therefore are to be called up early in the Morning, it will follow of Course, that they must go to Bed betimes; whereby they will be accustomed to avoid the unhealthy and unsafe Hours of Debauchery, which are those of the Evenings; and they who keep good Hours, seldom are guilty of any great Disorders. I do not say this, as if your Son, when grown up, should never be in Company past Eight, nor ever chat over a Glass of Wine till Midnight. You are now, by the accustoming of his tender Years, to indispose him to those Inconveniences, as much as you can; and it will be no small Advantage, that contrary Practice having made sitting up uneasy to him, it will make him often avoid, and very seldom propose Midnight-Revels. But if it should not reach so far, but Fashion and Company should prevail, and make him live as others do above Twenty, it is worth the while to accustom him to *early Rising* and early going to Bed, between this and that, for the present Improvement of his Health, and other Advantages.

Though I have said a large Allowance of *Sleep*, even as much as they will take, should be made to Children when they are little, yet I do not mean, that it should always be continued to them in so large a Proportion, and they suffered to indulge a drowzy Laziness in their Bed, as they grow up bigger. But whether they should begin to be restrained at Seven, or Ten Years old, or any other Time, is impossible to be precisely determined. Their Tempers, Strength, and Constitutions, must be considered. But some Time between Seven and Fourteen, if they are too great Lovers of their Beds, I think it may be seasonable to begin to reduce them, by Degrees, to about eight Hours, which is generally Rest enough for healthy grown People. If you have accustomed him, as you should do, to rise constantly very early in the Morning, this Fault of being too long in Bed will easily be reformed, and most Children will be froward enough to shorten that Time themselves, by coveting to sit up with the Company at Night, though if they be not looked after, they will be apt to take it out in the Morning, which should by no Means be permitted. They should constantly be called up and made to rise at their early Hour; but great Care should be taken in waking them, that it be not done hastily, nor with a loud or shrill Voice, or any other sudden violent Noise. This often affrights Children, and does them great Harm; and sound *Sleep* thus broke off, with sudden Alarms, is apt enough to discompose any one. When Children are to be wakened out of their *Sleep*, be sure to begin with a low Call, and some gentle Motion, and so draw them out of it by Degrees, and give them none but kind Words and Usage, till they are come perfectly to themselves, and being quite dressed, you are sure they are thoroughly awake. The being forced from their *Sleep*, how gently soever you do it, is Pain enough to them; and Care should be taken not to add any other Uneasiness to it, especially such that may terrify them.

Bed. — Let his *Bed* be *hard*, and rather Quilts, than Feathers. Hard Lodging strengthens the Parts, whereas being buryed every Night in Feathers melts and dissolves the Body, is often the Cause of Weakness, and the Forerunner of an early Grave. And, besides the Stone, which has often its Rise from this warm Wrapping of the Reins, several other Indispositions, and that which is the Root of them all, a tender, weakly Constitution, is very much owing to *Down Beds*. Besides, he that is used to hard Lodging at home, will not miss his Sleep (where he has most Need of it) in his Travels abroad, for Want of his soft Bed, and his Pillows laid in Order. And therefore, I think it would not be amiss, to *make* his *Bed* after different Fashions; sometimes lay his Head higher, sometimes lower, that he may not feel every little Change he must be sure to meet with, who is not designed to lie always in my young Master's Bed at home, and to have his Maid lay all Things in Print, and tuck him in warm. The great Cordial of Nature is *Sleep*. He that misses that, will suffer by it; and he is very unfortunate, who can take his Cordial only in his Mother's fine gilt Cup, and not in a wooden Dish. He that can sleep soundly, takes the Cordial; and it matters not, whether it be on a soft *Bed*, or the hard Boards. 'Tis *Sleep* only that is the Thing necessary.

And thus I have done with what concerns the Body and Health, which reduces itself to these few and easy observable Rules. Plenty of open *Air*, *Exercise*, and *Sleep*, plain *Diet*, no *Wine* or *strong Drink*, and very little or no Physick, not too warm and strait *Clothing*, especially the *Head* and *Feet* kept cold, and the *Feet* often used to cold Water, and exposed to Wet.

Mind. — Due Care being had to keep the Body in Strength and Vigour, so that it may be able to obey and execute the Orders of the *Mind;* the next and principal Business, is, to set the *Mind* right, that on all Occasions it may be disposed to consent to nothing, but what may be suitable to the Dignity and Excellency of a rational Creature.

If what I have said in the Beginning of this Discourse, be true, as I do not doubt but it is, *viz.* That the Difference to be found in the Manners and Abilities of Men is owing more to their *Education*, than to any thing else, we have Reason to conclude, that great Care is to be had of the forming Childrens *Minds*, and giving them that Seasoning early, which shall influence their Lives always after: For when they do well or ill, the Praise or Blame will be laid there; and when any thing is done awkwardly, the common Saying will pass upon them, that it is suitable to their *Breeding.*

As the Strength of the Body lies chiefly in being able to endure Hardships, so also does that of the Mind. And the great Principle and Foundation of all Virtue and Worth, is placed in this, That a Man is able to *deny himself* his own Desires, cross his own Inclinations, and purely follow what Reason directs as best, though the Appetite lean the other Way.

Early. — The great Mistake, I have observed in Peoples Breeding their Children, has been, that this has not been taken Care enough of in its *due Season;* that the Mind has not been made obedient to Discipline, and pliant to Reason, when at first it was most tender, most easy to be bowed. Parents, being wisely ordained by Nature to love their Children, are very apt, if Reason watch not that natural Affection very warily, are apt, I say, to let it run into Fondness. They love their little Ones, and it is their Duty; but they often, with them, cherish their Faults too. They must not be crossed forsooth; they must be permitted to have their Wills in all Things; and they being, in their Infancies, not capable of great Vices, their Parents think they may safely enough indulge their little Irregularities, and make themselves Sport with that pretty Perverseness, which they think well enough becomes that innocent Age. But to a fond Parent, that would not have his Child corrected for a perverse Trick, but excused it, saying it was a small Matter, *Solon* very well replyed: *Aye, but Custom is a great one.*

The Foundling must be taught to strike and call Names, must have what he calls for, and do what he pleases. Thus Parents, by humouring and cockering them when *little*, corrupt the Principles of Nature in their Children, and wonder afterwards to taste their bitter Waters, when they themselves have poisoned the Fountain; for, when their Children are grown up, and these ill Habits with them; when they are now too big to be daudled, and their Parents can no longer make Use of them as Play-things; then they complain that the Brats are untoward and perverse; then they are offended to see them wilful, and are troubled with those ill Humours which they themselves infused and fomented in them; and then, perhaps too late, would be glad to get out those Weeds, which their own Hands have planted, and which now have taken too deep Root, to be easily extirpated. For he that has been used to have his Will in every Thing, as long as he was in Coats, why should we think it strange that he should desire it, and contend for it still, when he is in Breeches? Indeed, as he grows more towards a Man, Age shews his Faults the more; so that there be few Parents then so blind, as not to see them; few so insensible, as not to feel the ill Effects of their own Indulgence. He had the Will of his Maid before he could speak, or go; he had the Mastery of his Parents ever since he could prattle; and why, now he is grown up, is stronger and wiser than he was then, why now of a sudden must he be restrained and curbed? Why must he at seven, fourteen, or twenty Years old, lose the Privilege, which the Parents Indulgence, till then so largely allowed him? Try it in a Dog, or an Horse, or any other Creature, and see whether the ill and resty Tricks, they have learned when young, are easily to be mended when they are knit; and yet none of those Creatures are Half so wilful and proud, or Half so desirous to be Masters of themselves and others, as Man.

We are generally wise enough to begin with them when they are *very young*, and discipline *betimes* those other Creatures we would make useful and good for somewhat. They are only our own Offspring, that we neglect in this Point; and having made them ill Children, we foolishly expect they should be good Men. For if the Child must have Grapes or Sugar-Plumbs when he has a Mind to them, rather than make the poor Baby cry, or be out of Humour; why, when he is grown up, must he not be satisfied too, if his Desires carry him to Wine or Women? They are Objects as suitable to the Longing of one of more Years, as what he cried for, when little, was to the Inclinations of a Child. The having Desires accommodated to the Apprehensions and Relish of those several Ages, is not the Fault; but the not having them subject to the Rules and Restraints of Reason: The Difference lies not in having or not having Appetites, but in the Power to govern, and deny ourselves in them. He that is not used to submit his Will to the Reason of others, *when he is young*, will scarce hearken or submit to his own Reason, when he is of an Age to make Use of it. And what a Kind of a Man such an one is likely to prove, is easy to foresee.

These are Oversights usually committed by those who seem to take the greatest Care of their Childrens Education. But if we look into the common Management of Children, we shall have Reason to wonder, in the great Dissoluteness of Manners which the World complains of, that there are any Foot-Steps at all left of Virtue. I desire to know what Vice can be named, which Parents, and those about Children, do not season them with, and drop into them the Seeds of, as soon as they are capable to receive them? I do not mean by the Examples they give, and the Patterns they set before them, which is Encouragement enough; but that which I would take Notice of here, is, the downright teaching them Vice, and actually putting them out of the Way of Virtue. Before they can go, they principle them with Violence, Revenge, and Cruelty. *Give me a Blow, that I may beat him*, is a Lesson which most Children every Day hear; and it is thought nothing, because their Hands have not Strength to do any Mischief. But I ask, does not this corrupt their Mind? Is not this the Way of Force and Violence, that they are set in? And if they have been taught, when little, to strike and hurt others by Proxy, and encouraged to rejoice in the Harm they have brought upon them, and see them suffer, are they not prepared to do it, when they are strong enough to be felt themselves, and can strike to some Purpose?

The Coverings of our Bodies, which are for Modesty, Warmth, and Defence, are, by the Folly or Vice of Parents, recommended to their Children for other Uses. They are made Matters of Vanity and Emulation. A Child is set a longing after a new Suit, for the Finery of it; and when the little Girl is tricked up in her new Gown and Commode, how can her Mother do less than teach her to admire herself, by calling her, *her little Queen*, and *her Princess?* Thus the little ones are taught to be *proud* of their Clothes, before they can put them on. And why should they not continue to value themselves for this outside Fashionableness of the Taylor or Tire-woman's making, when their Parents have so early instructed them to do so?

Sauces and Ragoos, and Food disguised by all the Arts of Cookery, must tempt their Palates, when their Bellies are full; and then, for Fear the Stomach should be overcharged, a Pretence is found for the other Glass of Wine to help Digestion, though it only serves to increase the Surfeit.

Is my young Master a little out of Order, the first Question is: *What will my Dear eat? What shall I get for thee?* Eating and Drinking are instantly pressed; and every Body's Invention is set on work to find out something, luscious and delicate enough to prevail over that Want of Appetite, which Nature has wisely ordered in the Beginning of Distempers, as a Defence against their Increase, that being freed from the ordinary Labour of digesting any new Load in the Stomach, she may be at Leisure to correct and master the peccant Humours.

And where Children are so happy in the Care of their Parents, as by their Prudence to be kept from the Excess of their Tables, to the Sobriety of a plain and simple Diet, yet there too they are scarce to be preserved from the Contagion that poisons the Mind; though, by a discreet Management, whilst they are under Tuition, their Healths perhaps may be pretty well secure, yet their Desires must needs yield to the Lessons which every where will be read to them upon this Part of Epicurism. The Commendation, that *eating well* has every where, cannot fail to be a successful Incentive to natural Appetite, and bring them quickly to the Liking and Expence of a fashionable Table. This shall have from every one, even the Reprovers of Vice, the Title of *Living well.* And what shall sullen Reason dare to say against the publick Testimony? Or can it hope to be heard, if it should call that *Luxury*, which is so much owned, and universally practised by those of the best Quality?

This is now so grown a Vice, and has so great Supports, that I know not whether it do not put in for the Name of Virtue; and whether it will not be thought Folly, or Want of Knowledge of the World, to open one's Mouth against it. And, truly, I should suspect, that what I have here said of it might be censured as a little Satyre out of my Way, did I not mention it with this View, that it might awaken the Care and Watchfulness of Parents in the Education of their Children, when they see how they are beset on every Side, not only with Temptations, but Instructors to Vice, and that, perhaps, in those they thought Places of Security.

I shall not dwell any longer on this Subject, much less run over all the Particulars that would shew what Pains are used to corrupt Children, and instil Principles of Vice into them: But I desire Parents soberly to consider, what Irregularity or Vice there is, which Children are not visibly taught, and whether it be not their Duty and Wisdom to provide them other Instructions.

Craving. — It seems plain to me, that the Principle of all Virtue and Excellency lies in a Power of denying ourselves the Satisfaction of our own Desires, where Reason does not authorize them. This Power is to be got and improved by Custom, made easy and familiar by an *early* Practice. If, therefore, I might be heard, I would advise, that, contrary to the ordinary Way, Children should be used to submit their Desires, and go without their Longings, even *from their very Cradles*. The very first Thing they should learn to know, should be, that they were not to have any Thing because it pleased them, but because it was thought fit for them. If Things suitable to their Wants were supplied to them, so that they were never suffered to have what they once cried for, they would learn to be content without it; would never, with Bawling and Peevishness, contend for Mastery, nor be half so uneasy to themselves and others, as they are, because *from the first*

Beginning they are not thus handled. If they were never suffered to obtain their Desire by the Impatience they expressed for it, they would no more cry for other Things, than they do for the Moon.

I say not this, as if Children were not to be indulged in any Thing, or that I expected they should in Hanging-Sleeves have the Reason and Conduct of Counsellors. I consider them as Children, who must be tenderly used, who must play, and have Playthings. That which I mean, is, that whenever they craved what was not fit for them to have or do, they should not be permitted it, because they were *little*, and desired it: Nay, whatever they were importunate for, they should be sure, for that very Reason, to be denied. I have seen Children at a Table, who, whatever was there, never asked for any Thing, but contentedly took what was given them: And, at another Place, I have seen others cry for every Thing they saw; must be served out of every Dish, and that first too. What made this vast Difference, but this; That one was accustomed to have what they called or cried for, the other to go without it? The *younger* they are, the less I think are their unruly and disorderly Appetites to be complied with; and the less Reason they have of their own, the more are they to be under the absolute Power and Restraint of those in whose Hands they are. From which, I confess, it will follow, that none but discreet People should be about them. If the World commonly does otherwise, I cannot help that. I am saying what I think should be; which, if it were already in Fashion, I should not need to trouble the World with a Discourse on this Subject. But yet I doubt not, but when it is considered, there will be others of Opinion with me, that the *sooner* this Way is begun with Children, the easier it will be for them, and their Governors too; and that this ought to be observed as an inviolable Maxim, that whatever once is denied them, they are certainly not to obtain by Crying or Importunity, unless one has a Mind to teach them to be impatient and troublesome, by rewarding them for it when they are so.

Early. — Those therefore that intend ever to govern their Children, should begin it whilst they are *very little*, and look that they perfectly comply with the Will of their Parents. Would you have your Son obedient to you, when past a Child? Be sure then to establish the Authority of a Father, *as soon* as he is capable of Submission, and can understand in whose Power he is. If you would have him stand in Awe of you, imprint it in his *Infancy;* and, as he approaches more to a Man, admit him nearer to your Familiarity; so shall you have him your obedient Subject (as is fit) whilst he is a Child, and your affectionate Friend when he is a Man. For methinks they mightily misplace the Treatment due to their Children, who are indulgent and familiar when they are little, but severe to them, and keep them at a Distance, when they are grown up: For Liberty and Indulgence can do no Good to *Children;* their Want of Judgement makes them stand in Need of Restraint and Discipline; and, on the contrary, Imperiousness and Severity is but an ill Way of treating Men, who have Reason of their own to guide them, unless you have a Mind to make your Children, when grown up, weary of you, and secretly to say with themselves: *When will you die, Father?*

I imagine every one will judge it reasonable, that their Children, *when little*, should look upon their Parents as their Lords, their absolute Governors, and as such stand in Awe of them; and that, when they come to riper Years, they should look on them as their best, as their only sure Friends, and as such love and reverence them. The Way I have mentioned, if I mistake not, is the only one to obtain this. We must look upon our Children, when grown up, to be like ourselves, with the same Passions, the same Desires. We would be thought rational Creatures, and have our Freedom; we love not to be uneasy under constant Rebukes and Brow-beatings; nor can we bear severe Humours, and great Distance in those we converse with. Whoever has such Treatment when he is a Man, will look out other Company, other Friends, other Conversation, with whom he can be at Ease. If therefore a strict Hand be kept over Children *from the Beginning*, they will in that Act be tractable, and quietly submit to it, as never having known any other: And if, as they grow up to the Use of Reason, the Rigour of Government be, as they deserve it, gently relaxed, the Father's Brow more smoothed to them, and the Distance by Degrees abated; his former Restraints will increase their Love, when they find it was only a Kindness to them, and a Care to make them capable to deserve the Favour of their Parents, and the Esteem of every Body else.

Thus much for the settling your Authority over your Children in general. Fear and Awe ought to give you the first Power over their Minds, and Love and Friendship in riper Years to hold it: For the Time must come, when they will be past the Rod and Correction; and then, if the Love of you make them not obedient and dutiful, if the Love of Virtue and Reputation keep them not in laudable Courses, I ask, what Hold will you have upon them to turn them to it? Indeed, Fear of having a scanty Portion if they displease you, may make them Slaves to your Estate; but they will be nevertheless ill and wicked in private; and that Restraint will not last always. Every Man must, some Time or other, be trusted to himself, and his own Conduct; and he that is a good, a virtuous and able Man, must be made so within. And therefore, what he is to receive from Education, what is to sway and influence his Life, must be something put into him betimes; Habits woven into the very Principles of his Nature, and not a counterfeit Carriage, and dissembled Outside, put on by Fear, only to avoid the present Anger of a Father, who perhaps may disinherit him.

Punishments. — This being laid down in general, as the Course ought to be taken, it is fit we now come to consider the Parts of the Discipline to be used, a little more particularly. I have spoken so much of carrying a *strict Hand* over Children, that perhaps I shall be suspected of not considering enough, what is due to their tender Age and Constitutions. But that Opinion will vanish, when you have heard me a little farther: For I am very apt to think, that *great Severity* of Punishment does but very little Good, nay, great Harm in Education; and I believe it will be found, that, *cæteris paribus*, those Children, who have been most *chastised*, seldom make the best Men. All that I have hitherto contended for is, that whatsoever *Rigour* is necessary, it is more to be used the younger Children are, and having by a due Application wrought its Effect, it is to be relaxed, and changed into a milder Sort of Government.

Awe. — A Compliance and Suppleness of their Wills, being by a steady Hand introduced by Parents, before Children have Memories to retain the Beginnings of it, will seem natural to them, and work afterwards in them, as if it were so, preventing all Occasions of struggling or repining. The only Care is, that it be begun early, and inflexibly kept to, till *Awe* and *Respect* be grown familiar, and there appears not the least Reluctancy in the Submission, and ready Obedience of their Minds. When this *Reverence* is once thus established, (which it must be early, or else it will cost Pains and Blows to recover it; and the more, the longer it is deferred) it is by it, mixed still with as much Indulgence as they make not an ill Use of, and not by *Beating*, *Chiding*, or other *servile Punishments*, they are for the future to be governed as they grow up to more Understanding.

Self-denial. — That this is so, will be easily allowed, when it is but considered, what is to be aimed at in an ingenuous Education, and upon what it turns.

1. He that has not a Mastery over his Inclinations, he that knows not how to *resist* the Importunity of *present Pleasure or Pain*, for the Sake of what Reason tells him is fit to be done, wants the true Principle of Virtue and Industry, and is in Danger of never being good for any Thing. This Temper therefore, so contrary to unguided Nature, is to be got betimes; and this Habit, as the true Foundation of future Ability and Happiness, is to be wrought into the Mind, as early as may be, even from the first Dawnings of any Knowledge, or Apprehension in Children, and so to be confirmed in them, by all the Care and Ways imaginable, by those who have the Oversight of their Education.

2. *Dejected.* — On the other Side, if the *Mind* be curbed, and *humbled* too much in Children; if their *Spirits* be abased and *broken* much, by too strict an Hand over them, they lose all their Vigour and Industry, and are in a worse State than the former. For extravagant young Fellows, that have Liveliness and Spirit, come sometimes to be set right, and so make able and great Men; but *dejected Minds*, timorous and tame, and *low Spirits*, are hardly ever to be raised, and very seldom attain to any Thing. To avoid the Danger that is on either Hand, is the great Art; and he that has found a Way how to keep up a Child's Spirit easy, active, and free, and yet, at the same Time, to restrain him

from many Things he has a Mind to, and to draw him to Things that are uneasy to him; he, I say, that knows how to reconcile these seeming Contradictions, has, in my Opinion, got the true Secret of Education.

Beating. — The usual, lazy, and short Way by Chastisement, and the Rod, which is the only Instrument of Government that Tutors generally know, or ever think of, is the most unfit of any to be used in Education, because it tends to both those Mischiefs, which, as we have shewn, are the *Scylla* and *Charybdis*, which on the one Hand or the other ruin all that miscarry.

1. This Kind of Punishment contributes not at all to the Mastery of our natural Propensity to indulge corporal and present Pleasure, and to avoid Pain at any Rate, but rather encourages it, and thereby strengthens that in us, which is the Root from whence spring all vicious Actions, and the Irregularities of Life. For what other Motive, but of sensual Pleasure and Pain, does a Child act by, who drudges at his Book against his Inclination, or abstains from eating unwholesome Fruit, that he takes Pleasure in, only out of Fear of *Whipping?* He in this only prefers the greater, *corporal Pleasure*, or avoids the greater *corporal Pain*. And what is it, to govern his Actions, and direct his Conduct, by such Motives as these? What is it, I say, but to cherish that Principle in him, which it is our Business to root out, and destroy? And therefore I cannot think any Correction useful to a Child, where the Shame of suffering, for having

done amiss, does not work more upon him than the Pain.

2. This Sort of Correction naturally breeds an Aversion to that which it is the Tutor's Business to create a Liking to. How obvious is it to observe, that Children come to hate Things which were at first acceptable to them, when they find themselves *whipped*, and *chid*, and teazed about them? And it is not to be wondered at in them, when grown Men would not be able to be reconciled to any Thing by such Ways. Who is there that would not be disgusted with any innocent Recreation, in itself indifferent to him, if he should with *Blows* or ill Language be *haled* to it, when he had no Mind? or be constantly so treated, for some Circumstances in his Application to it? This is natural to be so. Offensive Circumstances ordinarily infect innocent Things, which they are joined with; and the very Sight of a Cup, wherein any one uses to take nauseous Physick, turns his Stomach; so that nothing will relish well out of it, though the Cup be ever so clean and well-shaped, and of the richest Materials.

3. Such a Sort of *slavish Discipline* makes a *slavish Temper*. The Child submits, and dissembles Obedience, whilst the Fear of the Rod hangs over him; but when that is removed, and, by being out of Sight, he can promise himself Impunity, he gives the greater Scope to his natural Inclination; which, by this Way, is not at all altered, but, on the contrary, heightened and increased in him; and, after

such Restraint, breaks out usually with the more Violence. Or,

4. If *Severity* carried to the highest Pitch does prevail, and works a Cure upon the present unruly Distemper, it is often bringing in the room of it a worse and more dangerous Disease, by breaking the Mind; and then, in the Place of a disorderly young Fellow, you have a *low-spirited, moped* Creature; who, however with his unnatural Sobriety he may please silly People, who commend tame unactive Children, because they make no Noise, nor give them any Trouble, yet, at last, will probably prove as uncomfortable a Thing to his Friends, as he will be all his Life an useless Thing to himself and others.

Rewards. — Beating them, and all other Sorts of slavish and corporal Punishments, are not the Discipline fit to be used in the Education of those we would have wise, good, and ingenious Men; and therefore very rarely to be applied, and that only in great Occasions, and Cases of Extremity. On the other Side, to flatter Children by *Rewards* of Things that are pleasant to them, is as carefully to be avoided. He that will give to his Son *Apples* or *Sugar-plums*, or whatever else of this Kind he is most delighted with, to make him learn his Book, does but authorize his Love of Pleasure, and cocker up that dangerous Propensity, which he ought by all Means to subdue and stifle in him. You can never hope to teach him to master it, whilst you compound for the Check you give his Inclination in one Place, by the Satisfaction you propose to it in another. To make a good, a wise, and a virtuous Man, it is fit he should learn to cross his Appetite, and deny his Inclinations to *Riches*, *Finery*, or *pleasing his Palate*, &c. whenever his Reason advises the contrary, and his Duty requires it. But when you draw him to do any Thing that is fit by the Offer of *Money*, or reward the Pains of learning his Book, by the Pleasure of a luscious Morsel; when you promise him a *Lace-Cravat*, or a *fine new Suit*, upon Performance of some of his little Tasks; what do you, by proposing these as *Rewards*, but allow them to be the good Things he should aim at, and thereby encourage his Longing for them, and accustom him to place his Happiness in them? Thus People, to prevail with Children to be industrious about their Grammar, Dancing, or some other such Matter of no great Moment to the Happiness or Usefulness of their Lives, by misapplyed *Rewards* and *Punishments*, sacrifice their Virtue, invert the Order of their Education, and teach them Luxury, Pride, or Covetousness, &c. For in this Way, flattering those wrong Inclinations which they should restrain and suppress, they lay the Foundations of those future Vices, which cannot be avoided, but by curbing our Desires, and accustoming them early to submit to Reason.

I say not this, that I would have Children kept from the Conveniencies or Pleasures of Life, that are not injurious to their Health or Virtue. On the contrary, I would have their Lives made as pleasant, and as agreeable to them, as may be in a plentiful Enjoyment of whatsoever might innocently delight them; provided it be with this Caution, that they have those Enjoyments, only as the Consequences of the State of Esteem and Acceptation they are in with their Parents and Governors; but they should never be offered or bestowed on them, as the *Reward of this or that particular Performance*, that they shew an Aversion to, or to which they would not have applied themselves without that Temptation.

But if you take away the Rod on one Hand, and these little Encouragements, which they are taken with, on the other, how then, (will you say) shall Children be governed? Remove Hope and Fear, and there is an End of all Discipline. I grant that Good and Evil, *Reward* and *Punishment*, are the only Motives to a rational Creature. These are the Spur and Reins, whereby all Mankind are set on Work, and guided; and therefore they are to be made Use of to Children too. For I advise their Parents and Governors always to carry this in their Minds, that Children are to be treated as rational Creatures.

Rewards, I grant, and *Punishments* must be proposed to Children, if we intend to work upon them. The Mistake, I imagine, is, that those that are generally made Use of are *ill chosen*. The Pains and Pleasures of the Body are, I think, of ill Consequence when made the Rewards and Punishments whereby Men would prevail on their Children; for, as I said before, they serve but to increase and strengthen those

Inclinations, which it is our Business to subdue and master. What Principle of Virtue do you lay in a Child, if you will redeem his Desires of one Pleasure by the Proposal of another? This is but to enlarge his Appetite, and instruct it to wander. If a Child cries for an unwholesome or dangerous Fruit, you purchase his Quiet by giving him a less hurtful Sweetmeat. This, perhaps, may preserve his Health, but spoils his Mind, and sets that farther out of Order. For here you only change the Object, but flatter still his *Appetite*, and allow that must be satisfied, wherein, as I have shewed, lies the Root of the Mischief; and 'till you bring him to be able to bear a Denial of that Satisfaction, the Child may at present be quiet and orderly, but the Disease is not cured. By this Way of Proceeding you foment and cherish in him that which is the Spring from whence all the Evil flows, which will be sure on the next Occasion to break out again with more Violence, give him stronger Longings, and you more Trouble.

Reputation. — The *Rewards* and *Punishments* then, whereby we should keep Children in Order, *are* quite of another Kind, and of that Force, that when we can get them once to work, the Business, I think, is done, and the Difficulty is over. *Esteem* and *Disgrace* are, of all others, the most powerful Incentives to the Mind, when once it is brought to relish them. If you can once get into Children a Love of Credit, and an Apprehension of Shame and Disgrace, you have put into them the true Principle, which will constantly work, and incline them to the right. But it will be asked, How shall this be done?

I confess, it does not at first Appearance want some Difficulty; but yet I think it worth our while, to seek the Ways (and practise them when found) to attain this, which I look on as the great Secret of Education.

First, Children (earlier perhaps than we think) are very sensible of *Praise* and Commendation. They find a Pleasure in being esteemed and valued, especially by their Parents, and those whom they depend on. If therefore the Father *caress and commend them when they do well, shew a cold and neglectful Countenance to them upon doing ill;* and this accompanied by a like Carriage of the Mother, and all others that are about them, it will, in a little Time, make them sensible of the Difference, and this, if constantly observed, I doubt not but will of itself work more than Threats or Blows, which lose their Force when once grown common, and are of no Use when Shame does not attend them; and therefore are to be forborn, and never to be used, but in the Case hereafter mentioned, when it is brought to Extremity.

But *secondly*, To make the Sense of *Esteem* or *Disgrace* sink the deeper, and be of the more Weight, *other agreeable or disagreeable Things should constantly accompany these different States;* not as particular Rewards and Punishments of this or that particular Action, but as necessarily belonging to, and constantly attending one, who by his Carriage has brought himself into a State of Disgrace or Commendation. By which

Way of treating them, Children may as much as possibly be brought to conceive, that those that are commended, and in Esteem for doing well, will necessarily be beloved and cherished by every body, and have all other good Things as a Consequence of it; and on the other Side, when any one by Miscarriage falls into Disesteem, and cares not to preserve his Credit, he will unavoidably fall under Neglect and Contempt; and, in that State, the Want of whatever might satisfy or delight him will follow. In this Way the Objects of their Desires are made assisting to Virtue, when a settled Experience from the Beginning teaches Children that the Things they delight in belong to, and are to be enjoyed by, those only who are in a State of Reputation. If by these Means you can come once to shame them out of their Faults, (for, besides that, I would willingly have no Punishment) and make them in love with the Pleasure of being well thought on, you may turn them as you please, and they will be in love with all the Ways of Virtue.

The great Difficulty here, is, I imagine, from the Folly and Perverseness of Servants, who are hardly to be hindered from crossing herein the Design of the Father and Mother. Children discountenanced by their Parents for any Fault, find usually a Refuge and Relief in the Caresses of those foolish Flatterers, who thereby undo whatever the Parents endeavour to establish. When the Father or Mother looks sour on the Child, every body else should put on the same Coldness to him, and no body give him Countenance till Forgiveness asked, and a Reformation of this Fault has set him right again, and restored him to his former Credit. If this were constantly observed, I guess there would be little Need of Blows or Chiding: Their own Ease and Satisfaction would quickly teach Children to court Commendation, and avoid doing that which they found every body condemned, and they were sure to suffer for, without being chid or beaten. This would teach them Modesty and Shame; and they would quickly come to have a natural Abhorrence for that which they found made them slighted and neglected by every body. But how this Inconvenience from Servants is to be remedied, I must leave to Parents Care and Consideration: Only I think it of great Importance, and that they are very happy, who can get discreet People about their Children.

Shame. — Frequent *Beating* or *Chiding* is therefore carefully *to be avoided;* because this Sort of Correction never produces any Good, farther than it serves to raise *Shame* and Abhorrence of the Miscarriage that brought it on them: And if the greatest Part of the Trouble be not the Sense that they have done amiss, and the Apprehension that they have drawn on themselves the just Displeasure of their best Friends, the Pain of Whipping will work but an imperfect Cure. It only patches up for the present, and skins it over, but reaches not to the Bottom of the Sore. Ingenuous *Shame,* and the Apprehensions of Displeasure, are the only true Restraint. These alone ought to hold the Reins, and keep the Child in Order. But corporal

Punishments must necessarily lose that Effect, and wear out the Sense of *Shame*, where they frequently return. Shame in Children has the same Place that Modesty has in Women, which cannot be kept, and often transgressed against. And as to the Apprehension of *Displeasure in the Parents*, that will come to be very insignificant, if the Marks of that Displeasure quickly cease, and a few Blows fully expiate. Parents should well consider what Faults in their Children are weighty enough to deserve the Declaration of their Anger: But when their Displeasure is once declared to a Degree that carries any Punishment with it, they ought not presently to lay by the Severity of their Brows, but to restore their Children to their former Grace with some Difficulty, and delay a full Reconciliation, till their Conformity, and more than ordinary Merit, make good their Amendment. If this be not so ordered, *Punishment* will, by Familiarity, become a mere Thing of Course, and lose all its Influence; offending, being chastised, and then forgiven, will be thought as natural and necessary as Noon, Night, and Morning, following one another.

Concerning *Reputation* I shall only remark this one Thing more of it, that though it be not the true Principle and Measure of Virtue, (for that is the Knowledge of a Man's Duty, and the Satisfaction it is to obey his Maker, in following the Dictates of that Light God has given him, with the Hopes of Acceptation and Reward) yet it is that which comes nearest to it: And being the Testimony and Applause that other

Peoples Reason, as it were by a common Consent, gives to virtuous and well-ordered Actions, it is the proper Guide and Encouragement of Children, till they grow able to judge for themselves, and to find what is right by their own Reason.

This Consideration may direct Parents how to manage themselves in reproving and commending their Children. The Rebukes and Chiding, which their Faults will sometimes make hardly to be avoided, should not only be in sober, grave, and unpassionate Words, but also alone and in private: But the Commendations Children deserve, they should receive before others. This doubles the Reward, by spreading their Praise; but the Backwardness Parents shew in divulging their Faults will make them set a greater Value on their Credit themselves, and teach them to be the more careful to preserve the good Opinion of others, whilst they think they have it: But when, being exposed to Shame, by publishing their Miscarriages, they give it up for lost, that Check upon them is taken off, and they will be the less careful to preserve others good Thoughts of them, the more they suspect that their Reputation with them already blemished.

Let your *Rules* to your Son be as few as is possible, and rather fewer than more than seem absolutely necessary. For if you burden him with many *Rules*, one of these two Things must necessarily follow, that either he must be very often punished, which will be of ill Consequence, by making Punishment too frequent and familiar; or else you must let the Transgressions of some of your Rules go unpunished, whereby they will, of Course, grow contemptible; and your Authority become cheap to him. Make but few *Laws*, but see they be well observed, when once made. Few Years require but few Laws, and as his Age increases, when one Rule is by Practice well established, you may add another.

Habits. — But pray remember, Children are *not* to be *taught by Rules*, which will be always slipping out of their Memories. What you think necessary for them to do, settle in them by an indispensible Practice, as often as the Occasion returns: and, if it be possible, make Occasions. This will beget *Habits* in them, which, being once established, operate of themselves easily and naturally, without the Assistance of the Memory. But here let me give two Cautions: 1. The one is, that you keep them to the Practice of what you would have grow into Habit in them, by kind Words, and gentle Admonitions, rather as minding them of what they forget, than by harsh Rebukes and Chiding, as if they were wilfully guilty. 2. Another Thing you are to take Care of, is, not to endeavour to settle too many *Habits* at once, lest by Variety you confound them, and so perfect none. When constant Custom has made any one Thing easy and natural to them, and they practise it without Reflection, you may then go on to another.

Practice. — This Method of teaching Children by a repeated *Practice*, and the same Action done over and over again, under the Eye and the Direction of the Tutor, till they have got the Habit of doing it well, and not by relying on *Rules* trusted to their Memories, has so many Advantages, which Way soever we consider it, that I cannot but wonder (if ill Customs could be wondered at in any Thing) how it could possibly be so much neglected. I shall name one more that comes now in my Way. By this Method we shall see, whether what is required of him be adapted to his Capacity, and any Way suited to the Child's natural Genius and Constitution; for that too must be considered in a right Education. We must not hope wholely to change their original Tempers, nor make the Gay pensive and grave, nor the Melancholy sportive, without spoiling them. God has stampt certain Characters upon Men's Minds, which, like their Shapes, may perhaps be a little mended, but can hardly be totally altered, and transformed into the contrary.

He, therefore, that is about Children, should well study their Nature and Aptitudes, and see, by often Trials, what Turn they easily take, and what becomes them: Observe what their native Stock is, how it may be improved, and what it is fit for: He should consider what they want, whether they be capable of having it wrought into them by Industry, incorporated there by Practice; and whether it be worth while to endeavour it. For, in many Cases, all that we can do, or should aim at, is, to make the best of what Nature has given, to prevent the Vices and Faults to which such a Constitution is most inclined, and give it all the Advantages it is capable of. Every one's natural Genius should be carried as far as it could; but, to attempt the putting another upon him, will be but Labour in vain; and what is so plastered on, will, at best, sit but untowardly, and have always hanging to it the Ungracefulness of Constraint and Affectation.

Manners. Dancing. — *Manners*, as they call it, about which Children are so often perplexed, and have so many goodly Exhortations made them by their wise Maids and Governesses, I think, are rather to be learnt by Example, than Rules; and then Children, if kept out of ill Company, will take a Pride to behave themselves prettily, after the Fashion of others, perceiving themselves esteemed and commended for it. But if, by a little Negligence in this Part, the Boy should not put off his Hat, nor make Legs very gracefully, a Dancing-master will cure that Defect, and wipe off all that Plainness of Nature, which the a-la-mode People call Clownishness: And, since nothing appears to me to give Children so much becoming Confidence and Behaviour, and so to raise them to the Conversation of those above their Age, as *Dancing*, I think they should be taught to dance as soon as they are capable of learning it. For, though this consists only in outward Gracefulness of Motion, yet, I know not how, it gives Children manly Thoughts and Carriage, more than any Thing. But otherwise I would not have little Children much tormented about Punctilio's, or Niceties of Breeding.

Never trouble yourself about those Faults in them, which you know Age will cure: And therefore Want of well-fashioned Civility in the Carriage, whilst *Civility* is not wanting in the Mind, (for there you must take Care to plant it early) should be the Parents least Care, whilst they are young. If his tender Mind be filled with a Veneration for his Parents and Teachers, which consists in Love and Esteem, and a Fear to offend them; and with *Respect and Good-Will* to all People; that Respect will of itself teach those Ways of expressing it, which he observes most acceptable. Be sure to keep up in him the Principles of Good Nature and Kindness; make them as habitual as you can, by Credit and Commendation, and the good Things accompanying that State: And, when they have taken Root in his Mind, and are settled there by a continued Practice, fear not; the Ornaments of Conversation, and the Outside of fashionable Manners, will come in their due Time; if, when they are removed out of their Maid's Care, they are put into the Hands of a well bred Man to be their Governor.

Whilst they are very young, any *Carelessness* is to be born with in Children, that carries not with it the Marks of Pride or Ill-Nature; but those, whenever they appear in any Action, are to be corrected immediately, by the Ways above-mentioned. What I have said concerning Manners, I would not have so understood, as if I meant, that those who have the Judgement to do it, should not gently fashion the Motions and Carriage of Children, when they are very young. It would be of great Advantage, if they had People about them from their being first able to go, that had the Skill, and would take the right Way to do it. That which I complain of, is, the wrong Course that is usually taken in this Matter. Children, who were never taught any such Thing as Behaviour, are often (especially when Strangers are present) chid for having some Way or other failed in Good Manners, and have thereupon Reproofs and Precepts heaped upon them, concerning putting off their Hats, or making of Legs, &c. Though in this, those concerned pretend to correct the Child, yet, in Truth, for the most Part, it is but to cover their own Shame; and they lay the Blame on the poor little Ones, sometimes passionately enough to divert it from themselves, for fear the Bystanders should impute to their want of Care and Skill the Child's ill Behaviour.

For, as for the Children themselves, they are never one Jot bettered by such occasional Lectures. They at other Times should be shewn what to do, and, by reiterated Actions, be fashioned before-hand into the Practice of what is fit and becoming, and not told and talked to do upon the Spot, of what they have never been accustomed, nor know how to do as they should. To hare and rate them thus at every Turn, is not to teach them, but to vex and torment them to no Purpose. They should be let alone, rather than chid for a Fault, which is none of theirs, nor is in their Power to mend for speaking to. And it were much better their natural childish Negligence or Plainness should be left to the Care of riper Years, than that they should frequently have Rebukes misplaced upon them, which neither do, nor can give them graceful Motions. If their Minds are well-disposed, and principled with inward Civility, a great Part of the Roughness, which sticks to the Outside for Want of better Teaching, Time and Observation will rub off, as they grow up, if they are bred in good Company; but, if in ill, all the Rules in the World, all the Correction imaginable, will not be able to polish them. For you must take this for a certain Truth, that let them have what Instructions you will, and ever so learned Lectures of Breeding daily inculcated into them, that which will most influence their Carriage, will be the Company they converse with, and the Fashion of those about them. Children (nay, and Men too) do most by Example. We are all a Sort of Camelions, that still take a Tincture from Things near us; nor is it to be wondered at in Children, who better understand what they see, than what they hear.

Company. — I mentioned about one great Mischief that came by Servants to Children, when by their Flatteries they take off the Edge and Force of the Parents Rebukes, and so lessen their Authority. And here is another great Inconvenience which Children receive from the ill Examples which they meet with amongst the meaner Servants.

They are wholely, if possible, to be kept from such Conversation; for the Contagion of these ill Precedents, both in Civility and Virtue, horribly infects Children, as often as they come within Reach of it. They frequently learn from unbred or debauched Servants, such Language, untowardly Tricks and Vices, as otherwise they possibly would be ignorant of all their Lives.

It is a hard Matter wholely to prevent this Mischief. You will have very good Luck, if you never have a clownish or vicious Servant, and if from them your Children never get any Infection: But yet, as much must be done towards it as can be, and the Children kept as much as may be *in the Company of their Parents*, and those to whose Care they are committed. To this Purpose, their being in their Presence should be made easy to them; they should be allowed the Liberties and Freedom suitable to their Ages, and not be held under unnecessary Restraints, when in their Parents or Governors Sight. If it be a Prison to them, it is no Wonder they should not like it. They must not be hindered from being Children, or from playing, or doing as Children, but from doing ill; all other Liberty is to be allowed them. Next, to make them in Love with the *Company of their Parents*, they should receive all their good Things there, and from their Hands. The Servants should be hindered from making court to them, by giving them strong Drink, Wine, Fruit, Play-Things, and other such Matters, which may make them in Love with their Conversation.

Company. — Having named *Company*, I am almost ready to throw away my Pen, and trouble you no farther on this Subject: For since that does more than all Precepts, Rules, and Instructions, methinks it is almost wholely in vain to make a long Discourse of other Things, and to talk of that almost to no Purpose. For you will be ready to say, What shall I do with my Son? If I keep him always at home, he will be in Danger to be my young Master; and, if I send him abroad, how is it possible to keep him from the Contagion of Rudeness and Vice, which is every where so in Fashion? In my House he will perhaps be more innocent, but more ignorant too of the World. Wanting there Change of Company, and being used constantly to the same Faces, he will, when he come abroad, be a sheepish or conceited Creature.

I confess, both Sides have their Inconveniences. Being abroad, it is true, will make him bolder, and better able to bustle and shift amongst Boys of his own Age; and the Emulation of School-fellows often puts Life and Industry into young Lads. But, till you can find a School, wherein it is possible for the Master to look after the Manners of his Scholars, and can shew as great Effects of his Care of forming their Minds to Virtue, and their Carriage to Good Breeding, as of forming their Tongues to the learned Languages, you must confess, that you have a strange Value for Words, when preferring the Languages of the antient *Greeks* and *Romans*, to that which made them such brave Men, you think it worth while to hazard your Son's Innocence and Virtue, for a little *Greek* and *Latin*. For, as for that Boldness and Spirit which Lads get amongst their Play-fellows at School, it has ordinarily such a Mixture of Rudeness and ill-turned Confidence, that those misbecoming and disingenuous Ways of shifting in the World must be unlearnt, and all the Tincture washed out again, to make Way for better Principles, and such Manners, as make a truely-worthy Man. He that considers how diametrically opposite the Skill of living well, and managing, as a Man should do, his Affairs in the World, is to that Malapertness, Tricking, or Violence learnt amongst School-Boys, will think the Faults of a privater Education infinitely to be preferred to such Improvements, and will take Care to preserve his Child's Innocence and Modesty at home, as being nearer of Kin, and more in the Way of those Qualities which make an useful and able Man. Nor does any one find, or so much as suspect, that that Retirement and Bashfulness, which their Daughters are brought up in, makes them less knowing or less able Women. Conversation, when they come into the World, soon gives them a becoming Assurance; and whatsoever, beyond that, there is of rough and boisterous, may in Men be very well spared too; for Courage and Steadiness, as I take it, lie not in Roughness and Ill-breeding.

Example.— Having under Consideration how great the Influence of *Company* is, and how prone we are all, especially Children, to Imitation, I must here take the Liberty to mind Parents of this one Thing, *viz.*: that he that will have his Son have a Respect for him, and his Orders, must himself have a great Reverence for his Son; "*Maxima debetur Pueris Reverentia.*" You must do nothing before him, which you would not have him imitate. If any Thing escape you, which you would have pass for a Fault in him, he will be sure to shelter himself under your Example, and shelter himself so as that it will not be easy to come at him, to correct it in him the right Way. If you punish him for what he sees you practise yourself, he will not think that Severity to proceed from Kindness in you, or Carefulness to amend a Fault in him; but will be apt to interpret it, the Peevishness and arbitrary Imperiousness of a Father, who, without any Ground for it, would deny his Son the Liberty and Pleasures he takes himself. Or, if you assume to yourself the Liberty you have taken, as a Privilege belonging to riper Years, to which a Child must not aspire, you do but add new Force to your Example, and recommend the Action the more powerfully to him. For you must always remember, that Children affect to be Men earlier than is thought; and they love Breeches, not for their Cut or Ease, but because the having them is a Mark or Step towards Manhood. What I say of the Father's Carriage before his Children, must extend itself to all those who have any Authority over them, or for whom he would have them have any Respect.

Punishment. — But to return to the Business of *Rewards* and *Punishments*. All the Actions of Childishness and unfashionable Carriage, and whatever Time and Age will of itself be sure to reform, being (as I have said) exempt from the Discipline of the Rod, there will not be so much need of beating Children, as is generally made Use of. To which, if we add learning to read, write, dance, foreign Language, &c. as under the same Privilege, there will be but very rarely any Occasion for Blows or Force in an ingenuous Education. The right Way to teach them those Things, is, to give them a Liking and Inclination to what you propose to them to be learned, and that will engage their Industry and Application. This I think no hard Matter to do, if Children be handled as they should be, and the Rewards and Punishments above-mentioned be carefully applyed, and with them these few Rules observed in the Method of instructing them.

Task. — None of the Things, they are to learn, should ever be made a Burthen to them, or imposed on them as a *Task*. Whatever is so proposed, presently becomes irksome; the Mind takes an Aversion to it, though before it were a Thing of Delight or Indifferency. Let a Child be but ordered to whip his Top at a certain Time every Day, whether he has or has not a Mind to it; let this be but required of him as a Duty, wherein he must spend so many Hours Morning and Afternoon, and see whether he will not soon be weary of any Play at this Rate. Is it not so with grown Men? What they do chearfully of themselves, do they not presently grow sick of, and can no more endure, as soon as they find it is expected of them as a Duty? Children have as much a Mind to shew that they are free, that their own good Actions come from themselves, that they are absolute and independent, as any of the proudest of you grown Men, think of them as you please.

Disposition. — As a Consequence of this, they should seldom be put about doing even those Things you have got an Inclination in them to, but when they have a Mind and *Disposition* to it. He that loves Reading, Writing, Musick, etc. finds yet in himself certain Seasons wherein those Things have no Relish to him; and if at that Time he forces himself to it, he only pothers and wearies himself to no Purpose. So it is with Children. This Change of Temper should be carefully observed in them, and the favourable *Seasons of Aptitude and Inclination* be heedfully laid hold of: And, if they are not often enough forward of themselves, a good Disposition should be talked into them, before they be set upon any Thing. This, I think, no hard Matter for a discreet Tutor to do, who has studied his Pupil's Temper, and will be at little Pains to fill his Head with suitable Ideas, such as may make him in Love with the present Business. By this Means, a great deal of Time and Tiring would be saved; for a Child will learn three times as much when he is *in Tune*, as he will, with double the Time and Pains, when he goes aukwardly, or is dragged unwillingly to it. If this were minded as it should, Children might be permitted to weary themselves with Play, and yet have Time enough to learn what is suited to the Capacity of each Age. But no such Thing is considered in the ordinary Way of Education, nor can it well be. That rough Discipline of the Rod is built upon other Principles, has no Attraction in it, regards not what Humour Children are in, nor looks after favourable

Seasons of Inclination. And, indeed, it would be ridiculous, when Compulsion and Blows have raised an Aversion in the Child to his Task, to expect he should freely, of his own Accord, leave his Play, and with Pleasure court the Occasions of Learning; whereas, were Matters ordered right, learning any Thing they should be taught, might be made as much a Recreation to their Play, as their Play is to their Learning: The Pains are equal on both Sides: Nor is it that which troubles them; for they love to be busy, and the Change and Variety is that which naturally delights them. The only Odds is in that which we call Play; they act at Liberty, and employ their Pains (whereof you may observe them never sparing) freely; but what they are to learn, is forced upon them; they are called, compelled, and driven to it. This is that, which at first Entrance balks and cools them; they want their Liberty: Get them but to ask their Tutor to teach them, as they do often their Play-fellows, instead of his calling upon them to learn, and they being satisfied, that they act as freely in this, as they do in other Things, they will go on with as much Pleasure in it, and it will not differ from their other Sports and Play. By these Ways, carefully pursued, a Child may be brought to desire to be taught any Thing you have a Mind he should learn. The hardest Part, I confess, is with the first or eldest; but when once he is set right, it is easy by him to lead the rest whither one will.

Though it be past Doubt, that the fittest Time for Children to learn any Thing, is, when their *Minds* are in *Tune*, and *well disposed* to it; when neither Flagging of Spirit, nor Intentness of Thought upon something else, makes them aukward and averse; yet two Things are to be taken Care of, 1. That these Seasons either not being warily observed, and laid hold on, as often as they return; or else, not returning as often as they should, the Improvement of the Child be not thereby neglected, and so he be let grow into an habitual Idleness, and confirmed in this Indisposition. 2. That though other Things are ill learned, when the Mind is either indisposed, or otherwise taken up, yet it is of great Moment, and worth our Endeavours, to teach the Mind to get the Mastery over itself, and to be able, upon Choice, to take itself off from the hot Pursuit of one Thing, and set itself upon another with Facility and Delight; or at any Time to shake off its Sluggishness, and vigorously employ itself about what Reason, or the Advice of another shall direct. This is to be done in Children, by trying them sometimes, when they are by Laziness unbent, or by Avocation bent another Way, and endeavouring to make them buckle to the Thing proposed. If by this Means the Mind can get an habitual Dominion over itself, lay by *Ideas* or Business, as Occasion requires, and betake itself to new and less acceptable Employments, without Reluctance or Discomposure, it will be an Advantage of more Consequence than Latin or Logick, or most of those Things Children are usually required to learn.

Compulsion. — Children being more active and busy in that Age, than in any other Part of their Life, and being indifferent to any Thing they can do, so they may be but doing, *Dancing* and *Scotch-Hoppers* would be the same Thing to them, were the Encouragements and Discouragements equal. But to Things we would have them learn, the great and only Discouragement I can observe, is, that they are called to it, it is *made their Business*, they are *teazed* and *chid* about it, and do it with Trembling and Apprehension; or, when they come willingly to it, are kept too long at it, till they are quite tired: All which intrenches too much on that natural Freedom they extremely affect. And it is that Liberty alone which gives the true Relish and Delight to their ordinary Play-Games. Turn the Tables, and you will find, they will soon change their Application; especially if they see the Examples of others, whom they esteem and think above themselves. And if the Things which they observe others to do, be ordered so, that they insinuate themselves into them, as the Privilege of an Age or Condition above theirs, then Ambition, and the Desire still to get forward and higher, and to be like those above them, will set them on work, and make them go on with Vigour and Pleasure, Pleasure in what they have begun by their own Desire; in which Way the Enjoyment of their dearly-beloved Freedom will be no small Encouragement to them. To all which, if there be added the Satisfaction of Credit and Reputation, I am apt to think there will need no other Spur to excite their Application and Assiduity, as much as is necessary. I confess there needs Patience and Skill, Gentleness and Attention, and a prudent Conduct to attain this at first. But why have you a Tutor, if there needed no Pains? But when this is once established, all the rest will follow, more easily than in any more severe and imperious Discipline. And I think it no hard Matter to gain this Point: I am sure it will not be, where Children have no ill Example set before them. The great Danger, therefore, I apprehend, is only from Servants, and other ill-ordered Children, or such other vicious or foolish People, who spoil Children both by the ill Pattern they set before them in their own ill Manners, and by giving them together the two Things they should never have at once; I mean vicious Pleasures and Commendation.

Chiding. — As Children should very seldom be corrected by Blows, so I think frequent, and especially passionate *Chiding* of almost as ill Consequence. It lessens the Authority of the Parents, and the Respect of the Child; for I bid you still remember, they distinguish early betwixt Passion and Reason: And, as they cannot but have a Reverence for what comes from the latter, so they quickly grow into a Contempt of the former; or, if it causes a present Terror, yet it soon wears off, and natural Inclination will easily learn to slight such Scare-Crows, which make a Noise, but are not animated by Reason. Children being to be restrained by the Parents only in vicious (which, in their tender Years, are only a few) Things, a Look or Nod only ought to correct them, when they do amiss; or, if Words are sometimes to be used, they ought to be grave, kind, and sober, representing the Ill or Unbecomingness of the Faults, rather than a *hasty Rating* of the Child for it; which makes him not sufficiently distinguish, whether your Dislike be not more directed to him, than his Fault. Passionate Chiding usually carries rough and ill Language with it, which has this further ill Effect, that it teaches and justifies it in Children: And the Names that their Parents or Preceptors give them, they will not be ashamed or backward to bestow on others, having so good Authority for the Use of them.

Obstinacy. — I foresee here it will be objected to me, What then, will you have Children never beaten, nor chid for any Fault? This will be to let loose the Reins to all Kind of Disorder. Not so much as is imagined, if a right Course has been taken in the first Seasoning of their Minds, and implanting that Awe of their Parents above-mentioned; for Beating, by constant Observation, is found to do little Good, where the Smart of it is all the Punishment that is feared or felt in it; for the Influence of that quickly wears out with the Memory of it: But yet there is one, and but one Fault, for which, I think, Children should be beaten; and that is, *Obstinacy* or *Rebellion*. And in this too, I would have it ordered so, if it can be, that the Shame of the Whipping, and not the Pain, should be the greatest Part of the Punishment. Shame of doing amiss, and deserving Chastisement, is the only true Restraint belonging to Virtue. The Smart of the Rod, if Shame accompanies it not, soon ceases, and is forgotten, and will quickly, by Use, lose its Terror. I have known the Children of a Person of Quality kept in Awe, by the Fear of having their Shoes pulled off, as much as others by Apprehensions of a Rod hanging over them. Some such Punishment I think better than Beating; for, it is a Shame of the Fault, and the Disgrace that attends it, that they should stand in Fear of, rather than Pain, if you would have them have a Temper truly ingenuous. But *Stubbornness*, and an *obstinate Disobedience*, must be mastered with Force and Blows; for this there is no other Remedy. Whatever particular Action you bid him do, or forbear, you must be sure to see yourself obeyed: No Quarter in this Case, no Resistance. For when once it comes to be a Trial of Skill, a Contest for Mastery betwixt you, as it is if you command, and he refuses, you must be sure to carry it, whatever Blows it costs, if a Nod or Words will not prevail; unless, for ever after, you intend to live in Obedience to your Son. A prudent and kind Mother, of my Acquaintance, was, on such an Occasion, forced to whip her little Daughter, at her first coming home from Nurse, eight Times successively the same Morning, before she could master her *Stubbornness*, and obtain a Compliance in a very easy and indifferent Matter. If she had left off sooner, and stopped at the seventh Whipping, she had spoiled the Child forever, and, by her unprevailing Blows, only confirmed her *Refractariness*, very hardly afterwards to be cured: But wisely persisting, till she had bent her Mind, and suppled her Will, the only End of Correction and Chastisement, she established her Authority thoroughly in the very first Occasions, and had ever after a very ready Compliance and Obedience in all Things from her Daughter; for as this was the first Time, so I think it was the last too she ever struck her.

The Pain of the Rod, *the first* Occasion that requires it, continued and increased, without leaving off till it has thoroughly prevailed, should first bend the Mind, and settle the Parent's Authority; and then Gravity, mixed with Kindness, should for ever after keep it.

This, if well reflected on, would make People more wary in the Use of the Rod and the Cudgel, and keep them from being so apt to think Beating the safe and universal Remedy to be applyed at Random, on all Occasions. This is certain, however, if it does no Good, it does great Harm; if it reaches not the Mind, and makes not the Will supple, it hardens the Offender; and whatever Pain he has suffered for it, it does but indear to him his beloved *Stubbornness*, which has got him this Time the Victory, and prepares him to contest, and hope for it for the future. Thus, I doubt not, but by ill-ordered Correction, many have been taught to be *obstinate* and *refractary*, who otherwise would have been very pliant and tractable: For if you punish a Child so, as if it were only to revenge the past Fault, which has raised your Choler, what Operation can this have upon his Mind, which is the Part to be amended? If there were no *sturdy Humour*, or *Wilfulness* mixed with his Fault, there was nothing in it that required the Severity of Blows. A kind or grave Admonition is enough to remedy the Slips of Frailty, Forgetfulness, or Inadvertency, and is as much as they will stand in Need of: But if there were a *Perverseness* in the Will, if it were a designed, resolved Disobedience, the Punishment is not to be measured by the Greatness or Smallness of the Matter wherein it appeared, but by the Opposition it carries, and stands in, to that Respect and Submission that is due to the Father's Orders; which must always be rigorously exacted, and the Blows by Pauses laid on, till they reach the Mind, and you perceive the Signs of a true Sorrow, Shame, and Purpose of Obedience.

This, I confess, requires something more than setting Children a Task, and whipping them without any more ado, if it be not done, and done to our Fancy. This requires Care, Attention, Observation, and a nice Study of Children's Tempers, and weighing their Faults well, before we come to this Sort of Punishment. But is not that better, than always to have the Rod in Hand, as the only Instrument of Government; and by frequent Use of it on all Occasions, misapply and render inefficacious this last and useful Remedy, where there is Need of it? For what else can be expected, when it is promiscuously used upon every little Slip? When a Mistake in *Concordance*, or a wrong *Position* in Verse, shall have the Severity of the Lash, in a well-tempered and industrious Lad, as surely as a wilful Crime in an obstinate and perverse Offender, how can such a Way of Correction be expected to do Good on the Mind, and set that right? which is the only Thing to be looked after; and, when set right, brings all the rest that you can desire along with it.

Where a *wrong Bent of the Will* wants not Amendment, there can be no Need of Blows. All other Faults, where the Mind is rightly disposed, and refuses not the Government and Authority of the Father or Tutor, are but Mistakes, and may often be over-looked; or, when they are taken Notice of, need no other but the gentle Remedies of Advice, Direction, and Reproof, till the repeated and wilful Neglect of those, shews the Fault to be in the Mind, and that a manifest *Perverseness* of the Will lies at the Root of their Disobedience. But whenever *Obstinacy*, which is an open Defiance, appears, that cannot be winked at, or neglected, but must, in the first Instance, be subdued and mastered; only Care must be had, that we mistake not; and we must be sure it is Obstinacy, and nothing else.

But since the Occasions of Punishment, especially Beating, are as much to be avoided as may be, I think it should not be often brought to this Point. If the Awe I spoke of be once got, a Look will be sufficient in most Cases. Nor indeed should the same Carriage, Seriousness, or Application be expected from young Children, as from those of riper Growth. They must be permitted, as I said, the foolish and childish Actions suitable to their Years, without taking Notice of them. Inadvertency, Carelessness, and Gaiety is the Character of that Age. I think the Severity I spoke of is not to extend itself to such unseasonable Restraints; nor is that hastily to be interpreted Obstinacy or Wilfulness, which is the natural Product of their Age or Temper. In such Miscarriages they are to be assisted, and helped towards an Amendment, as weak People under a natural Infirmity; which, though they are warned of, yet every Relapse must not be counted a perfect Neglect, and they presently treated as obstinate. Faults of Frailty, as they should never be neglected, or let pass without minding, so, unless the Will mix with them, they should never be exaggerated, or very sharply reproved; but with a gentle Hand set right, as Time and Age permit. By this Means, Children will come to see what it is in any Miscarriage that is chiefly offensive, and so learn to avoid it. This will encourage them to keep their Wills right, which is the great Business, when they find that it preserves them from any great Displeasure, and that, in all their other Failings, they meet with the kind Concern and Help, rather than the Anger, and passionate Reproaches of their Tutor and Parents. Keep them from Vice, and vicious Dispositions, and such a Kind of Behaviour in general will come with every Degree of their Age, as is suitable to that Age, and the Company they ordinarily converse with; and, as they grow in Years, they will grow in Attention and Application. But that your Words may always carry Weight and Authority with them, if it shall happen, upon any Occasion, that you bid him leave off the doing of any, even childish Things, you must be sure to carry the Point, and not let him have the Mastery. But yet, I say, I would have the Father seldom interpose his Authority and Command in these Cases, or in any other, but such as have a Tendency to vicious

Habits. I think there are better Ways of prevailing with them: And a gentle Perswasion in Reasoning, (when the first Point of Submission to your Will is got) will most Times do much better.

Reasoning. — It will perhaps be wondered, that I mention *Reasoning* with Children; and yet I cannot but think that the true Way of dealing with them. They understand it as early as they do Language; and, if I mis-observe not, they love to be treated as rational Creatures, sooner than is imagined. It is a Pride should be cherish'd in them, and, as much as can be, made the greatest Instrument to turn them by.

But when I talk of *Reasoning*, I do not intend any other, but such as is suited to the Child's Capacity and Apprehension. No Body can think a Boy of three or seven Years old should be argued with, as a grown Man. Long Discourses, and Philosophical Reasonings, at best amaze and confound, but do not instruct Children. When I say, therefore, that they must be *treated as rational Creatures*, I mean, that you should make them sensible, by the Mildness of your Carriage, and the Composure even in your Correction of them, that what you do is reasonable in you, and useful and necessary for them; and that it is not out of *Caprichio*, Passion, or Fancy, that you command or forbid them any Thing. This they are capable of understanding; and there is no Virtue they should be excited to, nor Fault they should be kept from, which I do not think they may be convinced of; but it must be by such *Reasons* as their Age and Understanding are capable of, and those propose always *in* very *few and plain Words*. The Foundations on which several Duties are built, and the Fountains of Right and Wrong from which they spring, are not perhaps easily to be let into the Minds of grown Men, not used to abstract their Thoughts from common received Opinions. Much less are Children capable of *Reasonings* from remote Principles. They cannot conceive the Force of long Deductions. The *Reasons* that move them must be *obvious*, and level to their Thoughts, and such as may (if I may so say) be felt and touched. But yet, if their Age, Temper and Inclinations, be considered, there will never want such Motives, as may be sufficient to convince them. If there be no other more particular, yet these will always be intelligible, and of Force, to deter them from any Fault, fit to be taken Notice of in them, (*viz.*) That it will be a Discredit and Disgrace to them, and displease you.

Examples. — But of all the Ways whereby Children are to be instructed, and their Manners formed, the plainest, easiest, and most efficacious, is, to set before their Eyes the *Examples* of those Things you would have them do or avoid; which, when they are pointed out to them, in the Practice of Persons within their Knowledge, with some Reflexions on their Beauty or Unbecomingness, are of more Force to draw or deter their Imitation, than any Discourses which can be made to them. Virtues and Vices can by no Words be so plainly set before their Understandings, as the Actions of other Men will shew them, when you direct their

Observation, and bid them view this or that good or bad Quality in their Practice. And the Beauty or Uncomliness of many Things, in good and ill Breeding, will be better learnt, and make deeper Impressions on them, in the *Examples* of others, than from any Rules or Instructions can be given about them.

This is a Method to be used, not only whilst they are young, but to be continued even as long as they shall be under another's Tuition or Conduct; nay, I know not whether it be not the best Way to be used by a Father, as long as he shall think fit, on any Occasion, to reform any thing he wishes mended in his Son; nothing sinking so gently, and so deep, into Men's Minds, as *Example*. And what Ill they either overlook, or indulge in themselves, they cannot but dislike, and be ashamed of, when it is set before them in another.

Whipping. — It may be doubted, concerning *Whipping*, when, as the last Remedy, it comes to be necessary; at what Times, and by whom it should be done; whether presently upon the committing the Fault, whilst it is yet fresh and hot; and whether Parents themselves should beat their Children. As to the first, I think it should *not* be done *presently*, lest Passion mingle with it; and so, though it exceed the just Proportion, yet it lose of its due Weight; for even Children discern when we do Things in Passion. But, as I said before, that has most Weight with them, that appears sedately to come from their Parents Reason; and they are not without this Distinction. Next, if you have any discreet Servant capable of it, and has the

Place of governing your Child, (for, if you have a Tutor, there is no Doubt) I think it is the best the *Smart* should come more immediately *from another's Hand*, though by the Parents Order, who should see it done; whereby the Parent's Authority will be preserved, and the Child's Aversion, for the Pain it suffers, rather to be turned on the Person that immediately inflicts it: For I would have a *Father seldom strike his Child*, but upon very urgent Necessity, and as the last Remedy; and then, perhaps, it will be fit to do it so, that the Child should not quickly forget it.

But, as I said before, *Beating* is the worst, and therefore the last Means to be used in the Correction of Children; and that only in Cases of Extremity, after all gentler Ways have been tried, and proved unsuccessful; which, if well observed, there will be very seldom any Need of Blows: For, it not being to be imagined, that a Child will often, if ever, dispute his Father's present Command in any particular Instance; and the Father not interposing his absolute Authority, in peremptory Rules concerning either childish or indifferent Actions, wherein his Son is to have his Liberty, or concerning his Learning or Improvement, wherein there is no Compulsion to be used; there remains only the Prohibition of some vicious Actions, wherein a Child is capable of *Obstinacy*, and consequently can deserve Beating; and so there will be but very few Occasions of that Discipline to be used by any one, who considers well, and orders his Child's Education as it should be. For the first seven Years, what Vices can a Child be guilty of, but Lying, or some ill-natured Tricks, the repeated Commission whereof, after his Father's direct Command against it, shall bring him into the Condemnation of *Obstinacy*, and the Chastisement of the Rod? If any vicious Inclination in him be, in the first Appearances and Instances of it, treated as it should be, first with your Wonder, and then, if returning again a second Time, discountenanced with the severe Brow of the Father, Tutor, and all about him, and a Treatment suitable to the State of Discredit beforementioned, and this continued till he be made sensible, and ashamed of his Fault, I imagine there will be no Need of any other Correction, nor ever any Occasion to come to Blows. The Necessity of such Chastisement is usually the Consequence only of former Indulgencies or Neglects. If vicious Inclinations were watched from the Beginning, and the first Irregularities, which they caused, corrected by those gentler Ways, we should seldom have to do with more than one Disorder at once; which would be easily set right, without any Stir or Noise, and not require so harsh a Discipline as Beating. Thus, one by one, as they appeared, they might all be weeded out, without any Signs or Memory that ever they had been there. But we letting their Faults (by indulging and humouring our little Ones) grow up, till they are sturdy and numerous, and the Deformity of them makes us ashamed and uneasy, we are fain to come to the Plough and the Harrow; the Spade and the Pix-Ax, must go deep to come at the Roots; and all the Force, Skill, and Diligence we can use, is scarce enough to cleanse the viciated Seed-Plat, overgrown with Weeds, and restore us the Hopes of Fruits, to reward our Pains in its Season.

This Course, if observed, will spare both Father and Child the Trouble of repeated Injunctions, and multiply'ed Rules of Doing and Forbearing: For I am of Opinion, that of those Actions which tend to vicious Habits, (which are those alone that a Father should interpose his Authority and Commands in) none should be forbidden Children, till they are found guilty of them. For such untimely Prohibitions, if they do nothing worse, do at least so much towards teaching and allowing them, that they suppose, that Children may be guilty of them, who would possibly be safer in the Ignorance of any such Faults: And the best Remedy to stop them, is, as I have said, to shew *Wonder* and *Amazement* at any such Action, as hath a vicious Tendency, when it is first taken Notice of in a Child. For Example; when he is first found in a Lye, or any ill-natured Trick, the first Remedy should be, to talk to him of it as a *strange monstrous Matter*, that it could not be imagined he would have done; and so shame him out of it.

It will be (it is like) objected, that whatsoever I fancy of the Tractableness of Children, and the Prevalency of those softer Ways of Shame, and Commendation, yet there are many, who will never apply themselves to their Books, and to what they ought to learn, unless they are scourged to it. This, I fear, is nothing but the Language of ordinary Schools and Fashion, which have never suffered the other to be tryed as it should be, in Places where it could be taken Notice of. *Why, else, does the Learning of* Latin *and* Greek *need the Rod, when* French *and* Italian *need it not?* Children learn to dance and fence without Whipping; nay, Arithmetick, Drawing, etc. they apply themselves well enough to without Beating: Which would make one suspect, that there is something strange, unnatural, and disagreeable to that Age, in the Things required in Grammar-Schools, or in the Methods used there, that Children cannot be brought to, without the Severity of the Lash, and hardly with that too; or else, that it is a Mistake, that those Tongues could not be taught them without beating.

But let us suppose some so negligent or idle, that they will not be brought to learn by the gentle Ways proposed; for we must grant, that there will be Children found of all Tempers; yet it does not thence follow, that the rough Discipline of the Cudgel is to be used to all. Nor can any one be concluded unmanageable by the *milder Methods* of Government, till thy have been *thoroughly tryed* upon him; and if they will not prevail with him to use his Endeavours, and do what is in his Power to do, we make no Excuses for the Obstinate. Blows are the proper Remedies for those; but Blows laid on in a Way different from the ordinary. He that willfully neglects his Book, and stubbornly refuses any Thing he can do, required of him by his Father, expressing himself in a positive serious Command, should not be corrected with two or three angry Lashes, for not performing his Task, and the same Punishment repeated again and again upon every the like Default: But when it is brought to that Pass, that Wilfulness evidently shews itself, and makes Blows necessary, I think the Chastisement should be a little more sedate, and a little more severe, and the Whipping (mingled with Admonition between) so continued, till the Impressions of it on the Mind were found legible in the Face, Voice, and Submission of the Child, not so sensible of the Smart, as of the Fault he has been guilty of, and melting in true Sorrow under it. If such a Correction as this, tryed some few Times at fit Distances, and carried to the utmost Severity, with the visible Displeasure of the Father all the while, will not work the Effect, turn the Mind, and produce a future Compliance, what can be hoped from *Blows*, and to what Purpose should they be any more used? *Beating*, when you can expect no Good from it, will look more like the Fury of an enraged Enemy, than the Good-Will of a compassionate Friend and such Chastisement carries with it only Provocation, without any Prospect of Amendment. If it be any Father's Misfortune to have a Son thus perverse and untractable, I know not what more he can do, but pray for him. But, I imagine, if a right Course be taken with Children from the Beginning, very few will be found to be such; and when there are any such Instances, they are not to be the Rule for the Education of those, who are better natured, and may be managed with better Usage.

Familiarity. — Though I have mentioned the Severity of the Father's Brow, and the Awe settled thereby in the Mind of Children when young, as one main Instrument whereby their Education is to be managed; yet I am far from being of an Opinion that it should be continued all along to them, whilst they are under the Discipline and Government of Pupilage. I think it should be relaxed as fast as their Age, Discretion, and good Behaviour could allow it; even to that Degree, that a Father will do well, as his Son grows up, and is capable of it, to *talk familiarly* with him; nay, *ask his Advice*, *and consult* with him about those Things wherein he has any Knowledge or Understanding. By this the Father will gain two Things, both of great Moment: The one is, that it will put serious Considerations into his Son's Thoughts, better than any Rules or Advices he can give him. The sooner you *treat him as a Man*, the sooner he will begin to be one: And if you admit him into serious Discourses sometimes with you, you will insensibly raise his Mind above the usual Amusements of Youth, and those trifling Occupations which it is commonly wasted in. For it is easy to observe, that many young Men continue longer in the Thought and Conversation of School-Boys, than otherwise they would, because their Parents keep them at that Distance, and in that low Rank, by all their Carriage to them.

Another Thing of greater Consequence, which you will obtain by such a Way of treating him, will be *his Friendship*. Many Fathers, though they proportion to their Sons liberal Allowances, according to their Age and Condition, yet they keep the Knowledge of their Estates and Concerns from them, with as much Reservedness, as if they were guarding a Secret of State from a Spy or an Enemy. This, if it looks not like Jealousy, yet it wants those Marks of Kindness and Intimacy which a Father should shew to his Son, and no Doubt often hinders or abates that Cheerfulness and Satisfaction wherewith a Son should address himself to, and rely upon his Father. And I cannot but often wonder to see Fathers, who love their Sons very well, yet so order the Matter by a constant Stiffness, and a Mien of Authority and Distance to them all their Lives, as if they were never to enjoy, or have any Comfort from those they love best in the World, untill they had lost them, by being removed into another. Nothing cements and establishes Friendship and Good-Will so much as *confident Communication* of Concernments and Affairs. Other Kindnesses, without this, leave still some Doubts: But when your Son sees you open your Mind to him; when he finds, that you interest him in your Affairs, as Things you are willing should in their Turns come into his Hands, he will be concerned for them, as for his own, wait his Season with Patience, and love you in the mean Time, who keep him not at the Distance of a Stranger. This will also make him see, that the Enjoyment you have, is not without Care; which the more he is sensible of, the less will he envy you the Possession, and the more think himself happy under the Management of so favourable a Friend, and so careful a Father. There is scarce any young Man of so little Thought, or so void of Sense, that would not be glad of a *sure Friend*, that he might have Recourse to, and freely consult on Occasion. The Reservedness and Distance that Fathers keep, often deprive their Sons of that Refuge, which would be of more Advantage to them than an hundred Rebukes and Chidings. Would your Son engage in some Frolick, or take a Vagary, were it not much better he should do it with, than without your Knowledge? For since Allowances for such Things must be made to young Men, the more you know of his Intrigues and Designs, the better will you be able to prevent great Mischiefs; and by letting him see what is like to follow, take the right Way of prevailing with him to avoid less Inconveniences. Would you have him open his Heart to you, and ask your Advice, you must begin to do so with him first, and by your Carriage beget that Confidence.

But whatever he consults you about, unless it lead to some fatal and irremediable Mischief, be sure you advise only as a Friend of more Experience; but with your Advice, mingle nothing of Command or Authority, nor more than you would to your Equal, or a Stranger. That would be to drive him for ever from any farther demanding, or receiving Advantage from your Counsel. You must consider, that he is a young Man, and has Pleasures and Fancies, which you are passed. You must not expect his Inclinations should be just as yours, nor that at twenty he should have the same Thoughts you have at fifty. All that you can wish, is, that since Youth must have some

Liberty, some Out-leaps, they might be with the Ingenuity of a Son, and *under the Eye of a Father*, and then no very great Harm can come of it. The Way to obtain this, as I said before, is (according as you find him capable) to talk with him about your Affairs, propose Matters to him *familiarly*, and ask his Advice; and when he ever lights on the Right, follow it as his; and if he succeeds well, let him have the Commendation. This will not at all lessen your Authority, but increase his Love and Esteem of you. Whilst you keep your Estate, the Staff will still be in your own Hands; and your Authority the surer, the more it is strengthened with *Confidence* and *Kindness*. For you have not that Power you ought to have over him, till he comes to be more afraid of offending so good a Friend, than of losing some Part of his future Expectation.

Familiarity of Discourse, if it can become a Father to his Son, may much more be condescended to by a Tutor to his Pupil. All their Time together should not be spent in reading of Lectures, and magisterially dictating to him, what he is to observe and follow. Hearing him in his Turn, and using him to reason about what is proposed, will make the Rules go down the easier, and sink the deeper, and will give him a Liking to Study and Instruction: And he will then begin to value Knowledge, when he sees, that it enables him to discourse, and he finds the Pleasure and Credit of bearing a Part in the Conversation, and of having his Reasons sometimes approved, and hearkened to: Particularly in Morality, Prudence, and Breeding,

Cases should be put to him, and his Judgment asked. This opens the Understanding better than Maxims, how well soever explained, and settles the Rules better in the Memory for Practice. This Way lets Things into the Mind, which stick there, and retain their Evidence with them; whereas Words at best are faint Representations, being not so much as the true Shadows of Things, and are much sooner forgotten. He will better comprehend the Foundations and Measures of Decency and Justice, and have livelier, and more lasting Impressions of what he ought to do, by giving his Opinion on Cases proposed, and reasoning with his Tutor on fit Instances, than by giving a silent, negligent, sleepy Audience to his Tutor's Lectures; and much more than by captious logical Disputes, or set Declamations of his own, upon any Question. The one sets the Thoughts upon Wit and false Colours, and not upon Truth; the other teaches Fallacy, Wrangling, and Opiniatrey; and they are both of them Things that spoil the Judgment, and put a Man out of the Way of right and fair Reasoning; and therefore carefully to be avoided by one who would improve himself, and be acceptable to others.

Reverence. — When, by making your Son sensible that he depends on you, and is in your Power, you have established your Authority; and by being inflexibly severe in your Carriage to him, when obstinately persisting in any ill-natured Trick, which you have forbidden, especially Lying, you have imprinted on his Mind that Awe, which is necessary: And, on the other Side, when (by permitting him the full Liberty due to his Age, and laying no Restraint in your Presence to those childish Actions and Gaiety of Carriage, which, whilst he is very young, are as necessary to him as Meat or Sleep) you have reconciled him to your Company, and made him sensible of your Care and Love of him, by Indulgence and Tenderness, especially caressing him on all Occasions wherein he does any thing well, and being kind to him after a thousand Fashions, suitable to his Age, which Nature teaches Parents better than I can: When I say, by these Ways of Tenderness and Affection, which Parents never want for their Children, you have also planted in him a particular Affection for you, he is then in the State you could desire, and you have formed in his Mind that true *Reverence* which is always afterwards carefully to be continued, and maintained in both Parts of it, *Love* and *Fear*, as the great Principles whereby you will always have Hold upon him, to turn his Mind to the Ways of Virtue and Honour.

Temper. — When this Foundation is once well laid, and you find this Reverence begin to work in him, the next Thing to be done, is carefully to consider his *Temper*, and the particular Constitution of his Mind. Stubbornness, Lying, and ill-natured Actions, are not (as has been said) to be permitted in him from the Beginning, whatever his Temper be. Those Seeds of Vices are not to be suffered to take any Root, but must be carefully weeded out, as soon as ever they begin to shew themselves in him; and your Authority is to take place, and influence his Mind from the very

Dawning of Knowledge in him, that it may operate as a natural Principle, whereof he never perceived the Beginning, never knew that it was, or could be otherwise. By this, if the *Reverence* he owes you be established early, it will always be sacred to him, and it will be as hard for him to resist it, as the Principles of his Nature.

Having thus very early set up your Authority, and, by the gentler Applications of him, shamed him out of what leads towards any immoral Habit, as soon as you have observed it in him, (for I would by no Means have Chiding used, much less Blows, until Obstinacy and Incorrigibleness make it absolutely necessary) it will be fit to consider which Way the natural Make of his *Mind inclines* him. Some Men, by the unalterable Frame of their Constitutions, are *stout*, others *timorous;* some *confident*, others *modest*, *tractable*, or *obstinate*, *curious* or *careless*, *quick* or *slow*. There are not more Differences in Men's Faces, and the outward Lineaments of their Bodies, than there are in the Makes and Tempers of their Minds; only there is this Difference, that the distinguishing Characters of the Face, and the Lineaments of the Body, grow more plain and visible with Time and Age; but the peculiar *Physiognomy of the Mind* is most discernable in Children, before Art and Cunning have taught them to hide their Deformities, and conceal their ill Inclinations, under a dissembled Outside.

Begin therefore betimes nicely to observe your Son's *Temper;* and that, when he is under least Restraint, in his Play, and as he thinks out of your

Sight: See what are his *predominant Passions*, and *prevailing Inclinations;* whether he be fierce or mild, bold or bashful, compassionate or cruel, open or reserved, etc. for as these are different in him, so are your Methods to be different, and your Authority must hence take Measures to apply itself different Ways to him. These *native Propensities*, these Prevalencies of Constitution, are not to be cured by Rules, or a direct Contest, especially those of them that are the humbler and meaner Sort, which proceed from Fear and Lowness of Spirit, though with Art they may be much mended, and turned to good Purposes. But this, be sure, after all is done, the Byass will always hang on that Side that Nature first placed it: And if you carefully observe the Characters of his Mind, now in the first Scenes of his Life, you will ever after be able to judge which Way his Thoughts lean, and what he aims at even hereafter, when, as he grows up, the Plot thickens, and he puts on several Shapes to act it.

Dominion. — I told you before, that Children love *Liberty;* and therefore they should be brought to do the Things that are fit for them, without feeling any Restraint laid upon them. I now tell you, they love something more, and that is *Dominion:* And this is the first Original of most vicious Habits, that are ordinary and natural. This Love of *Power* and Dominion shews itself very early, and that in these two Things.

1. We see Children, (as soon almost as they are born, I am sure long before they can speak)

cry, grow peevish, sullen, and out of Humour, for nothing but to have their *Wills*. They would have their Desires submitted to by others; they contend for a ready Compliance from all about them, especially from those that stand near, or beneath them in Age or Degree, as soon as they come to consider others with those Distinctions.

Another Thing wherein they shew their Love of Dominion, is, their Desire to have Things to be theirs: They would have *Property* and *Possession*, pleasing themselves with the Power which that seems to give, and the Right, they thereby have, to dispose of them as they please. He that has not observed these two Humours working very betimes in Children, has taken little Notice of their Actions: And he who thinks that these two Roots of almost all the Injustice and Contention that so disturb Human Life are not early to be weeded out, and contrary Habits introduced, neglects the proper Season to lay the Foundations of a good and worthy Man.

Recreation. — However strict an Hand is to be kept upon all Desires of Fancy, yet there is one Case wherein Fancy must be permitted to speak, and be hearkened to also. *Recreation* is as necessary as Labour or Food. But because there can be no *Recreation* without Delight, which depends not always on Reason, but oftner on Fancy, it must be permitted Children not only to divert themselves, but to do it after their own Fashion, provided it be innocently, and without Prejudice to their Health; and therefore in this Case they should not be denied, if they proposed any particular Kind of *Recreation*. Though, I think, in a well-ordered Education, they will seldom be brought to the Necessity of asking any such Liberty: Care should be taken, that what is of Advantage to them, they should always do with Delight; and before they are wearyed with one, they should be timely *diverted* to some other useful Employment. But if they are not yet brought to that Degree of Perfection, that one Way of Improvement can be made a *Recreation* to them, they must be let loose to the childish Play they fancy; which they should be weaned from, by being made surfeit of it: But from Things of Use, that they are employed in, they should always be sent away with an Appetite, at least be dismissed before they are tired, and grow quite sick of it, that so they may return to it again, as to a Pleasure that diverts them. For you must never think them set right, till they can find Delight in the Practice of laudable Things; and the useful Exercises of the Body and Mind, taking their Turns, make their Lives and Improvement pleasant in a continued Train of *Recreations*, wherein the wearyed Part is constantly relieved and refreshed. Whether this can be done in every Temper, or whether Tutors and Parents will be at the Pains, and have the Discretion and Patience to bring them to this, I know not; but that it may be done in most Children, if a right Course be taken to raise in them the Desire of Credit, Esteem, and Reputation, I do not at all doubt. And when they have so much true Life put into them, they may freely be talked with about what most *delights* them, and be directed, or let loose to it; so that they may perceive that they are beloved and cherished, and that those under whose Tuition they are, are not Enemies to their Satisfaction. Such a Management will make them in Love with the Hand that directs them, and the Virtue they are directed to.

This farther Advantage may be made by a free Liberty permitted them in their *Recreations*, that it will discover their natural Tempers, shew their Inclinations and Aptitudes, and thereby direct wise Parents in the Choice, both of the Course of Life and Employment they shall design them for, and of fit Remedies, in the mean Time, to be applied to whatever Bent of Nature they may observe most likely to mislead any of their Children.

2. *Complaints.* — Children who live together, often strive for Mastery, whose Wills shall carry it over the rest. Whoever begins the *Contest*, should be sure to be crossed in it. But not only that, but they should be taught to have all the *Deference*, *Complaisance*, and *Civility* one for another imaginable. This, when they see it procures them Respect, Love and Esteem, and that they lose no Superiority by it, they will take more Pleasure in, than in insolent Domineering; for so plainly is the other.

The Accusations of Children one against another, which usually are but the Clamours of Anger and Revenge, desiring Aid, should not be favourably received, nor hearkened to. It weakens and effeminates their Minds to suffer them to *complain*; and if they endure something crossing, or Pain from others, without being permitted to think it strange or intolerable, it will do them no Harm to learn Sufferance, and harden them early. But though you give no Countenance to the *Complaints* of the *Querulous*, yet take Care to curb the Insolence and Ill-Nature of the Injurious. When you observe it yourself, reprove it before the injured Party: But if the *Complaint* be of something really worthy your Notice, and Prevention another Time, then reprove the Offender by himself alone, out of Sight of him that complained, and make him go and ask Pardon, and make Reparation: Which coming thus, as it were from himself, will be the more cheerfully performed, and more kindly received, the Love strengthened between them, and a Custom of Civility grow familiar amongst your Children.

3. *Liberality. Justice.* — As to the having and possessing of Things, teach them to part with what they have easily and freely to their Friends, and let them find by Experience, that the most *liberal* has always the most Plenty, with Esteem and Commendation to boot, and they will quickly learn to practise it. This, I imagine, will make Brothers and Sisters kinder and civiller to one another, and consequently to others, than twenty Rules about good Manners, with which Children are ordinarily perplexed and cumbered. Covetousness, and the Desire of having in our Possession, and under our Dominion, more than we have Need of, being the Root of all Evil, should be early and carefully weeded out, and the contrary Quality of a Readiness to impart to others implanted. This should be encouraged by great Commendation and Credit,

and constantly takeing Care, that he loses nothing by his *Liberality*. Let all the Instances he gives of such Freeness be always repayed, and with Interest; and let him sensibly perceive, that the Kindness he shews to others is no ill Husbandry for himself; but that it brings a Return of Kindness both from those that receive it, and those who look on. Make this a Contest among Children, who should out-do one another this Way: And by this Means, by a constant Practice, Children having made it easy to themselves to part with what they have, good Nature may be settled in them into an Habit, and they may take Pleasure, and pique themselves in being *kind*, *liberal*, and *civil* to others.

If Liberality ought to be encouraged, certainly great Care is to be taken, that Children transgress not the Rules of *Justice:* And whenever they do, they should be set right, and, if there be Occasion for it, severely rebuked.

Our first Actions being guided more by Self-love, than Reason or Reflection, it is no Wonder that in Children they should be very apt to deviate from the just Measures of Right and Wrong; which are in the Mind the Result of improved Reason and serious Meditation. This, the more they are apt to mistake, the more careful Guard ought to be kept over them; and every the least Slip in this great social Virtue taken Notice of, and rectified; and that in Things of the least Weight and Moment, both to instruct their Ignorance, and prevent ill Habits; which, from small Beginnings, in Pins and Cherry-stones, will, if let alone, grow up to higher Frauds, and be in Danger to end at last in down-right hardened Dishonesty. The first Tendency to any *Injustice* that appears must be suppressed, with a shew of Wonder and Abhorrency in the Parent and Governors. But because Children cannot well comprehend what *Injustice* is, till they understand Property, and how particular Persons come by it, the safest Way to secure *Honesty*, is to lay the Foundations of it early in Liberality, and an Easiness to part with to others whatever they have or like themselves. This may be taught them early, before they have Language and Understanding enough to form distinct Notions of Property, and to know what is theirs by a peculiar Right, exclusive of others. And since Children seldom have any Thing but by Gift, and that for the most Part from their Parents, they may be at first taught not to take or keep any Thing, but what is given them by those whom they take to have a Power over it: And as their Capacities enlarge, other Rules and Cases of *Justice*, and Rights concerning *Meum* and *Tuum*, may be proposed and inculcated. If any Act of *Injustice* in them appears to proceed not from Mistake, but a Perverseness in their Wills, when a gentle Rebuke and Shame will not reform this irregular and covetous Inclination, rougher Remedies must be applied: And it is but for the Father or Tutor to take and keep from them something that they value, and think their own, or order somebody else to do it; and by such Instances, make them sensible what little Advantage they are like to make, by possessing themselves *unjustly* of what is another's, whilst there are in the World stronger and more Men than they. But if an ingenuous Detestation of this shameful Vice be but carefully and early instilled into them, as I think it may, that is the true and genuine Method to obviate this Crime; and will be a better Guard against *Dishonesty*, than any Considerations drawn from Interest; Habits working more constantly, and with greater Facility, than Reason; which, when we have most Need of it, is seldom fairly consulted, and more rarely obeyed.

Fortitude. — *Fortitude* is the Guard and Support of the other Virtues; and without Courage a Man will scarce keep steady to his Duty, and fill up the Character of a truly-worthy Man.

Courage. — *Courage*, that makes us bear up against Dangers that we fear, and Evils that we feel, is of great Use in an Estate, as ours is in this Life, exposed to Assaults on all Hands: And therefore it is very adviseable to get Children into this Armour as early as we can. Natural Temper, I confess, does here a great deal: But even where that is defective, and the Heart is in itself weak and timorous, it may, by a right Management, be brought to a better Resolution. What is to be done to prevent breaking Childrens Spirits by frightful Apprehensions instilled into them when young, or bemoaning themselves under every little Suffering, I have already taken Notice: How to harden their Tempers, and raise their *Courage*, if we find them too much subject to Fear, is farther to be considered.

True Fortitude I take to be the quiet Possession of a Man's Self, and an undisturbed doing his Duty, whatever Evil besets, or Danger lies in his Way. This there are so few Men attain to, that we are not to expect it from Children. But yet something may be done: And a wise Conduct, by insensible Degrees, may carry them farther than one expects.

The Neglect of this great Care of them, whilst they are young, is the Reason, perhaps, why there are so few that have this Virtue in its full Latitude, when they are Men. I should not say this in a Nation so naturally brave, as ours is, did I think, that true Fortitude required nothing but Courage in the Field, and a Contempt of Life in the Face of an Enemy. This, I confess, is not the least Part of it, nor can be denied the Laurels and Honours always justly due to the Valour of those who venture their Lives for their Country. But yet this is not all: Dangers attack us in other Places, besides the Field of Battle; and, though Death be the King of Terrors, yet Pain, Disgrace and Poverty, have frightful Looks, able to discompose most Men, whom they seem ready to seize on: And there are those who contemn some of these, and yet are heartily frighted with the other. True Fortitude is prepared for Dangers of all Kinds, and unmoved, whatsoever Evil it be that threatens. I do not mean unmoved with any Fear at all. Where Danger shews itself, Apprehension cannot, without Stupidity, be wanting. Where Danger is, Sense of Danger should be, and so much Fear as should keep us awake, and excite our Attention, Industry and Vigour, but not disturb the calm Use of our Reason, nor hinder the Execution of what that dictates.

Hardiness. — The Way to harden, and fortify Children against Fear and Danger, is to accustom them to suffer Pain. This, it is possible, will be thought, by kind Parents, a very unnatural Thing towards their Children; and by most, unreasonable, to endeavour to reconcile any one to the Sense of Pain, by bringing it upon him. It will be said, it may perhaps give the Child an Aversion for him that makes him suffer, but can never recommend to him Suffering itself. This is a strange Method: You will not have Children whipped and punished for their Faults, but you would have them tormented for doing well, or for Tormenting's Sake. I doubt not but such Objections as these will be made, and I shall be thought inconsistent with myself, or phantastical, in proposing it. I confess it is a Thing to be managed with great Discretion, and therefore it falls not out amiss, that it will not be received and relished but by those who consider well, and look into the Reason of Things. I would not have Children much beaten for their Faults, because I would not have them think bodily Pain the greatest Punishment: And I would have them, when they do well, be sometimes put in Pain, for the same Reason, that they may be accustomed to bear it without looking on it as the greatest Evil. How much Education may reconcile young People to Pain and Sufferance, the Example of *Sparta* does sufficiently shew: And they who have once brought themselves not to think bodily Pain the greatest of Evils, or that which they ought to stand most in fear of, have made no small Advance towards Virtue. But I am not so foolish to propose the *Lacedæmonian* Discipline in our Age or Constitution. But yet I do say, that enuring Children gently to suffer some Degrees of Pain, without shrinking, is a Way to gain Firmness to their Minds, and lay a Foundation for Courage and Resolution, in the future Part of their Lives.

Not to bemoan them, or permit them to bemoan themselves, on every little Pain they suffer, is the first Step to be made. But of this I have spoken elsewhere.

The next Thing is sometimes designedly to put them in Pain: But Care must be taken that this be done when the Child is in good Humour, and satisfied of the good Will and Kindness of him that hurts him, at the Time that he does it. There must no Marks of Anger or Displeasure, on the one Side; nor Compassion, or Repenting, on the other, go along with it: And it must be sure to be no more than the Child can bear, without repining or taking it amiss, or for a Punishment. Managed by these Degrees, and with such Circumstances, I have seen a Child run away laughing, with good smart Blows of a Wand on his Back, who would have cried for an unkind Word, and been very sensible of the Chastisement of a cold Look, from the same Person. Satisfy a Child, by a constant Course of your Care and Kindness, that you perfectly love him, and he may, by Degrees, be accustomed to bear very painful and rough Usage from you, without flinching or complaining: And this we see Children do every Day in Play one with another. The softer you find your Child is, the more you are to seek Occasions, at fit Times thus to harden him. The great Art in this is to begin with what is but very little painful, and to proceed by insensible Degrees, when you are playing, and in Good-Humour with him, and speaking well of him: And when you have once got him to think himself made Amends for his Suffering, by the Praise is given him for his Courage; when he can take a Pride in giving such Marks of his Manliness, and can prefer the Reputation of being brave and stout, to the avoiding a little Pain, or the shrinking under it; you need not despair in Time, and by the Assistance of his growing Reason, to master his Timorousness, and mend the Weakness of his Constitution. As he grows bigger, he is to be set upon bolder Attempts than his natural Temper carries him to; and whenever he is observed to flinch from what one has Reason to think he would come off well in, if he had but Courage to undertake, that he should be assisted in at first, and by Degrees shamed to, till at last Practice has given more Assurance, and with it a Mastery; which must be rewarded with great Praise, and the good Opinion of others, for his Performance. When by these Steps he has got Resolution enough not to be deterred, from what he ought to do, by the Apprehension of Danger; when Fear does not, in sudden or hazardous Occurrences, discompose his Mind, set his Body a trembling, and make him unfit for Action, or run away from it, he has then the Courage of a rational Creature: And such an Hardiness we would endeavour, by Custom and Use, to bring Children to, as proper Occasions come in our Way.

Cruelty. — One Thing I have frequently observed in Children, that when they have got Possession of any poor Creature they are apt to use it ill: They often *torment*, and treat, very roughly young Birds, Butterflies, and such other poor Animals, which fall into their Hands, and that with a seeming Kind of Pleasure. This, I think, should be watched in them, and if they incline to any such Cruelty, they should be taught the contrary Usage: For the Custom of tormenting and killing of Beasts will, by Degrees, harden their Minds, even towards Men; and they who delight in the Suffering and Destruction of inferior Creatures, will not be apt to be very compassionate or benign to those of their own Kind. Our Practice takes Notice of this in the Exclusion of *Butchers* from Juries of Life and Death. Children should, from the Beginning, be bred up in an Abhorrence of *killing* or tormenting any living Creature; and be taught not to *spoil* or destroy any Thing, unless it be for the Preservation or Advantage of some other that is nobler. And truly, if the Preservation of all Mankind, as much as in him lies, were every one's Persuasion, as indeed it is every one's Duty, and the true Principle to regulate our Religion, Politicks, and Morality by, the World would be much quieter and better natured than it is. But to return to our present Business: I cannot but commend both the Kindness and Prudence of a Mother I knew, who was wont always to indulge her

Daughters, when any of them desired Dogs, Squirrels, Birds, or any such Things as young Girls use to be delighted with: But then, when they had them, they must be sure to keep them well, and look diligently after them, that they wanted nothing, or were not ill used: For if they were negligent in their Care of them, it was counted a great Fault, which often forfeited their Possession, or at least they failed not to be rebuked for it; whereby they were early taught Diligence and Good-Nature. And, indeed, I think People should be accustomed from their Cradles to be tender of all sensible Creatures, and to spoil or *waste* nothing at all.

This Delight they take in *doing of Mischief*, whereby I mean spoiling of any Thing to no Purpose, but more especially the Pleasure they take to put any Thing in Pain that is capable of it, I cannot persuade myself to be any other than a foreign and introduced Disposition, an Habit borrowed from Custom and Conversation. People teach Children to strike, and laugh, when they hurt, or see Harm come to others: And they have the Examples of most about them, to confirm them in it. All the Entertainment and Talk of History is of nothing almost but Fighting and Killing: And the Honour and Renown that is bestowed on Conquerors (who for the most Part are but the great Butchers of Mankind) farther mislead growing Youth, who by this Means come to think Slaughter the laudable Business of Mankind, and the most heroick of Virtues. By these Steps unnatural Cruelty is planted in us; and what Humanity abhors, Custom reconciles and recommends to us, by laying it in the Way to Honour. Thus, by Fashion and Opinion, that comes to be a Pleasure, which in itself neither is nor can be any. This ought carefully to be watched, and early remedied; so as to settle and cherish the contrary, and more natural Temper of Benignity and *Compassion* in the Room of it: But still by the same gentle Methods, which are to be applied to the other two Faults beforementioned. It may not perhaps be unreasonable here to add this farther Caution, *viz.* That the Mischiefs, or Harms, that come by Play, Inadvertency, or Ignorance, and were not known to be Harms, or designed for Mischief's Sake, though they may, perhaps, be sometimes of considerable Damage, yet are not at all, or but very gently, to be taken Notice of. For this, I think, I cannot too often inculcate, That whatever Miscarriage a Child is guilty of, and whatever be the Consequence of it, the Thing to be regarded, in taking Notice of it, is only what Root it springs from, and what Habit it is like to establish: And to that the Correction ought to be directed, and the Child not to suffer any Punishment for any Harm which may have come by his Play or Inadvertency. The Faults to be amended lie in the Mind; and if they are such, as either Age will cure, or no ill Habits will follow from, the present Action, whatever displeasing Circumstances it may have, is to be passed by, without any Animadversion.

Another Way to instill Sentiments of Humanity, and to keep them lively in young Folks, will be, to accustom them to Civility in their Language and

Deportment towards their Inferiors, and the meaner Sort of People, particularly Servants. It is not unusual to observe the Children in Gentlemen's Families treat the Servants of the House with domineering Words, Names of Contempt, and an imperious Carriage; as if they were of another Race and Species beneath them. Whether ill Example, the Advantage of Fortune, or their natural Vanity, inspire this Haughtiness, it should be prevented, or weeded out; and a gentle, courteous, affable Carriage towards the lower Ranks of Men placed in the Room of it. No Part of their Superiority will be hereby lost; but the Distinction increased, and their Authority strengthened; when Love in Inferiors is joined to outward Respect, and an Esteem of the Person has a Share in their Submission: And Domesticks will pay a more ready and cheerful Service, when they find themselves not spurned, because Fortune has laid them below the Level of others, at their Masters Feet. Children should not be suffered to lose the Consideration of human Nature, in the Shufflings of outward Conditions: The more they have, the better humoured should they be taught to be; and the more compassionate and gentle to those of their Brethren who are placed lower, and have scantier Portions. If they are suffered from their Cradles to treat Men ill and rudely, because, by their Father's Title, they think they have a little Power over them, at best it is ill-bred, and, if Care be not taken, will, by Degrees, nurse up their natural Pride into an habitual Contempt of those beneath them: And where will that probably end, but in Oppression and Cruelty?

Play-Games. — Play-things, I think, Children should have, and of divers Sorts; but still to be in the Custody of their Tutors, or somebody else, whereof the Child should have in his Power but one at once, and should not be suffered to have another but when he restored that. This teaches them betimes to be careful of not losing or spoiling the Things they have; whereas Plenty and Variety in their own keeping, makes them wanton and careless, and teaches them from the Beginning to be Squanderers and Wasters. These, I confess, are little Things, and such as will seem beneath the Care of a Governour; but nothing that may form Children's Minds is to be overlooked and neglected; and whatsoever introduces Habits, and settles Customs in them, deserves the Care and Attention of their Governours, and is not a small Thing in its Consequences.

One Thing more about Children's Play-things may be worth their Parents Care: though it be agreed they should have of several Sorts, yet, I think, they should have none bought for them. This will hinder that great Variety they are often overcharged with, which serves only to teach the Mind to wander after Change and Superfluity, to be unquiet, and perpetually stretching itself after something more still, though it knows not what, and never to be satisfied with what it hath. The Court that is made to People of Condition, in such Kind of Presents to their Children, does the little ones

ON EDUCATION. 375

great Harm: By it they are taught Pride, Vanity, and Covetousness, almost before they can speak: And I have known a young Child so distracted with the Number and Variety of his Play-Games, that he tired his Maid every Day to look them over; and was so accustomed to Abundance, that he never thought he had enough, but was always asking, What more? What more? What new Thing shall I have? A good Introduction to moderate Desires, and the ready Way to make a contented happy Man!

How then shall they have the Play-Games you allow them, if none must be bought for them? I answer, they should make them themselves, or at least endeavour it, and set themselves about it: Till then they should have none, and till then they will want none of any great Artifice. A smooth Pebble, a Piece of Paper, the Mother's Bunch of Keys, or any thing they cannot hurt themselves with, serves as much to divert little Children as those more chargeable and curious Toys from the Shops, which are presently put out of Order and broken. Children are never dull or out of Humour for want of such Play-Things, unless they have been used to them; when they are little, whatever occurs serves the Turn; and, as they grow bigger, if they are not stored by the expensive Folly of others, they will make them themselves. Indeed, when they once begin to set themselves to work about any of their Inventions, they should be taught and assisted; but should have nothing whilst they lazily sit still, expecting to be furnished from other Hands, without employing their own. And, if you help them where they are at a Stand, it will more endear you to them than any chargeable Toys you shall buy for them. Play-Things which are above their Skill to make, as Tops, Gigs, Battledors, and the like, which are to be used with Labour, should, indeed, be procured them. These it is convenient they should have, not for Variety, but Exercise; but these too should be given them as bare as might be. If they had a Top, the Scourge-Stick and Leather-Strap should be left to their own making and fitting. If they sit gaping to have such Things dropt in their Mouths, they should go without them. This will accustom them to seek for what they want in themselves, and in their own Endeavours; whereby they will be taught Moderation in their Desires, Application, Industry, Thought, Contrivance, and good Husbandry: Qualities that will be useful to them when they are Men, and therefore cannot be learned too soon, nor fixed too deep. All the Plays and Diversions of Children should be directed towards good useful Habits, or else they will introduce ill ones. Whatever they do leaves some Impression on that tender Age, and from thence they receive a Tendency to do Good or Evil: And whatever hath such an Influence ought not to be neglected.

Lying. — Lying is so ready and cheap a Cover for any Miscarriage, and so much in Fashion among all Sorts of People, that a Child can hardly avoid observing the Use is made of it on all Occasions, and so can scarce be kept, without great Care, from getting into it. But it is so ill a Quality, and the Mother of so many ill ones that spawn from it, and take Shelter under it, that a Child should be brought up in the greatest Abhorrence of it imaginable. It should be always (when occasionally it comes to be mentioned) spoke of before him with the utmost Detestation, as a Quality so wholly inconsistent with the Name and Character of a Gentleman, that no Body of any Credit can bear the Imputation of a Lye; a Mark that is judged the utmost Disgrace, which debases a Man to the lowest Degree of a shameful Meanness, and ranks him with the most contemptible Part of Mankind, and the abhorred Rascality; and is not to be endured in any one who would converse with People of Condition, or have any Esteem or Reputation in the World. The first Time he is found in a *Lye*, it should rather be wondered at as a monstrous Thing in him, than reproved as an ordinary Fault. If that keeps him not from relapsing, the next Time he must be sharply rebuked, and fall into the State of great Displeasure of his Father and Mother, and all about him, who take Notice of it. And if this Way work not the Cure, you must come to Blows; for after he has been thus warned, a premeditated *Lye* must always be looked upon as Obstinacy, and never be permitted to escape unpunished.

Excuses. — Children, afraid to have their Faults seen in their naked Colours, will, like the rest of the Sons of *Adam*, be apt to make *Excuses*. This is a Fault usually bordering upon, and leading to Untruth, and is not to be indulged in them; but yet it ought to be cured rather with Shame than Roughness. If therefore, when a Child is questioned for any Thing, his first Answer be an *Excuse*, warn him soberly to tell the Truth; and then, if he persists to shuffle it off with a *Falsehood*, he must be chastised; but if he directly confess, you must commend his Ingenuity, and pardon the Fault, be it what it will, and pardon it so that you never so much as reproach him with it, or mention it to him again: For if you would have him in Love with Ingenuity, and by a constant Practice make it habitual to him, you must take Care that it never procure him the least Inconvenience; but, on the contrary, his own Confession bringing always with it perfect Impunity, should be besides encouraged by some Marks of Approbation. If his *Excuse* be such at any Time that you cannot prove it to have any Falsehood in it, let it pass for true, and be sure not to shew any Suspicion of it. Let him keep up his Reputation with you as high as is possible; for when once he finds he has lost that, you have lost a great, and your best Hold upon him. Therefore let him not think he has the Character of a Lyar with you, as long as you can avoid it without flattering him in it. Thus some Slips in Truth may be over-looked. But after he has once been corrected for a *Lye* you must be sure never after to pardon it in him, whenever you find, and take Notice to him that he is guilty of it: For it being a Fault which he has been forbid, and may, unless he be wilful, avoid, the repeating of it is perfect Perverseness, and must have the Chastisement due to that Offence.

That which every Gentleman, that takes any Care of his Education, desires for his Son, besides the Estate he leaves him, is contained (I suppose) in these four Things, *Virtue*, *Wisdom*, *Breeding*, and *Learning*. I will not trouble myself whether these Names do not some of them sometimes stand for the same Thing, or really include one another. It serves my Turn here to follow the popular Use of these Words, which, I presume, is clear enough to make me be understood, and I hope there will be no Difficulty to comprehend my Meaning.

I place *Virtue* as the first and most necessary of those Endowments that belong to a Man or a Gentleman; as absolutely requisite to make him valued and beloved by others, acceptable or tolerable to himself. Without that, I think, he will be happy neither in this nor the other World.

God. — As the Foundation of this, there ought very early to be imprinted on his Mind a true Notion of *God*, as of the independent Supreme Being, Author and Maker of all Things, from whom we receive all our Good, who loves us, and gives us all Things. And consequent to this, instill into him a Love and Reverence of this supreme Being. This is enough to begin with, without going to explain this Matter any farther; for Fear, least by talking too early to him of Spirits, and being unseasonably forward to make him understand the incomprehensible Nature of that infinite Being, his Head be either filled with false, or perplexed with unintelligible Notions of him. Let him only be told upon Occasion, that *God* made and governs all Things, hears and sees every Thing, and does all Manner of Good to those that love and obey him. You will find, that being told of such a *God*, other Thoughts will be apt to rise up fast enough in his Mind about him; which, as you observe them to have any Mistakes, you must set right. And I think it would be better if Men generally rested in such an Idea of *God*, without being too curious in their Notions about a Being, which all must acknowledge incomprehensible; whereby many, who have not Strength and Clearness of Thought to distinguish between what they can and what they cannot know, run themselves into Superstition or Atheism, making *God* like themselves, or, because they cannot comprehend any thing else, none at all. And I am apt to think, the keeping Children constantly Morning and Evening to Acts of Devotion to God, as to their Maker, Preserver and Benefactor, in some plain and short Form of Prayer, suitable to their Age and Capacity, will be of much more Use to them in Religion, Knowledge, and Virtue, than to distract their Thoughts with curious Enquiries into his inscrutable Essence and Being.

Spirits. — Having by gentle Degrees, as you find him capable of it, settled such an Idea of God in his Mind, and taught him to *pray* to him, and *praise* him, as the Author of his Being, and of all the Good he does or can enjoy; forbear any Discourse of other *Spirits*, till the Mention of them coming in his Way, upon Occasion hereafter to be set down, and his reading the Scripture-History, put him upon that Enquiry.

Truth. Good-Nature. — Having laid the Foundations of Virtue in a true Notion of a God, such as the Creed wisely teaches, as far as his Age is capable, and by accustoming him to pray to him; the next Thing to be taken Care of, is to keep him exactly to speaking of *Truth*, and by all the Ways imaginable inclining him to be *good-natured*. Let him know that twenty Faults are sooner to be forgiven, than the *straining of Truth* to cover any one *by an Excuse*. And to teach him betimes to love, and be *good-natured* to others, is to lay early the true Foundation of an honest Man. All Injustice generally springing from too great Love of ourselves, and too little of others.

This is all I shall say of this Matter in general, and is enough for laying the first Foundations of Virtue in a Child. As he grows up, the Tendency of his natural Inclination must be observed; which, as it inclines him, more than is convenient, on one or t'other Side, from the right Path of Virtue, ought to have proper Remedies applied: For few of *Adam's* Children are so happy as not to be born with some Biass in their natural Temper, which it is the Business of Education either to take off, or counterbalance. But to enter into Particulars of this, would be beyond the Design of this short Treatise of Education. I intend not a Discourse of all the Virtues and Vices, and how each Virtue is to be attained, and every peculiar Vice by its peculiar Remedies cured; though I have mentioned some of the most ordinary Faults, and the Ways to be used in correcting them.

Wisdom. — *Wisdom*, I take, in the popular Acceptation, for a Man's managing his Business ably, and with Fore-sight in this World. This is the Product of a good natural Temper, Application of Mind, and Experience together, and so above the Reach of Children. The greatest Thing that in them can be done towards it, is to hinder them, as much as may be, from being *Cunning;* which being the Ape of *Wisdom*, is the most distant from it that can be: And as an Ape, for the Likeness it has to a Man, wanting what really should make him so, is by so much the uglier; *Cunning* is only the Want of Understanding; which, because it cannot compass its Ends by direct Ways, would do it by a Trick, and Circumvention; and the Mischief of it is, a *Cunning* Trick helps but once, but hinders ever after. No Cover was ever made either so big, or so fine as to hide its self. No Body was ever so *cunning* as to conceal their being so: And when they are once discovered, every Body is shy, every Body distrustful of *crafty* Men; and all the World forwardly join to oppose and defeat them: Whilst the open, fair, *wise* Man has every Body to make Way for him, and goes directly to his Business. To accustom a Child to have true Notions of Things, and not to be satisfied till he has them; to raise his Mind to great and worthy Thoughts; and to keep him at a Distance from Falsehood, and Cunning, which has always a broad Mixture of Falsehood in it, is the fittest Preparation of a Child for *Wisdom*. The rest, which is to be learned from Time, Experience, and Observation, and an Acquaintance with Men, their Tempers, and Designs, is not to be expected in the Ignorance and Inadvertency of Childhood, or the inconsiderate Heat and Unwariness of Youth: All that can be done towards it, during this unripe Age, is, as I have said, to accustom them to Truth and Sincerity; to a Submission to Reason; and as much as may be, to Reflection on their own Actions.

Though the managing ourselves well in this Part of our Behaviour has the Name of *Good-Breeding*, as if peculiarly the Effect of Education; yet, as I have said, young Children should not be much perplexed about it; I mean about putting off their Hats and making Legs modishly. Teach them Humility, and to be good-natured, if you can, and this Sort of Manners will not be wanting; *Civility* being, in Truth, nothing but a Care not to shew any Slighting or Contempt of any one in Conversation. What are the most allowed and esteemed Ways of expressing this, we have above observed. It is as peculiar and different, in several Countries of the World, as their Language; and therefore, if it be rightly considered, Rules and Discourses, made to Children about it, are as useless and impertinent, as it would be now and then to give a Rule or two of the *Spanish* Tongue to one that converses only with *Englishmen*. Be as busy as you please with Discourses of *Civility* to your Son, such as is his Company, such will be his Manners. A Ploughman of your Neighbourhood, that has never been out of his Parish, read what Lectures you please to him, will be as soon in his Language, as his Carriage, a Courtier; that is, in neither will be more polite than those he uses to converse with: And therefore of this no other Care can be taken till he be of an Age to have a Tutor put to him, who must not fail to be a well-bred Man: And, in good Earnest, if I were to speak my Mind freely, so Children do nothing out of Obstinacy, Pride, and Ill-Nature, it is no great Matter how they put off their Hats, or make Legs. If you can teach them to love and respect other People, they will, as their Age requires it, find Ways to express it acceptably to every one, according to the Fashions they have been used to: And, as to their Motions and Carriage of their Bodies, a Dancing-Master, as has been said, when it is fit, will teach them what is most becoming. In the mean Time, when they are young, People expect not that Children should be over-mindful of these Ceremonies; Carelessness is allowed to that Age, and becomes them as well as Compliments do grown People; or, at least, if some very nice People will think it a Fault, I am sure it is a Fault that should be overlooked, and left to Time, a Tutor, and Conversation, to cure: And therefore I think it not worth your while to have your Son (as I often see Children are) molested or chid about it: But, where there is Pride or Ill-Nature appearing in his Carriage, there he must be persuaded or shamed out of it.

Though Children, when little, should not be much

perplexed with Rules and ceremonious Part of *Breeding*, yet there is a Sort of Unmannerliness very apt to grow up with young People, if not early restrained; and that is a Forwardness to *interrupt* others that are speaking, and to stop them with some *Contradiction*. Whether the Custom of Disputing, and the Reputation of Parts and Learning usually given to it, as if it were the only Standard and Evidence of Knowledge, make young Men so forward to watch Occasions to correct others in their Discourse, and not to slip any Opportunity of shewing their Talents; so it is, that I have found Scholars most blamed in this Point. There cannot be a greater Rudeness, than to *interrupt* another in the Current of his Discourse; for if there be not impertinent Folly in answering a Man before we know what he will say, yet it is a plain Declaration, that we are weary to hear him talk any longer, and have a Disesteem of what he says, which we, judging not fit to entertain the Company, desire them to give Audience to us, who have something to produce worth their Attention. This shews a very great Disrespect, and cannot but be offensive: And yet, this is what almost all *Interruption* constantly carries with it. To which, if there be added, as is usual, a *Correcting* of any Mistake, or a *Contradiction* of what has been said, it is a Mark of yet greater Pride and Self-Conceitedness, when we thus intrude ourselves for Teachers, and take upon us, either to set another right in his Story, or shew the Mistakes of his Judgement.

I do not say this, that I think there should be no Difference of Opinions in Conversation, nor Opposition in Men's Discourses; This would be to take away the greatest Advantage of Society, and the Improvements that are to be made by ingenious Company; where the Light is to be got from the opposite Arguings of Men of Parts, shewing the different Sides of Things, and their various Aspects and Probabilities, would be quite lost, if every one were obliged to assent to, and say after, the first Speaker. It is not the owning one's Dissent from another, that I speak against, but the Manner of doing it. Young Men should be taught not to be forward to *interpose* their Opinions, unless asked, or when others have done and are silent; and then only by Way of Enquiry, not Instruction. The positive Asserting, and the magisterial Air should be avoided; and when a general Pause of the whole Company affords an Opportunity, they may modestly put in their Question as Learners.

This becoming Decency will not cloud their Parts, nor weaken the Strength of their Reason; but bespeak the more favourable Attention, and give what they say the greater Advantage. An ill Argument, or ordinary Observation thus introduced, with some civil Preface of Deference and Respect to the Opinions of others, will procure them more Credit, and Esteem, than the sharpest Wit, or profoundest Science, with a rough, insolent, or noisy Management, which always shocks the Hearers, and leaves an ill Opinion of the Man, though he get the better of it in the Argument.

This therefore should be carefully watched in young People, stopped in the Beginning, and the contrary

Habit introduced in all their Conversation; and the rather, because Forwardness to talk, frequent *Interruptions* in arguing, and loud *Wrangling*, are too often observable amongst grown People, even of Rank amongst us. The *Indians*, whom we call barbarous, observe much more Decency and Civility in their Discourses and Conversation, giving one another a fair silent Hearing, till they have quite done; and then answering them calmly, and without Noise or Passion. And if it be not so in this civilized Part of the World, we must impute it to a Neglect in Education, which has not yet reformed this ancient Piece of Barbarity amongst us. Was it not, think you, an entertaining Spectacle, to see two Ladies of Quality, accidentally seated on the opposite Sides of a Room, set round with Company, fall into a Dispute, and grow so eager in it that in the Heat of their Controversy, edging, by Degrees, their Chairs forwards, they were in a little Time got up close to one another in the Middle of the Room; where, for a good while, they managed the Dispute as fiercely as two Game-Cocks in the Pit, without minding or taking any Notice of the Circle, which could not all the while forbear smiling? This I was told by a Person of Quality, who was present at the Combat, and did not omit to reflect upon the Indecencies, that Warmth in *Dispute* often runs People into; which since Custom makes too frequent, Education should take more Care of. There is no body but condemns this in others, though they overlook it in themselves; and many, who are sensible of it in themselves, and resolve against it, cannot yet get rid of an ill Custom, which Neglect in their Education has suffered to settle into an Habit.

Conclusion. — There are a thousand other Things, that may need Consideration; especially if one should take in the various Tempers, different Inclinations, and particular Defaults, that are to be found in Children, and prescribe proper Remedies. The Variety is so great, that it would require a Volume; nor would that reach it. Each Man's Mind has some Peculiarity, as well as his Face, that distinguishes him from all others; and there are possibly scarce two Children, who can be conducted by exactly the same Method. Besides that, I think a Prince, a Nobleman, and an ordinary Gentleman's Son, should have different Ways of Breeding. But having had here only some general Views in Reference to the main End, and Aims in Education, and those designed for a Gentleman's Son, whom, being then very little, I considered only as white Paper, or Wax, to be molded and fashioned as one pleases; I have touched little more than those Heads, which I judged necessary for the Breeding of a young Gentleman of his Condition in general; and have now published these my occasional Thoughts with this Hope, that tho' this be far from being a complete Treatise on this Subject, or such as that every one may find what will just fit his Child in it, yet it may give some small Light to those, whose Concern for their dear little Ones makes them so irregularly bold, that they dare venture to consult their own Reason, in the Education of their Children, rather than wholly to rely upon old Custom.

VIII.

THOMAS GRAY.

1716—1771.

"Gray is one of the few, the very few of our greatest poets, who deserves to be studied in every line for the apprehension of that wonderful sweetness, power and splendour of versification, which has made him (scholastic and difficult as he is) one of the most popular of writers, though his rhymes are occasionally flat and his phrases heathen Greek to ordinary readers. The secret of his supremacy consists principally in the consummate art with which his diction is elaborated into the most melodious concatenation of syllables to form lines; and those lines so to implicate and evolve in progression, that the strain of one of Händel's Overtures is not more consecutively ordered to carry the mind onward, through every bar, to the march at the conclusion, when the hearer has been wrought to such a state of exaltation, that he feels as though he could mount the scaffold to the beaten time of such music."

James Montgomery in his "Lectures on Poetry" &c. p. 203.

GRAY'S POEMS.

ODES.

I. ON THE SPRING.

1 Lo! where the rosy-bosom'd Hours,
    Fair Venus' train, appear,
Disclose the long-expecting flowers,
    And wake the purple year!
The Attic warbler pours her throat
Responsive to the cuckoo's note,
    The untaught harmony of Spring;
While, whispering pleasure as they fly,
Cool Zephyrs through the clear blue sky
    Their gather'd fragrance fling.

2 Where'er the oak's thick branches stretch
    A broader, browner shade,
Where'er the rude and moss-grown beech
    O'ercanopies the glade,
Beside some water's rushy brink
With me the Muse shall sit, and think
    (At ease reclined in rustic state)
How vain the ardour of the crowd,
How low, how little, are the proud,
    How indigent the great!

3 Still is the toiling hand of Care,
    The panting herds repose;
Yet hark! how through the peopled air
    The busy murmur glows!

  The insect youth are on the wing,
  Eager to taste the honied spring,
   And float amid the liquid noon;
  Some lightly o'er the current skim,
  Some show their gaily gilded trim,
   Quick glancing to the sun.

4 To Contemplation's sober eye,
   Such is the race of Man,
  And they that creep, and they that fly,
   Shall end where they began.
  Alike the busy and the gay
  But flutter through life's little day,
   In Fortune's varying colours dress'd;
  Brush'd by the hand of rough Mischance,
  Or chill'd by Age, their airy dance
   They leave, in dust to rest.

5 Methinks I hear, in accents low,
   The sportive kind reply:
  Poor Moralist! and what art thou?
   A solitary fly!
  Thy joys no glittering female meets,
  No hive hast thou of hoarded sweets,
   No painted plumage to display:
  On hasty wings thy youth is flown,
  Thy sun is set, thy spring is gone —
   We frolic while 'tis May.

II. ON THE DEATH OF A FAVOURITE CAT,
DROWNED IN A CHINA TUB OF GOLD FISHES.

1 'Twas on a lofty vase's side,
  Where China's gayest art had dyed
   The azure flowers that blow,
  Demurest of the tabby kind,
  The pensive Selima, reclined,
   Gazed on the lake below.

2 Her conscious tail her joy declared;
  The fair round face, the snowy beard,
    The velvet of her paws,
  Her coat that with the tortoise vies,
  Her ears of jet, and emerald eyes,
    She saw, and purr'd applause.

3 Still had she gazed, but, 'midst the tide,
  Two angel-forms were seen to glide,
    The Genii of the stream;
  Their scaly armour's Tyrian hue,
  Through richest purple, to the view
    Betray'd a golden gleam.

4 The hapless nymph with wonder saw;
  A whisker first, and then a claw,
    With many an ardent wish,
  She stretch'd in vain to reach the prize;
  What female heart can gold despise?
    What cat's averse to fish?

5 Presumptuous maid! with looks intent,
  Again she stretch'd, again she bent,
    Nor knew the gulf between;
  Malignant Fate sat by and smiled;
  The slippery verge her feet beguiled —
    She tumbled headlong in.

6 Eight times emerging from the flood,
  She mew'd to every watery god
    Some speedy aid to send.
  No Dolphin came, no Nereid stirr'd,
  Nor cruel Tom or Susan heard:
    A favourite has no friend!

7 From hence, ye beauties! undeceived,
  Know one false step is ne'er retrieved,
    And be with caution bold;
  Not all that tempts your wandering eyes,
  And heedless hearts, is lawful prize,
    Nor all that glisters gold.

III. ON A DISTANT PROSPECT OF ETON COLLEGE.

Ἄνθρωπος· ἱκανὴ πρόφασις εἰς τὸ δυστυχεῖν.
MENANDER.

1   Ye distant spires! ye antique towers!
   That crown the watery glade
   Where grateful Science still adores
   Her Henry's holy shade;
And ye that from the stately brow
Of Windsor's heights the expanse below
   Of grove, of lawn, of mead survey,
   Whose turf, whose shade, whose flowers among
Wanders the hoary Thames along
   His silver-winding way:

2 Ah, happy hills! ah, pleasing shade!
   Ah, fields beloved in vain!
   Where once my careless childhood stray'd,
   A stranger yet to pain!
I feel the gales that from ye blow
A momentary bliss bestow,
   As, waving fresh their gladsome wing,
My weary soul they seem to soothe,
And, redolent of joy and youth,
   To breathe a second spring.

3 Say, father Thames! for thou hast seen
   Full many a sprightly race,
Disporting on thy margent green
   The paths of pleasure trace:
Who foremost now delight to cleave
With pliant arm thy glassy wave?
   The captive linnet which enthral?
What idle progeny succeed
To chase the rolling circle's speed,
   Or urge the flying ball?

4 While some, on earnest business bent,
    Their murmuring labours ply,
 'Gainst graver hours, that bring constraint,
    To sweeten liberty;
 Some bold adventurers disdain
 The limits of their little reign,
    And unknown regions dare descry;
 Still as they run they look behind,
 They hear a voice in every wind,
    And snatch a fearful joy.

5 Gay Hope is theirs, by Fancy fed,
    Less pleasing when possess'd;
 The tear forgot as soon as shed,
    The sunshine of the breast;
 Theirs buxom health of rosy hue,
 Wild wit, invention ever new,
    And lively cheer, of vigour born;
 The thoughtless day, the easy night,
 The spirits pure, the slumbers light,
    That fly the approach of morn.

6 Alas! regardless of their doom,
    The little victims play;
 No sense have they of ills to come,
    Nor care beyond to-day:
 Yet see how all around them wait,
 The ministers of human fate,
    And black Misfortune's baleful train!
 Ah! show them where in ambush stand,
 To seize their prey, the murderous band!
    Ah! tell them they are men!

7 These shall the fury Passions tear,
    The vultures of the mind,
 Disdainful Anger, pallid Fear,
    And Shame that skulks behind;
 Or pining Love shall waste their youth,
 Or Jealousy, with rankling tooth,

That inly gnaws the secret heart;
And Envy wan, and faded Care,
Grim-visaged, comfortless Despair,
And Sorrow's piercing dart.

8 Ambition this shall tempt to rise,
Then whirl the wretch from high,
To bitter Scorn a sacrifice,
And grinning infamy;
The stings of Falsehood those shall try,
And hard Unkindness' alter'd eye,
That mocks the tear it forced to flow;
And keen Remorse, with blood defiled,
And moody Madness, laughing wild
Amid severest woe.

9 Lo! in the vale of years beneath,
A grisly troop are seen,
The painful family of Death,
More hideous than their queen:
This racks the joints, this fires the veins,
That every labouring sinew strains,
Those in the deeper vitals rage;
Lo! Poverty, to fill the band,
That numbs the soul with icy hand,
And slow-consuming Age.

10 To each his sufferings; all are men
Condemn'd alike to groan:
The tender for another's pain,
The unfeeling for his own.
Yet ah! why should they know their fate,
Since sorrow never comes too late,
And happiness too swiftly flies?
Thought would destroy their paradise —
No more! Where ignorance is bliss,
'Tis folly to be wise.

IV. HYMN TO ADVERSITY.

*Ζῆνα . . . .
Τὸν φρονεῖν βροτοὺς ὁδώσαντα, τῷ πάθει μάθος
θέντα κυρίως ἔχειν.*
                                        ÆSCH. AG. 167.

1 DAUGHTER of Jove, relentless Power,
   Thou tamer of the human breast,
Whose iron scourge and torturing hour
   The bad affright, afflict the best!
Bound in thy adamantine chain,
The proud are taught to taste of pain,
And purple tyrants vainly groan
With pangs unfelt before, unpitied and alone.

2 When first thy Sire to send on earth,
   Virtue, his darling child, design'd,
To thee he gave the heavenly birth,
   And bade to form her infant mind:
Stern rugged nurse! thy rigid lore
With patience many a year she bore;
What sorrow was thou badest her know,
And from her own she learn'd to melt at others' woe.

3 Scared at thy frown, terrific fly
   Self-pleasing Folly's idle brood,
Wild Laughter, Noise, and thoughtless Joy,
   And leave us leisure to be good.
Light they disperse; and with them go
The summer-friend, the flattering foe;
By vain Prosperity received,
To her they vow their truth, and are again believed.

4 Wisdom, in sable garb array'd,
   Immersed in rapturous thought profound,
And Melancholy, silent maid!
   With leaden eye, that loves the ground,

Still on thy solemn steps attend;
Warm Charity, the general friend,
With Justice, to herself severe,
And Pity, dropping soft the sadly-pleasing tear.

5 Oh! gently on thy suppliant's head,
Dread Goddess! lay thy chastening hand,
Not in thy Gorgon terrors clad,
Nor circled with the vengeful band,
As by the impious thou art seen,
With thundering voice and threatening mien,
With screaming Horror's funeral cry,
Despair, and fell Disease, and ghastly Poverty.

6 Thy form benign, O Goddess! wear,
Thy milder influence impart,
Thy philosophic train be there,
To soften, not to wound, my heart:
The generous spark extinct revive;
Teach me to love and to forgive,
Exact my own defects to scan,
What others are to feel, and know myself a Man.

V. THE PROGRESS OF POESY.

PINDARIC.

ADVERTISEMENT.—When the author first published this and the following ode, he was advised, even by his friends, to subjoin some few explanatory notes, but had too much respect for the understanding of his readers to take that liberty.

Φωνάντα συνετοίσιν· ἐς
δὲ τὸ πᾶν ἑρμηνέων
Χατίζει.———
PINDAR, Olymp. II.

I.—1.

AWAKE, Æolian lyre! awake,
And give to rapture all thy trembling strings!
From Helicon's harmonious springs
A thousand rills their mazy progress take;

The laughing flowers, that round them blow,
Drink life and fragrance as they flow.
Now the rich stream of music winds along,
Deep, majestic, smooth, and strong,
Through verdant vales and Ceres' golden reign;
Now rolling down the steep amain,
Headlong, impetuous, see it pour;
The rocks and nodding groves rebellow to the roar.

I.—2.

Oh! Sovereign of the willing soul,
   Parent of sweet and solemn-breathing airs,
   Enchanting Shell! the sullen Cares
And frantic Passions hear thy soft control.
On Thracia's hills the Lord of War
Has curb'd the fury of his car,
And dropp'd his thirsty lance at thy command:
Perching on the sceptred hand
Of Jove, thy magic lulls the feather'd king
With ruffled plumes and flagging wing:
Quench'd in dark clouds of slumber lie
The terror of his beak and lightnings of his eye.

I.—3.

Thee the voice, the dance obey,
Temper'd to thy warbled lay;
   O'er India's velvet green
   The rosy-crownèd Loves are seen,
On Cytherea's day,
With antic Sports and blue-eyed Pleasures
Frisking light in frolic measures:
   Now pursuing, now retreating,
   Now in circling troops they meet;
   To brisk notes in cadence beating,
Glance their many-twinkling feet.
Slow-melting strains their Queen's approach declare;
   Where'er she turns, the Graces homage pay;

With arms sublime, that float upon the air,
  In gliding state she wins her easy way;
O'er her warm cheek and rising bosom move
The bloom of young Desire and purple light of Love.

II.—1.

Man's feeble race what ills await!
  Labour and Penury, the racks of Pain,
  Disease, and Sorrow's weeping train,
And Death, sad refuge from the storms of Fate!
The fond complaint, my Song! disprove,
And justify the laws of Jove.
Say, has he given in vain the heavenly Muse?
Night and all her sickly dews,
Her spectres wan, and birds of boding cry,
He gives to range the dreary sky,
Till down the eastern cliffs afar
Hyperion's march they spy, and glittering shafts of war.

II.—2.

In climes beyond the Solar road,
  Where shaggy forms o'er ice-built mountains roam,
  The Muse has broke the twilight-gloom
To cheer the shivering native's dull abode;
And oft beneath the odorous shade
Of Chili's boundless forests laid,
She deigns to hear the savage youth repeat,
In loose numbers, wildly sweet,
Their feather-cinctured chiefs and dusky loves.
Her track, where'er the Goddess roves,
Glory pursue, and generous Shame,
The unconquerable mind, and freedom's holy flame.

II.—3.

Woods that wave o'er Delphi's steep,
Isles that crown the Ægean deep,
  Fields that cool Ilissus laves,
  Or where Meander's amber waves

In lingering labyrinths creep,
How do your tuneful echoes languish,
Mute but to the voice of Anguish?
Where each old poetic mountain
  Inspiration breathed around;
Every shade and hallow'd fountain
  Murmur'd deep a solemn sound,
Till the sad Nine, in Greece's evil hour,
  Left their Parnassus for the Latian plains,
Alike they scorn the pomp of tyrant Power
And coward Vice, that revels in her chains.
When Latium had her lofty spirit lost,
They sought, O Albion! next thy sea-encircled coast.

III.—1.

Far from the sun and summer-gale,
  In thy green lap was Nature's darling laid,
  What time, where lucid Avon stray'd,
To him the mighty Mother did unveil
Her awful face; the dauntless child
Stretch'd forth his little arms, and smiled.
This pencil take (she said) whose colours clear
Richly paint the vernal year;
Thine, too, these golden keys, immortal Boy!
This can unlock the gates of Joy,
Of Horror that, and thrilling Fears,
Or ope the sacred source of sympathetic Tears.

III.—2.

Nor second He that rode sublime
  Upon the seraph-wings of Ecstasy;
  The secrets of the abyss to spy,
He pass'd the flaming bounds of place and time;
The living throne, the sapphire-blaze,
Where angels tremble while they gaze,
He saw; but, blasted with excess of light,
Closed his eyes in endless night.

Behold where Dryden's less presumptuous car
Wide o'er the fields of glory bear
Two coursers of ethereal race,
With necks in thunder clothed and long-resounding pace.

III.—3.

Hark! his hands the lyre explore!
Bright-eyed Fancy, hovering o'er,
    Scatters from her pictured urn
    Thoughts that breathe and words that burn;
But ah! 'tis heard no more.
O lyre divine! what dying spirit
Wakes thee now? though he inherit
Nor the pride nor ample pinion
    That the Theban eagle bear,
Sailing with supreme dominion
    Through the azure deep of air,
Yet oft before his infant eyes would run
    Such forms as glitter in the Muse's ray
With orient hues, unborrow'd of the sun;
    Yet shall he mount, and keep his distant way
Beyond the limits of a vulgar fate,
Beneath the good how far — but far above the great.

VI. THE BARD.

PINDARIC.

ADVERTISEMENT.— The following ode is founded on a tradition current in Wales, that Edward I., when he completed the conquest of that country, ordered all the bards that fell into his hands to be put to death.

I.—1.

"Ruin seize thee, ruthless King!
    Confusion on thy banners wait!
Though fann'd by Conquest's crimson wing,
    They mock the air with idle state.
Helm nor hauberk's twisted mail,
Nor even thy virtues, Tyrant! shall avail
To save thy secret soul from nightly fears
From Cambria's curse, from Cambria's tears!"

Such were the sounds that o'er the created pride
Of the first Edward scatter'd wild dismay,
As down the steep of Snowdon's shaggy side
He wound with toilsome march his long array;
Stout Glo'ster stood aghast in speechless trance;
To arms! cried Mortimer, and couch'd his quivering lance.

I.—2.

On a rock, whose haughty brow
  Frowns o'er old Conway's foaming flood,
Robed in the sable garb of woe,
  With haggard eyes the poet stood;
(Loose his beard and hoary hair,
Stream'd like a meteor to the troubled air,)
And with a master's hand and prophet's fire
Struck the deep sorrows of his lyre:
"Hark how each giant oak and desert cave
  Sighs to the torrent's awful voice beneath!
O'er thee, O King! their hundred arms they wave,
  Revenge on thee in hoarser murmurs breathe;
Vocal no more, since Cambria's fatal day,
To high-born Hoel's harp, or soft Llewellyn's lay.

I.—3.

"Cold is Cadwallo's tongue
  That hush'd the stormy main;
Brave Urien sleeps upon his craggy bed:
  Mountains! ye moan in vain
Modred, whose magic song
Made huge Plinlimmon bow his cloud-topp'd head.
  On dreary Arvon's shore they lie,
  Smear'd with gore and ghastly pale;
Far, far aloof the affrighted ravens sail;
  The famish'd eagle screams and passes by.
Dear lost companions of my tuneful art!
  Dear as the light that visits these sad eyes,
Dear as the ruddy drops that warm my heart,
  Ye died amidst your dying country's cries —

No more I weep. They do not sleep!
  On yonder cliffs, a grisly band,
  I see them sit; they linger yet,
    Avengers of their native land:
With me in dreadful harmony they join
And weave with bloody hands the tissue of thy line.

II.—1.
'Weave the warp and weave the woof,
  The winding-sheet of Edward's race!
Give ample room and verge enough
  The characters of Hell to trace.
Mark the year and mark the night
When Severn shall re-echo with affright
The shrieks of death through Berkley's roofs that ring,
Shrieks of an agonising king!
She-wolf of France, with unrelenting fangs
  That tear'st the bowels of thy mangled mate,
From thee be born who o'er thy country hangs
  The scourge of Heaven. What terrors round him wait!
Amazement in his van, with Flight combined,
And Sorrow's faded form, and Solitude behind.

II.—2.
'Mighty Victor, mighty Lord,
  Low on his funeral couch he lies!
No pitying heart, no eye afford
  A tear to grace his obsequies!
Is the sable warrior fled? —
Thy son is gone; he rests among the dead.
The swarm that in thy noontide beam were born,
Gone to salute the rising morn;
Fair laughs the morn, and soft the Zephyr blows,
  While, proudly riding o'er the azure realm,
In gallant trim the gilded vessel goes,
  Youth on the prow, and Pleasure at the helm,
Regardless of the sweeping whirlwind's sway,
That, hush'd in grim repose, expects his evening prey.

II.—3.

'Fill high the sparkling bowl,
  The rich repast prepare!
Reft of a crown, he yet may share the feast.
  Close by the regal chair
  Fell Thirst and Famine scowl
A baleful smile upon the baffled guest.
Heard ye the din of battle bray,
Lance to lance and horse to horse?
Long years of havoc urge their destined course,
And through the kindred squadrons mow their way;
Ye Towers of Julius! London's lasting shame,
  With many a foul and midnight murder fed,
Revere his consort's faith, his father's fame,
  And spare the meek usurper's holy head.
Above, below, the Rose of snow,
  Twined with her blushing foe, we spread;
The bristled Boar in infant gore
  Wallows beneath the thorny shade;
Now, Brothers! bending o'er the accursed loom,
Stamp we our vengeance deep, and ratify his doom.

III.—1.

'Edward, lo! to sudden fate
  (Weave we the woof, the thread is spun!)
Half of thy heart we consecrate;
  (The web is wove, the work is done!')
."Stay, oh stay! nor thus forlorn
Leave me unbless'd, unpitied, here to mourn,
In yon bright track, that fires the western skies,
They melt, they vanish from my eyes.
But oh! what solemn scenes on Snowdon's height,
  Descending slow, their glittering skirts unroll!
Visions of glory! spare my aching sight!
  Ye unborn ages crowd not on my soul!
No more our long-lost Arthur we bewail:
All hail, ye genuine Kings! Britannia's issue, hail!

III.—2.

"Girt with many a baron bold,
    Sublime their starry fronts they rear;
And gorgeous dames and statesmen old
    In bearded majesty appear;
In the midst a form divine,
Her eye proclaims her of the Briton-line,
Her lion-port, her awe-commanding face,
Attemper'd sweet to virgin-grace.
What strings symphonious tremble in the air!
    What strains of vocal transport round her play!
Hear from the grave, great Taliessin, hear!
    They breathe a soul to animate thy clay.
Bright Rapture calls, and, soaring as she sings,
Waves in the eye of Heaven her many-colour'd wings.

III.—3.

"The verse adorn again,
    Fierce War and faithful Love,
And Truth severe, by fairy Fiction dress'd.
    In buskin'd measures move
Pale Grief, and pleasing Pain,
    With Horror, tyrant of the throbbing breast.
A voice as of the cherub-choir
Gales from blooming Eden bear,
And distant warblings lessen on my ear,
    That lost in long futurity expire.
Fond, impious man! think'st thou yon sanguine cloud,
    Raised by thy breath, has quench'd the orb of day?
To-morrow he repairs the golden flood,
    And warms the nations with redoubled ray.
Enough for me: with joy I see
    The different doom our Fates assign;
Be thine despair and sceptred care;
    To triumph and to die are mine."
He spoke, and headlong from the mountain's height,
Deep in the roaring tide, he plunged to endless night.

VII. THE FATAL SISTERS.

FROM THE NORSE TONGUE.

"Vitt er orpit
Fyrir valfalli."

ADVERTISEMENT. — The author once had thoughts (in concert with a friend) of giving a history of English poetry. In the introduction to it he meant to have produced some specimens of the style that reigned in ancient times among the neighbouring nations, or those who had subdued the greater part of this island, and were our progenitors: the following three imitations made a part of them. He afterwards dropped his design; especially after he had heard that it was already in the hands of a person well qualified to do it justice both by his taste and his researches into antiquity.

PREFACE. — In the eleventh century, Sigurd, Earl of the Orkney Islands, went with a fleet of ships, and a considerable body of troops, into Ireland, to the assistance of Sigtryg with the Silken Beard, who was then making war on his father-in-law, Brian, King of Dublin. The Earl and all his forces were cut to pieces, and Sigtryg was in danger of a total defeat; but the enemy had a greater loss by the death of Brian, their king, who fell in the action. On Christmas-day (the day of the battle) a native of Caithness, in Scotland, saw, at a distance, a number of persons on horseback riding full speed towards a hill, and seeming to enter into it. Curiosity led him to follow them, till, looking through an opening in the rocks, he saw twelve gigantic figures, resembling women: they were all employed about a loom; and as they wove they sung the following dreadful song, which, when they had finished, they tore the web into twelve pieces, and each taking her portion, galloped six to the north, and as many to the south.

1 Now the storm begins to lower,
   (Haste, the loom of Hell prepare!)
  Iron-sleet of arrowy shower
   Hurtles in the darken'd air.

2 Glittering lances are the loom
   Where the dusky warp we strain,
  Weaving many a soldier's doom,
   Orkney's woe and Randver's bane.

3 See the grisly texture grow,
   'Tis of human entrails made,
  And the weights that play below,
   Each a gasping warrior's head.

4 Shafts for shuttles, dipp'd in gore,
   Shoot the trembling cords along:
Sword, that once a monarch bore,
   Keep the tissue close and strong.

5 Mista, black, terrific maid!
   Sangrida and Hilda see,
Join the wayward work to aid:
   'Tis the woof of victory.

6 Ere the ruddy sun be set,
   Pikes must shiver, javelins sing,
Blade with clattering buckler meet,
   Hauberk crash, and helmet ring.

7 Weave the crimson web of war!
   Let us go, and let us fly,
Where our friends the conflict share,
   Where they triumph, where they die.

8 As the paths of Fate we tread,
   Wading through th'ensanguined field,
Gondula and Geira spread
   O'er the youthful king your shield.

9 We the reins to Slaughter give,
   Ours to kill and ours to spare:
Spite of danger he shall live;
   Weave the crimson web of war!

10 They whom once the desert beach
   Pent within its bleak domain,
Soon their ample sway shall stretch
   O'er the plenty of the plain.

11 Low the dauntless earl is laid,
   Gored with many a gaping wound:
Fate demands a nobler head;
   Soon a king shall bite the ground.

12 Long his loss shall Eirin weep,
    Ne'er again his likeness see;
  Long her strains in sorrow steep,
    Strains of immortality!

13 Horror covers all the heath,
    Clouds of carnage blot the sun:
  Sisters! weave the web of death!
    Sisters, cease, the work is done!

14 Hail the task and hail the hands!
    Songs of joy and triumph sing!
  Joy to the victorious bands,
    Triumph to the younger king!

15 Mortal! thou that hear'st the tale,
    Learn the tenor of our song!
  Scotland! through each winding vale
    Far and wide the notes prolong!

16 Sisters! hence with spurs of speed!
    Each her thundering falchion wield,
  Each bestride her sable steed:
    Hurry, hurry, to the field!

VIII. THE DESCENT OF ODIN.

FROM THE NORSE TONGUE.

"Uprois Odinn
Allda gautr."

UPROSE the King of Men with speed,
And saddled straight his coal-black steed;
Down the yawning steep he rode
That leads to Hela's drear abode.
Him the Dog of Darkness spied;
His shaggy throat he open'd wide,
While from his jaws, with carnage fill'd,

Foam and human gore distill'd;
Hoarse he bays with hideous din,
Eyes that glow and fangs that grin,
And long pursues with fruitless yell
The Father of the powerful spell.
Onward still his way he takes,
— The groaning earth beneath him shakes, —
Till full before his fearless eyes
The portals nine of Hell arise.
   Right against the eastern gate,
By the moss-grown pile he sate,
Where long of yore to sleep was laid
The dust of the prophetic maid.
Facing to the northern clime,
Thrice he traced the Runic rhyme,
Thrice pronounced, in accents dread,
The thrilling verse that wakes the dead,
Till from out the hollow ground
Slowly breathed a sullen sound.
   Proph. What call unknown, what charms presume
To break the quiet of the tomb?
Who thus afflicts my troubled sprite,
And drags me from the realms of Night?
Long on these mouldering bones have beat
The winter's snow, the summer's heat,
The drenching dews and driving rain!
Let me, let me sleep again.
Who is he, with voice unblest,
That calls me from the bed of rest?
   Odin. A traveller, to thee unknown,
Is he that calls, a warrior's son.
Thou the deeds of light shalt know;
Tell me what is done below,
For whom yon glittering board is spread;
Dress'd for whom yon golden bed?
   Proph. Mantling in the goblet see
The pure beverage of the bee,

O'er it hangs the shield of gold;
'Tis the drink of Balder bold;
Balder's head to death is given;
Pain can reach the sons of Heaven!
Unwilling I my lips unclose;
Leave me, leave me to repose!
   Odin. Once again my call obey:
Prophetess! arise, and say,
What dangers Odin's child await,
Who the author of his fate?
   Proph. In Hoder's hand the hero's doom;
His brother sends him to the tomb.
Now my weary lips I close;
Leave me, leave me to repose.
   Odin. Prophetess! my spell obey;
Once again arise, and say,
Who the avenger of his guilt,
By whom shall Hoder's blood be spilt?
   Proph. In the caverns of the west,
By Odin's fierce embrace compress'd,
A wondrous boy shall Rinda bear,
Who ne'er shall comb his raven hair,
Nor wash his visage in the stream,
Nor see the sun's departing beam,
Till he on Hoder's corse shall smile,
Flaming on the funeral pile.
Now my weary lips I close;
Leave me, leave me to repose.
   Odin. Yet a while my call obey:
Prophetess! awake, and say,
What virgins these, in speechless woe,
That bend to earth their solemn brow,
That their flaxen tresses tear,
And snowy veils that float in air?
Tell me whence their sorrows rose,
Then I leave thee to repose.

Proph. Ha! no traveller art thou;
King of Men, I know thee now;
Mightiest of a mighty line —
   Odin. No boding maid of skill divine
Art thou, no prophetess of good,
But mother of the giant-brood!
   Proph. Hie thee hence, and boast at home,
That never shall inquirer come
To break my iron-sleep again,
Till Lok has burst his tenfold chain!
Never till substantial Night
Has re-assumed her ancient right;
Till, wrapp'd in flames, in ruin hurl'd,
Sinks the fabric of the world.

IX. THE DEATH OF HOEL.

HAD I but the torrent's might,
With headlong rage, and wild affright
Upon Deïra's squadrons hurl'd,
To rush and sweep them from the world!
Too, too secure in youthful pride,
By them my friend, my Hoel, died,
Great Cian's son; of Madoc old
He ask'd no heaps of hoarded gold;
Alone in Nature's wealth array'd,
He ask'd and had the lovely maid.
   To Cattraeth's vale, in glittering row,
Twice two hundred warriors go;
Every warrior's manly neck
Chains of regal honour deck,
Wreath'd in many a golden link;
From the golden cup they drink
Nectar that the bees produce,
Or the grape's ecstatic juice.

Flush'd with mirth and hope they burn:
But none from Cattraeth's vale return, 20
Save Aëron brave and Conan strong,
— Bursting through the bloody throng —
And I, the meanest of them all,
That live to weep and sing their fall.

X. THE TRIUMPH OF OWEN:
A FRAGMENT FROM THE WELSH.

ADVERTISEMENT. — Owen succeeded his father Griffin in the Principality of North Wales, A.D. 1120; this battle was near forty years afterwards.

Owen's praise demands my song,
Owen swift, and Owen strong,
Fairest flower of Roderick's stem,
Gwyneth's shield and Britain's gem.
He nor heaps his brooded stores,
Nor on all profusely pours;
Lord of every regal art,
Liberal hand and open heart.
  Big with hosts of mighty name,
Squadrons three against him came; 10
This the force of Eirin hiding;
Side by side as proudly riding
On her shadow long and gay
Lochlin ploughs the watery way;
There the Norman sails afar
Catch the winds and join the war;
Black and huge, along they sweep,
Burthens of the angry deep.
  Dauntless on his native sands
The Dragon son of Mona stands; 20
In glittering arms and glory dress'd,
High he rears his ruby crest;
There the thundering strokes begin,
There the press and there the din:

Talymalfra's rocky shore
Echoing to the battle's roar!
Check'd by the torrent-tide of blood,
Backward Meinai rolls his flood;
While, heap'd his master's feet around,
Prostrate warriors gnaw the ground.
Where his glowing eye-balls turn,
Thousand banners round him burn;
Where he points his purple spear,
Hasty, hasty rout is there;
Marking, with indignant eye,
Fear to stop and Shame to fly.
There Confusion, Terror's child,
Conflict fierce, and Ruin wild,
Agony, that pants for breath,
Despair and honourable Death.

* * * * *

XI. FOR MUSIC.

I.

"Hence, avaunt! 'tis holy ground,
　Comus and his midnight crew,
And Ignorance, with looks profound,
　And dreaming Sloth, of pallid hue,
Mad Sedition's cry profane,
Servitude that hugs her chain,
Nor in these consecrated bowers,
Let painted Flattery hide her serpent-train in flowers;

CHORUS.

Nor Envy base, nor creeping Gain,
Dare the Muse's walk to stain,
While bright-eyed Science watches round;
Hence, away! 'tis holy ground."

II.

From yonder realms of empyrean day
Bursts on my ear the indignant lay;
There sit the sainted sage, the bard divine,
The few whom Genius gave to shine
Through every unborn age and undiscover'd clime.
Rapt in celestial transport they,
Yet hither oft a glance from high
They send of tender sympathy,   20
To bless the place where on their opening soul
First the genuine ardour stole.
'Twas Milton struck the deep-toned shell,
And, as the choral warblings round him swell,
Meek Newton's self bends from his state sublime,
And nods his hoary head, and listens to the rhyme.

III.

Ye brown o'er-arching groves!
That Contemplation loves,
Where willowy Camus lingers with delight;
Oft at the blush of dawn   30
I trod your level lawn,
Oft wooed the gleam of Cynthia, silver-bright,
In cloisters dim, far from the haunts of Folly,
With Freedom by my side, and soft-eyed Melancholy.

IV.

But hark! the portals sound, and pacing forth,
With solemn steps and slow,
High potentates, and dames of royal birth
And mitred fathers, in long orders go:
Great Edward, with the Lilies on his brow
From haughty Gallia torn,   40
And sad Chatillon, on her bridal morn,
That wept her bleeding love, and princely Clare,
And Anjou's heroine, and the paler Rose,
The rival of her crown, and of her woes,

And either Henry there,
The murder'd saint, and the majestic lord
That broke the bonds of Rome, —
(Their tears, their little triumphs o'er,
Their human passions now no more,
Save Charity, that glows beyond the tomb,)
All that on Granta's fruitful plain
Rich streams of regal bounty pour'd,
And bade those awful fanes and turrets rise,
To hail their Fitzroy's festal morning come;
And thus they speak in soft accord
The liquid language of the skies.

V.

"What is grandeur, what is power?
Heavier toil, superior pain,
What the bright reward we gain?
The grateful memory of the good.
Sweet is the breath of vernal shower,
The bee's collected treasures sweet,
Sweet Music's melting fall, but sweeter yet
The still small voice of Gratitude."

VI.

Foremost, and leaning from her golden cloud,
The venerable Margaret see!
"Welcome, my noble son!" she cries aloud,
"To this thy kindred train, and me:
Pleased, in thy lineaments we trace
A Tudor's fire, a Beaufort's grace.
Thy liberal heart, thy judging eye,
The flower unheeded shall descry,
And bid it round Heaven's altars shed
The fragrance of its blushing head;
Shall raise from earth the latent gem
To glitter on the diadem.

VII.

"Lo! Granta waits to lead her blooming band;
Not obvious, not obtrusive, she
No vulgar praise, no venal incense flings:
Nor dares with courtly tongue refined   80
Profane thy inborn royalty of mind:
She reveres herself and thee.
With modest pride, to grace thy youthful brow,
The laureate wreath that Cecil wore she brings,
And to thy just, thy gentle hand
Submits the fasces of her sway;
While spirits blest above, and men below,
Join with glad voice the loud symphonious lay.

VIII.

"Through the wild waves, as they roar,
With watchful eye, and dauntless mien,   90
Thy steady course of honour keep,
Nor fear the rock, nor seek the shore:
The Star of Brunswick smiles serene,
And gilds the horrors of the deep."

MISCELLANEOUS.

A LONG STORY.

ADVERTISEMENT. — Gray's "Elegy," previous to its publication, was handed about in MS., and had, amongst other admirers, the Lady Cobham, who resided in the mansion-house at Stoke-Pogeis. The performance inducing her to wish for the author's acquaintance, Lady Schaub and Miss Speed, then at her house, undertook to introduce her to it. These two ladies waited upon the author at his aunt's solitary habitation, where he at that time resided, and not finding him at home, they left a card behind them. Mr. Gray, surprised at such a compliment, returned the visit; and as the beginning of this intercourse bore some appearance of romance, he gave the humorous and lively account of it which the "Long Story" contains.

1 In Britain's isle, no matter where,
    An ancient pile of building stands:
The Huntingdons and Hattons there
    Employ'd the power of fairy hands,

2 To raise the ceiling's fretted height,
    Each pannel in achievements clothing,
Rich windows that exclude the light,
    And passages that lead to nothing.

3 Full oft within the spacious walls,
    When he had fifty winters o'er him,
My grave Lord-Keeper led the brawls,[1]
    The seal and maces danced before him.

4 His bushy beard and shoe-strings green,
    His high-crown'd hat and satin doublet,
Moved the stout heart of England's Queen,
    Though Pope and Spaniard could not trouble it.

---

[1] "Brawls" were a sort of figure-dance, in vogue in the times of Queen Elizabeth, when Sir Christopher Hatton was Lord-Keeper.

5 What, in the very first beginning,
  Shame of the versifying tribe!
Your history whither are you spinning?
  Can you do nothing but describe?

6 A house there is, and that's enough,
  From whence one fatal morning issues
A brace of warriors, not in buff,
  But rustling in their silks and tissues.

7 The first came *cap-à-pie* from France,
  Her conquering destiny fulfilling,
Whom meaner beauties eye askance,
  And vainly ape her art of killing.

8 The other Amazon kind Heaven
  Had arm'd with spirit, wit, and satire;
But Cobham had the polish given,
  And tipp'd her arrows with good nature.

9 To celebrate her eyes, her air —
  Coarse panegyrics would but tease her;
Melissa is her *nom de guerre;*
  Alas! who would not wish to please her!

10 With bonnet blue and capuchine,
  And aprons long, they hid their armour;
And veil'd their weapons, bright and keen,
  In pity to the country farmer.

11 Fame, in the shape of Mr. P—t,
  (By this time all the parish know it),
Had told that thereabouts there lurk'd
  A wicked imp they call a Poet,

12 Who prowl'd the country far and near,
  Bewitch'd the children of the peasants,
Dried up the cows, and lamed the deer,
  And suck'd the eggs, and kill'd the pheasants.

13 My Lady heard their joint petition,
    Swore by her coronet and ermine,
    She'd issue out her high commission
    To rid the manor of such vermin.

14 The heroines undertook the task;
    Through lanes unknown, o'er stiles they ventured,
    Rapp'd at the door, nor stay'd to ask,
    But bounce into the parlour enter'd.

15 The trembling family they daunt;
    They flirt, they sing, they laugh, they tattle,
    Rummage his mother, pinch his aunt,
    And upstairs in a whirlwind rattle.

16 Each hole and cupboard they explore,
    Each creek and cranny of his chamber,
    Run hurry-scurry round the floor,
    And o'er the bed and tester clamber;

17 Into the drawers and china pry,
    Papers and books, a huge imbroglio!
    Under a tea-cup he might lie,
    Or creased like dog's-ears in a folio!

18 On the first marching of the troops,
    The Muses, hopeless of his pardon,
    Convey'd him underneath their hoops
    To a small closet in the garden.

19 So Rumour says; (who will believe?)
    But that they left the door a-jar,
    Where safe, and laughing in his sleeve,
    He heard the distant din of war.

20 Short was his joy: he little knew
    The power of magic was no fable;
    Out of the window, whisk! they flew,
    But left a spell upon the table.

21 The words too eager to unriddle,
    The Poet felt a strange disorder;
  Transparent birdlime form'd the middle,
    And chains invisible the border.

22 So cunning was the apparatus,
    The powerful pothooks did so move him,
  That will-he, nill-he, to the great house
    He went as if the devil drove him.

23 Yet on his way (no sign of grace,
    For folks in fear are apt to pray)
  To Phœbus he preferr'd his case,
    And begg'd his aid that dreadful day.

24 The godhead would have back'd his quarrel:
    But with a blush, on recollection,
  Own'd that his quiver and his laurel
    'Gainst four such eyes were no protection.

25 The court was set, the culprit there;
    Forth from their gloomy mansions creeping,
  The Lady Janes and Joans repair,
    And from the gallery stand peeping:

26 Such as in silence of the night
    Come sweep along some winding entry,
  (Styack has often seen the sight)
    Or at the chapel-door stand sentry;

27 In peaked hoods and mantles tarnish'd,
    Sour visages enough to scare ye,
  High dames of honour once that garnish'd
    The drawing-room of fierce Queen Mary!

28 The peeress comes: the audience stare,
    And doff their hats with due submission;
  She curtsies, as she takes her chair,
    To all the people of condition.

29 The Bard with many an artless fib
    Had in imagination fenced him,
Disproved the arguments of Squib,
    And all that Grooms could urge against him.

30 But soon his rhetoric forsook him,
    When he the solemn hall had seen;
A sudden fit of ague shook him;
    He stood as mute as poor Maclean.[1]

31 Yet something he was heard to mutter,
    How in the park, beneath an old tree,
(Without design to hurt the butter,
    Or any malice to the poultry,)

32 He once or twice had penn'd a sonnet,
    Yet hoped that he might save his bacon;
Numbers would give their oaths upon it,
    He ne'er was for a conjuror taken.

33 The ghostly prudes, with hagged face,
    Already had condemn'd the sinner:
My Lady rose, and with a grace —
    She smiled, and bid him come to dinner.

34 "Jesu-Maria! Madam Bridget,
    Why, what can the Viscountess mean?"
Cried the square hoods, in woeful fidget;
    "The times are alter'd quite and clean!

35 "Decorum's turn'd to mere civility!
    Her air and all her manners show it:
Commend me to her affability!
    Speak to a commoner and poet!"

                [*Here* 500 *stanzas are lost.*]

36 And so God save our noble king,
    And guard us from long-winded lubbers,
That to eternity would sing,
    And keep my lady from her rubbers.

---

[1] A famous highwayman, hanged some days before.

ELEGY WRITTEN IN A COUNTRY CHURCHYARD.

1 The curfew tolls the knell of parting day,
   The lowing herd wind slowly o'er the lea,
The ploughman homewards plods his weary way,
   And leaves the world to darkness and to me.

2 Now fades the glimmering landscape on the sight,
   And all the air a solemn stillness holds,
Save where the beetle wheels his droning flight,
   And drowsy tinklings lull the distant folds:

3 Save that, from yonder ivy-mantled tower,
   The moping owl does to the moon complain
Of such as, wandering near her secret bower,
   Molest her ancient solitary reign.

4 Beneath those rugged elms, that yew-tree's shade,
   Where heaves the turf in many a mouldering heap,
Each in his narrow cell for ever laid,
   The rude forefathers of the hamlet sleep.

5 The breezy call of incense-breathing Morn,
   The swallow twittering from the straw-built shed,
The cock's shrill clarion, or the echoing horn,
   No more shall rouse them from their lowly bed.

6 For them no more the blazing hearth shall burn,
   Or busy housewife ply her evening care;
No children run to lisp their sire's return,
   Or climb his knees, the envied kiss to share.

7 Oft did the harvest to their sickle yield,
   Their furrow oft the stubborn glebe has broke;
How jocund did they drive their team afield!
   How bow'd the woods beneath their sturdy stroke!

8 Let not Ambition mock their useful toil,
   Their homely joys, and destiny obscure;
Nor Grandeur hear with a disdainful smile
   The short and simple annals of the poor.

9 The boast of heraldry, the pomp of power,
   And all that beauty, all that wealth e'er gave,
Await alike the inevitable hour:
   The paths of glory lead but to the grave.

10 Nor you, ye Proud! impute to these the fault,
   If Memory o'er their tomb no trophies raise,
Where, through the long-drawn aisle and fretted vault,
   The pealing anthem swells the note of praise.

11 Can storied urn or animated bust
   Back to its mansion call the fleeting breath?
Can Honour's voice provoke the silent dust,
   Or Flattery soothe the dull cold ear of death?

12 Perhaps in this neglected spot is laid
   Some heart once pregnant with celestial fire;
Hands that the rod of empire might have sway'd,
   Or waked to ecstasy the living lyre.

13 But Knowledge to their eyes her ample page,
   Rich with the spoils of Time, did ne'er unroll;
Chill Penury repress'd their noble rage,
   And froze the genial current of the soul.

14 Full many a gem of purest ray serene
   The dark unfathom'd caves of ocean bear;
Full many a flower is born to blush unseen,
   And waste its sweetness on the desert air.

15 Some village Hampden, that with dauntless breast
   The little tyrant of his fields withstood,
Some mute inglorious Milton here may rest,
   Some Cromwell, guiltless of his country's blood.

16 The applause of listening senates to command,
  The threats of pain and ruin to despise,
  To scatter plenty o'er a smiling land,
  And read their history in a nation's eyes,

17 Their lot forbade; nor circumscribed alone
  Their growing virtues, but their crimes confined;
  Forbade to wade through slaughter to a throne,
  And shut the gates of Mercy on mankind;

18 The struggling pangs of conscious Truth to hide,
  To quench the blushes of ingenuous Shame,
  Or heap the shrine of Luxury and Pride
  With incense kindled at the Muse's flame.

19 Far from the madding crowd's ignoble strife,
  Their sober wishes never learn'd to stray;
  Along the cool sequester'd vale of life
  They kept the noiseless tenor of their way.

20 Yet e'en these bones, from insult to protect,
  Some frail memorial still erected nigh,
  With uncouth rhymes and shapeless sculpture deck'd,
  Implores the passing tribute of a sigh.

21 Their name, their years, spelt by the unletter'd Muse,
  The place of fame and elegy supply,
  And many a holy text around she strews,
  That teach the rustic moralist to die.

22 For who, to dumb Forgetfulness a prey,
  This pleasing, anxious being e'er resign'd,
  Left the warm precincts of the cheerful day,
  Nor cast one longing, lingering look behind?

23 On some fond breast the parting soul relies,
  Some pious drops the closing eye requires;
  E'en from the tomb the voice of Nature cries,
  E'en in our ashes live their wonted fires.

24 For thee, who, mindful of the unhonour'd dead,
 Dost in those lines their artless tale relate,
If chance, by lonely Contemplation led,
 Some kindred spirit shall inquire thy fate,

25 Haply some hoary-headed swain may say,
 "Oft have we seen him, at the peep of dawn,
Brushing with hasty steps the dews away,
 To meet the sun upon the upland lawn.

26 "There, at the foot of yonder nodding beech,
 That wreathes its old fantastic root so high,
His listless length at noontide would he stretch,
 And pore upon the brook that babbles by.

27 "Hard by yon wood, now smiling as in scorn,
 Muttering his wayward fancies, he would rove;
Now drooping, woeful, wan, like one forlorn,
 Or crazed with care, or cross'd in hopeless love.

28 "One morn I miss'd him on the accustom'd hill,
 Along the heath, and near his favourite tree;
Another came, nor yet beside the rill,
 Nor up the lawn, nor at the wood, was he:

29 "The next, with dirges due, in sad array,
 Slow through the churchway-path we saw him borne.
Approach, and read (for thou canst read) the lay
 Graved on the stone beneath yon aged thorn:"

THE EPITAPH.

30 Here rests his head upon the lap of Earth,
 A youth to Fortune and to Fame unknown:
Fair Science frown'd not on his humble birth,
 And Melancholy mark'd him for her own.

31 Large was his bounty, and his soul sincere;
 Heaven did a recompense as largely send:
He gave to misery all he had — a tear;
 He gain'd from Heaven—'twas all he wish'd—a friend.

32 No further seek his merits to disclose,
   Or draw his frailties from their dread abode,
(There they alike in trembling hope repose)
   The bosom of his Father and his God.

EPITAPH ON MRS. JANE CLARKE.

Lo! where this silent marble weeps,
A friend, a wife, a mother sleeps;
A heart, within whose sacred cell
The peaceful Virtues loved to dwell:
Affection warm, and faith sincere,
And soft humanity were there.
In agony, in death resign'd,
She felt the wound she left behind.
Her infant image here below
Sits smiling on a father's woe:
Whom what awaits while yet he strays
Along the lonely vale of days?
A pang, to secret sorrow dear,
A sigh, an unavailing tear,
Till time shall every grief remove
With life, with memory, and with love.

STANZAS,

SUGGESTED BY A VIEW OF THE SEAT AND RUINS AT KINGSGATE,
IN KENT, 1766.

1 OLD, and abandon'd by each venal friend,
   Here Holland took the pious resolution,
To smuggle a few years, and strive to mend
   A broken character and constitution.

2 On this congenial spot he fix'd his choice;
   Earl Goodwin trembled for his neighbouring sand;
Here sea-gulls scream, and cormorants rejoice,
   And mariners, though shipwreck'd, fear to land.

3 Here reign the blustering North, and blasting East,
  No tree is heard to whisper, bird to sing;
Yet Nature could not furnish out the feast,
  Art he invokes new terrors still to bring.

4 Now mouldering fanes and battlements arise,
  Turrets and arches nodding to their fall,
Unpeopled monasteries delude our eyes,
  And mimic desolation covers all.

5 "Ah!" said the sighing peer, "had Bute been true,
  Nor C—'s, nor B—d's promises been vain,
Far other scenes than this had graced our view,
  And realised the horrors which we feign.

6 "Purged by the sword, and purified by fire,
  Then had we seen proud London's hated walls:
Owls should have hooted in St. Peter's choir,
  And foxes stunk and litter'd in St. Paul's."

TRANSLATION FROM STATIUS.

Third in the labours of the disc came on,
With sturdy step and slow, Hippomedon;
Artful and strong he poised the well-known weight,
By Phlegyas warn'd, and fired by Mnestheus' fate,
That to avoid and this to emulate,
His vigorous arm he tried before he flung,
Braced all his nerves, and every sinew strung,
Then with a tempest's whirl and wary eye
Pursued his cast, and hurl'd the orb on high;
The orb on high, tenacious of its course,
True to the mighty arm that gave it force,
Far overleaps all bound, and joys to see
Its ancient lord secure of victory:
The theatre's green height and woody wall
Tremble ere it precipitates its fall;

The ponderous mass sinks in the cleaving ground,
While vales and woods and echoing hills rebound.
As when, from Ætna's smoking summit broke,
The eyeless Cyclops heaved the craggy rock,
Where Ocean frets beneath the dashing oar,   20
And parting surges round the vessel roar;
"Twas there he aim'd the meditated harm,
And scarce Ulysses 'scaped his giant arm.
A tiger's pride the victor bore away,
With native spots and artful labour gay,
A shining border round the margin roll'd,
And calm'd the terrors of his claws in gold.

    CAMBRIDGE, May, 8, 1736.

GRAY ON HIMSELF.

Too poor for a bribe, and too proud to importune,
He had not the method of making a fortune;
Could love and could hate, so was thought something odd;
No very great wit, he believed in a God;
A post or a pension he did not desire,
But left church and state to Charles Townshend and Squire.

THE END.

PRINTING OFFICE OF THE PUBLISHER.

www.ingramcontent.com/pod-product-compliance
Lightning Source LLC
Chambersburg PA
CBHW051732300426
44115CB00007B/526